From Christians to Europe

CW01497227

Providing the first in-depth examination of Pope Pius II's development of the concept of Europe and what it meant to be 'European', *From Christians to Europeans* charts his life and work from his early years as a secretary in Northern Europe to his papacy.

This volume introduces students and scholars to the concept of Europe by an important and influential early thinker. It also provides Renaissance specialists who already know him with the fullest consideration to date of how and why Pius (1405–1464) constructed the idea of a unified European culture, society, and identity. Author Nancy Bisaha shows how Pius's years of travel, his emotional response to the fall of Constantinople in 1453, and the impact of classical ethnography and other works shaped this compelling vision—with close readings of his letters, orations, histories, autobiography, and other works. Europeans, as Pius boldly defined them, shared a distinct character that made them superior to the inhabitants of other continents. The reverberations of his views can still be felt today in debates about identity, ethnicity, race, and belonging in Europe more generally. This study explores the formation of this problematic notion of privilege and separation—centuries before the modern era, where most scholars have erroneously placed its origins. *From Christians to Europeans* adds substantially to our understanding of the Renaissance as a critical time of European self-fashioning and the creation of a modern "Western" identity.

This book is essential reading for students and scholars interested in the formation of modern Europe, intellectual history, cultural studies, and the history of Renaissance Europe, late medieval Italy, and the Ottoman Empire.

Nancy Bisaha is Professor of History at Vassar College. She works on Renaissance humanism and identity and is the author of *Creating East and West: Renaissance Humanists and the Ottoman Turks* (2004), and co-author of a translation of Pope Pius II's *Europe, c. 1400–1458* (2013).

From Christians to Europeans

Pope Pius II and the Concept of the
Modern Western Identity

Nancy Bisaha

 Routledge
Taylor & Francis Group

LONDON AND NEW YORK

Designed cover image: Frescoes (1502) in Piccolomini Library in Siena Cathedral, Tuscany, Italy, by Pinturicchio, depicting Pope Pius II leaving for the Council of Basel. Joris Van Ostaeyen / Alamy Stock Photo

First published 2023
by Routledge
4 Park Square, Milton Park, Abingdon, Oxon OX14 4RN

and by Routledge
605 Third Avenue, New York, NY 10158

Routledge is an imprint of the Taylor & Francis Group, an informa business

British Library Cataloguing-in-Publication Data
A catalogue record for this book is available from the British Library

Library of Congress Cataloging-in-Publication Data
Names: Bisaha, Nancy, author.
Title: From Christians to Europeans : Pope Pius II and the concept of the modern Western identity / Nancy Bisaha.
Description: New York : Routledge, 2023. | Includes bibliographical references and index. | Contents: Acknowledgements -- Timeline of ley events in Pius II's life -- Chapter 1: From Siena to Vienna: the foundations of Aeneas's worldview -- Chapter 2: 1453-1455: "Europe vs. Asia" -- Chapter 3: "The German Cardinal" at the Roman Curia -- Chapter 4: Papacy and Crusade (1458-1464) -- Conclusion -- Bibliography.
Identifiers: LCCN 2022057486 (print) | LCCN 2022057487 (ebook) | ISBN 9781032326153 (hardback) | ISBN 9781032326160 (paperback) | ISBN 9781003315865 (ebook)
Subjects: LCSH: Europe--Civilization--15th century. | Europeans--Ethnic identity--History. | Europe--Intellectual life--15th century. | Pius II, Pope, 1405-1464. | Europe--History--15th century. | East and West. | Civilization, Western.
Classification: LCC D203 .B57 2023 (print) | LCC D203 (ebook) | DDC 940.2/1--dc23/eng/20230111
LC record available at https://lccn.loc.gov/2022057486
LC ebook record available at https://lccn.loc.gov/2022057487

ISBN: 978-1-032-32615-3 (hbk)
ISBN: 978-1-032-32616-0 (pbk)
ISBN: 978-1-003-31586-5 (ebk)

DOI: 10.4324/9781003315865

Typeset in Times New Roman
by SPi Technologies India Pvt Ltd (Straive)

To John M. Najemy

Contents

Acknowledgements

Many people have contributed to this book in large and small ways over the years. I am humbled by their generosity and grateful for their time and expertise. Their support and suggestions have significantly improved this book and helped me to shape it. All errors and shortcomings are, of course, my own.

Several colleagues read portions of this book at various stages. First and foremost, I want to thank Rob Brown for his help with Latin questions and his review of my translations. I cannot count the times he came to my aid, and always with kindness and encouragement. Jim Merrell, Josh Schreier, and Tom Izbicki read early drafts of this book and offered much-needed observations, questions, and advice as I tried to plot its direction and find my footing. Emily O'Brien, Marc Epstein, Zoltan Markus, and Curtis Dozier read later drafts and offered valuable suggestions and guidance on a number of questions.

Several other colleagues helped with questions along the way and were instrumental in pushing the project forward. They include Ron Patkus, Deb Bucher, Rebecca Edwards, Bob Brigham, Steve Taylor, Carollynn Costella, Nabil Matar, Julia Hairston, Christine Shaw, Stefan Stantchev, Maarten Halff, Mootacem Mhiri, David d'Avray, Larissa Juliet Taylor, Eric Dursteler, Palmira Brummett, Gerry Milligan, and Erika Harlitz-Kern. Thanks also go to Yvonne Elet, Mita Choudhury, John Tolan, Thomas Fudge, Febe Armanios, Bogac Ergene, Giuseppe Cecere, John Monfasani, Chris Celenza, Margaret Meserve, and Suzanne Conklin-Akbari for important insights and support.

I want to thank my wonderful students who inquired about my work and inspired me every step of the way as we traded stories of highs and lows about our research. Many thanks as well to my research assistants, whose help was invaluable: Alix Gonzales, Lestra Atlas, Emma Iadanza, J.D. Nichols, and Noah Ross. I am also profoundly grateful to all the members of the Vassar History Department and the Medieval and Renaissance Studies Program for their collegiality and support.

Important institutional assistance came from Vassar College in the form of semester sabbaticals and support from the Lucy Maynard Salmon Research Fund and from Dean Jon Chenette via the Anne McNiff Tatlock '61 Fund. Thanks to the Max Planck Institute in Berlin and McGill University, I attended several workshops on the 'Before Copernicus' project that greatly expanded my understanding of both Ottoman and Western European culture and science. I am grateful to Jamil Ragep and Rivka Feldhay for inviting me to join that stimulating group and to all the members involved. The Leverhulme Foundation supported another series of workshops on the later crusades that helped me think through this project in many ways. Thanks to Norman Housley for organizing these events and to all the members involved for their excellent input as I zeroed in on the parameters of this book; additional thanks to Norman for his help with various research questions along the way. I also received beneficial feedback at a number of other conferences and speaking events over the years hosted by the Renaissance Society of America, Barnard and Columbia University, Trinity College, Bard College, the University of Bologna, and discussion groups at Vassar and LACOL on antiracism.

I am enormously grateful to the scholars who have edited and translated Pius's works in recent years. By producing reliable texts, they have made his works more accessible for deeper exploration. I especially want to thank Michael von Cotta-Schönberg, whose editions and translations of Pius's many orations have been a gift to students and scholars. This work could not have taken place, moreover, without the help of many librarians and interlibrary loan specialists who located and procured countless critical sources. I am especially indebted to Vassar Library's ILL department and Special Collections. I also wish to thank the Siena Biblioteca Communale and the Watkinson Library at Trinity College.

At Routledge Press, I wish to thank my editor Laura Pilsworth for her interest in this project from the start and her encouragement, guidance, and remarkable patience. Many thanks also go to Andrea K. Harris, Louise Ingham, Isabel Voice, and Yassar Arafat Abdulnasser for all their help with copyediting and production of this book.

Last but not least, I want to thank my family and friends who sustained me throughout the years I worked on this book and helped me stay the course, many of whom are already noted. To Susan and Mark Cooper, Simon and Geeta Gorwara, Mark Seidl, Susan Kassouf, and Martin Hampel, and my wonderful book club friends who kept my joy of reading alive and offered many pleasant breaks, Jessica Nowlin, Stacey Mesler, Michelle Robbin, Leigh Williams, Andrea Sayago, and Astrid Storm: thank you all for inspiring me in more ways than you can know and for making me laugh when I most needed it. Special thanks to my family, Joan Bieler, and Joe, Sarah, Jack, and Michael Bisaha, and my many cousins, who always asked how my book was coming along and let me know they were thinking of me. To my daughter Jocelyn, who cheered me on and showed me in so many ways what it means to follow your heart, thank you for putting up with me and the demands of this project. My husband, Dave Bieler, read portions of the manuscript and offered rich insights, and he answered technical questions of every sort, but much more than that, his love, support, patience, and daily belief in me were the greatest foundation of this project. And to John Najemy, who read an early version of this manuscript and to whom this book is dedicated: I could not have asked for a better mentor or example of what it means to love and to "do" history. I am so grateful to have known you as my teacher and now, my good friend. Thank you for taking a chance on a Jersey girl with a great deal to learn many years ago.

During the period when I wrote this book I lost my dear mother, we experienced a global pandemic, and I changed homes and towns and sent my only child off to college. Through it all, Pius's works have been a comfort to me in many strange and wonderful ways. His lively letters and dedications embodied the Republic of Letters as we struggled to teach and do much of our work remotely. While I may question some of the directions his rhetoric on Europe took, I have always admired his humanity, warmth, persistence, and humor in the darkest of times.

Timeline of Key Events in Pius II's Life

1405   Pius is born Aeneas Silvius Piccolomini in Corsignano on October 18
1423   Begins his studies at the University of Siena
1432   Arrives at the Council of Basel in Switzerland
1436   Delivers the oration "Audivi" at the Council of Basel
1442   Enters the service of Emperor Frederick III
1443   Writes the *Pentalogus*
1446   Writes "On the Origin and Authority of the Roman Empire" (*De ortu*)
1446   Enters the priesthood
1447   Is named Bishop of Trieste
1451   Is named Bishop of Siena
1452   Delivers the oration "Moyses vir Dei" to Pope Nicholas V in Rome
1453   Constantinople is conquered by the Ottoman Turks
1454   Delivers "Quamvis omnibus" at the Diet of Regensburg
1454   Delivers "Constantinopolitana clades" at the Diet of Frankfurt
1455   Delivers "In hoc florentissimo" at the Diet of Wiener-Neustadt
1455   Delivers "Solent plerique" to Pope Calixtus III
1456   Is created Cardinal of Santa Sabina
1458   Writes *Germania*, *Europe*, and *History of Bohemia*
1458   Is elected pope on August 19
1458   Issues papal bull "Vocavit nos Pius" calling for crusade
1459   Congress of Mantua
1459   Delivers "Cum bellum hodie" at Mantua
1461   Writes *Asia*
1461   Writes "Letter to Mehmed II"
1462   Begins the *Commentaries*
1463   Issues papal bull, "Ezechielis"
1464   Journeys to Ancona, Italy to take part in crusade
1464   Dies at Ancona on August 14

Introduction

On September 3, 1458, Aeneas Silvius Piccolomini was crowned Pope Pius II at the age of fifty-two. Recently returned to Italy after two decades abroad, poor, and prematurely aged by gout, he must have seemed an odd choice to become the new prince of the Church. But he was esteemed by many for his witty and graceful humanist writings, his connections in Northern Europe, and his ardent support for a crusade against the Ottoman Turks. This last quality made him a fitting successor to the hawkish Pope Calixtus III. In his autobiographical *Commentaries*, Pius described how the Romans, in their usual style, greeted his election with raucous celebration that could turn violent in an instant. On his coronation day, he stated, "he went in solemn procession to the Lateran where he narrowly escaped death in the mob who fought with swords for the horse he had ridden. He was saved by the mercy of heaven."[1] The fanfare continued with a royal banquet attended by cardinals, princely ambassadors, nobles, and magnates, but when the festivities concluded, he returned to the Vatican palace and went to work. "Among all the concerns that occupied his heart," the text continues, "none was greater than his desire to arouse Christians against the Turks and wage war on them."[2] Within weeks of his coronation Pius issued a bull calling all Christians to join or support this holy war. At long last, he was in a position to "drive the Turks out of Europe," as he had repeatedly urged fellow Christians to do—or so he thought.[3]

Pius would spend his papacy trying to cajole, persuade, and pressure Christian governments to commit to holy war, with no measurable results—until he announced that he himself would go on crusade: "It is not good to say 'Go'; perhaps they will listen better to 'Come.'"[4] No pontiff before or since has ever done such a thing, but it elicited a response. Thousands of individuals took the cross, and small forces from several regions committed to the crusade, which was set to depart from Ancona, Italy in August 1464. Unfortunately, the bold decision to accompany the campaign in the summer of 1464 was costly to Pius's fragile health. He received his death wound not in battle, but on the exhausting journey across Italy to join the gathering forces and died at the port of Ancona as Venetian warships docked in the harbor beyond his window. It has been argued that when Pius II died, so did the future of crusading, and his idealistic efforts were little more than "a noble failure."[5]

DOI: 10.4324/9781003315865-1

Likewise, his memory has suffered in the intervening centuries among the general population. Well-known to Renaissance specialists for his learning and ambition, Pius pales in comparison to the flashy, unapologetically corrupt men who succeeded him on the throne of St. Peter.[6] The vain and brash warrior Julius II (Giuliano della Rovere) and the sybaritic Alexander VI (Rodrigo Borgia), who boldly brought his illegitimate adult children into the Vatican, have become the stuff of novels, movies, and more than one racy miniseries; Leo X (Giovanni de' Medici), whose wealth and privilege blinded him to the threat posed by a humble monk from Germany named Martin Luther, also stands out for obvious reasons. Among such men, Pius seems an awkward fit: neither hero nor villain in this heady age, he is harder to place on the Hollywood spectrum. Pius II may have been proud, controlling, and somewhat nepotistic, but his failings recede when juxtaposed to those of popes whose actions paved the way for the Protestant Reformation. Nor can he be numbered among the more glamorous papal builders and patrons like Nicholas V, who created the Vatican Library.

But scholars who judge Pius's impact on both Europe and the Ottoman Empire by his inglorious death and failed crusade are, quite simply, looking in the wrong direction. Their narrow focus on his papal program of crusade ignores Pius's biggest legacy: his copious, authoritative, and well-circulated writings on Europe, the Ottoman Empire, and Asia.[7] Pius's texts contain a compelling vision of Europe whose echoes can still be felt today. "Europe" has become a powerful, yet amorphous, concept—employed without hesitation to designate both a continent and a people. It connotes a cultural, political, or social collective, but it is also a term of exclusion for those deemed unworthy of its lofty pretensions. One measure of Pius's influence is the adjective "European," which he appears to have coined.[8] This etymological twist was Pius's attempt to express not only what it meant to be *in* Europe, but *of* it. Unfortunately, Pius's early articulations of European identity are as little known to the broader population as the man himself.

In the past few decades, a good deal of work has been published on the construction of European identity.[9] The two periods that receive the most attention, however, are separated by two millennia. Many scholars point to the fifth century BCE when Herodotus described the Greek and Persian wars of his day as the natural outcome of centuries of enmity and difference between "Europe" and "Asia." Others choose the modern colonial era, when brute imperial force cloaked in post-Enlightenment "reason" enabled writers to brashly position Europe and increasingly, "the West" (a term Pius also freely used), above all other cultures.[10] Important though these two eras were, a great deal took place in the centuries that separated them.[11] Surely the fifteenth century—when the Ottomans seemed poised to conquer half the continent and humanist scholars offered bold new definitions of culture and society—played a part in the evolution of the concept of Europe?[12]

In the modern era, one would be hard pressed to find an earlier developed vision of European identity than the one that emerges from Pius's writings.[13] Two key points, in my view, suggest his impact on the way Europeans came to describe themselves: a strong tendency to view the Ottomans as the consummate other, and the use of that same anti-Ottoman discourse to help define the European self. Regarding the first point, consider the way most modern Europeans and Americans view the Ottoman Empire—when they think about it at all. For over five hundred years, the Ottomans were an integral part of Eastern Europe: they profoundly shaped and were shaped by the peoples they ruled, and scholars today see them as part of a "shared world."[14] But for nonspecialists, the historical memory of the Ottoman era is far from settled. A discourse of separation and difference ebbs and flows but never disappears. The tendency to cast the Ottomans as foreign intruders and their reign in Europe as a blip is still pronounced in western countries, and not only in discussions of the deep past: this dogma influences recent debates about immigration, refugees, citizenship, the E.U., and the nationalistic language of some of the world's most powerful leaders.[15] Individuals who insist that the Ottomans never truly belonged in Europe often say the same for non-European peoples today.

No one shaped this early mantra of otherness more, I contend, than Pius. As an imperial secretary in Austria, within days of hearing of the shocking conquest of Constantinople in 1453, he described the sophisticated, successful Ottomans as "a Scythian people from the midst of a barbarous region."[16] One year later, despite his access to reports from Eastern European countries, he upped the ante with a stirring oration at Frankfurt, which later circulated widely, describing the Turks as effeminate, reluctant warriors, and Mehmed as barbaric, unlearned, and full of "Asian arrogance."[17]

These examples provide a small taste of the ways in which Pius's dream to "drive the Turks out of Europe"—or at least the imaginations of many Europeans—arguably came true. Mehmed II and other sultans remained well known to Pius's contemporaries for several generations, but one wonders if his dismissive rhetoric helped diminish their place in European histories over time. How many sultans can be named today (without a technological crutch) by westerners who easily recite the names and deeds of Roman emperors and Christian kings? Why is Mehmed so little known and admired among the other great premodern conquerors and rulers? Ottomanist Linda Darling frames this paradox by describing the Ottomans as active participants in the Renaissance, while also noting a marked tendency among contemporary observers to view them as distinctly other. One way that both Christian Europe and the Ottomans dealt with their "increasingly intense and intimate" contact, she states, was to "thicken the imagined wall between them." That distancing, she adds, "seems to have begun on the European side."[18]

This leads to my second point: Europe itself. In order to prove that the Turks did not belong in Europe, Pius first had to define what "Europe" was. Few Christians regularly used the term before Pius was born, preferring the medieval catch-alls "Christians" or "Christendom" instead.[19] Different concepts of Europe had been evoked by earlier authors, but before 1400, there was little agreement about what it meant beyond a geographical concept.[20] In the fifteenth century, this rapidly began to change, with Pius as one of the leading voices. He passionately described Europe to Christian audiences as "our soil"; he praised the unique attributes of its nations and their potential to work together as an unstoppable team; and he portrayed the continent as the heart and natural leader of the Christian world. As this study will show, Pius ascribed a formidable personality to Europe and "the West"—one that was strong, masculine, highly educated, polished, and almost entirely Christian.[21]

By the early sixteenth century, it was much more common to speak of "Europe," to map its features, and even to personify the continent as the mythical Europa. The self-awareness of Europeans became so pronounced that by 1600 Samuel Purchas claimed that "the Qualitie of Europe exceeds her Quantitie, in this the least, in that best of the world," touting the superior culture, sciences, and technology of "Europeans."[22] It evoked a feeling of belonging so recognizable that Francis Bacon could confidently pen the phrase "we Europeans" in 1623 without fear of being misunderstood.[23] Pius's exact role in this shift is complicated, and other factors certainly played a part, but he clearly stood at the early stages of the change and, therefore, deserves our attention. Specialists strongly agree. To scholars of the medieval and Renaissance periods, Pius's importance to the early concept of European identity is widely accepted.

This view has long prevailed among medieval and Renaissance historians, owing in large part to Denys Hay, who called attention to Pius's rhetoric in 1957 in his wonderfully compact *Europe: The Emergence of an Idea*. Federico Chabod in 1961 and others also noted Pius's role.[24] More recently, Barbara Baldi usefully discussed Pius's political vision for Europe and Christendom, particularly his diplomatic efforts as cardinal and pope. Norman Housley remarked on Pius's efforts to blend his humanism and spiritual leadership in order to promote crusade, calling it "a remarkable achievement of synthesis, with substantial implications for the formation of a European identity." Anthony Molho, Jacques Le Goff, and others have recently affirmed Pius's importance here as well, with Karl Enenkel calling him "the father of Europe."[25] More recently, Isabella Walser-Bürgler has also argued strongly for Pius's impact, stating, "Piccolomni's significance with regard to the early modern Europe discourse cannot be stressed enough."[26] These studies have been incredibly helpful to my research, yet they open the door to more questions. Is Pius's part so well known among specialists that it has been taken for granted? The consensus among so many scholars about Pius's imprint on the concept of Europe begs a deeper understanding of precisely *how* and *why* he developed these strong concepts. What made him, of all his contemporaries, so single-minded and persistent in his quest to comprehend and celebrate Europe? This is the premise of this book. I hope to introduce Pius's work to scholars of European and "Western" identity who do not know him, and for those who do, to offer an in-depth analysis of how his views evolved and their possible impact on later generations. His writings help us to understand a pivotal moment in time that has been too often overlooked.

By rallying Europeans to make common cause against the Ottomans, Pius created and asserted a purportedly unique and superior European *identity*.

Colonialism, the Protestant Reformation, and other later phenomena helped this notion harden into a truism, but as this study will show, modern writers did not invent these concepts out of thin air. The first clear argument of European greatness and self-determination began in Pius's time as a bold rallying cry against a superior military and political power. I contend that Pius created a European identity largely for the purpose of excluding the Ottomans, and the notion took on a life of its own in the process. To be clear, less exclusionary and hierarchical notions of Europe certainly existed. The borders between Europe and Asia or "East and West" meant little to people whose worlds were defined more by interaction and coexistence than warfare and harsh rhetoric; many writers continued to prefer the idea of "Christendom" or simply used more localized terms to describe their home writ large. The discourse that Pius helped shape was but one view of European identity, but the consequences of this viewpoint even today are abundantly clear.[27]

One might reasonably ask if it was unusual for a pope to express such emphatic concern for "Europe." In this period in history, it was.[28] Like other popes before and after him, Pius used terms like "Christendom" and "Roman Catholic Church," but his vision of Europe was uniquely strong and some-times startling. In 1459, at a gathering of princes and dignitaries in Mantua to plan a joint crusade, Pope Pius addressed the crowd, at one point urging them: "Let all of Asia and Africa pass away, and let us look only to Europe and take account of the present."[29] One of the great orators of his age, Pius did not mince words. This statement was novel in its preference for the safety of one group of Christ's followers and its blatant disregard for all the others. It evokes a region that was much smaller than the tri-continental expanse of "Christendom," and yet larger than the reach of the Roman Catholic Church. Whether Pius held his audience in the Northern Italian city in "rapt atten-tion," as he later claimed, throughout his three-hour–long oration (in Latin, no less),[30] his mantra about the security and common bonds of "Europeans" spread across the continent via copies of this broadly disseminated oration. His conflation of continent and religious faith, here and in other texts, reflect a significant ideological shift.

This is not to claim that Pius stood alone in these concerns. Many other Renaissance humanists vilified the Ottomans and some also gestured to the boundaries of Europe and the West in the process. There is little doubt that Pius was engaging in a discourse that was larger than himself, and it is unlikely that he was the first.[31] One can argue, however, that of all his contemporaries, Pius left the biggest imprint. He deserves special attention for three reasons. First, the sheer amount that he wrote on the notion of Europe and the Ottomans (before and after his elevation to the papacy) was unmatched. Second, of all these humanists, only he became pope—an office that lent his pronouncements an authority that few other writers enjoyed. Lastly, Pius was one of the most widely read authors in Western Europe during the Renaissance, and possibly the most widely read humanist of his era.[32] A well-known writer before 1458, his attainment of the highest office in Christendom multiplied the circulation of his works, in both manuscript and print. Other voices held forth on the Turks, but Pius's was the most resounding, and none of his contemporaries spoke in quite the same way to the subjects of European and national identity. In reality, Pius's grasp of current affairs in the East was rather shaky. As Mustafa Soykut argues, Pius and other European writers crafted this image of Islam and the Ottomans in a period when access to reliable information about both were in decline. Nonetheless, in their day, they were regarded as trusted sources and "makers of the contemporary public opinion."[33]

In addition to Pius's exceptional circumstances, political and technological developments at the time converged in a way that amplified his message on Europe and the West and facilitated its spread. The fifteenth century was an era of conceptual transition: educated Christians increasingly questioned authorities and notions of identity that had previously seemed solid and fixed. In 1300, the pope and the Holy Roman Emperor were widely regarded as universal spiritual and secular leaders of western "Christendom." But by 1450, the popes' move to Avignon and the papal Schism, the emperor's waning authority over large swathes of central Europe, and the rising power of centralized monarchies had altered that dynamic. Pius offered new concepts of group identity at a time when state boundaries were forcefully contested and apologists for kings and city-states began to tout the special qualities of their peoples, their founding myths, and their political destinies.[34] The essential appeal of the words "Europe" and "West," one imagines, was that they conjured a collective without a clear leader—neither pope, nor emperor, nor king. The benefits of this neutrality only increased as the Protestant Reformation fragmented the Christian fold and exploration and colonization made differentiations between continents and their peoples objects of intense interest.[35] Lastly, the printing press played an enormous role in increasing and sustaining Pius's audience. Within two decades of his death, Pius's still popular writings began to circulate more rapidly (and affordably) across Europe via this new medium.[36] In addition to the printing of separate works and letter collections, his massive *Opera omnia* was published twice in Basel in the sixteenth century, in 1551 and 1571.

This study will examine how Pius's personal experiences, learning, and major events in his day all came together in his powerful characterization of "Europe," as an entity that embraced some and excluded many, in ways that reverberate in our time when representations of this continent and the entire "West" are still hotly debated. Wherever our own present moment leads us, the ability of the words "Europe" and "West" to inspire, intimidate, unite, or exclude are unlikely to fade away. As Gerard Delanty has stated, "every age [has] reinvented the idea of Europe in the mirror of its own identity."[37] Thoughtful interrogation of the history of these terms and the ways in which we use them must be ongoing.

Key Themes of Pius's Life and this Study

Three factors in Pius's life were crucial to the formation of his views of identity—first and foremost, decades of travel and observation of international politics. Before entering the Church, Pius worked as a secretary, taking his first job with a cardinal on his way to the Council of Basel in Switzerland. Apart from a few visits to Italy, Pius remained north of the Alps for over twenty years. As a secretary, he served bishops, cardinals, an anti-pope, and even the Holy Roman Emperor. His work required considerable travel—to France, England, Scotland, the Netherlands, Slovenia, Italy, and Bohemia— in addition to years spent living and traveling locally in Switzerland, Austria, and Germany. These professional travels gave him chronic arthritis (i.e., gout), nearly shipwrecked him twice, and provided the occasion to sire two children out of wedlock, neither of whom survived infancy—but they also taught him a great deal about his corner of the world. Few men of his age visited as many regions, so carefully observed local inhabitants and cultures, or enjoyed close contact with the most powerful men and women of his time. Even fewer were positioned to receive news and meet visitors from all over Europe and beyond as Pius regularly did in the chanceries where he worked. His years of travel and diplomatic experience created a storehouse of memories, knowledge, and emotional connections that provided fodder for his later views on Europe, its peoples, and the Ottomans.

A second key component in Pius's evolving cultural views was his humanist education—comprised primarily of grammatical and rhetorical training and the study of ancient texts. While competency in Latin was a professional requirement for many vocations, Pius's immersion in the language and literature of ancient Rome was far from utilitarian. This passion for ancient learning connected him to a vibrant international community of like-minded scholars whose training in Latin and Greek texts created a rich pool of historical examples, literary references, and shared language to explore and frame the issues of their time.[38] In direct opposition to today's worship of all that is new, to humanists and their readers, a source's advanced age generally increased its authority. Despite a gap of hundreds of years, in which kingdoms rose and fell, peoples migrated en masse, and great technological and intellectual shifts took place, scholars regularly looked to ancient texts to help navigate contemporary questions.

When Pius wrote about the Germans, for instance, he did not prioritize what he had personally observed or read in contemporary sources, but drew heavily from Tacitus's *Germania* (98 CE), which flattened differences between the many Germanic tribes and treated them as part barbarian, part noble savage. And when Pius wrote about the Turks, he did not stick to recent reports, but included information from texts over a millennium old like Strabo's *Geography* (c. 7 BCE) and the bizarre early medieval *Cosmography* of Aethicus Ister, who described the supposed ancestors of the Turks in the most lurid terms. Even in the face of the radically new, be it the Ottomans or the Indigenous peoples of the Americas, ancient texts were often consulted like reference books.[39] For centuries, the standards that European readers absorbed from classical texts so thoroughly shaped their views of cultural identity and civilization that scholars long mistook these tropes for historical truth. The Ottomans suffered most unfairly from such comparisons. While they were no less sophisticated than other Renaissance Europeans, many humanists like Pius forged a discourse that set a tone of "Western" superiority for centuries to come. Hence, Pius's selective use of ancient texts to describe modern peoples is a crucial thread of this study.[40]

The third and final puzzle piece in Pius's evolving cultural views was his explosive reaction to the Ottoman advance, particularly the conquest of Constantinople in 1453. He had been idly following the Ottomans' progress for years and was serving the uninspiring Frederick III in the sleepy town of Graz, Austria, when news of the cataclysm arrived in July. The siege and sack of the second capital of the Roman Empire rocked him to his core: "But what is that horrible news just reported about from Constantinople?" he wrote in letter to Pope Nicholas V. "My hand trembles as I write these things, my spirit shudders, and neither indignation allows me to be quiet, nor does sadness permit me to speak. Alas, poor Christendom."[41] Overnight, the bored secretary stopped seeking an excuse to return to his homeland in Italy and became one of the most vocal and determined advocates of a large-scale crusade, with the emperor as its would-be leader. Something about the sack of this illustrious and ancient Christian city clearly affected Pius in ways that other battles in war-torn Europe had not.[42]

From this time forward, both the Ottomans and Europe dominated Pius's compositions. If many had only known him before as a writer of poems, erotic fiction, and elegant letters, they would come to see him now as a serious-minded expert on geopolitical and cultural matters. The fall of Constantinople quite simply flipped a switch in him: for all his extensive travels around Europe, before 1453 Pius wrote next to nothing about most places he visited and comparatively little about the Ottomans. From the summer of 1453 on, however, he became obsessed not just with crusade, but with a need to define the nature of the Ottomans and the Christian peoples he hoped would stop them. During his cardinalate in Rome, five years later, with the inspiration of ancient ethnographic texts, he became especially prolific. This is not to say Pius's message about identity and belonging was always neat and clear. Some of his histories and treatises fed early stirrings of national pride with his glib thumbnail sketches of the peoples of Europe and their local peculiarities—a response that undercut Pius's message of European unity.[43] With his oft-times fluid notions of identity, he did not perceive the tensions we identify today between nationalist leanings and cosmopolitanism. As such, Pius contributed to both national myths and a broader notion of Europe as the antithesis of the "Eastern" worlds of Islam and Asia.

More important than any one of the preceding components—experience, humanistic studies, or the jolt of 1453—was their combination. Pius's humanist training and extensive knowledge of contemporary events and peoples from across the continent gave him the means to quickly articulate a forceful response to the fall of Constantinople. By the same token, the Ottomans provided the impetus for Pius to reexamine his views of Europe and its nation states. It was the Turks—and their heightened threat after May 29, 1453—that awakened Pius to the geographical, political, and cultural significance of the countries he visited years before and inspired him to write copiously about the continent that they inhabited. Without the Turks, I believe that Pius would never have conceived of "Europeans" in the same way. Similarly, without his travels and classical studies, he would not have envisioned the Turks as he did. The joint effect of these three components on Pius's notions of identity are traced in this study.

Having sketched the key components of Pius's personal history that shaped his views on identity, I want to step back and say a few words about the broader context of the Renaissance as a time of transition. What does it mean to move from Christendom to Europe, and was it, in fact, a clean break? Despite the attention scholars have given to the idea of Europe, the shift away from Christianity as a primary identity is less often examined or problematized—most scholars assume it happened sometime in the Enlightenment and gained momentum through the political and economic forces of imperialism. Pius's work suggests that this was not an either-or proposition. While much of his worldview resonates with modern secular assumptions about European identity, he also preserved the centrality of Christianity. Since his time, education and other cultural aspects have become less religious in nature, but the Christian components are still palpable.[44] Whether or not most European citizens practice Christianity is secondary to the notion that it undergirds society and forms a connection to a mythical shared "Judeo-Christian" past—a past that deliberately erases Muslims, who also lived in Europe from the eighth century onward. As Talal Asad aptly put it, "Muslims [today] are present in Europe and yet absent from it. The problem of understanding Islam in Europe is primarily, so I claim, a matter of understanding how 'Europe' is conceptualized by Europeans."[45] These powerful words written in the year 2000 are curiously reminiscent of Pius's statement in 1458 about the Ottomans in his history of Europe: "The Turkish race is Scythian and uncivilized. Although I may seem to be digressing from my plan, I think it not irrelevant to describe their origin and expansion."[46] Pius's apology for addressing the Ottomans' origins in a history of Europe reveals an inability to see them as part of the same continent that he and his audience inhabited. Pius had much less to say about Jews in his works, but his brief mentions of them contain a sense of belonging in European society that is missing in his discussions of Muslims or pagans.[47]

One last theme that I explore in this book may come as a surprise given my emphasis up to this point on Pius's ethnocentric views. A subtle, perhaps unconscious, thread also runs through several of his texts: a quiet acknowledgment of the Ottomans' entrenchment in European society. His discursive efforts to "expel the Turks from Europe" mingle with details, large and small, that undermine his mantra of otherness and separation: their alliances with Christian princes, their reputation as fair rulers, and their seamless integration into European diplomacy and trade. Pius's obsession with the Ottomans was equal parts fear and fascination—sometimes chauvinistic and exoticizing—but other times it was soberly observational. As a result, Pius's readers were presented with two contrasting pictures: they could choose to believe one or the other, or remain ambivalent. Pius's efforts to understand the enemy, with the aim of exiling them from Europe, ironically led to works that made them more familiar to Europeans and showed how embedded they were in the continent. This narrative theme will be discussed throughout the book. In addition, Pius's controversial letter to Mehmed II, about which I have previously written, receives new consideration as a complicated offer of conversion.

Similarly, Pius conveys his ambivalence about the Christians of Europe. While he urged princes to fight the Ottomans together as brothers, he fully recognized the fragility of their loyalties to one another. It is the tensions in many of his works that show him to be a more careful historian than the high-flown rhetoric in his better-known speeches and letters would suggest. This malleability makes for lively and unpredictable reading, and it reveals a nuanced view of Christian Europe. Pius's mixed feelings about Christian leaders certainly complicate any serious use of the "self and other" paradigm, which ignores a vast middle ground of tense negotiation and belonging.[48]

Approach and Chapter Overview

This book is an intellectual biography of Pius II's notions of cultural, ethnic, and religious identity. I do not examine his works on love, rhetoric, conciliarism, and other topics, nor is it my goal to tell his life story in detail—many other biographers have done an excellent job on that front—but each chapter follows the main arc of his movements and highlights key moments to bring the man, his milieu, and his words to life.[49] I explore his influences and theorize about his impact, but my central focus is a close reading of his works that pertain to group identity. By reading Pius's creative visions of Europe and Asia against the backdrop of his life, one gains a better understanding of the unique blend of experiences that not only shaped his forceful views, but created a receptive audience.

Because this is not a traditional biography of Pius, I have taken some liberties with the common practice of parceling out his life decade by decade or work by work. Instead, I have divided it into what I see as distinct intellectual periods vis-à-vis his notions of Europe and its nations, and their perceived opposites. As a result, some of the periods are long and lighter on direct evidence of his evolving cultural views, while other phases are brief, but dense in material. Rather than devoting a chapter to his early life, one to his university years, another to his decade with the Council of Basel, and another to his decade in Austria and Germany serving Frederick III, I have condensed this material into Chapter 1. My reasoning is simple: Pius had far less to say about group identity at this time than one would expect. His views on national, continental, and even religious belonging did not fully cohere until after the fall of Constantinople. Everything that preceded it matters largely in retrospect; hence, it can be covered at a brisk pace with attention to some key themes and texts rather than a host of events. Chapter 2 is devoted to Pius's reception of the news of Constantinople, his actions in response, and his copious writings from 1453 to 1455—mainly letters and crusade orations.

Chapter 3 focuses on his time in Rome and his elevation to the cardinalate (1455–58)—a period in which he completed three critical works on Germany, Europe, and Bohemia, in addition to letters and orations. Chapter 4 considers his pontificate (1458–64) from the standpoint of his views on identity as seen in his writings and pursuit of crusade. Chief among these works are his crusade bulls and orations, his enigmatic letter to Mehmed II, his treatise on Asia, and his famous autobiography, the *Commentaries*.

This study concludes with an overview of how these periods and influences fit together, along with suggestions of ways that Pius's writings may have carried forward in time among later writers. I had at one point thought to track Pius's influence more directly, showing who exactly read him and how, but I feared that any attempt to do this would obscure as much as it revealed. It is very hard to know for certain who read Pius or heard echoes of his rhetoric when they spoke of European identity, or whether they were moved by other authors or sociopolitical factors. Getting a firm grasp of his readership, moreover, would require a large-scale study of its own. Until such a study appears, I hope the timing and spread of Pius's works, and the growing confidence with which sixteenth-century Europeans described their home and its qualities, provide enough reason to give him a larger place in studies of the discourse of Europe and the West. Whether readers believe that he provoked and shaped or simply participated in this shift, my hope is that they will find Pius "good to think with."

A Note on Terminology and Language

In a study centered on the epistemology of terms like "Europe," "Asia," "West," and "East," one makes choices on how to use them. Whenever a term appears as a construct, I have tried to signal it in some way or set it apart. Heavy usage of quotation marks, however, can become unruly. I opted for the compromise of limiting straightforward usage of these terms to geographical regions, problematic though that sometimes is. I also needed to choose how to refer to Pius himself and when it was appropriate to use "Aeneas" instead. In this introduction and the conclusion, I have used "Pius" for the sake of consistency and clarity, but in Chapters 1–3, I refer to him as "Aeneas," switching in Chapter 4 to "Pius" with his elevation to the papacy.

I should also address my use of "Turks" as well as "Ottomans." The Ottoman Empire was comprised of multiple ethnic and religious groups; it is, indeed, more accurate to use "Ottoman" rather than narrower designation "Turk"—a term that is freighted with modern nationalist agendas and which the Ottomans themselves did not use. Yet for Pius and so many of his European contemporaries, "Turk" was the designation that they most often used. In order to convey his viewpoint, it seems useful to employ it as well. Most Europeans thought of "the Turks" as a cohesive ethnic group—misleading though this may have been, it was an essential part of their outlook.[50]

Regarding language, like most humanists of his time, Pius wrote almost exclusively in Latin, which made his works both more and less accessible. On the one hand, Latin was an international language that enabled Europeans across the continent to read his works. His simple yet elegant Latin style, a refreshing alternative to the ornate prose of some of his humanist contemporaries, contributed to his popularity. Some of Pius's works, moreover, were translated into German, Italian, and other languages.[51] For the most part, however, only the well-educated could read his texts. Given the spread of his works, one could argue that their availability in Latin did not hinder the reception of his ideas—at least during the Renaissance. Over time, as vernaculars started to replace Latin in documents, government records, and literary tastes, humanists like Pius fell further in popularity behind writers like Dante, Tasso, and Machiavelli.[52] A decline in the study of Latin in the past century has further contributed to what Christopher Celenza has called, "the lost Italian Renaissance."[53] That being said, we lack a full understanding of the use of Neo-Latin by Renaissance and early modern writers and readers, as Walser-Bürgler has noted; her study suggests a widespread usage of the concept of Europe in Latin sources of this period that deserves fuller attention.[54]

* * *

This book seeks to show that it was during the Renaissance, and not the modern colonial era, when a strong sense of Europe and even "the West" began to emerge in the imagination of Europeans. With Pope Pius II's works helping to set the tone, many inhabitants of the continent started to see the region and its peoples as having a shared identity—even a personality. This was a huge shift in thinking from previous eras. Before the fifteenth century, both Muslims and Christians spoke of their worlds as separate places, and occasionally Christians spoke of "the East," yet there was comparatively little use of the words "Europe" or "West," and rarely in the sense of a group identity. But many of the people who came to be called Western Europeans began to see the world differently after 1453—some marveled at the Ottomans and treated them as neighbors, others regarded them as enemies and sought to distance themselves from them. Definitions of Europe and the West would continue to evolve in the modern period, but the belief in inherent difference and cultural superiority fostered by Pius remained fixed for many thinkers. In that crucial sense, their origins date much earlier—to a time when the Ottomans appeared to have the upper hand, and a humanist pope struggled to turn the tables.

Note on translations

All translations in this work, unless otherwise noted, are my own.

Notes

1 "... petiitque ipsa die Lateranum solemni pompa. Quo in loco vix necem evasit inter eos qui propter equum, quo insederat, gladiis decertabant; servatus est divina ope." Pius II, *Commentaries*, ed. Margaret Meserve and Marcello Simonetta (Cambridge, MA: Harvard University Press, 2003), 1, 208–9.

2 "… eademque nocte in suas aedes ad Vaticanum rediit. Atque inter omnes curas quae animum eius invasere, nulla maior fuit quam ut in Turchos excitare Christianos posset atque illis bellum inferre." *Commentaries*, ed. Meserve and Simonetta, 1, 208; English tr., my own. See also ibid., 209.

3 To cite one example, on Jan 1, 1454, he wrote to Pope Nicholas V, asking him to help the emperor "drive the foul Muslims from the borders of Europe," (ad … propulsandos de finibus Europe impuros Mahumeti cultores). See Rudolph Wolkan, ed., *Der Briefwechsel des Eneas Silvius Piccolomini*, in *Fontes Rerum Austriacarum*, ser. 2, vol. 68 (1918), 601.

4 "Non belle dicitur: ite! Fortasse melius audient: venite!" *Commentarii*, ed. Adrian Van Heck (Vatican City: Biblioteca Apostolica Vaticana, 1984), 2, 772; English tr., *Commentaries of Pius II*, tr. Florence Alden Gragg, ed. Leona C. Gabel (Northampton, MA: Smith College, 1937–1957), 824.

5 For a summary of these scholarly views, see Norman Housley, "Pope Pius II and Crusading," *Crusades* 11 (2012): 209. This view of both crusading and Pius has been changing thanks to Housley and others. A more positive estimation of Pius's papacy and its steadying impact on the Church can be found in Marco Pellegrini, "Pio II, il Collegio cardinalizio e la Dieta di Mantova," in *Il Sogno di Pio II e il viaggio da Roma a Mantova*, ed. Arturo Calzona, Francesca Paolo Fiore, Alberto Tenenti, Cesare Vasoli (Florence: Leo S. Olschki, 2003), 15–76; see also Emily O'Brien, *Commentaries of Pope Pius II (1458–1464) and the Crisis of the Fifteenth-Century Papacy* (Toronto: University of Toronto Press, 2015), 9–10.

6 Several recent conferences and proceedings show the interest he generates among specialitsts. See, for example, *Pio II nell'epistolografia del Rinascimento*, ed. Luisa Secchi Tarugi (Florence: Franco Cesati Editore, 2015); *Pio II Piccolomini: il Papa del Rinascimento a Siena*, ed. Fabrizio Nevola (Siena: Protagon Editore, 2009); *Enea Silvio Piccolomini: Pius Secundus Laureatus Pontifex Maximus*. Ed. Manlio Sodi and Arianna Antoniutti (Rome: Libreria Editrice Vaticana, 2007); *Enea Silvio Piccolomini: Arte, Storia e Cultura nell'Europa di Pio II*, ed. Roberta Di Paola, Arianna Antoniutti, and Marco Gallo (Rome: Libreria Editrice Vaticana, 2006); *Il Sogno di Pio II e il viaggio da Roma a Mantova*, ed. Arturo Calzona, Francesca Paolo Fiore, Alberto Tenenti, and Cesare Vasoli (Florence: Leo S. Olschki, 2003).

7 The dissemination of Pius's works is discussed later in this chapter.

8 Denys Hay, *Europe: The Emergence of an Idea* (Edinburgh: Edinburgh University Press, 1957), 86. For increasing uses of "European" in different vernaculars in the later sixteenth century, see ibid., 106–7. Klaus Oschema has recently shown that Lampo Birago used the term Europeans (*Europaei*) in a little-known 1455 treatise, which Pius may have seen; *Bilder von Europe im Mittelalter* (Ostfildern: Jan Thorbecke Verlag, 2013), 442–43. Whether Birago inspired Pius or he came up with the wording independently, scholars agree that Pius "ended up being the one to spread the term and render it respectable among intellectuals and the broad public," as Isabella Walser-Bürgler puts it. See her *Europe and Europeanness in Early Modern Latin Literature: Fuitne Europa tunc unita?* (Leiden: Brill, 2021), 34. On Pius's importance regarding the word "European," see also Nicolas Detering and Dennis Pulina, "Rivalry of Lament: Early Personifications of Europe in Neo-Latin Panegyrics for Charles V and Francis I," in *Contesting Europe: Comparative Perspectives on Early Modern Discourses on Europe, 1400–1800*, ed. Detering, Clementina Marsico, and Isabella Walser-Bürgler Leiden: Brill, 2020), 13–14; Marco Pellegrini, "Unità europea, primato romano. Riflessi della teologia politica di Pio II Piccolomini," in *Enea Silvio Piccolomini: Arte, Storia e Cultura nell'Europa di Pio II*, ed. Roberta Di Paola, Arianna Antoniutti, and Marco Gallo (Rome: Libreria Editrice Vaticana, 2006), 423; Barbara Baldi, "Enea Silvio Piccolomini e il *De Europa*: umanesimo, religione e politica." *Archivio Storico Italiano* 598 (2003): 619.

9 See, for instance, Gerard Delanty, *Inventing Europe: Idea, Identity, Reality* (London: Palgrave Macmillan, 1995); Anthony Pagden, ed., *The Idea of Europe from Antiquity to the European Union* (Cambridge University Press, 2002); *Finding Europe: Discourses on the Margins, Communities, Images, ca. 13th–18th Centuries*, ed. Anthony Molho, Diogo Ramada Curto, and Niki Koniordos (New York: Bergahn Books, 2007); Hay, *Europe.* On the problematic nature of some of the early studies on Europe and the West, see Lynn Hunt, *History: Why it Matters* (Cambridge: Polity Press, 2018), 54–61. For a summary of earlier opinions on the question, including Federico Chabod and Lucien Febvre, see Molho, introduction to *Finding Europe.*

10 Herodotus, *The Histories*, tr. Aubrey de Selincourt, revised by John Marincola (New York: Penguin Books, 1972), 4. For the colonial era, particularly, see Kwame Anthony Appiah, "There is no such thing as western civilization," *The Guardian*, Nov. 9, 2016. (https://www.theguardian.com/world/2016/nov/09/western-civilisation-appiah-reith-lecture); Edward Said, *Culture and Imperialism* (New York: Vintage Books, 1994); Maxime Rodinson dates Eurocentrism to the Enlightenment, but believes it was softened by universalist ideology prevalent at the time. See *Europe and the Mystique of Islam*, tr. Roger Veinus (Seattle: University of Washington Press, 1987), 65. Peter Burke acknowledges the fifteenth century and Pius's writings as a moment of increased usage, tied to the threat of invasion, but does not see a clear sense of European consciousness before 1700. See "Did Europe Exist Before 1700?" *History of European Ideas* 1, no. 1 (1980): 21–9.

11 Some important studies have been done on the medieval period. The evolution of early continental coherence was proposed by Henri Pirenne in *Mahomet et Charlemagne* (1937). The notion of "Christendom" as an important precursor to the idea of Europe is explored in detail by Robert Bartlett in *The Making of Europe: Conquest, Colonization and Cultural Change 950–1350* (Princeton: Princeton University Press, 1993); a more recent treatment is John Tolan, "Constructing Christendom," in *The Making of Europe: Essays in Honour of Robert Bartlett*, ed. John Hudson and Sally Crumplin (Leiden: Brill, 2016), 277–98; Klaus Oschema's recent book explores a variety of medieval usages of "Europe"; see *Bilder von Europe*. Jacques Le Goff has also argued for the development of Europe in the later Middle Ages, while noting that an awareness of it only came later, with Pius's works representing that turning point; see *The Birth of Europe*, tr. Janet Lloyd (Malden, Mass.: Blackwell, 2005), 1.

12 Many studies of the concept of Europe, the West, or related topics ignore both Pius and the fifteenth century. See, for example, *The European Way Since Homer: History, Memory, and Identity*, ed. Valérie Rosoux and Akiyoshi Nishiyama (London: Bloomsbury Academic, 2021); Stuart Elden, *The Birth of Territory* (Chicago: University of Chicago Press, 2013); *Engaging Europe: Rethinking a Changing Continent*, eds. Evlyn Gould and George Sheridan (Lanham, MD: Rowman and Littlefield, 2005); Pagden, ed., *The Idea of Europe.* Even a handful of Renaissance scholars overlook the fifteenth century as a key moment and focus on the sixteenth century. See J.G.A. Pocock, "Some Europes in Their History," in *Idea of Europe*, ed. Pagden, 55–71, and John R. Hale, *The Civilization of Europe in the Renaissance* (New York: Atheneum, 1994).

13 Detering and Pulina state that examples of the notion of Europe Pius describes "remain scarce before 1500"; see "Rivalry of Lament," 13–4.

14 See Molly Greene, *A Shared World: Christians and Muslims in the Early Modern Mediterranean* (Princeton: Princeton University Press, 2000); Palmira Brummett, *Mapping the Ottomans: Sovereignty, Territory, and Identity in the Early Modern Mediterranean* (Cambridge: Cambridge University Press, 2015); Eric Dursteler, *Renegade Women: Gender, Identity and Boundaries in the Early Modern Mediterranean* (Baltimore: Johns Hopkins University Press, 2011); E. Nathalie Rothman, *Brokering Empire: trans-imperial subjects between Venice and Istanbul* (Ithaca, NY: Cornell University Press, 2012).

15 See Talal Asad, *Formations of the Secular: Christianity, Islam, Modernity* (Stanford, Calif.: Stanford University Press, 2003). On former Trump adviser Stephen Bannon's obsessive polarization of Europe and Islam, for example, see Scott Shane, "Stephen Bannon in 2014: We Are at War With Radical Islam," *New York Times*, Feb. 1, 2017. https://www.nytimes.com/interactive/2017/02/01/us/ste phen-bannon-war-with-radical-islam.html

16 Letter to Nicholas of Cusa (July 21, 1453) "Scitharum ex media barbarie genus profectum est ..." Wolkan, *Briefwechsel*, 68: 209.

17 Aeneas Silvius Piccolomini, "Constantinopolitana clades" (15 October 1454, Frankfurt), ed. and tr. Michael von Cotta-Schönberg. 3rd ed.: (Orations of Enea Silvio Piccolomini/Pius II; 19). Ed. and transl. by Michael von Cotta-Schönberg. 2nd ed. 2015. <hal-01097147v3>. See 106–9 for "Asiana superbia" and 90–1 for his depiction of Turkish soldiers, discussed at greater length in Chapter 2.

18 Linda Darling, "The Renaissance and the Middle East," in *A Companion to the Worlds of the Renaissance*, ed. Guido Ruggiero, ed. (Oxford: Blackwell Publishing, 2002), 65.

19 The Ottomans did not begin to use "Europe" (*Avrupa*) until much later—despite the fact that they were clearly part of the same continent. See Veinstein, "The Great Turk and Europe,"184; Cemal Kafadar, "The Ottomans and Europe," in *Handbook of European History 1400–1600*, vol. 1, eds. Thomas A. Brady, Jr., Heiko A. Oberman, James D. Tracy (Leiden: Brill, 1994), 589–636.

20 Oschema's learned *Bilder von Europe* shows many medieval usages of "Europe" that suggest the creation of an identity, but Walser-Bürgler sees medieval usages as "overinterpreted" and lacking a clear message. She views the fifteenth century as a turning point, describing it as "the big bang" for its unprecedented usage of Europe, with Pius's treatise *Europe* (1458) as an important part of the promotion of the term; see Walser-Bürgler *Europe and Europeanness*, 29–32.

21 Suzanne Conklin Akbari sees the period around 1450 as a turning point in the growing consciousness of the West as a distinct center of attention, but describes it as the work of many thinkers; see *Idols in the East: European Representations of Islam and the Orient, 1100*–1450 (Ithaca: Cornell University Press, 2009), 19.

22 Samuel Purchas, *Hakluytus posthumus, or Purchas his Pilgrimes: contayning a history of the world in sea voyages and lande travells by Englishmen and others* (Glasgow: J. MacLehose and Sons, 1905–1907), 248–52.

23 Randolph Starn, "The European Renaissance," in *Companion to the Worlds of the Renaissance*, ed. Guido Ruggiero (Oxford: Blackwell Publishing, 2002), 44. See also Hale, *Civilization of Europe*, 3 and ff; Hay, *Europe*, chs. 5–7, esp. page 117; Delanty, *Inventing Europe*, ch 4. Ottomans, by contrast, preferred other terms such as *Rūm* (Rome), "the lands of the Christians," or sometimes "the Franks." For more on this see Nabil Matar, *Lands of the Christians: Arabic Travel Writing in the Seventeenth Century* (New York: Routledge, 2003); Gilles Veinstein, "Ottoman Europe: An Ancient Fracture," in *Europe and the Islamic World: A History*, ed. John Tolan, Gilles Veinstein, and Henry Laurens (Princeton: Princeton University Press, 2013), 184–85.

24 Hay, *Europe*, 83–87; Federico Chabod, *Storia dell'idea d'Europa* (1961. Rev. ed. by Ernest Sestan and Armando Saitta, 4th edition. Rome: Edizioni Laterza, 2001), 44–6.

25 Barbara Baldi, *Pio II e le trasformazioni dell'Europa Cristiana (1457–1464)* (Milan: Edizioni Unicopli, 2006). Housley, "Pius II," 245; Anthony Molho "Harlequin's Dress: Reflections on Europe's Public Discourse," in *Finding Europe*, ed. Molho et al., 2. Le Goff, *Birth of Europe*, 1, 186. Karl Enenkel, "Landeskunde als Politische Argumentation: Enea Silvio Piccolominis *De Europa*," *Monumenta Illustrata Raumwissen und antiquarische Gelehrsamkeit*, ed. Dietrich Boschung and Alfred Schäfer (Leiden: Wilhelm Fink, 2019), 13. See also Johannes Helmrath, "Political-Assembly Speeches, German Diets, and Aeneas Sylvius Piccolomini,"

in *Beyond Reception: Renaissance Humanism and the Transformation of Classical Antiquity*, ed. Patrick Baker, Johannes Helmrath, and Craig Kallendorf (Berlin: De Gruyter, 2019), 92–93. See also other studies cited *supra* in note 8.

26 Walser-Bürgler, *Europe and Europeanness*, 41. She goes on to say, "Unfortunately, a comprehensive investigation of Piccolomini's life and works still constitute a big research desideratum"; ibid. I hope that my book helps to fill that gap.

27 A growing number of studies demonstrate the porousness between Christian Europe and the Ottoman Empire, and the fluidity of Mediterranean culture. See, for instance, Eric Dursteler "Language and Gender in the Early Modern Mediterranean," *Renaissance Quarterly* 75: 1 (Spring, 2022): 1–45; Giovanni Ricci, *Appeal the to the Turk: The Broken Boundaries of the Renaissance* (Rome: Viella, 2018); *A Companion to Mediterranean History*, ed. Peregrine Horden and Sharon Kinoshita (Malden, MA: Wiley Blackwell, 2014); Brummett, *Mapping the Ottomans*.

28 Other popes before and after Pius expressed occasional concern for Europe, but Pius's writings surpassed them in frequency, degree, and detail.

29 "Transeat omnis Asia, omnis Africa; Europam saltem inspiciamus, et nostri temporis rationem reddamus." Michael von Cotta-Schönberg, ed. and tr., "Cum bellum hodie" of Pope Pius II (26 September 1459, Mantua). Preliminary edition, 4th version. (Orations of Enea Silvio Piccolomini / Pope Pius II; 45). 2015. <hal-01184169v4>. 68; Eng. tr. 69, with some modifications.

30 "… atque imperato silentio horis circiter tribus peroravit tanta auditorum attentione ut nullum exciderit non intellectum verbum" *Commentaries*, ed. and tr. Meserve and Simonetta, 2: 136–37.

31 See Nancy Bisaha, *Creating East and West: Renaissance Humanists and the Ottoman Turks* (Philadelphia: University of Pennsylvania Press, 2004); Margaret Meserve, *Empires of Islam in Renaissance Historical Thought* (Cambridge, MA: Harvard University Press, 2008); James Hankins, "Renaissance Crusaders: Humanist Crusade Literature in the Age of Mehmed II," *Dumbarton Oaks Papers* 49 (1995): 111–207. For a fuller discussion of some of the differences between Pius's usages and those of his contemporaries, see Chapter 2.

32 Thomas J. Mauro covers this subject extensively in "*Praeceptor Austriae*: Aeneas Sylvius Piccolomini (Pius II) and the Transalpine Diffusion of Italian Humanism before Erasmus" (PhD diss., University of Chicago, 2003), 2–7; 19. See also Paul Weinig, *Aeneam suscipite, Pium recipite: Aeneas Silvius Piccolomini, Studien zur Rezeption eines humanistischsen Schriftstellers im Deutschland des 15. Jahrhunderts* (Wiesbaden: Harrasowitz Verlag, 1998); Meserve, Empires, 292, n. 129; Helmrath, "Political Assembly Speeches," 82–83; Norman Housley, *Crusading and the Ottoman Threat, 1453–1505* (Oxford: Oxford University Press, 2012), 159–60.

33 Mustafa Soykut, *The Image of the "Turk" in Italy: A History of the "Other" in Early Modern Europe: 1453–1683* (Berlin: Klaus Schwarz Verlag, 2001), 18, 147. As Soykut argues, access to more reliable information was not regained in Europe until the seventeenth century; see ibid., 18.

34 Hay, *Europe*, 63–72; William Chester Jordan, "'Europe' in the Middle Ages," in *Idea of Europe*, ed. Pagden, 82–83, 88. Other studies that point to the impact of fourteenth century developments on questions of local and larger identity: Peter Rietbergen, *Europe: A Cultural History* (London: Routledge, 1998), 139; Caspar Hirschi, *The Origins of Nationalism: An Alternative History from Ancient Rome to Modern Germany* (Cambridge: Cambridge University Press, 2012). Le Goff and Bartlett argue for an earlier inflection point in the making of Europe, if not the consciousness of it: see Le Goff, *Birth of Europe*; Bartlett, *Making of Europe*. See also Luisa Passerini, for a more modern comparison on the role of the loss of bodily "health," in "From the Ironies of Identity to the Identities of Irony," in *Europe*, ed. Pagden, 193.

35 Hay, *Europe*, 97–100; Jeremy Black, *Maps and History: Constructing Images of the Past* (New Haven, Conn.: Yale University Press, 1997), 6–7.

36 See Mauro, "*Praeceptor Austriae*," on Pius's works in print. See also Catherine Kikuchi, "Des humanists italiens au-delà des Alpes des imprimés voyageurs entre le xvᵉ et le début du xviᵉ siècle," in *L'humanisme à l'épreuve de 'Europe (xvᵉ- xviᵉ siècle)*, ed. Denis Crouzet, Elisabeth Crouzet-Pavan, Philippe Desan, Clémence Revest (Ceyzérieu: Champs Vallon, 2019), 41, 45–46. On the importance of the intersection of reading practices, evolving ideas of race in the early modern period, and the impact of printing, see Elizabeth Spiller, *Reading and the History of Race in the Renaissance* (Cambridge: Cambridge University Press, 2011).

37 Delanty, *Inventing Europe*, 1.

38 For a fuller discussion of humanism, see Chapter 1.

39 Meserve, *Empires*; Anthony Grafton, April Shelford, and Nancy Siraisi, *New Worlds, Ancient Texts: The Power of Tradition and the Shock of Discovery* (Cambridge, Mass.: Belknap Press, 1992).

40 See Meserve, *Empires*, for examples of humanists who readily used medieval sources and demonstrated more complex views of the Ottomans and central Asian powers.

41 "Sed quid illud horribile novum modo allatum de Constantinopoli? Tremit manus, dum hec scribo, horret animus neque tacere indignatio sinit neque dolor loqui permittit. Heu miseram Christianitatem." Wolkan, *Briefwechsel* 68: 199.

42 In his Letter to Nicholas of Cusa (July 21, 1453) he claims Mehmed "killed all the adults and has now afflicted the Christian people with *disasters of such a size as I think has been previously unheard of for many centuries*," (emphasis, mine). ("Puberes omnes occidit tantisque nunc cladibus Christianum populum affecit, quantis ante hac multis seculis inauditum arbitror.") Wolkan, *Briefwechsel* 68: 212; Eng. tr., mine, but see also *Reject Aeneas*, 315.

43 See Hirschi, *Origins of Nationalism*; Rolando Montecalvo, "The New *Landesgeschichte*: Aeneas Silvius Piccolomini on Austria and Bohemia," in *Pius II: 'El Più Expeditivo Pontifice: Selected Studies on Aeneas Silvius Piccolomini*, ed. Zweder Von Martels and Arjo Vanderjagt (Leiden: Brill, 2003), 55–86.

44 On the continuing significance of Christianity in Europe and uses of "Christendom," including Pius's pronounced use of such terms, see Hay, *Europe*, 96, 120. On the durability of the association of Europe with Christianity into present times, see Walser-Bürgler, *Europeans and Europeanness*, 38–39.

45 Talal Asad, "Muslims and European Identity: Can Europe Represent Islam?" in *Idea of Europe*, ed. Pagden, 209. Asad focuses more on recent decades, although he takes note of the Ottoman period. Another study suggests that the combination of Europe and religion, at least in an academic sense, is "only very recent." See Chiara Bottici and Benoit Challand, *Imagining Europe: Myth, Memory, and Identity* (Cambridge: Cambridge University Press, 2013), 146.

46 "Turcorum gens scythica et barbara est. De cuius origine atque progressu, quamvis propositum egredi videar, dicere haud alienum existimo, quando sub evo nostro in tantum hoc genus hominum auctum est, ut Asiam Greciamque tenens latinum christianumque nomen late perterreat," *De Europa*, ed. Adrian Van Heck (Vatican City: Biblioteca Apostolica Vaticana, 2001), 62; Eng. tr. *Europe (c. 1400–1458)*, tr. Robert Brown, intro. and notes, Nancy Bisaha (Washington D.C.: Catholic University of America Press, 2013), 72.

47 See Chapter 4 for discussion of Pius's references to European Jews.

48 On recent challenges to the self and other model, see Brummett, *Mapping the Ottomans*; Jonathan M. Elukin, *Living Together, Living Apart: Rethinking Jewish-Christian Relations in the Middle Ages* (Princeton: Princeton University Press, 2007); Paul Freedman, "The Medieval Other" in Timothy S. Jones and David Sprunger, eds. *Marvels, Monsters, and Miracles* (Kalamazoo, Mich.: Medieval Institute Publications, 2002), 1–24. While Pius did not succeed in creating one clear "self" to stand against all others, his attempt to do so with a definition of "Europeans" is all the more ambitious considering the array of categories of identity in his period.

49 Readers who wish to obtain a more detailed understanding of Pius's life should consult one of the many fine biographies that have been written on him in several languages. See, for example, Arthur White, *Plague and Pleasure: The Renaissance World of Pius II* (Washington DC: Catholic University of America Press, 2014); Serge Stolf, *Les lettres et la tiare: E.S. Piccolomini, un humaniste au XVe siècle* (Paris: Classiques Garnier 2012); Gioacchino Paparelli, *Enea Silvio Piccolomini: l'umanesimo sul soglio di Pietro* (Ravenna: Longo Editore, 1978); R.J. Mitchell, *The Laurels and the Tiara* (New York: Doubleday and Co., 1962); Berthe Widmer, *Enea Silvio Piccolomini Papst Pius II* (Basel: Benno Schwabe & Co. Verlag, 1960); Cecilia M. Ady, *Pius II: (Aeneas Silvius Piccolomini) The Humanist Pope* (London: Methuen and Co., 1913); Georg Voigt, *Enea Silvio de' Piccolomini als Papst Pius II und sein Zeitalter*, 3 vols. (Berlin: De Gruyter, 1856–1863). Despite its age, I find Ady's biography to be particularly thorough on biographical details and sources.

50 On the problems with using "Turks" for this period, see Cemal Kafadar, *Between Two Worlds: The Construction of the Ottoman State* (Berkeley, Calif.: University of California Press, 1995), 26–27. For an argument on its validity when discussing Western-based perceptions, see Andrei Pippidi, *Visions of the Ottoman World in Renaissance Europe* (London: Hurst and Co., 2012), 2.

51 A portion of his *Europe* was translated into German in the 1490s, and both his *Europe* and *Asia* were translated into Italian in the mid sixteenth century. His papal bulls, especially *Ezechielis* (1463), were immediately translated into several languages.

52 On Latinity in the Renaissance, see Christopher Celenza, "What Did It Mean to Live in the Long Fifteenth Century?" in *Before Copernicus: The Cultures and Contexts of Scientific Learning in the Fifteenth Century*, ed. Rivka Feldhay and F. Jamil, Ragep (Montreal: McGill University Press, 2017), 25–27.

53 Christopher Celenza, *The Lost Italian Renaissance: Humanists, Historians, and Latin's Legacy* (Baltimore: Johns Hopkins University Press, 2004); see also Patrick J. Geary "What Happened to Latin?" *Speculum* 84, no. 4 (Oct. 2009): 859–873.

54 Walser-Bürgler, *Europe and Europeanness*, 4. After describing a range of Neo-Latin sources that deal with this subject, she insightfully adds, "early modern Europe as an entity was not conceived in the offices of politicians and diplomats but on the desks of poets, scholars, and intellectuals." Ibid., 7.

1   From Siena to Vienna
The Foundations of Aeneas's Worldview

In 1435, when Pius II was just a humble secretary named Aeneas Silvius Piccolomini, he embarked on a long and dangerous journey from France to Scotland. The Hundred Years War was still raging, and Aeneas's employer, a pro-French cardinal, sent the clever young Italian on a secret mission to entreat King James I to distract the English by launching raids across his southern border. Aeneas risked being captured by the English as a spy and was nearly drowned in a shipwreck, but by the grace of heaven, he survived both travails. He showed his gratitude for his safe landing at Dunbar by walking barefoot to the nearest shrine to the Virgin at Whitekirk—a distance of ten miles over frozen pathways. As a result, Aeneas contracted gout (or frostbite arthritis), which would plague his feet for the rest of his life. The journey was not all bad, however. In his *Commentaries* he later marveled at "the rich and populous city of London" and the beauty and forwardness of the Scottish women—one of whom later bore him a son who died in infancy like so many children of the time.[1] Scotland and England had clearly made an impression on him.

Yet, despite his adventures, Aeneas wrote next to nothing about the lands across the Channel upon his return. All that survives from that period is a single sentence in a letter of 1436 to the government of Siena:

> for seven months I have been outside the world in the kingdom of Scotland, to which Cardinal Albergati had sent me, and there was no means of writing from that place, nor was there need to write since nothing was done there pertaining to your republic [Siena].[2]

The words "outside the world" (*extra terrarum orbem*) raise a host of unanswered questions—from modern readers and, one imagines, his continental contemporaries, the vast majority of whom would never venture so far. Perhaps he thought it unwise to elaborate on his covert mission at the time, but this does not explain why Aeneas wrote little about most places he visited or resided in during his two decades in Northern Europe—at least not until many years had passed and he had permanently settled in Rome.

Biographers of Aeneas, seemingly untroubled by his lack of early writing about his travels, have drawn freely from his lush, descriptive, and much later

DOI: 10.4324/9781003315865-2

Commentaries (1462–64), paraphrased above. While noting the dangers of taking the pope at his word in his grandiloquent autobiography, they largely accept what he says about the *places* he saw—as if his views in the 1460s were identical to his impressions in the 1430s and 1440s. In the pages ahead, I will avoid that trap by focusing as much as possible on his works at the time he penned them. This approach compels me to hasten over almost five decades in order to glean a sense of bigger issues: how did Aeneas's early experiences compare to his later views of identity—of continents, nations, and religions?[3] In truth, without the scaffolding of the *Commentaries* or *Europe* (1458), the story of his early views becomes shorter, if not easier, to tell. Before proceeding, the reader would do well to put aside for now the rich scene conjured in the first paragraph since nothing like it, I believe, existed in Aeneas's mind in 1436. In order to reconstruct Aeneas's trajectory from the youngest son of poor Sienese nobles to the man who would craft a compelling vision of Europe, one must pay close attention to his early testimonies and not rush to fill in his silences.

Part I: An Overview of Aeneas's Life From 1405–1453

The scope and structure of this chapter differs from the others in this book. First, it quickly covers nearly fifty years in Aeneas's life. If five decades seems excessive for one chapter, recall that this is an intellectual, not a traditional biography, with an emphasis on Aeneas's concept of Europe—an idea he wrote little about before 1453, but a great deal afterward. Of necessity, his post-1453 years must be carefully unpacked. Yet, the early decades were formative in ways that require some attention: one cannot understand Aeneas or his views without a basic comprehension of his early life, education, secretarial career, and travels. Second, this chapter is structurally different from the others, which focus more directly on Aeneas's writings while weaving in biographical details along the way—an elegant solution when one is covering a few years at a time, but ungainly when the expanse is forty-eight years and there are several recurring themes. In this chapter the biographical material appears up front so as to avoid unnecessary repetition and to provide an understanding of the experiences and ideas that shaped Aeneas, not just in his first forty-eight years, but throughout his life.

Early Life and Student Years: From Corsignano to Siena

To visit Aeneas's place of birth today is to step back in time. The town of Corsignano, known today as Pienza, so charmed director Franco Zeffirelli that he used it to film scenes from 'Romeo and Juliet' (1968). Though it was not Verona, Pienza seemed in many ways to be the perfect Renaissance city with its winding cobblestone streets, graceful homes, high-walled gardens, and unobstructed views of the Tuscan countryside below the town. Some of the grander Renaissance buildings, however, were not yet there when Aeneas was born—he built up much of the town during his papacy and, eschewing false modesty, renamed it after himself. His beginnings in Corsignano/Pienza, however, were much humbler. There were few aristocratic trappings in Aeneas's early life except for his name. The Piccolomini had been a prominent Sienese noble family two generations earlier but lost their political sway and, soon thereafter, their property when they and other aristocrats were exiled in 1385 by the republican city government. All that remained was the modest family farm in Corsignano where Aeneas grew up.[4] The town is but an hour's drive south of Siena today, but in Aeneas's time, the distance felt far greater. His first taste of his ancestral capital, in fact, may have only occurred in 1420 when the university or *Studio* of Siena temporarily transferred there to escape the plague.

Aeneas was born in Corsignano on October 18, 1405 the youngest of eighteen children—only three of whom survived to adulthood. He received a respectable education from his parish priest and spent a great deal of time exploring the fields and woods and helping his father on their farm. His early life in this bucolic setting may explain why Aeneas's adult writings reflect such pleasure at escapes to the countryside and conversations with members of the peasantry. Despite the serene tones with which the *Commentaries* paint Aeneas's youth, the Piccolomini's lack of money and frequent visitations of the plague, which took several of his siblings, must have caused significant anxiety.[5]

In 1423, eighteen-year-old Aeneas traveled to Siena to begin his studies. The city bristled with towers and magnificent buildings like the (uncompleted) Duomo and Palazzo Pubblico, rich family homes, fountains, and brick-paved streets. Before the Palazzo stretched the Piazza del Campo, a broad oval space used for markets surrounded by elegant buildings and graced by the recently completed Fonte Gaia, bedecked with sculptures by Jacopo della Quercia. Located along Via Francigena, the pilgrimage route to Rome, Siena brought pious travelers, merchants, and, of course, students and faculty from all over the peninsula and continent.[6] Aeneas must have been dazzled not only by the city, but by the cosmopolitan culture of the university. The school was expanding thanks to the commune's decision to increase funding and establish a student residence. In this period, it attracted prominent legal scholars like Mariano Sozzini and Ugo Benzi, and some humanist scholars to its faculty. Aeneas was drawn to both types of study.[7] Like Petrarch before him, he planned to earn a degree in civil law—a path with stable career prospects. But, also like Petrarch (and many other would-be jurists), he became fixated on the study of the Latin language and classical texts.[8]

At the time, Aeneas did not cut a dashing figure. Small in stature and poor, he boarded with his aunt's family to save money, and his unstylish clothes purportedly provoked the mockery of a beautiful (married) woman whom he dared approach. At least she inspired him to write love poems, only a few of which survive.[9] The price of books was also dear, and Aeneas often skipped meals to save for them or copied long extracts from borrowed volumes.[10] The greatest hardship, however, must have been the academic deficits that Aeneas's poverty had already incurred. He struggled to keep pace with privileged students who had received better primary educations. Many of these young men wrote more polished Latin, had read more ancient texts, and some were even learning Greek, while Aeneas worked furiously to catch up. His younger cousin, Goro Lolli, with whom Aeneas lived, later described how Aeneas fell asleep one night over his books and accidentally set fire to his bedclothes—a hazard of late hours spent in study.[11]

While his *Commentaries* portray a calm, untroubled education, one catches a rare glimpse of his state of mind in an early letter to Barnabeo da Siena (c. 1427), written near the end of his undergraduate years. He commiserates with his close friend over a recent scolding from one of their teachers:

> Three days ago, when I heard Master Antonio[12] was strongly reproving our folly and weak devotion to study, I was ready to return home immediately. Calling myself to my senses, I began to ask, 'What spirit has plagued you now, what inclination, what desire? Did you not resolve to always work hard at studies? Did you not determine to wed yourself to Pallas? Did you not often put Venus, raging against you, to flight with the shield of that same Pallas? Why is it that you have now forgotten all this? Or does the vast extent of knowledge prevent you from studying? Ah, what a little heart you have! What is so very difficult that assiduous practice cannot master? Do you suppose that scholarly distinction [can be achieved] without the greatest labor, sweat, and anxiety ....'[13]

Clearly, Aeneas was sensitive to accusations of sloth and distraction, but he made no excuses for himself. How much time and further study, one wonders, would it have taken for him to comfortably claim that he had achieved an adequate level of knowledge (*scientia*)? How often was he on the verge of giving up and going home? One can only admire his perseverance in the face of such challenges.

Fortunately for Aeneas, there was no standardized curriculum for the humanities in the early fifteenth century against which he or others could clearly measure his attainments. Many of the better-known male and female humanists, including Aeneas, taught themselves for some period of time. Some of this learning, for men at least, took place within the university, but not always in the most obvious of ways. Aeneas, for example, learned much about the classics from Sozzini, a professor of law.[14] Even the word "humanism" is misleading: it is a later term for studies that contemporaries described as "good letters," "good arts," "the study of humanity," or Aeneas's favorite, "literary studies."[15] Aeneas, like many other students, never formally graduated, but a degree was arguably less important than the acceptance of one's scholarly peers; humanism was as much an attitude as a loosely defined course of studies that included a set of common authors and readings like Virgil and Cicero, to name two of Aeneas's favorites.

Nonetheless, some basic definition of humanism should be offered.[16] In the broadest sense, humanists were scholars of ancient Roman literature and learning who mastered classical Latin and reproduced its style in writing and speaking; by the end of the fifteenth century, mastery of ancient Greek was also expected. Beyond these basic points, modern scholars often diverge in their opinions. In the twentieth century, two competing theories portrayed humanism as either professional in nature with an emphasis on rhetoric, or as a philosophical movement.[17] More recently, the pursuit of eloquence as a goal in itself has received more attention. As Ronald Witt argues, the "litmus for identifying a humanist was his intention to imitate ancient Latin style."[18] Other scholars, like Hanna Gray and Kenneth Gouwens have demonstrated the emotional attachment and moral purpose that many humanists drew from their studies and work.[19] For such devotees, the pursuit of eloquence was more than aesthetic. As Patrick Baker states, it was "intimately related to human, cultural, moral, political—in short, civilizational—ideals and flourishing that, according to the humanists, had been absent during the Middle Ages."[20] This not only held true for Aeneas in his younger years, but it intensified when he came to grips with the Ottoman advance and the fate of Europe as a whole.[21]

Fortunately for Aeneas, his late nights and self-discipline resulted in a firm yet graceful command of Latin. He developed an engaging, witty, and accessible writing style which won the admiration of his contemporaries well before his rise to the papacy.[22] He also earned the support and affection of his professors and fellow students in his university years. His preserved correspondence with many of these men, maintained over decades and great distances, offers an early example of the Republic of Letters. But Aeneas could only be a student for so long: he had to consider his future. He thought about joining the Franciscan order and claimed that he traveled to Rome to meet with the Saint Bernardino of Siena who kindly dissuaded him from that calling, perhaps detecting too much worldly attachment in the spirited young man.[23] Unfortunately, Aeneas had little property to inherit, a fact that must have rendered good marriage prospects all but impossible, despite his illustrious name. Economic and social mobility in the Renaissance, even in the dynamic urban centers of Northern Italy, were not easily achieved.[24] Hence, life in Siena, it would seem, simultaneously expanded Aeneas's world and laid bare the depressing narrowness of his options.

The lack of prospects in Siena, a thirst to see more of Italy, and a desire to expand his education in the liberal arts spurred Aeneas to leave the city in his mid-twenties. After studying grammar, rhetoric, and civil law in Siena, he spent two years off and on (c. 1429–31) as an itinerant scholar traveling "in true medieval fashion" to Florence, Padua, Bologna, and Ferrara.[25] The contacts he made on this journey were primarily with other humanists, including such luminaries as Francesco Filelfo, famed teacher Guarino da Verona, and Sicilian poet Giovanni Aurispa. A letter from late 1431 to Aurispa, whom he met in Ferrara, conveys Aeneas's awe among the stars of his field and his efforts to build short acquaintances into enduring friendships—using all the charm, wit, and eloquence he could muster. He praises Aurispa's humanity, refinement, charity, and benevolence toward all, even the lowly people: "no one could be kinder or more favorable than you, for you wished to number me, too, among your friends."[26] This letter, though possibly edited later by Aeneas, poignantly reveals his longing to become a member of this elite group. Aeneas's many short biographies of scholars in his *On Famous Men* (1445–50) and his descriptions of scholars throughout Italy in his *De Europa* (1458) give some indication of connections he forged during this period.[27]

At the time, however, his exposure to top universities and scholars must have also brought the grim realization that he was unlikely to find employment as a teacher. For all its excitement, his period of wandering demonstrates the downside to the freedom of early humanism. The flexibility of classical studies may have created a large and open community, but it fostered insecurity and competition among its devotees when it came to jobs and recognition. Even the most successful humanists—chancellors, prelates, or university chairs—experienced brief or extended periods of precariousness when they sought new positions.[28] We can comfortably assume that Aeneas's path was no different, but his writings provide few details on this phase. His *Commentaries* later state that he had been attending lectures on civil law when he was forced to leave Siena due to the outbreak of war with Florence, omitting any record of his scholarly peregrinations, and creating the impression that he was determined to complete his legal studies, but was somehow prevented.[29] His vagueness in the *Commentaries* on this entire period was either a cover for a lackluster resumé, or the erasure of unpleasant memories of failed ambitions.[30] But his luck would soon change. Not long after Aeneas returned to Siena in late 1431, he met Cardinal Domenico Capranica, who was traveling to the Council of Basel in Switzerland and looking to hire a secretary. If some young men at the time saw classical studies as merely a path toward employment, as Kristeller has suggested, Witt and Baker come closer to Aeneas's experience when they argue that humanists were employable *because* they had already mastered these texts and the *ars rhetorica*.[31] Secretarial work was a solid 'plan B' for many lovers of antiquity.

The Life of a Secretary, From Basel to Austria

Aeneas crossed the Alps just as the Council of Basel (1431–49) was getting underway, arriving in a well-ordered and maintained Rhineland city with elegant homes and beautiful churches.[32] This was the first major council since the resolution of the Papal Schism (1378–1417) at the Council of Constance (1414–1417).[33] The gathering at Basel, in fact, was supposed to be the first of many general councils to follow it. Unlike most Church councils, it was neither called nor led by the current pope and was broader based and more representative in nature. Hopes were high in the early years that delegates at Basel would push through long overdue reforms of the Church and its hierarchy and, thereby, "transform the papacy into a constitutional monarchy."[34] Aeneas's letters capture that feeling of common enterprise. Popes in this period, however, saw Basel differently; Eugenius IV (r. 1431–47) spent much of his papacy opposing the council's efforts to regulate his actions. While the council waited for Eugenius to come around, representatives from governments across Europe gathered: according to Aeneas, they came from Spain, Scotland, Poland, France, Italy, and even Hussite-riven Bohemia.[35]

If Siena gave Aeneas his first glimpse of the larger world, Basel offered wider exposure to the diversity of the Christian peoples of Europe. In this city he observed and interacted with delegates individually and in groups, and perhaps most powerfully in the "nations" that assembled there—i.e., groups of voting clergy organized by country and region. He also made several life-long friends like Piero da Noceto, a young fellow secretary who traveled in Capranica's entourage from Italy to Basel. Piero would later serve in the papal curia in Rome and remain a knowledgeable contact for Aeneas.[36]

As a young foreigner amidst the busy, sometimes frenetic, doings at Basel, Aeneas has aptly been described as "star struck."[37] He understandably sided with the council as Pope Eugenius's resistance to it mounted. Less than a year after arriving, he wrote to the Sienese government in late 1432 roundly criticizing the pope's efforts to dissolve the council and urged his home state to condemn papal actions: "Already, a year has elapsed since [Eugenius] issued the dissolution [of the council]; and, since that time, he never has ceased to alarm the council. And so, he must be proceeded against, pronounced contumacious, and stripped of all obedience."[38] Siena, like most governments in Europe, demurred, but the council pushed on and refused to disband when Pope Eugenius transferred it to Ferrara in 1438. The conciliarists at Basel went so far as to depose Eugenius in 1439 and elect another pope, Felix V. Hence, what started out as a means to improve the Church and to give voice to more of its members nearly ended with another schism.

For all the excitement of Basel, Aeneas's personal concerns were more mundane and pressing: namely, finding steady employment among bishops and cardinals whose needs or finances could change overnight. His job with Capranica ended shortly after their arrival in Basel due to the cardinal's unexpected loss of funds, but Aeneas managed to find work serving two bishops for short periods of time—the Bishop of Freising, Nicodemo della Scala, and the Bishop of Novara, Bartolomeo Visconti.[39] Meanwhile, he tried to maintain a network of support back home as his many letters to the government of Siena and other contacts in Italy show. While it probably took Aeneas years to become an adept and confident secretary, he demonstrated one valuable skill from an early age: letter writing. As its Latin name implies, the *ars dictaminis* was an art form that required training and subtlety; in an age where correspondence might be the first or only form of contact on matters of import, powerful men were eager to employ talented writers with polished Latin.[40]

Travel was another component of Aeneas's secretarial jobs. He accompanied the bishop of Freising to the Diet of Frankfurt and the bishop of Novara to Milan. His situation improved when he was hired by Cardinal Niccolò Albergati, whom he served for four years starting around the end of 1434. He visited France, the Netherlands, England, and Scotland in the cardinal's service, in addition to his trips to Austria and Germany. If the gathering at Basel offered a preview of the far corners of Europe, the miles that Aeneas covered by land and sea and the time he spent in each of these places gave him the most direct experience possible—his early impressions of some of these places will be discussed later in this chapter. Within a few years of arriving at Basel, he rose through the ranks and began to serve the Council directly, drafting its letters and documents; in 1439 he was appointed to serve the pope himself, or rather, the anti-pope, Felix V.[41] In addition to all this activity, Aeneas wrote his first history, an account the council titled *Two Books on the Proceedings of the Council of Basel* (1439–40).[42]

The 1430s was a dynamic decade for Aeneas: he travelled extensively and acquired skill and subtlety as a secretary, orator, and diplomat, earning the trust of some of the most powerful men in both Church and state along the way.[43] In his letters, he began to reflect upon the nature of political and religious power, the dynamics of group identity, and the health and unity of Christendom. But in the early 1440s, the future of the Council of Basel began to look uncertain. No major power fully and openly supported Felix, whose fortunes continued to sink as his rival's rose with the triumphant Council of Florence (1438–39). This elaborate council, which hosted some 700 Byzantine delegates, was called and presided over by Eugenius; it began in Ferrara then moved to Florence with the Medici's financial support. There, Eugenius accomplished what several popes before him had failed to do by concluding a union with the Greek Church on July 6, 1439.[44] Back in Basel, the antipope Felix scored no comparable victories, but Aeneas hung on for a few more years even as he likely considered other options for employment.

The chance to leave Basel finally arose when he accepted a position serving the Holy Roman Emperor, Frederick III (r. 1440–93).[45] Aeneas had visited Frankfurt on behalf of the council in the summer of 1442 and was crowned poet laureate on July 27 by the emperor. In November of that same year, Frederick visited the Council of Basel and, while there, asked Aeneas to return with him to Austria as a secretary in the imperial chancery. Aeneas would spend over a decade in Frederick's service.

Aeneas, now thirty-seven, came to the imperial court as a seasoned diplomat, a skilled secretary, and a writer whose fame was steadily growing. Within a short time, he was trading letters with famous humanists like Lorenzo Valla.[46] His knowledge of European politics and cultures at this age already exceeded that of most men, and through his extensive correspondence it would continue to increase. He diligently maintained a network of connections and friendships across the continent from his Basel days—including the powerful Cardinal Giuliano Cesarini, Juan de Segovia, and Nicholas of Cusa as well as a host of fellow secretaries who also served high-ranking clergy and lay rulers.[47] In addition, his humanist training and knowledge of the German language made him a rare commodity among secretaries.[48]

Despite all this, Aeneas would spend the first several months in his new position feeling out of place and overlooked. He alludes to his predicament with a playful exchange in the *Pentalogus* (1443), a dialogue between himself, the emperor, the chancellor, and two bishops on the merits of a humanist education and issues facing the Church and empire. The work opens with the emperor walking past Aeneas, who was sitting in the corner, and summoning him from the shadows to come speak. It takes him a few moments to recall that this functionary is the same man he crowned as poet laureate and hired as secretary! When asked why he had not come to see Frederick, Aeneas offers an amusing story about a deaf door keeper who would not let him through.[49] A few years after leaving his service, Aeneas would describe Frederick as having "a fine physique and an appearance of a worthy emperor," but he also said he was slow to act and more interested in his gardens and gemstones than more pressing matters, presumably ruling and fighting.[50] Judging from the *Pentalogus*, it did not take Aeneas long to realize he had thrown in his lot with an absent-minded, hesitant man.

Another famous work by Aeneas from this period, his popular *Miseries of Courtiers* (1444), seems a thinly veiled lament on his own life at court, with tales of bad food, sleeping on poor straw mattresses, and other indignities.[51] For all the satire of these works, it is clear from his letters to trusted correspondents that his living and working conditions in his first two years did not please him. In a letter to Sigismund of Tyrol (Dec. 5, 1443) in which he urges the young duke resume his studies, he ends by excusing his brevity with a complaint about the cramped, noisy chancery in which he worked, comparing his cohort to bees, sheep, magpies, and frogs.[52] Aeneas's situation improved, however, through the offices of imperial chancellor Kaspar Schlick, whose family ties to Italy made him more appreciative than his colleagues of Aeneas's talents and elegant writing style.[53] Within a couple of years, Aeneas received his own salary and a seat at Schlick's well-appointed table and became second in command when the chancellor was away. Through patient cultivation of allies and opportunities, Aeneas improved his position at the imperial court. In time, he became a trusted envoy and adviser to Emperor Frederick himself.

Life changed in other important ways during Aeneas's imperial service. Within four years, he left the camp of the conciliarists and became both a papalist and a priest. Pope Eugenius looked favorably on Aeneas's efforts to mend his ways and absolved him in 1445. In the year 1446, at the age of forty-one, Aeneas took holy orders; in 1447 he received his first major benefice, the bishopric of Trieste in northern Italy, which still holds a manuscript collection of his works and related materials.[54] In 1451 he became bishop of his beloved Siena. These were substantial alterations for such a short span of time, and for some scholars, the change seems too abrupt to have been sincere. Not only was he an ardent supporter of conciliarism a few years earlier, but his recent romantic adventures have raised flags. Aeneas's second child was born out of wedlock to a woman he wooed over the course of several days at an inn where they were both staying in Strasbourg in 1444—the same year he penned his famous and erotic *Tale of Two Lovers*.

The motives behind these shifts may not have been wholly selfless, but his letters prove that neither decision was abrupt nor ill considered. His new identity as a clergyman and papal supporter would play major roles in his developing view of the broader world, the collective interests of Christians of Europe, and the question of who might best lead them toward greater unity. Among his biggest accomplishments during this time was his painstakingly brokered reconciliation between Emperor Frederick and Pope Eugenius from 1446 to 1447. Trieste was his reward from a grateful Eugenius.

During his decade with the imperial chancery Aeneas made further strides as an author and a political thinker.[55] He became more reflective in letters and other works regarding cultural differences between Germany and Italy, internal and external threats to European security, and notions of universal authority on the continent. Aeneas's observation of both the inner workings of government at the imperial chancery and the wider world of European diplomacy certainly kept him apprised of current events. His renown continued to grow with the publication of several important works including *On the Origin and Authority of the Roman Empire* (1446), *On Famous Men* (1445–50), *The Education of Boys* (1450), *The Miseries of Courtiers* (1444), and the *Tale of Two Lovers* (1444). Despite occasional homesickness and lack of promotion at court, the years he spent in Austria and Germany were productive. These experiences advanced his career in the Church and his formidable reputation as an authority on "the world" as most Western Europeans defined it at the time.

Finally, we should consider the role that Aeneas's profession played in shaping his views and writings—especially his elegant epistolary style. Secretaries have all too frequently been taken for granted and ignored, but they are incredibly keen observers. Renaissance secretaries moved freely among all of the three estates of clergy, nobility, and peasantry/townspeople without clearly belonging to any one of them. This liminality may have enabled Aeneas to transition fluidly from religious to secular masters; to navigate between politics, law, and theology; and finally, to move unobtrusively through so many different countries and classes of people. The writings of Renaissance secretaries contain some of the most insightful analyses of powerful people and events of their day, couched in well-crafted, compelling prose. This comes as no surprise given the number of humanists who filled the profession's ranks. Some of them later found fame as chancellors, political advisers, bishops, and even popes: Petrarch, Salutati, Bruni, Poggio, Pope Nicholas, and Machiavelli all worked as secretaries. It was a position filled with unwritten rules, conventions, and constant negotiation between the powerful masters they served and the people who wanted access to them.[56] Having reviewed the first five decades of Aeneas's life at a brisk pace, it is now time to let him speak for himself on questions of identity, culture, and related issues.

Part II: Aeneas's Early Works on Culture, Identity, and Universal Authority

Travels and Observations: Aeneas's Letters

In the fifteenth century, travel was slow, grueling, unpredictable, and dangerous. Few Europeans of any station traveled more than Aeneas.[57] Whereas travel today suggests adventure and leisure, its medieval etymology conjured only joylessness: *travail* in French meant labor and toil as well as travel; the English word "travail" is a close equivalent.[58] Illness and brigandage were constant threats, and shipwrecks all too frequent. Aeneas himself had two near brushes with death on the high seas: first in the Ligurian Sea heading toward Genoa in early 1432 and again in the North Sea sailing to Scotland in 1435.[59] On the brighter side, the slow pace of journeys enabled observant travelers to register subtle changes as they crossed from port to port and region to region—a cognitive advantage that modern transportation has all but erased.[60] Being a resourceful secretary likely helped Aeneas adapt, make connections, and gain assistance from clergy and laypeople in the many places he visited. This is not to say he was invisible to locals; foreigners generally stood out.[61] He claimed years later in his *Commentaries* (perhaps an exaggeration) that the northern English found him so exotic they were not sure if he was a Christian.[62] While Aeneas rarely wrote about the places he visited at this time in his life, there are a few rich exceptions. All of them were framed in Aeneas's favorite genre of this period, the letter.

Renaissance letters occupy a special niche among historical sources. The tremendous value of these sources is only matched by the challenge of interpreting them. On their face, letters are honest, unfiltered, and speak directly to readers across the centuries with a form and function that mirror today's correspondence—even if our present medium is largely electronic. But the resemblances between modern letters and those of Renaissance Europe can be deceptive. Letters that claim to be private and informal, for example, were often carefully crafted, intended for public consumption, and filled with "ritualized emotions" that were governed by a "social code"—all of which can escape the modern reader's notice.[63] In addition to these complexities, humanist letter writers often aspired or felt pressured to replicate the style of classical epistolary masters like Cicero and St. Jerome, who collected and edited their letters. When Petrarch began selecting and revising his own familiar letters, he deliberately copied the "familiar style" he found in Cicero's letters to Atticus. By the early fifteenth century, Salutati had collected his letters and Bruni and Poggio were doing the same. Hence, when Aeneas wrote a letter of any kind, the choices and signals that he navigated were considerable.[64]

Aeneas's letters are prolific and expressive. They speak to a range of issues in a style that contemporaries praised for its simplicity and clarity.[65] Agostino Dati attests to Aeneas's early reputation for mastery of the genre when he asked Aeneas in or around 1442 for precepts on the art of letter writing.[66] There was nothing off-handed, then, about the way Aeneas wrote his epistles, especially the surviving ones—the majority of which are known to us because he chose to copy and, almost certainly, edit them. He first began collecting and circulating his own letters between 1443–1444.[67] What survives is a carefully curated selection of epistles he wrote and received; they reflect not only his tastes but those of his associates, relatives, and later editors who ensured that some letters became very well known while others were lost or forgotten.[68] Their content, moreover, was wide ranging. Like Petrarch and others,

Aeneas used them as a form of autobiography and history, not to mention a showcase for rhetorical prowess and storytelling.[69] The inherent flexibility of the genre was one of its greatest attractions. As John Najemy shows, Renaissance letter writing "became a field of freer play and greater experimentation" because it was bound by no single template.[70] In many ways, Aeneas found his true voice in his familiar letters, so it is no surprise that he employed this genre to explore his earliest efforts at travel writing. Three cities received lengthy descriptions in Aeneas's early letters: Genoa, Basel, and Vienna. Each of these letters speak to Aeneas's curiosity and talent for travel writing—they follow similar themes that provide a preview of Aeneas's later, more developed views of cultures and societies.

The letter on Genoa, addressed to Aeneas's Sienese friend, Andreozio Petrucci, is the earliest and shortest of Aeneas's urban descriptions. Written on March 24, 1432, in Milan, shortly after he left the bustling coastal city on his journey north, it conveys Aeneas's curiosity and sense of wonder at what must have been his first visit.[71] As a student, Aeneas had recently traveled to several cities in Italy, but Genoa stood out as a wealthy, cosmopolitan port city and the capital of a Mediterranean trading empire rivalled only by Venice: "Ships busily come and go, these from the east, those from the west, so that every day you may see different races [*genera*] of men, with strange and unpolished manners, and merchants arriving with every kind of wares."[72] Though impressed by the industry of the Genoese, Aeneas criticized their attitude toward learning: "Too little desirous of knowledge, they study grammar out of necessity, and value other sorts of studies but little."[73] He also condemned the frequent dissension and conspiracies in Genoa, saying the one thing the city lacked was peace.[74] Still, the size, bustle, and beauty of Genoa (and its women) left him entranced.[75] Comparing the city to Florence, he claims that Genoa surpassed it, just as Florence surpassed Arezzo.[76] While it is unclear how much of this letter was written in 1432 or added later, if even parts of it date from 1432 it shows Aeneas's early gift for vivid portraits of places and people.

Aeneas's accounts of Basel expand on some of these themes. The Swiss city is the subject of two letters that are almost identical in form and content. The first, to Cardinal Giuliano Cesarini (July 1434), was written from Milan while Aeneas was in the service of the bishop of Novara, and the second, to the archbishop of Tours, Philippe Coetquis (Oct. 28, 1438).[77] He describes the northwestern Swiss city as a strikingly modern, neatly planned city—a result of mid-fourteenth–century earthquakes that left fewer than one hundred buildings standing. The position of the city, surrounding rivers abounding in fish, and fields rich with vines and grain are treated at length, revealing his fascination with geography and the belief he shared with Strabo that it was intimately connected with the destiny of a region.[78] He favorably compares the richly adorned churches to those of Italy, but for their lack of paintings, and notes the practice of women praying with their maidservants from the comfort of wooden cubicles, which, he presumes, was for protection from the cold rather than for privacy.[79] The homes of Basel's citizens, at least the wealthier ones, receive high praise for their elegance and comforts like glazed windows, warmth in cold winters, caged singing-birds, gardens, and fountains. His aside that, "Florentine homes are not greater," suggests constant comparison on his travels to the wonders he once saw in that city—and perhaps a desire to knock Siena's Tuscan rival off its pedestal.[80] Regarding the Baselers themselves, they are unostentatious but well dressed, learned, upright, and honest; he accuses them of little vice save for the peccadilloes of Venus and Dionysus.[81] When it comes to security, if Italian cities have thicker walls, he argues, the unity of Basel's citizens render the city strong against attack.[82] There is nothing, in short, to suggest that Aeneas looked down his nose at the northern city.

Vienna, which he visited in 1437 with the bishop of Novara, receives a less positive review.[83] In a letter to an unnamed friend (c. April 1438), he describes the city's layout and buildings, commending its thick and high walls, its towers, and the comfort and beauty of private homes—marred only by unattractive wooden roofs. For the most part "Whichever house you enter, you will think you are in the palace of a prince."[84] As for the inhabitants, he found them more colorful than respectable. He admired the university, but he found the bulk of the citizenry to be rather coarse:

> Common people worship their bellies and are gluttonous. What a man has earned during the week by the work of his hands, he squanders down to the last penny on Sunday. This is a ragged, boorish lot, and there is a very great number of whores. Rare is the woman who is content with one husband.[85]

Ex-prostitutes were given the chance to rehabilitate at the convent of St. Jerome, but those who reverted to their former ways were cruelly thrown into the Danube. Murders were common occurrences along with excessive drinking, and piety was in short supply with the regular sale of meat on fasting days and little fear of excommunication in general.

One might reasonably ask if ethnic bias sparked these harsh generalizations, but elitism seems a likelier explanation, as seen in Aeneas's comment that few old families lived in the city—most were immigrants or foreigners. And yet, Aeneas is not insensitive to the plight of the poor, noting that (unlike in Basel) justice is harsh only to the poor who lack the means to manipulate or bribe their way out of it.[86] If Aeneas truly found Vienna to be such a den of iniquity, one can imagine his mixed emotions when he accepted his new position with the emperor, who kept a residence there. Fortunately for Aeneas, his initial distaste would change as he came to know the region better.[87]

When read as a group, some common topics emerge in these descriptive letters, particularly education and government. Aeneas shows his scholarly bias in judging cities by the level and type of learning they promoted. The Genoese did not pursue higher learning enough in his view, but the citizens of Basel come off slightly better. In his letter to Coetquis, he praises the Baselers' love of religion but sees the commitment to classical studies as deficient, particularly the fields of rhetoric and poetry. He positively notes, however, the expansive access to education in Basel: many youths come to the city from neighboring towns because they are given sustenance through charity while the school master is supported by public funds.[88] Similarly, he offers mixed opinions about education in Vienna, praising the university but noting that "the greatest flaw is that they give too much attention to dialectic and too much time to study which is not very fruitful."[89] Yet, he also claims that the students were partying pleasure seekers who rarely attended to their studies. These brief comments may not add up to much at this stage, but they suggest an early connection in Aeneas's mind between learning and culture—with an emphasis on the liberal arts and classical studies as the ultimate yardstick of accomplishment and civility.

Aeneas's letters are important records of his impressions of the appearance, functioning, and inhabitants of three European cities; a fourth letter about the Czech town of Tabor will be discussed later in this chapter. And yet, considering his extensive travels over the course of two decades, the survival of a handful of letters on three cities and one town seems rather paltry. For some reason, Aeneas did not set himself to the task of writing a description of his fascinating new home in Basel until two years after arriving there; in fact, it was only in Milan with time to spare and perhaps the example of Bruni's *Laudatio* on the city of Florence (1404) to stimulate him that he turned to this task.[90] Whether his general silence on his travels stemmed from a lack of time or a perception that readers were not interested in descriptions of other cities is hard to say. In fairness, the Council of Basel was international, so perhaps his focus was less on the citizens and local culture than on the business of foreign visitors. Regardless, what appears to be lacking is the motivation to write more about foreign places at this time in Aeneas's life—a circumstance that would obviously change. Also missing is a clear sense of cities as microcosms of the larger nation. Instead, he keenly observes the individualistic qualities of each city—perhaps owing to Italy's unique context as a land of so many independent city-states. These writings, then, reveal Aeneas's early interest in foreign cities, but also the limited scope of his thinking at this time.

Politics and Universal Authority

From 1432 to 1455 Aeneas served or came into contact with several types of government including, but not limited to, the Republic of Siena, a Church council, city government in Basel, the Holy Roman Empire, and the papacy. He witnessed a wide spectrum of power structures, political theory, law, and procedure: from popular and representative, to feudal and princely, to ecclesiastical. Yet Aeneas's early political views are far from clear. His letters to the government of Siena from Basel show a willingness to serve the state, but not a passion for republicanism.[91] His letters and historical treatise on the Council of Basel show enthusiasm for its mission and outbursts of support for conciliar principles, but also doubts about the council's ability to find consensus. He had similarly undecided views of the state of the empire. It is hard to know, in short, if Aeneas had a strong political philosophy at this stage or simply served his masters as a loyal secretary.

At Basel, Aeneas was exposed to a democratic model of government. The council contained a diversity of voices, representing a range of social classes, nations, and theological views. Clergymen from around Europe regularly met in four "deputations" or committees to deliberate matters of heresy, peace, reform, and general business. A president and a promoter were elected monthly in each deputation. A council of twelve was also elected monthly, drawing three members from each deputation; it acted as the steering committee and oversaw business of the council. In many ways, the Council mirrored the shape and procedures of communal governments, except that it was more diverse and popular in composition, with lower clergy outnumbering the higher ranks.

Adding to the Council of Basel's broad-based structure was its international character. Lay and clerical envoys constantly arrived from around Europe, pushing the agendas of their cities and nation states. Perspectives and concerns of different regions in Europe were further defined by the division of delegates to the Council according to blocks of "nations." The clergy who attended were sorted into one of four (roughly constituted) nations: France, Italy, Spain, and Germany, which were evenly distributed across the deputations.[92] Aeneas seems to have written little about the nations at the time, but the council must have given him valuable insight into the different countries of Europe and the regional and international concerns that brought them together.[93]

At least one scholar has argued that Aeneas was "pro-democracy" given his support of the council.[94] On its face, this seems a reasonable supposition. When the wheels of the Council turned efficiently, it must have been impressive for young Aeneas to witness. He defended its principles of broad-based government as late as 1443, a year after he left Basel, in a letter to a papalist:

> The pope is one. The council is a gathering of many experienced people where more eyes than one see, and all know all things, although no one knows everything. No one is so arrogant that he thinks himself to understand better than all others.[95]

At other times, however, Aeneas questioned the Council's ability to bring so many opinions into productive dialogue. In a letter of 1437 to his friend Piero da Noceto he describes arguments over the location of the council's next meeting and the abuses the esteemed president Cardinal Cesarini had to suffer:

> Once he was accustomed to nothing other than to guide the council with his speech, just as Cicero once did the senate, and they wondered at his eloquence no less than the Athenians wondered at the orations of Demosthenes. Now all heckled him when speaking and condemned him when silent.[96]

In the same letter, he recounts another meeting where archbishops insulted one another and the lesser men shouted like common folk in a tavern; he later describes some participants of the council as a mob of the "basest people" (*vilissime plebis*) and their descent into a shoving match.[97] Only the intervention of the townspeople prevented bloodshed. His exasperation peaks with the statement: "How utterly ridiculous that those who gathered to give the world peace should lack it themselves, and that those who boast that they give concord to the laity should seek it from the laity."[98] The literary flair of this letter notwithstanding, his elitism is unmistakable.

Aeneas's disdain for the lower classes and even for popular government emerges in other works as well, like an oration he gave at Basel in 1436 promoting the Duke of Milan's request to hold the next meeting in his dominion and dismissing the bids of republican cities to host it themselves. Such towns are not populated with free men, he states, but "slaves ... who believe that freedom is to have many masters."[99] Whether this outburst had anything to do with his disappointment in the Republic of Siena or his (likely paid) support of the duke of Milan, or both, is hard to say, but the same view prevails in his letter describing Basel to Coetquis (1438). Unlike the earlier version to Cesarini, he elaborates harshly on the class differences between Basel and Italian cities. Among Italians, he states,

> individuals wish to rule, [and] all are forced to serve, as those who spurn the king or emperor are subjected to the lowest people. As a result, there is no long-lasting rule among them, and nowhere more than in Italy does fortune jest.

At least in Basel, he continues, the popular government demonstrates cooperation between nobles and commoners, who share tasks or appointments in peace.[100] Recall, as well, his disdain for boorish Vienna, assigning some of the blame to its lack of old, presumably elite, families in the city.

If Aeneas was ever pro-democracy, it was a short-lived flirtation. As the descendant of noble exiles, he may have always mistrusted popular government, and the mayhem of the council in 1437 and the loss of Cesarini's steadying leadership likely increased his antipathy. Still, there seems little reason to force these views under the label of a firm political ideology. Whatever his personal views, he stayed with the Council for several more years and defended its work in his flattering history, *The Deeds of the Council of Basel* (1439–40), where he orchestrated the cacophony of voices into a seductive vision of harmony and benevolence.[101] His most serious criticisms of the council were only written years later.[102]

The prospect of social change or conflict elicited little excitement in Aeneas. Unlike Machiavelli, who viewed dissension as a feature of strong and healthy government, Aeneas only felt anxiety and discomfort whenever he witnessed it. To be fair, few Renaissance republicans can be said to have enjoyed conflict, but most continued to trust in the principle of shared government; Aeneas, however, increasingly looked to the guiding hand of centralized authority. Some hint of this may be seen in his letter to Emperor Sigismund (1437) asking him to intervene to help restore unity to the council.[103] While Aeneas did not abandon conciliarism and embrace papalism until 1445, by 1443 he started to accept the need for a centralized, universal authority.[104] The only potential source of secular universal leadership in Christian Europe was the Holy Roman Emperor. After years of stalemate at Basel, Aeneas appeared hopeful that the emperor could heal at least some of the wounds of a divided Christendom.

Aeneas made several attempts to convince his new master Frederick to take advantage of his position as Holy Roman Emperor to unify central Europeans and inspire other Christian nations. The earliest was his *Pentalogus* (1443). In truth, it is an odd text: it did not circulate widely during Aeneas's life or for centuries after, and its premise seems ham-fisted. Aeneas's character spends much of the dialogue trying to persuade Frederick to invade Italy—an idea that Frederick in no way appears to have considered.[105] Even stranger than his call to invade Italy is the reason why: Aeneas seems to suggest that that if Frederick conquered Italy, German princes and burghers would better respect and obey him. Yet, he does not consider how Frederick could conquer Italy in the first place without the Germans firmly behind him.[106] This fantasy, moreover, clashed with the agendas that Frederick and other German princes were trying to pursue at this time, like agitating for a large-scale diet, even a third general council at Nuremberg to end the schism and to assert imperial claims in Eastern Europe.[107]

Yet beneath Aeneas's provocative suggestions lies a more serious message: a longing to repair the damage of the latest schism, for which he was partially to blame, and hope that the emperor could be a force for Christian unity.[108] While the *Pentalogus* was not a serious call for caesaropapism on Aeneas's part, it reflects his growing desire for centralized leadership in Europe—for an individual who could bring the nations and factions together.[109] Just as important, it shows his increased reflection on the relationship between the empire, the German people, and the Italian peninsula. His repeated references to the German *natio* (nation) or *patria* (fatherland, homeland, or native land), while undeveloped here, show an early interest in the German people as a political collective that extended beyond their membership in the empire.[110] More will be said about the concept of nation in Chapter 3.

A more extensive treatment of the prerogatives and duties of the emperor appears in a treatise dedicated to Frederick called "On the Origin and Authority of the Roman Empire" (*De ortu et auctoritate imperii Romani*) (1446). When he composed this work, Aeneas had been at the court for approximately four years and was eager to see Frederick take more decisive action. He also hoped that the emperor and leading princes would decide whether to support the pope or the council and abandon their current position of neutrality. Neutrality (and division) may have suited the princes' local needs better, but the impact on the empire was damaging. In 1444, Aeneas started to lean toward the papalists and began taking steps to reconcile personally with Eugenius. He received formal absolution in 1445.[111] Still, he was not yet ready to throw his lot in completely with the pope, and he explored the basis on which Frederick could assert greater leadership among Christians; the question was still open as the emperor had not yet fully reconciled with the pope nor had the schism ended—it would drag on until anti-pope Felix agreed to step down in 1449.

At first glance, *De ortu* seems a standard medieval defense of imperial power. Aeneas describes empire as a system anointed by God when he sent his only son to live among mankind just as Rome was experiencing its zenith under Augustus Caesar.[112] Biblical references to the Psalms and Job shore up this traditional feel: "there is nothing which is of more concern to the supreme God … than the neglect of justice and the unmerited oppression of the poor."[113] In some ways, Aeneas seems to fall in line with the medieval and Renaissance belief in the role of divine intervention as a stabilizing force in worldly affairs and the moral guidance of Christianity in political practice.[114]

But as Cary Nederman argues, there is more to *De ortu* than meets the eye. A closer reading shows Aeneas carefully weighing political problems of his day and using classical sources, namely Cicero, in an innovative and decidedly humanistic way.[115] Aeneas, in fact, exposes a limitation in Cicero's political model which few republican thinkers of his time grasped: while republican rule offered a path to stability within states, the weakness of this model, as Aeneas frames it, appears whenever there is a conflict between states. Republican governments are not designed to ensure peace beyond their own borders and face conflict whenever they or their neighbors seek to expand.[116] What is needed, Aeneas argues, is an arbiter who stands above all these republics and principalities to help keep the peace. It is a model that blends (Ciceronian) reason and observation of human nature with medieval ideologies, and I would add, his own personal perspectives.[117]

The goal of government, Aeneas argues, is not power, but peace:

> If we were living under one head, if all of us followed one obedience, if we recognized only one supreme prince in temporal affairs, the best sort of peace would flourish everywhere on earth; and all of us would enjoy sweet concord.[118]

The most logical manifestation of this "one head" is, of course, empire. Aeneas anticipates certain problems with this call for reason and obedience, but boldly asserts that if the emperor acts unjustly, it "must be suffered patiently; and redress must be awaited from his successor, or from the correction of the celestial judge."[119] For all his realism on the fallibility of emperors, it was a bit absurd to ask powerful men to tolerate these wrongs and wait for better times. And, indeed, Frederick turned out to be one of the longest reigning Habsburgs! At such moments, Aeneas shows his conditioning as a civil servant instead of his sobering experience with princes. Nonetheless, Aeneas ultimately believed that if the princes empowered the emperor to adjudicate disputes between his subjects, long and complicated wars would be circumvented—a small price to pay for the occasional injustice, in his mind.[120]

These ideas may sound "medieval," but they are arguably the product of his decade and a half as a secretary and diplomat, witnessing the failures of compromise. By 1446, whatever sympathies for broad-based government that Aeneas might have harbored had given way to the necessity for strong, centralized authority, imperfect though it was. He makes this clear in *De ortu*: "For neither a popular regime, which is called civil, or that of the best citizens, which is called aristocratic government, can be as just and peaceful as a monarchic one."[121] Yet his use of Cicero is revealing: Aeneas could not join Bruni and others in their republican answers to political problems of the day, but *De ortu* proves that he engaged with their arguments.[122]

De ortu also shows a change of heart on the papacy and its role in Europe. In the *Pentalogus*, he ceded no ground to the papacy, but in *De ortu*, he edges closer to accepting the role of universal papal authority, at least on spiritual matters. Both pope and emperor are needed in Christendom, he argues, and neither should be questioned: "No one has the right to make void a judgement of the Roman pontiff. No one can impugn the will of the Roman prince."[123] Among the supporting principles for this claim, he cites the famous "two swords" passage in the Gospel of Luke:

> Thus, too those words of Christ are cited here: when a disciple said to him *Behold, here are two swords* [Luke 22:38], He said, *it is enough.* By these words, as the doctors of the Church interpret [them], He subjected spiritual matters to the supreme pontiff and temporal matters to Caesar, as if He had said, 'Let there be two powers …[124]

Though not a full endorsement for the pope as peacemaker and unifier of Europe, it opens the door to a far greater role than Aeneas had previously allowed to pontiffs. The idea of a universal authority, or two such authorities, to put an end to the petty bickering and eruptions of war increasingly appealed to Aeneas.[125] His worldview was continuing to expand.

It is important to ask what terms Aeneas used to describe the larger Christian/political collective. There is almost no use of "Europe" or "Asia" in either *Pentalogus* or *De ortu* except when Aeneas mentions Alexander the Great in the latter. Germany appears several times in *Pentalogus*, but there is little mention of it in *De ortu*. What Aeneas does speak of repeatedly in *De ortu* is the Roman Empire, in both the ancient Italic and medieval Germanic incarnations. He also uses both *Romanum genus* and *Romanus populus*, with perhaps a slight preference for the latter—both roughly translate to "Roman people," with subtle differences.[126] In *De ortu*, he does not speak of "Christendom" or "Christians" as a collective, but he does employ the notion a few times in *Pentalogus*. Either way, "Europe" was not regularly invoked at this time—by him or other writers—but "Roman Empire" often served as a proximate sense of a larger community.[127] Also noteworthy in *De ortu* is the way that Aeneas questions the autonomy of nations, even Germanic kingdoms, who proudly claimed their ancestral right to rule by rescuing the faltering Roman provinces. Showing little interest in the complexities that led to the dissolution of the empire, both internal and external, Aeneas argues that the Germans were unjustly stealing from a broken empire.[128] This cavalier attitude toward national sovereignty would undergo considerable transformation after the crisis of 1453 and his move to Rome. Immature though some of Aeneas's political views were at this time, they are certainly creative and deserving of more attention. During his time at the imperial court, he began to reflect more seriously on these matters and to expand his lens wider.[129] It is no coincidence that he eagerly tried to secure a copy of Aristotle's *Politics*, translated by Bruni between 1443–1446, as several of his letters show.[130]

Cultural and Ethnic Observations

Aeneas's time north of the Alps must have been full of surprises. One imagines the Sienese humanist adjusting to both colder temperatures and linguistic challenges with locals who spoke neither Latin nor Italian, and trading wine for beer along with other dietary novelties. Sadly, Aeneas wrote not a word about the Swiss or their culture while he was at Basel—at least in anything that survives. Perhaps the young secretary was eager to blend in or convince others that he was doing so. Germany and Austria, however, elicited more of a response. At the imperial court, cultural observations finally began to emerge in his writings. If the international character of the council created a culture of its own at Basel where foreigners forged common bonds, in Austria and Germany Aeneas seems to have felt more alone and aware of his own differences. He even downplayed or denied his proficiency in the German language, though evidence exists to the contrary, and one sensibly assumes it was a requirement for employment in the chancery.[131] For whatever reason, Aeneas was modest about his linguistic ability—except in Latin, of course.

On the whole, Aeneas seems to have admired the Germans. In his epistolary novel, *The Tale of Two Lovers* (1444), he presents dashing chivalric portraits of Emperor Sigismund and his noble courtiers, who impressed even the urbane Sienese; the romantic hero, Euryalus, may have been based on Kaspar Schlick, whom Aeneas knew well and admired.[132] He also repeatedly invokes the honor of the German nation in his proposal to invade Italy in *Pentalogus* and defends the imperial crown as part of the Germanic national identity. "National honor" is not well developed here, but it is a theme Aeneas raises in later writings in ways that Caspar Hirschi has argued presage nationalism. In short, his time at the imperial court clearly impressed him.[133]

Nor did Aeneas limit his admiration to contemporary Germans; he portrayed Charlemagne in *De ortu* as the savior of the Roman people and the rightful recipient of the title of Roman Emperor in the year 800 at a time when the Greeks were "neglecting" it:

> That Roman people, which had achieved by its blood so great an empire, and which had established by its virtues the monarchy of the world, acclaimed—with the pope's consent— Charlemagne, king of the Franks,

a German by birth, who coming to their aid had defended the city ... patrician first, afterwards Augustus. It is agreed that in such a manner the Roman Empire was transferred to the Germans.[134]

With this statement Aeneas declares the legitimacy of Charlemagne and all his Germanic successors, up to and including Frederick III, whom he pointedly called Caesar and King of the Romans in letters and other works.[135] There is no hint in Aeneas's writings at this time of Italian snobbery or doubt regarding the German claim to the emperor's title.

Aeneas was less enthusiastic about German learning, but praised their growing attention to the humanities. In a letter to his frequent rival Gregor Heimburg (Jan. 31, 1449) he compares Heimburg's speech to a story about Cicero by Plutarch where an old Greek man weeps at Cicero's eloquence, claiming that he has carried it away from Greece and transferred it to the Latins:

> This occurred to me today about you, when you were discussing in the palace those studies which they call humanities. For you were overcoming the lawyer and German in you and exuding an air of Italian oratory and eloquence. But what was sorrowful to the Greek brought me joy. For if Germany shines forth in letters, which [Cicero] handed down, it is not that Italy has less of them.[136]

He goes on to posit that Italy, as well as Switzerland and Germany, suffered losses to learning when "the ignorance of the barbarians dominated"; if Heimburg and men like him continued to work very hard on oratory, the future of Germany would be bright.[137] On the one hand, it is an acknowledgment that Italy, too, suffered from invasions and changes in rule, but Aeneas seems to indicate that this had not been the case in Italy for at least a hundred years, whereas in Germany and Switzerland, Latin eloquence was only just being rediscovered. Aeneas, moreover, takes little trouble to conceal his condescension with comments about "overcoming the German." Given Heimburg's later treatment of Aeneas as pope, one suspects he did not appreciate Aeneas's attitude or airs.[138]

Some letters to fellow Italians are even less tactful. Writing to the Archbishop of Milan, Francesco Pizzolpasso (1442), he defended his practice of signing his letters with the term "poet" partly as a calculated move to inspire himself and others in Germany to greater attention to studies.[139] While Aeneas was impressed by the overall level of learning in Germany, he did not find a paradise of humanistic eloquence—something he worked to change. Called "'the apostle of humanism' in the Germanic North" by modern scholars, his impact was also appreciated by contemporaries like Nicholas von Wyle; Aeneas certainly did much to stimulate the growth of classical studies in Germany.[140] And yet, considering some of the stereotypes other Italians perpetuated about Germans, such as drunkenness and a propensity for violence, Aeneas was mild in his judgements. His most critical comments appear in a missive to his friend Giovanni Campisio (1445), where he expresses his desire to return to Italy and regrets about moving north, such as the dearth of cultivated men among the German court:

> Are there not, you say, those around you to be associates? There certainly are good men and true, but not lovers of literature in my fashion, nor those who would be pleased by what pleases me. The clash about food is also very great, although it is easier for an Italian to gorge like a German than for a German to sup [lit. "lick"] like an Italian.[141]

This remark about food is one of the few indications that he may have found some Germans to be indelicate—given its presence in a letter professing his homesickness, one should treat this aside with caution. Petrarch and other Italian humanists who made snide comments about the Germans spent little or no time among them, quite unlike Aeneas. If he found the Viennese a bit unsophisticated at first glance in 1437, that view seems to have changed over time.[142] Even his buffoonish rendering of amorous, vaguely Germanic clerics at the Council of Basel in his comedic play *Chrysis* (1444) was probably meant more as a jab at the clergy than German stereotypes.[143] Aeneas yearned for Italy at times, as his letters show, but Cecilia Ady's suggestion that he despised the atmosphere of Germany or had trouble making Germanic friends seems unfounded.[144] Indeed, by the end of his time there, he spoke very warmly of Germany and the many friends and contacts he had made throughout the empire and Slavic-speaking areas of Central and Eastern Europe.[145] Even after he became a cardinal, he proudly described himself as more German than Italian. Perhaps there was some truth to that statement: by the time Aeneas returned to Italy for good in 1455, he had spent almost half his life in Germany and Switzerland. His few comments on Germanic society noted previously pale in comparison to the copious amount he would write in 1457–1458, but they show that he was increasingly drawn to questions of cultural difference.

If Aeneas rejected the trope of the Germanic "barbarian," he had no problem applying the term to other European Christians. He disparages the region of modern-day Slovenia with an offhanded remark in a letter to apostolic secretary Giovanni Peregallo (Apr. 18, 1444). As an excuse for his late response, he states,

> your letter to me is old, and I have not responded because having settled now in Styria, now in Carinthia, now in Carniola in the midst of barbaric and savage peoples, and now passing time around Istria and above the regions of the Adriatic near Trieste, I have had no one to whom I could entrust a letter for delivery to you.[146]

It is hard to know how seriously to take this comment, which may only be an impatient swipe at the region's relative isolation from other parts of Europe and its lack of long-distance travelers to carry his letters to friends. Either way, it reads as an urbane expression of amusement between two worldly Italian friends. His uncharitable remark may have had more to do with the bizarre and slovenly ruler of Carinthia than most of the inhabitants, as his later writing suggests.[147]

Aeneas also characterized some of the Bohemian Hussites as barbaric, but his writings also suggest a deeper fascination with its people.[148] The Hussites had faced war and oppression for their beliefs, which included aligning religious practices and institutions with Scripture, frequent reception of communion in both forms, and general calls for reform of clerical corruption.[149] The founder of this movement, Jan Hus, was judged to be a heretic and executed in 1415 at the Council of Constance—an act that only fueled the Bohemian Hussites' resistance.[150] Rather than submit to pressure from the pope and emperor, the Hussites steadfastly pressed for acceptance of their beliefs and practices. Aeneas's first contacts with the sect actually date back to the negotiations between the Council of Basel and moderate Hussites. These talks resulted in the compromises of the *Compactata* or Prague Compacts (1436), which were formulated without the papacy's involvement or blessing. In 1451, Aeneas was sent to the diet at Benešov in Bohemia as an imperial spokesman. There he met with George Podiebrad, who would later become king of Bohemia; at this time Podiebrad was the influential leader of the Utraquists, a moderate Hussite branch that believed the laity should receive both bread and wine at communion.

But it was Aeneas's visit to the fortified settlement of Tabor that made the most vivid impression on him. He describes it in a letter to his friend Cardinal Juan Carvajal (Aug. 21, 1451) as a town full of artisans who largely worked in the wool and cloth trade and attended an unadorned church. Their rejection of pomp manifested itself in the simplicity of church services and the priests' vestments as well as the clergy's closeness to the people. The community had a central role in decisions and their guiding principle was the Gospels. Aeneas also noted the high level of learning in the town where many students and citizens knew Latin and even women showed familiarity with the Bible. What perhaps unsettled him the most was how freely the citizens could disagree on precise matters of the faith—something that Aeneas, now a bishop, writing to a cardinal, could never abide.[151]

Whether the religious freedom of Tabor troubled Aeneas more than certain cultural and social differences is hard to determine, but he closed the letter with a dramatic flourish:

> It seemed to me that I had been among barbarians, beyond the Sauromatians and the Glacial Ocean, among the man-eaters or the monstrous people of India and Lybia. Nor indeed in the whole world encircled by Amphitrite is there any people more monstrous than the Taborites; for they say that the Ethiopians, Scythians, and Taprobanians are monstrous by fault of their bodies, but Taborites are made monstrous by fault of their depraved minds and innumerable blemishes of soul.[152]

It is interesting that he references racial tropes assigned to "exotic" northern and eastern peoples but ranks physical difference or monstrosity as less concerning than deformities of the soul.[153] He would go on in later years to write much more about Bohemia and the Hussites, but for now, two points stand out regarding his cultural views. First, as late as 1451, he seems to think only of the characteristics of towns and cities, not of nations. Second, despite his fascination with the Taborites, he does not go into great detail about them as culturally barbaric. The word barbarian is tacked on at the end for literary effect, but the concept of barbarism does not yet appear to hold significant interest for him. This is true for his views of the Ottomans as well—before 1453, at any rate.

Crusade and the Ottoman Turks

A part of Europe which Aeneas never visited but grew increasingly preoccupied with was the western Ottoman Empire, comprised of Bulgaria and expanding portions of the Balkans. When Aeneas was born, the Ottoman advance had come to a halt. After Bayezid I's defeat and capture by Timur Lenk followed by his death (1402–1403), the interregnum and civil war that ensued brought years of peace and even growth to Byzantium—a welcome respite after decades of pressure and incursions. For a brief period of time, it seemed possible to reverse Ottoman conquests entirely. But in 1421 an energetic new sultan, Murad II, took the throne with a plan to recapture and expand Ottoman possessions in Europe, the Mediterranean, and Western Asia; he reasserted Ottoman suzerainty over the Byzantine emperor with alarming shows of force. The first sign of danger was his blockade of Constantinople in 1422, followed in 1430 by his conquest of the large, bustling port city of Thessalonica in northeastern Greece. Thousands of Greeks were killed or taken captive as the Venetians, to whom the city had recently been ceded for its protection, watched from their ships and refused to engage. Clearly, the Greeks would need much more help against Murad. Once again, the idea of a union with the Roman Catholics gained traction.

In the 1430s, Byzantine Emperor John VIII Paleologus began to send out feelers to both the Council of Basel and the pope. A major council was needed to negotiate a union, but with the growing chasm between Basel and the pope, it was unclear where it should be held and whom should preside. The Greeks indicated their preference for a site in Italy to help minimize the distance of their journey.[154] It was at this unlikely juncture that Aeneas became directly involved. In 1436, he presented the aforementioned oration, titled *Audivi*, to the council on behalf of Duke Filippo Maria Visconti of Milan, who craved the honor of hosting the council in Pavia or another one of his cities. This became Aeneas's first major public speech. It touches on numerous issues and even briefly praises Pope Eugenius IV, whom the council hoped would attend, but it is largely an extended panegyric of the duke and his dominions. Nonetheless, the oration offers rich insight to this study as it contains one of Aeneas's earliest statements on the Ottoman Turks.

The Greeks, he argues, would be well disposed to come to Pavia, since they preferred that the council take place in the duke's territory: "They are in fact acting with good reason, knowing that the duke has a hereditary friendship with the Turks, from whom he derives his most ancient ancestry—a thing that cannot be disparaged in good faith." This purported common descent from the ancient Trojans could enable the duke to write a letter on the Greeks' behalf to the Ottoman sultan to reassure him that the purpose of the Greek visit to Italy was not political, but purely religious, thereby forestalling any plans the sultan might have to attack Constantinople in their absence. He adds, "almost all Greeks are subject to the power of the Turks ... [and] no one can bring the Greeks over against the will of the Turks."[155] This is a fascinating set of assertions. First, it shows familiarity with the Greeks' difficult position under Turkish suzerainty and the risks they faced if their burgeoning alliance with Latin Christians were discovered. More intriguing is Aeneas's gesture toward the notion of Trojan origins—which the Milanese and other Christian peoples claimed for themselves and some Europeans even attributed to the Turks. The Turks as Trojan descendants is an idea Aeneas would later roundly reject, but in several of his early works, and in some manuscripts of this very oration one finds the classical spelling "Teucri" to designate both the Trojans and the Turks.[156] As Margaret Meserve has shown, humanist historian Andrea Biglia, one of Aeneas's teachers in Siena and author of the unpublished *Commentaries* on Eastern History (1433), seems a likely source for Aeneas on the origins of the Turks.[157] One might dismiss Aeneas's rosy invocation of ancestral ties between Milan and the Turks as rhetorical opportunism, but the next passage suggests that there is more to his thinking:

> For great is the realm of the Turks, immense is the power of the Asiatics and enormous their riches. They have extended their empire from Asia to Europe and they have occupied the whole of Greece as if they were the avengers of the destruction of Troy. To expel them from Greece would not be the task of a single city or state, but of the entire Christian world.[158]

Interestingly, Aeneas has little to say about other issues that may have mattered to the Greeks beyond their position as vassals of the Turks and their supposed desire to have the duke of Milan's assistance.

Two points stand out here. For one, Aeneas's views of the Ottomans were neither hostile nor heavily biased. The Turks in this oration were not "barbarians," but rather civilized, wealthy heirs to Troy; they present as powerful rulers who would welcome the diplomacy and even friendship of the duke of Milan. How and why this view of the Ottomans would change after the fall of Constantinople in 1453 is an important theme of this book. Second, his comment on the need for a large-scale force to expel the Turks from Greece has been seen as early evidence of his thinking on the need for a multistate crusade; here he speaks for the first time of the great force required to expel the Turks from Greece. It is hard to know how seriously Aeneas had thought about crusade or the Turks at this early stage, but his strategic assessment of them in 1436 differs little from his appraisal of any other *European* power. Finally, it is worth noting that the opposing force he conjures against the Ottomans is not Europe but "the entire Christian world."

During his years in Austria, Aeneas began to devote more attention to the Turks and crusade. The Ottoman advance escalated in the 1440s, with some important pauses and counteroffensives by the Hungarians and other local forces. Dispatches and messengers to the imperial court regularly reported Murad's attacks on Transylvania, Hungary, and Serbia and the capture and enslavement of thousands of Christians. Standing at the forefront of the battle against the Ottomans was John Hunyadi, governor or *voivode* of Transylvania and a highly effective general. Of equal importance was the crusade called by Pope Eugenius IV to aid the Greeks in exchange for their return to papal obedience in 1439 at the Council of Florence.

Despite the steady encroachment of the Ottomans, Aeneas had many doubts about crusade. He resented the Hungarian and papal campaigns because they complicated Frederick's political aims and furthered the interests of the young king Vladislas IV of Hungary, who also ruled Poland as King Wladyslaw III (r. 1434–44). Wladyslaw accepted the throne of Hungary in 1440 from a majority of Hungarian nobles who wanted an adult male on the throne after the death of Albert II in 1439. But Albert's wife, Elizabeth, the daughter of king and emperor Sigismund, was pregnant at the time, and a faction of nobles supported her plan to elevate her child to the throne if she delivered a son. She personally crowned the child, Ladislas Postumus, with the Holy Crown and fled (with her son and the crown) to the court of her relative Frederick; upon her death in 1442, Frederick became Ladislas's guardian and hoped to gain control of Hungary through him.[159] This dynastic rivalry concerned Aeneas far more than crusade at this time. While it is often assumed that Aeneas was always pro-crusade, this was far from the case.

At first, Aeneas saw crusade in purely local terms, as witnessed by his churlish silence in 1439 about the extraordinary union between the Greek Orthodox Church and Rome at the Council of Florence and the crusade that it promised; he could only see the union and crusade as a win for Eugenius and a loss for Basel—which Eugenius had also dissolved. In the lead-up to the Crusade of Varna, his view on any given day hinged entirely on how he saw the Christian leaders. To his mind, each victory helped legitimate Wladyslaw's claim to the throne of Hungary, which Frederick III refused to recognize.[160] After breaking a truce with the Ottomans, King Wladyslaw, Hunyadi, and Cardinal Giuliano Cesarini led a crusade with assistance from a Venetian fleet that attempted (unsuccessfully) to block an Ottoman relief army from crossing the Bosphorus. The crusade army was soundly defeated at the Battle of Varna in Bulgaria on Nov. 10, 1444, and the king and cardinal were both killed, although their fates were uncertain for months afterward; Hunyadi managed to escape.[161] The loss at Varna, however, does not tell the full story of the strong resistance Hunyadi led or the broad cross-section of Christian Europe that it represented with "contingents from every Balkan country threatened by the Turks, as well as Czech and Moldavian mercenaries, and Italian, French, and German volunteers."[162] Indeed, historians have long misrepresented this period as one long, doomed losing streak.

Aeneas's letters provide useful insights into his ambivalent views at this time. Writing in or around 1443 to Niccolò Amidano, a jurisconsult and friend from his Basel days, he discusses Cardinal Cesarini, a man he had praised in the past and whose loss in the Crusade of Varna he would later lament. Yet here, he describes Cesarini's efforts to raise troops for the crusade in Hungary as a diversionary war to distract from the illegitimacy of both Eugenius and Wladyslaw, who sought only to prop up their actions and win followers:

> He [Giuliano] has chosen the king of Poland who, by invading another's kingdom, also [i.e., like Giuliano] desires to establish a good reputation, as the best instrument for this work. And so Gabriel [Pope Eugenius], under the cloak of an expedition [i.e., crusade],[163] desires to hold another's pontificate, while he [Wladyslaw] desires to hold another's kingdom. Giuliano is the minister of these affairs, for whom we ought not to weep because this man is not accustomed to be fortunate in wars, as Bohemia showed.[164] God looks not at the work but at the end, and so, I hope, he will fall short of success.[165]

This is a stunning assertion. It depicts crusade, at least this particular one, in wholly secular terms—to the point where Aeneas rooted for the opposition in order to embarrass Christian enemies. On the other hand, it may show, as Housley has argued, a genuine appreciation of crusade as something that required selfless intention—a quality Aeneas judged to be sorely lacking in this war.[166] While he may have harbored a purer view of crusade as a pious endeavor, it is hard to look past the incredible cynicism of this letter and others.

Aeneas's tone began to mellow, however, as he reconciled with the pope. In a friendly letter dated May 28, 1444, to Cesarini, he questions the usefulness of neutrality and concedes, "as far as I can perceive, all Christendom follows the party of Eugenius."[167] Not only does he support the pope here, but also speaks of a united Christendom. His stance on Cesarini's crusade also changed after it became clear that both he and Wladyslaw had perished at Varna. He describes Cesarini in a letter of May 21, 1445, to Giovanni Campisio as "the splendor of his age," and goes on to say "I judge that he, who was defending Christ's cause, made a good end."[168] Whatever doubts he had harbored two years earlier about Cesarini's intentions had melted away: he was now a martyr. Wladyslaw, however, achieved no saintly status in Aeneas's eyes; he would continue to be skeptical of the king for years to come.[169]

When it came to John Hunyadi, Aeneas's views were more complicated. Before the Battle of Varna, he wrote positively about the Transylvanian general, though not the king he served.[170] In a letter to his friend Giovanni Campisio (Jan. 13, 1444), Aeneas describes Hunyadi's successes in the "long campaign" against the Ottomans in the winter of 1443–1444. He seems genuinely uplifted by the news and conveys a shared anticipation that Turks would be "expelled from Europe" through his efforts.[171] This is perhaps his earliest usage of the trope of the Turks being expelled from "Europe"; Aeneas had spoken only of their expulsion from Greece in his Basel oration of 1436. But while he admired Hunyadi's prowess and desire to combat the Turks, he resented his quest for power in Hungary; Aeneas also criticized his uncanny ability to flee battle at just the right moment. In a later letter to Pope Nicholas V (Nov. 25, 1448), he mentions Hunyadi's failed campaign against the Ottomans at Varna, depicting him as "a Wallachian, knowledgeable about the region and quick of wits, [but he] avoided without trouble the peril in which he had ensnared others."[172]

Despite this criticism, Aeneas presents a nobler view of Hunyadi's leadership at the Battle of Kosovo (Oct. 17–20, 1448) in the same letter. A speech he attributes to Hunyadi begins, "Today, comrades in arms, either we will liberate Europe from the violent domination of the Turks, or, falling for Christ, will be crowned with martyrdom."[173] Describing the battle, Aeneas gives Hunyadi credit for the damage his troops inflicted on the Turks and blames their ultimate defeat on the Hungarians who defected in the night after the first day of battle—not on Hunyadi. Yet, his praise of Hunyadi even here had its limits. At the end of the letter, he portrays the loss as the just judgment of God and casts doubt on the intentions of the crusaders, repeating the rumor that Hunyadi had plotted to seize the throne from young Ladislas Postumus after Wladyslaw's death.[174]

The mention of "Europe" in both of these letters deserves comment. Aeneas was likely influenced by the Hungarians in the depiction of Europe as an entity to be defended or liberated. Earlier evocations of Europe can be found as far back as the reign of King Béla IV (r. 1235–70) in battles against the Mongols, and Hunyadi seems to have been fond of this phrasing. He or his representatives employed this dramatic phrasing on at least one occasion, as a letter from Hunyadi to Pope Eugenius in late 1448 attests. Pope Eugenius and Cesarini had also used this expression.[175] Hence, while Aeneas would later popularize the notion of expelling the Turks from Europe, he did not invent it. He clearly found the concept appealing and would invest deeper and more expansive meaning into it after the fall of Constantinople.

Importantly, Aeneas affirms his newfound commitment to crusade in the letter, urging Pope Nicholas that the next battle "should be waged not just by the forces of the Hungarians but by those of all Christendom .... To effect this, just like correcting the Hussites, is your function and the task of the Jubilee."[176] With these articulations of "Europe" and "Christendom," Aeneas now paints crusade not as a local problem, but one that concerns the larger collective. The failures at Varna and Kosovo and the knowledge he likely gained of military matters from Kaspar Schlick at the imperial court appear to have raised his awareness about the magnitude of a campaign to stop the

Ottomans.[177] By 1448, Aeneas seemed less content to let local princes deal with the problem on their own.

While nothing inspired Aeneas as much as the fall of Constantinople in 1453 to support crusade and articulate a defense of Europe, an oration he delivered to Pope Nicholas V in 1452 can be seen as a bridge to those ideas. The occasion of this speech was Frederick III's lengthy, pageant-filled trip to Italy, where he met and married Eleanora of Portugal, and visited the pope and other rulers along the way. Aeneas traveled to Italy in advance of Frederick to pave his way and help smooth his reception. His oration, titled *Moyses vir Dei* (April 24, 1452), was delivered at Rome and designed to praise both the pontiff and the emperor; it exhorts the pope to call a crusade against the Ottomans and offers Frederick III's assistance. The piece shows little awareness of the Ottomans' military threat to Constantinople in 1452, and it contains no mention of the young sultan Mehmed II who recently came to the throne in 1451 at the age of nineteen.[178] To be fair, Mehmed was still an unknown quantity for most Western Europeans at this time, but the oration is equally vague on fundraising, costs, and other logistics of planning a large-scale crusade. Nor is there a specific destination: the Holy Land, Greece, Hungary, and the Mediterranean are all mentioned as viable targets.[179] As such, *Moyses vir Dei* presents a contrast to his post-1453 writings where he displays a firmer grasp of such details and greater focus on weakening the Ottomans in Eastern Europe.

Putting aside the ambiguities in this oration, three points offer a preview of some of his later thinking. One is an imaginative reflection on Greek versus Ottoman culture, which occurs during his discussion of the motives for crusade:

> What about Greece, who is the mother of letters, who invented laws, who nursed culture, who is the teacher of the good arts? Who would not pity this afflicted, oppressed, and ruined people? Their empire was mighty and flourishing not only under Alexander the Macedonian and his successors, but also under the Athenians, the Thebans, and the Lacedaemonians: now it is forced to serve the *effeminate* Turks everywhere [emphasis mine].[180]

This romantic view of Greece as the homeland of ancient sages and Aeneas's silence on the long Byzantine period were not uncommon for humanists at the time; he would expand upon the idealization of ancient Greece in his later works.[181]

Aeneas's characterization of the Ottomans as effeminate, moreover, was no random word choice, as a later passage arguing the ease of the expedition for the manly Christians shows:

> For the peoples of Europe are warlike and ferocious, and they do not know how to be at peace …. If the Christians should have peace between them, war should be turned against foreigners. In this matter, neither the

shining spirit of the Germans, nor the noble heart of the French people, nor the lofty mind of the Spaniards, nor the honor-loving spirit of the Italians will be lacking. All will single mindedly obey Your Holiness's commands. Who can doubt that a crusade is possible when it has been decreed by the authority of the Roman Pontiff and summoned by the order of the Emperor?[182]

By way of contrast, he makes the following claim about the Turks and other Muslims:

His Imperial Majesty knows the Assyrian and Egyptian people: they are weak, impotent, and effeminate, and they are warlike neither in temperament nor in planning. *The Sarmatian spoils will be without sweat or blood.*[183] Who would fear the Turks in their robes and turbans or the Egyptians in their flowing garments? ... If our armies were beaten by them in former times, it was not because of their strength or their military skills, but because of their numbers.[184]

The gendered ethnic stereotypes and the distinct personalities he assigns to different countries alone provided much fodder for his audience's imagination. But Aeneas thought even bigger. With the phrase, "the peoples of Europe," he argues for an inherent sense of European, not just Christian, unity—with a cast of national characteristics that loosely unites the men of the continent. This is the first time we see Aeneas using this team-like analogy of European peoples possessing different characters that could easily combine into an effective whole—a concept that would appear repeatedly and with increasing vigor in other writings. It is also the first of many times that he invokes the idea of European national attributes. Meanwhile, the (Muslim) men of the East are assumed to be undifferentiated: they are all equally weak and unmanly. Whether Aeneas believed that culture or bloodline was driving these characteristics or an ancient Greek sense of climate and geography as racial determinants is hard to say at this stage.[185]

Two other aspects about these passages stand out. First is Aeneas's shift regarding the Turks. There is no sense of the Ottomans as strong rulers of a rich and powerful state, as he described them in his Basel oration of 1436 or in the sober reports on their movements and victories found in his letters. He simultaneously diminishes them as soft Easterners and elevates all European peoples to a position of strength and dignity. Perhaps the pro-crusade objective of the speech or a growing concern over recent Ottoman victories drove this rhetorical pivot, but the desire to denigrate the Turks in this way was certainly new for him. These are undeveloped, but provocative pronouncements, showing a preference for the comforting myth of Eastern effeminacy over that of barbarism—a term he only invokes once here and imprecisely.[186]

Second, this oration moves beyond the simple bifurcations of Christian and Muslim to incorporate a sense of geography as a political and cultural marker. For Aeneas in 1452, it was not enough to ask the pope to summon all

Christians; he needed to promote a vision of Europeans fighting on the same side: "The worship of Christ that once filled the whole world has been reduced to the corner of Europe. We have lost Africa and Asia. Even in Europe we are being oppressed."[187] Altogether, he invokes Europe three times in this oration. Such claims show that Aeneas was already engaging with questions of borders and identity—just over a year before the unthinkable took place and his attention sharply focused on Constantinople. Where did the impulse for this new geographical turn arise? Was the idea of Hunyadi "driving the Turks out of Europe" growing on him? Did he enter into conversations in Rome with other humanists who also used Europe in this fashion, like Flavio Biondo or the Greek refugee George of Trebizond, and if so, who was first, or was this simply the common influence of the classics bubbling up?[188] Regardless, it is important to remember that during these years, the Ottomans were but one piece of a larger puzzle in the struggle for control of the council and local politics in Eastern Europe. For most of the period before 1453, Aeneas maintained a fairly open-minded view of the Ottomans and watched Christian powers more warily as they sought to use Church Union or crusade for their own ends.

Conclusion

From the 1430s to the early 1450s, Aeneas did not fully appreciate the impact the Germans and other northern Europeans made on him personally, nor had he wrestled with the unique role they played in Christendom or Europe. His early writings rarely speak of cultural variations, but when they do, he generally echoes ancient Roman writers with their ideas of one-way exchange of high culture (in his case, the humanities) to other areas of Europe.[189] Apart from differences in the study of the humanities, Aeneas may have seen more cultural similarities between Northern Europe and Italy than differences. Both regions had vibrant urban centers and shared similar governing systems and norms. Most important, all these areas, with the exception of Hussite strongholds, had the same familiar infrastructure of churches, monasteries, and feast days that gave the towns and villages Aeneas visited a certain predictability in both physical space and the observance of the Roman Catholic calendar; indeed, Robert Bartlett's work has shown the many similarities that could be found throughout Europe by the later Middle Ages.[190] Aeneas's early works do not suggest that he perceived sizable local cultural differences in these years. His political views, moreover, show a growing desire to find stability and unity among European Christians, but his suggestions, as yet, lacked coherence.

   After 1453, however, this would change. As a result of the momentous loss of the Byzantine capital, Aeneas began to reflect on his home writ large in a profoundly new way. There was a new urgency to think critically about regional differences and to dwell upon the larger similarities. Modern biographies of Aeneas, which make heavy use of his *Commentaries* (1462–64), ascribe many of its impressions to his years in Northern Europe *as he was living them*—this is an error that I hope to have corrected here. At least in regard to his views of identity, it is very important that we do not elide decades of changing thought into one flat picture of cognitive stasis.

Moreover, the silences in Aeneas's writings at this time are as important as his pronouncements. Almost completely missing from these early works is a sense of nationality, a strong support of crusade, or a hatred of the Ottomans. Toward the end of this period, there is a slight uptick in his use of "Europe" and interest in the welfare of "Christendom" and crusade, but these ideas are still loose and unformed. His tantalizing but brief evocations of Europe and Asia in his 1452 oration to Pope Nicholas V might have undergone expansion and development without the cataclysm of 1453, but—importantly—there is little or no evidence of these notions in his writings between April 1452 and July 1453. As the next two chapters will show, the shock of the conquest of Constantinople and his time in Rome reading works of ancient Roman and Greek ethnographers would light a spark to the storehouse of observations and experiences he had accumulated over these years.

Perhaps the best way to end this chapter is with a quote from Norbert Ohler, who captures the simultaneous opening and closing of the mind that could take place for the medieval (and Renaissance) traveler:

> The countries of the west became interlinked, a common European feeling arose. This had a negative effect, when it became an arrogant dismissal of 'the others,' and a positive one when it enabled a member of this 'international brotherhood' to feel at home even when he was living in another country.[191]

While I question what Ohler means by "European feeling" at this time, his point about a growing sense of common culture is well taken. So much potential from Aeneas's journeys and time abroad was stored in his memory—ready to be drawn upon, edited, and embellished in a host of new ways. Other travelers besides Aeneas may have felt a similar sense of recognition, but few if any of them would articulate it as early or as fully as Aeneas.

Notes

1 For a later description of his journey to England and Scotland, see Pius II, *Commentaries*, tr. and ed. Margaret Meserve and Marcello Simonetta (Cambridge, MA: Harvard University Press, 2003), 1, 17–29.

2 "... fui jam septem mensibus extra terrarum orbem in regno Scotie, quo me dominus meus, cardinalis sancte crucis, transmiserat, quo ex loco nec scribendi facultas erat, nec opus erat scribere, cum nihil ibi ageretur ad vestram rem publicam pertinens." (Letter to Sienese government, April 9, 1436); Rudolph Wolkan, ed., *Der Briefwechsel des Eneas Silvius Piccolomini*, in *Fontes Rerum Austriacarum*, ser. 2, vol. 61 (1909): 41; Eng. tr., *Reject Aeneas, Accept Pius: Selected Letters of Aeneas Sylvius Piccolomini (Pope Pius II)*, intr. and tr. Thomas M. Izbicki, Gerald Christianson, and Philip Krey (Washington, D.C.: Catholic University of America Press, 2006), 83–84.

3 A host of rich biographies of Aeneas's life have been published. See the intro-duction for a partial list.

4 Cecilia M. Ady, *Pius II: (Aeneas Silvius Piccolomini) The Humanist Pope* (London: Methuen and Co., 1913), 2–3; R.J. Mitchell, *The Laurels and the Tiara* (New York: Doubleday and Co., 1962), 24–25. Arthur White, *Plague and Pleasure: The Renaissance World of Pius II* (Washington, DC: Catholic University of America Press, 2014), 48–51.

5 Mitchell, *Laurels*, 25–29. Aeneas's *Commentaries*, book I, presents a romantic and very brief portrait of his youth and Siena years. For an interpretation of the role that both plague and country life played in Aeneas's development see White, *Plague and Pleasure*.

6 Fabrizio Nevola, *Siena: Constructing the Renaissance City* (New Haven, CT: Yale University Press, 2007), 12–27; Ady, *Pius II*, 8–10. See also Fabrizio Nevola, ed. *Pio II Piccolomini: il Papa del Rinascimento a Siena* (Siena: Protagon Editore, 2009).

7 On the university of Siena, see Paul F. Grendler, *Universities of the Italian Renaissance* (Baltimore: Johns Hopkins University Press, 2002), 45–49; Mitchell, *Laurels*, 36–37. Paolo Nardi uses archival sources to pinpoint dates when certain instructors were at the university and provide other details; see "Enea Silvio Piccolomini e lo *Studium* di Siena nel terzo decennio Quattrocento," in *Pio II Piccolomini*, ed. Nevola, 151–66. A good recent study on experiences and per-ceptions of early humanism is Patrick Baker's, *Italian Renaissance Humanism in the Mirror* (Cambridge: Cambridge University Press, 2015), see especially 5, 38–53.

8 Aeneas appears to have continued his legal studies and briefly lectured on civil law at Siena; Ady, *Pius II*, 24. Very few accomplished humanists became doctors of law. Leon Battista Alberti is one of the exceptions; see David Lines, *Humanism and Creativity in the Renaissance*, ed. Christopher Celenza and Kenneth Gouwens (Leiden: Brill, 2006), 331. The flamboyant humanist Francesco Filelfo briefly taught at Siena, but there is no evidence that he taught Aeneas there, although he appears to have instructed him in some capacity at another time.

9 We know little about his romantic pursuits and rejections, but Aeneas repeatedly described Siena as the city of Venus. See Ady, *Pius II*, 7, 18; Mitchell, *Laurels*, 48; Gioacchino Paparelli, *Enea Silvio Piccolomini: l'umanesimo sul soglio di Pietro* (Ravenna: Longo Editore, 1978), 22; Giuseppe Cugnoni, *Aeneae Silvii Piccolomini Senensis qui postea fuit Pius II Pont. Max., Opera Inedita* (Rome: Salviucci, 1883), 342.

10 Ady, *Pius II*, 14. On the *pecia* or piece system of borrowing and copying books a portion at a time and the debts that book lovers incurred, see Andrew Petegree, *The Book in the Renaissance* (New Haven: Yale University Press, 2010), 9–10.

11 Ady, *Pius II*, 14.

12 Grammar teacher Master Antonio d'Arezzo or Antonio di Niccolò dei Burletti. See Nardi, "Piccolomini e lo *Studium* di Siena," 153.

13 This letter is revealing because it survives only in part, and Aeneas did not col-lect and edit it, unlike others that may have been polished by him later. "Nudius tertius, cum audivissem vecordiam nostram atque minimam studendi volun-tatem a magistro Antonio vehementer reprehendi, domum confestim reversurus vocansque me ad me, quis, cepi, animus in presentiarum accidit tibi morbo, que voluntas, quod desiderium? Nunquid studiis semper operam dare statuisti? Nunquid Palladem tibi nubere decrevisti? Nunquid Venerem contra te sevientem eiusdem Palladis clipeo sepius fugavisti? Quid est, quod nunc omnium sis obli-tus? An te ipsa scientie a studio arcet longitudo? Ha, corculum habes! Quid dif-ficilimum est, quod non perficiat assiduus usus? Putasne quenquam musarum sublimitatem sine summo labore sudoreque et anxietate non mi ...." Wolkan, *Briefwechsel*, 61: 1–2. The undated letter breaks off at the end of the page and

comes from a manuscript of letters to and from Barnabeo in the Siena Biblioteca Communale, now catalogued as D.VI.5. Wolkan dates the letter to 1431; Nardi suggests 1427. See "Piccolomini e lo *Studium* di Siena," 153–54. Nardi's date of 1427 seems more likely as the context reflects a student in the midst of his studies, not one at the end who had just returned from travels abroad and was seeking employment. The Latin has a poetic flair with three successive lines ending in *statuisti, decrevisti,* and *fugavisti.* Thanks to Rob Brown for his helpful insights.

14 There were, of course famous humanist teachers like Guarino da Verona, Vittorino da Feltre, Gasparino da Barzizza, and others, but they were accessible only to the wealthy, and their engagements were often short. Italian universities did play an important role in humanistic training, however, as Lines argues in "Humanism and the Italian Universities." See also Baker's exploration of the ways in which early humanists like Aeneas and Bruni defined their craft just as humanism was crystallizing as a movement; *Italian Renaissance Humanism*, 17, 22–23.

15 The terms are *bonae litterae, bonae artes, studia humanitatis,* and *litterarum studia,* respectively. See Baker, *Italian Renaissance Humanism*, 85.

16 The scholarship on humanism is vast, and I make no attempt to offer a comprehensive overview in the pages that follow. Introductions to this field may be found in Robert Black, ed., *Renaissance Thought: A Reader* (London: Routledge, 2001); Jill Kraye, ed., *Renaissance Humanism* (Cambridge: Cambridge University Press, 1996); Albert Rabil Jr., ed., *Renaissance Humanism: Foundations, Forms, and Legacy* (Philadelphia: University of Pennsylvania Press, 1988), 3 vols.

17 These two camps roughly correspond to the ideas of Paul Oskar Kristeller and Eugenio Garin, respectively. The advantage of Kristeller's definition is that it avoids the thorny question of *which* philosophical views define humanism, but its drawback is that it disregards the passion many humanists brought to their work, making them seem like dreary functionaries. Baker presents a useful overview of humanist scholarship from the nineteenth century forward; *Italian Renaissance Humanism*, 5–15. A third definition is often added with Hans Baron's civic humanism, which was shaped by its service to the state; see *The Crisis of the Early Italian Renaissance Civic Humanism and Republican Liberty in an Age of Classicism and Tyranny* (Princeton: Princeton University Press, 1966). Baron never claimed this was "the" definition of humanism, broadly speaking, nor does this category fit well with Aeneas's work, although Rolando Montecalvo sees aspects of it in Aeneas's commitment to his work and rejection of cynical opportunism; Montecalvo, "Between Empire and Papacy: Aeneas Silvius and German Regional Historiography (PhD diss., University of California, Berkeley, 2000), 19–20.

18 Ronald G. Witt, *In the Footsteps of the Ancients: The Origins of Humanism from Lovato to Bruni* (Leiden: Brill Academic Publishers, 2003), 22. Baker reaches a similar conclusion. Looking at collective biographies written by Aeneas and others, he finds a common "linguistic enterprise, its medium Latin, its object eloquence"; *Italian Renaissance Humanism*, 25.

19 See Kenneth Gouwens, "Perceiving the Past: Renaissance Humanism After the 'Cognitive Turn'," *American Historical Review* 103, no. 1 (1998): 55–82; Hanna Gray, "Renaissance Humanism: The Pursuit of Eloquence," *Journal of the History of Ideas* 24 (1963): 497–514. See also Riccardo Fubini's description of humanism in *Humanism and Secularization* (Durham, N.C. Duke University Press, 2003), 1–8.

20 Baker, *Italian Renaissance Humanism*, 80, 240. See also Fubini on the "horizontal ties linking contemporary texts or those of the same general historical period," *Humanism and Secularization*, 2.

21 Baker claims that Aeneas did not state a position on the meaning of the revival of classical Latin to his age; *Italian Renaissance Humanism*, 241. This may be true for *On Famous Men*, on which he focuses, but not. I believe, for Aeneas's later works.

22 Ady, *Pius II*, 15; Mitchell, *Laurels*, 36. For more on Aeneas's style, see Adrian Van Heck, "Amator vetusti ritus et observator diligens. Stile e modelli stilistici di Pio II," *In Pio II e la cultura del suo tempo*, ed. Luisa Rotondi Secchi Tarugi (Milan: Guerini e Associati, 1991), 119–49; Aeneas Silvius Piccolomini, *Europe (c. 1400–1458)*, tr. Robert Brown, intro. and notes, Nancy Bisaha (Washington D.C.: Catholic University of America Press, 2013), 38–41.

23 Aeneas was inspired by the sermons of the famous friar, who began preaching in Siena in 1425. He describes his decision to join the Franciscans, his friends' efforts to dissuade him, and his meeting with Bernardino later in Rome in his short biographical sketch of Bernardino in his *De viris illustribus* (1445–50): Adrian Van Heck, ed. *De viris illustribus* (Vatican City: Biblioteca Vatican Apostolica, 1991), 38, 41. Some have questioned the veracity of the dramatic Rome meeting; see *Reject Aeneas*, Izbicki et al., 13.

24 For a sense of how social and economic markers worked in neighboring Florence, see Lauro Martines, *The Social World of the Florentine Humanists 1390–1460* (Princeton: Princeton University Press, 1963), ch. 2.

25 Mitchell, *Laurels*, 49–51; *Commentaries*, ed. Meserve and Simonetta, 1: 388 n. 4.

26 "... tantum in te urbanitatis esse cognovi, tantum caritatis ac benivolentie in omnes etiam infimos, ut opiner, te nullum fore benigniorem facilioremque, nam et me voluisti inter amicos tuos connumerare." Wolkan, *Briefwechsel* 61: 2. Mitchell aptly refers to this letter as a "graceful Collins," evoking the obsequious character in Jane Austen's *Pride and Prejudice*; see *Laurels*, 51.

27 Mitchell, *Laurels*, 50. For more on Aeneas's relationships with other humanists, see Riccardo Fubini, "Enea Silvio Piccolomini nei suoi rapporti con la cultura umanistica del tempo," in *Pio II Piccolomini*, ed. Nevola, 131–50.

28 See Caspar Hirschi's insightful comments in *The Origins of Nationalism: An Alternative History from Ancient Rome to Modern Germany* (Cambridge: Cambridge University Press, 2012), 124–25. On the vagaries of university positions and pay scale, see Lines, "Humanism and the Italian Universities," 333–34.

29 While Aeneas may have later exaggerated his desire to complete his degree, Guido Kisch has shown his legal training was not inconsequential and that he continued to hold jurists in high opinion; "Enea Silvio Piccolomini e la giurisprudenza," in *Enea Silvio Piccolomini Papa Pio II*, ed. Domenico Maffei (Siena. Varese, 1968), 195–97. For a similar discussion of differences in Aeneas's letters vs. his *Commentaries*, see Zweder Von Martels, "The Fruit of Love. Aeneas Silvius Piccolomini about his Illegitimate Child," in *Pius II 'El Più Expeditivo Pontifice*, eds. Zweder Von Martels and Arjo Vanderjagt (Leiden: Brill, 2003), 229–48.

30 See Christopher Celenza's portrait of Lapo da Castiglionchio, a contemporary of Aeneas who faced similar financial constraints and moved about in search of educational and employment prospects: *Renaissance Humanism and the Papal Curia: Lapo da Castiglionchio the Younger's "De curiae commodis"* (Ann Arbor, Mich: University of Michigan Press, 1999), 1–9.

31 Baker, *Italian Renaissance Humanism*, 89, 257–8; Witt, *Footsteps*, 497–98.

32 Aeneas's letters from this period describing the city of Basel will be discussed later in the chapter.

33 On the Council of Basel, see Johannes Helmrath, *Das Basler Konzil, 1431–1449* (Cologne: Böhlau Verlag, 1987); see also Joachim Stieber, *Pope Eugenius IV, The Council of Basel and the Secular and Ecclesiastical Authorities in the Empire* (Leiden: E.J. Brill, 1978); Denys Hay and W.K. Smith, ed. and tr., *De gestis concilii Basiliensis commentariorum libri II* (Oxford: Clarendon Press, 1967), xv; Emily O'Brien, *Commentaries of Pope Pius II (1458–1464) and the Crisis of the Fifteenth-Century Papacy* (Toronto: University of Toronto Press, 2015), 22.

34 Stieber, *Pope Eugenius*, 1.

35 See Aeneas's letter to the government of Siena (Nov. 11, 1432); *Reject Aeneas*, tr. Izbicki et al., 68–69; Wolkan, *Briefwechsel*, 61: 14–16.

36 Many of Aeneas's letters contain insights into the connections and lasting friendships he forged at Basel. See *Reject Aeneas*, tr. Izbicki et al.

37 *Reject Aeneas*, tr. Izbicki et al., 17.

38 Letter to the Sienese government (Dec. 18, 1432). "Jam annum elapsum, quo dissolutionem emiserit, neque ab eo tempore unquam cessasse perturbare. Procedendum itaque contra eum esse, pronuntiandam contumaciam, omni obedientia spoliandum." Wolkan, *Briefwechsel*, 61: 17; Eng. tr. with a slight modification, *Reject Aeneas*, tr. Izbicki et al., 71.

39 The council quickly granted Capranica his appeal to reclaim the title of cardinal, which Pope Eugenius IV had repudiated, but they were powerless to help him regain access to his position's property and income; hence, he could no longer afford to pay his staff.

40 See John M. Najemy, *Between Friends: Discourses of Power and Desire in the Machiavelli-Vettori Letters of 1513–1515* (Princeton, NJ: Princeton University Press, 1993), 23–24; Witt, *Footsteps*, 1–2, 133–38, and *passim*; see also Jerrold Seigel, *Rhetoric and Philosophy in Renaissance Humanism* (Princeton, NJ: Princeton University Press, 1968).

41 At the council, Aeneas was employed first as a scribe or secretary (*scriptor*), then as a supervisor, and beginning in 1436 he served the council directly as *abbreviator major*, drafting their letters and documents; in 1439 he was promoted clerk of the ceremonies, placing him at the center of important moments, namely the papal election. See *Reject Aeneas*, tr. Izbicki et al., 22, 123; O'Brien, *Commentaries*, 47; Barbara Baldi, *Il "cardinale tedesco": Enea Silvio Piccolomini fra impero, papato, Europa (1442–1455)* (Milan: Edizioni Unicopoli, 2012), 22.

42 *De gestis concilii*, ed. and tr. Hay and Smith. See also Aeneas's dialogue *Libellus dialogorum de generalis concilii auctoritate et gestis Basileensium* (1440), which sought to delegitimate Pope Eugenius's transfer of the council to Ferrara (and later Florence) and contains many arguments undermining papal authority; O'Brien, *Commentaries of Pope Pius II*, 48.

43 As Mitchell states, "During this period of his life he stored up a great wealth of experience of men and affairs." *Laurels*, 55. See also Ady, *Pius II*, 36–37; *Reject Aeneas*, tr. Izbicki et al., 16–18.

44 Aeneas had little to say on the Council of Florence when it occurred, seeing it only in political terms as a loss for Basel instead of an opportunity to both reunite with the Greeks and create a strong alliance against the Ottomans.

45 See Ady, *Pius II*, 70. Cardinal Cesarini had offered to take Aeneas and others with him when he left the council in 1438, but Aeneas still saw his fortunes as linked to Basel. After his publication of *De gestis* in 1440, his options were even slimmer. Ady, *Pius II*, 62–63; On the offer to leave Basel in 1438, see *Reject Aeneas*, tr. Izbicki et al., 121; Wolkan, *Briefwechsel*, 61: 79–80.

46 Lorenzo Valla's complimentary reply to Aeneas (April 5, 1443) can be found in *Correspondence*, tr. and ed. Brendan Cook (Cambridge, MA: Harvard University Press, 2013), 136–137; see also Wolkan, *Briefwechsel*, 61: 146–47.

47 See Ady, *Pius II*, 71, 80.

48 There has been some question about Aeneas's knowledge of German, due in large part to his own misleading comments about it. More will be said later in the chapter on the evidence.

49 Christoph Schingnitz, ed. *Pentalogus* (Hannover: Harrassowitz, 2009), 54–56; see also Barbara Baldi, *Il "cardinale tedesco": Enea Silvio Piccolomini fra impero, papato, Europa (1442–1455)* (Milan: Edizioni Unicopoli, 2012), 36.

50 *Europe*, tr. and ed. Bisaha and Brown, 134.

51 *Miseries* should not be read as directly autobiographical. It borrows from Juvenal, Lucan, and Peter of Blois. See *Reject Aeneas*, tr. Izbicki et al., 28; Keith Sidwell,

"Aeneas Silvius Piccolomini's De curialium miseriis and Peter of Blois," in *Pius II*, ed. Von Martels and Vanderjagt, 87–106; Sidwell, "Il De curialium miseriis di Enea Silvio Piccolomini e il De mercede conductis di Luciano," in *Pio II e la cultura*, ed. Tarugi, 329–42. Celenza posits that Aeneas may have drawn upon a more recent work, Lapo da Castiglionchio's *De curiae commodis* (1438), as a model; see Celenza, *Renaissance Humanism and the Papal Curia*, 36–41. Baldi argues that *Miseries* was less about Aeneas's disenchantment with court life than courtiers who advanced their own interests instead of advising rulers; *Cardinale tedesco*, 114.

52 Albert R. Baca, ed. and tr., *Selected Letters of Aeneas Silvius Piccolomini* (Northridge, Calif.: San Fernando Valley State College, 1969), 19; Wolkan, *Briefwechsel*, 61: 236. See also a letter to Francesco Pizzolpasso (Dec. 1442) where he describes himself as follows: "Caesar Augustus, Frederick, has summoned me to his secretariat in which I am now a servant in the least honored grade and position"; *Reject Aeneas*, tr. Izbicki et al., 135; Wolkan, *Briefwechsel*, 61: 119–20.

53 Schlick's mother was Italian, and he spent several months in Siena in Emperor Sigismund's entourage in 1432. Aeneas dedicated a poem and essay to Schlick in late 1442, and more importantly, helped the chancellor to secure his brother's bid for the vacant see of Freising in 1443. See Wolkan, *Briefwechsel*, 61: 121–25; Ady, *Pius II*, 74, 79–82.

54 For more on this transition see Thomas Izbicki, "The Missing Anti-pope: The Rejection of Felix V and the Council of Basel in the Writings of Aeneas Sylvius Piccolomini and the Piccolomini Library," *Viator* 41, no. 1 (2009): 301–14. On Aeneas's absolution by Eugenius in Rome in 1445, see Ady, *Pius II*, 87–88. Aeneas says a few words about his path to ordination in a letter to his friend, Giovanni Campisio, dated sometime in 1446; *Reject Aeneas*, tr. Izbicki et al., 231–33.

55 See Baldi, *Cardinale tedesco*, for an in-depth look at Aeneas's time at the imperial court and the development of his political leanings and perspectives.

56 See Marcello Simonetta, *Il Rinascimento segreto: Il mondo del segretario da Petrarca a Machiavelli* (Milan: Franco Angeli, 2004); Douglas Biow, *Doctors, Ambassadors, and Secretaries: Humanism and Professions in Renaissance Italy* (Chicago: University of Chicago Press, 2002); Peter Partner, *The Pope's Men: The Papal Civil Service in the Renaissance* (Oxford: Clarendon Press, 1990). Stephen Greenblatt evokes the unique position of this profession with his imaginative description of papal secretary Poggio Bracciolini's travels through the German countryside in 1417, on a break from the Council of Constance to visit monastic libraries. See *The Swerve: How the World Became Modern* (New York: W.W. Norton and Co., 2011), 14–5.

57 Monks and priests traveled, but mostly locally or, on occasion, to Rome. Merchants traveled but rarely beyond the continent at this time. University students were among the more mobile classes and helped create a sense of common culture with their use of Latin, an attribute that put Aeneas in good company with them. Still, most traveled to relatively few destinations for their studies. See Peter Rietbergen, *Europe: A Cultural History* (London: Routledge, 1998), 150–57. See also Christopher Celenza, "What Did It Mean to Live in the Long Fifteenth Century?" in *Before Copernicus" The Cultures and Contexts of Scientific Learning in the Fifteenth Century*, ed. Rivka Feldhay and F. Jamil Ragep (Montreal: McGill University Press, 2017), 19–20.

58 Norbert Ohler, *The Medieval Traveller*, tr. Caroline Hillier (Woodbridge, UK: Boydell Press, 1989), ix. For more recent studies of travel, see *Travels and Mobilities in the Middle Ages: From the Atlantic to the Black Sea*, ed. Marianne O'Doherty and Felicitas Schmieder (Turnhout: Belgium, 2015).

59 Aeneas describes both adventures later in his *Commentaries*, but he exaggerates the dangers and his supposed equanimity in the first instance and adds a great deal of detail to the second. His terror off the coast of Scotland was likely genuine, yet he does not mention it in his letter from the time (see below).

60 Hirschi, *Origins*, 29–30.

61 Rietbergen, *Europe*, 143.

62 *Commentaries*, ed. Meserve and Simonetta, 1: 24–25. See Chapter 4 for further discussion.

63 Najemy, *Between Friends*, 22. For an examination of the social coding of letters between two Trecento correspondents, see Richard C. Trexler, *Public Life in Renaissance Florence* (Ithaca, NY: Cornell University Press, 1980), 131–58.

64 In addition to humanist epistles and diplomatic official letters, there was also the genre of "everyday utilitarian letters" to which educated men of central Italy were accustomed—the categories were not "watertight"; see Najemy, *Between Friends*, 18.

65 I discuss the Cardinal of Krakow, Zbigniew Olesnicki's praise in "'Discourses of Power and Desire': The Letters of Aeneas Silvius Piccolomini (1453)," in *Florence and Beyond: Culture, Society, and Politics in Renaissance Italy*, ed. David Peterson and Daniel Bornstein (Toronto: Centre for Reformation and Renaissance Studies, 2008), 121–34. I am now less certain of my assertion in this article that that Olesnicki's praise of Aeneas's simple style was meant condescendingly.

66 Wolkan, *Briefwechsel*, 61: 111–12, dated Nov. 13 (possibly 1442).

67 Baldi, *Cardinale tedesco*, 80.

68 Cecil Clough discusses the range of possibilities on how Aeneas's letters were preserved, possibly altered, collected, disseminated, and starting in the 1470s, printed. See "The Chancery letter-files of Aeneas Silvius Piccolomini," in *Enea Silvio Piccolomini*, ed. Maffei, 117–131. A welcome addition to the study of Aeneas's letters is *Reject Aeneas, Accept Pius*, ed. and tr. Izbicki et al., which contains helpful introductions and notes as well as a selection of over seventy letters, mostly from 1430–1450. See also Baca, *Selected Letters*.

69 For a literary analysis of Aeneas's letters, see Antonio Musumeci, "L'epistolario di Enea Silvio Piccolomini: il discorso sulla letteratura," in *Pio II e la cultura*, ed. Tarugi, 373–93; for letters as autobiography, see Roberta Antognini, *Il progetto autobiografico delle Familiares di Petrarca* (Milan: Edizioni Universitarie di Lettere Economia Diritto, 2008). See also the recent essay collection, *Pio II nell'epistolografia del Rinascimento*, ed. Luisa Secchi Tarugi, (Florence: Franco Cesati Editore, 2015).

70 Najemy, *Between Friends*, 26.

71 Petrucci was also friends with several well-known humanists including Bruni, Filelfo, and Aurispa; Wolkan, *Briefwechsel*, 61: 7, n. 1a; Ady, *Pius II*, 29.

72 "Sedulo et vadunt et veniunt, he quidem ab orienti, ille ab occidenti sole, ut aspicias quotidie diversa hominum genera incognitosque et incultos mores, mercatores etiam cum universa merce adventantes." Wolkan, *Briefwechsel*, 61: 7; Eng. tr., Ady, *Pius II*, 29.

73 "Scientie parum cupidi grammaticen ad necessitatem student, cetera studiorum genera parvi faciunt." Wolkan, *Briefwechsel*, 61: 8.

74 "O urbem fortunatissimam, si civium concordiam habuisset." Wolkan, *Briefwechsel*, 61: 10.

75 Venus, he states, would choose to live in Genoa today if given the chance; Wolkan, *Briefwechsel*, 61: 9.

76 Wolkan, *Briefwechsel*, 61: 10; Ady, *Pius II*, 30.

77 The first letter is in Wolkan, *Briefwechsel*, 61, no. 16; the second, in ibid, no. 28. See Ady, 33–35 for a summary and analysis.

78 Strabo, *Geography*, 1.1.17–18. It is hard to know if Aeneas had access to partial translations or epitomes of Strabo at this time. He would begin to cite the text directly when he was at Rome in the later 1450s.

79 Wolkan, *Briefwechsel*, 61: 33.

80 "Civium edes partibus suis mirifice distincte, polite adeo ac delicate, ne Florentine quidem magis." Wolkan, *Briefwechsel*, 61: 34; see Ady, *Pius II*, 34.

81 "Viri magno, ut plurimum, corpore sunt urbanique, minus magnifice vestiuntur, delicate tamen. Pauci, forsitan ex militibus aliqui, utuntur ostro, primores vero civitatis, quibus magne divitie sunt amplaque supellex, nigro velantur panno." Wolkan, *Briefwechsel*, 61:37; see also ibid., 38.

82 Wolkan, *Briefwechsel*, 61: 34–35.

83 On Aeneas's visit to Vienna with Bishop Bartolomeo Visconti of Novara in 1438, see Baldi, *Cardinale tedesco*, 29. The letter was reproduced almost verbatim in Aeneas's *Historia Friderici* (1458); see *Portable Renaissance Reader*, ed. and tr. James Bruce Ross and Mary Martin McLaughlin (New York, Penguin Books, 1981; 1st ed. Viking Press, 1953), 208–13 for a translation of the latter account.

84 "Ingressus cujusque domum in edes te principis venisse putabis." Wolkan, *Briefwechsel*, 61: 81. Eng. tr., Ross and McLaughlin, *Portable Renaissance Reader*, 209.

85 "Plebs ventri dedita, vorax, quicquid hebdomada manu quesivit, id festo die totum absumit. Lacerum et incompositum vulgus, meretricum maximus numerus, raro mulier est uno contenta viro." Wolkan, *Briefwechsel*, 61: 83; Eng. tr., Ross and McLaughlin, *Portable Renaissance Reader*, 212.

86 Wolkan, *Briefwechsel*, 61: 84; *Portable Renaissance Reader*, 213.

87 See Vito Giustiniani, 'Gli umanisti Italiani e la Germania," in *Pio II e la cultura*, ed. Tarugi, 238.

88 "Nulla hic studia gentilium litterarum, poeticam oratoriamque prorsus ignorant, grammatice tamen ac dialectice operam adhibent. Confluunt huc ex vicinioribus opidis quamplures adolescentes, quibus ex elemosina victus est, magister ex publico." Wolkan, *Briefwechsel*, 61: 94.

89 "Maximum autem huius gymnasii vitium es, quod nimis diutinam operam in dialectica nimiumque temporis in re non magni fructus terunt." Wolkan, *Briefwechsel*, 61: 82; Eng. tr., Ross and McLaughlin, *Portable Renaissance Reader*, 210.

90 Aeneas states in his letter on Basel to Cesarini (1434) that it was prompted by an excess of time on his hands in Milan. Regarding Bruni's *Laudatio* on the city of Florence, Aeneas had access to the text in Francesco Pizzolpasso's library in Milan; see Giovanni Zippel, "E.S. Piccolomini e il mondo Germanico," *Cultura* 19 (1981): 274–75. Aeneas shares with Bruni a sense of history as directed toward common utility and the importance of place—a connection to his later *Europe*. Considering this, it is odd that he leaves all this description of Basel out of both of his later histories of the council. Ady describes it as intended to be used as an introduction to his history, *Pius II*, 34.

91 As several of his letters show, Aeneas urged Siena to make a competitive bid to host the council for the glory of the city, but the republic was unable or unwilling to outbid Florence or other cities. See *Reject Aeneas*, tr. Izbicki et al., 83–98. There is little evidence of the Sienese government's view of Aeneas as a go-between or adviser at Basel, but a summary of the *Concistoro* records has a brief entry remarking on Aeneas's exhortations that the republic should host the council in their city. See *Concistoro* no. 422 (May 1-June 30, 1436), fol. 5v., Archivio di Stato di Siena. Thanks to Christine Shaw and Julia Hairston for their assistance with this question.

92 See the introduction to Piccolomini, *De gestis* ed. and tr. Hay and Smith, xvii–xviii. Aeneas later claimed that he often presided over the deputation of faith (regarding concerns of heresy) and sat on the council of twelve, but he is the only source for this; see *Reject Aeneas*, tr. Izbicki et al., 22. Hirschi discusses the importance of the role of "nations" at the previous Council of Constance, but Hay and Smith argue that they played a lesser role at Basel; Hirschi, *Origins*, 82–88; Hay and Smith, ed. *De gestis*, xvii.

93 Aeneas does make a point of listing the representatives, nation by nation, at Basel who entered the conclave to elect anti-pope Felix V. See *De gestis*, ed. Hay and Smith, 208–18.

94 Zippel, "E.S. Piccolomini e il mondo Germanico," 273, 302–03.
95 "Papa unus est, concilium multorum est peritorum congregatio, unde plus vident oculi quam oculus et omnes omnia sciunt, nemo omnia. Nimiumque arrogans est, qui se melius discernere putat omnibus aliis ...." (Letter to Hartung von Kappel, April 1443), Wolkan, *Briefwechsel*, 61: 134; Eng. tr., *Reject Aeneas*, tr. Izbicki et al., 139.
96 "Non aliter olim sua oratione moderare hic concilium solebat, quam Cicero quondam senatum, nec minus isti suam eloquentiam quam Athenienses Demosthenis mirabantur orationem. Nunc loquenti omnes perstrepunt contempnuntque tacentem." (May 21, 1437), Wolkan 61: 64–65; Eng. tr., *Reject Aeneas*, tr. Izbicki et al., 106.
97 *Reject Aeneas*, tr. Izbicki et al., 104: 108–09; Wolkan, *Briefwechsel*, 61: 67.
98 "Ridiculum prorsus, ut, qui daturi orbi pacem convenerunt, iis ea opus sit, et qui dare concordiam laicis sese jactant, a laicis illam expectent." Wolkan, *Briefwechsel*, 61: 67; Eng. tr., *Reject Aeneas*, tr. Izbicki et al., 109.
99 "Audivi" (16 November 1436, Basel), ed. and tr. Michael v. Cotta-Schönberg (Final edition, 2nd version) (Orations of Enea Silvio Piccolomini / Pope Pius II; 1). 2019. ⟨hprints-00683151⟩, 138–39. See Cotta-Schönberg's comments on the question of Aeneas and democracy in ibid., 34.
100 "Italici vero ... dum imperare singuli volunt, omnes servire coguntur, ut qui regem aut cesarem aspernantur vilissime plebi subjiciuntur, unde nec ullum apud eos diuturnum imperium nec ullibi magis quam in Italia fortuna jocatur."; Wolkan, *Briefwechsel*, 61: 93. See also Ady's reading and translation; *Pius II*, 35.
101 See Norman Housley's astute analysis of Aeneas's political views in "Aeneas Silvius Piccolomini, Nicholas of Cusa, and the Crusade: Conciliar, Imperial, and Papal Authority," *Church History* 86, no. 3 (Sept., 2017): 646–47.
        Regarding Aeneas's *De gestis Basiliensis Concilii* (1439–40), see O'Brien, *Commentaries*, 48–54, and O'Brien, "Aeneas Sylvius Piccolomini and the Histories of the Council of Basel," in *The Church, the Councils, and Reform: The Legacy of the Fifteenth Century*, ed. Gerald Christianson, Thomas Izbicki, and Christopher Belitto (Washington, DC: Catholic University of America Press, 2008), 60–81.
102 The later embarrassment that *De gestis* created is clear from Aeneas's decision to write a revised history of the Council in 1450, where his criticisms come out in full. For more on Aeneas's shifting attitudes on conciliarism and the papacy, see O'Brien, *Commentaries*; Izbicki, "'Reject Aeneas!' Pius II on the Errors of his Youth" in *Pius II, ed.* Von Martels and Vanderjagt.
103 For the letter to Sigismund, which may or may not have been sent, see *Reject Aeneas*, tr. Izbicki et al., 117–20.
104 See Housley, "Piccolomini, Cusa, and Crusade," 650.
105 The *Pentalogus* was not among his early printed texts. Only two manuscripts of the work are known, and it was not printed until 1723. See Schingnitz, *Pentalogus*, 27–38; Harry Basten, "'Nationis Teutonicae': The German Nation and the Holy Roman Empire through the eyes of an Italian humanist" (Master's thesis, Leiden University, 2016), 33–34. For an overview of *Pentalogus*, see Basten, 43–49.
106 See *Pentalogus*, ed. Schingnitz, 252–58, 286; Basten, 'Nationis Teutonicae,' 46–47.
107 Housley, "Piccolomini, Cusa, and Crusade," 650.
108 *Pentalogus*, ed. Schingnitz, 198; 246; Basten, "'Nationis Teutonicae,'" 43; O'Brien, *Commentaries*, 91.
109 See *Pentalogus* ed. Schingnitz on the schism and the role of secular leaders, 114, 116; see also O'Brien, *Commentaries*, 91–92; Barbara Baldi, "Un umanista alla corte di Federico III. Il Pentalogus di Enea Silvio Piccolomini" *Cahiers d'études italiennes* 13 (2011): 161–71. http://cei.revues.org/85?lang=en
110 See especially *Pentalogus*, ed. Schingnitz, 252–62. Hirschi has remarked on the importance of this text, with its emphasis on the honor of Germans, as an early indication of nationalist thought; see *Origins*, 130–33.

111 See Aeneas's letter to his old employer, Domenico Capranica (1444), where he asks the cardinal to recommend him to Pope Eugenius, and his request to a friend to sell his secretarial job in Basel in a letter of April 18, 1444; see *Reject Aeneas*, tr. Izbicki et al., 185 and 188; Wolkan, *Briefwechsel*, 61: 294, and 312–14.

112 Wolkan, *Briefwechsel*, 67: 10–11; "On the Origin and Authority of the Roman Empire," in *De Ortu et auctoritate imperii Romani*, in *Three Tracts on Empire: Engelbert of Admont, Aeneas Silvius Piccolomini, and Juan de Torquemada*, tr. and ed., Thomas M. Izbicki and Cary J. Nederman (Bristol, UK: Thoemmes Press, 2000), 98–99.

113 "Nihil est enim, quod illi maximo deo ... gravius sit, quam justitie neglectus indignaque pauperum oppressio." Wolkan, *Briefwechsel*, 67: 23; Eng. tr., "Origin," 112.

114 See Vanita Seth on this concept, citing the work of Michel de Certeau, in *Europe's Indians: Producing Racial Difference, 1500–1900* (Durham, NC: Duke University Press, 2010), 188–89.

115 On Aeneas's possible medieval sources and ideas, see John Toewes, "The View of Empire in Aeneas Sylvius Piccolomini (Pope Pius II)," *Traditio* 24 (1968): 471–87; Zippel, "Piccolomini e il mondo Germanico," 311–12; For a more recent reading, see Baldi, *Cardinale tedesco*, 125–32.

116 Cary Nederman, "Humanism and Empire: Aeneas Sylvius Piccolomini, Cicero, and the Imperial Ideal," *The Historical Journal* 36, no. 3 (Sept. 1993): 509–10.

117 Nederman, "Humanism and Empire," 507.

118 "Quod si uno sub capite viveremus, si unam omnes sequeremur obedientiam, si unum dumtaxat in temporalibus summum principem recognosceremus, floreret ubique terrarum pax optima dulcique omnes concordia frueremur." Wolkan, *Briefwechsel*, 67: 15. Eng. tr., Nederman and Izbicki, "Origin," 103.

119 "Tolerandum est patienter, quod princeps facit, quamvis inique, expectandaque est successoris emenda vel superni correctio judicis ...." Wolkan, *Briefwechsel*, 67: 18; English tr., "Origin," 105–06, with some modification.

120 Wolkan, *Briefwechsel*, 67: 22–23; "Origin," 111.

121 "... nec enim vel populare regimen, quod politicum, vel optimorum civium, quod aristocraticum appellatur, tam justum tamque pacificum esse potest, quam monarchicum ...." Wolkan, *Briefwechsel*, 67: 13; Eng. tr., with some modification, "Origin," 101.

122 Nederman posits, "It can be argued, in fact, that Aeneas more nearly approaches the philosophical core of Cicero's own thought—and is, therefore, truer to the Ciceronian theoretical framework—than were quattrocento figures such as Leonardo Bruni." See "Humanism and Empire," 503.

123 "Romani pontificis sententiam nulli fas est in irritum revocare. Romani principis voluntatem nemo potest impugnare." Wolkan, *Briefwechsel*, 67: 23; Eng. tr., "Origin," 111, with some modification.

124 "Hinc etiam illa Christi verba trahuntur, cum dicenti discipulo, ecce gladii duo hic, sufficit, inquit. Quo dicto et spiritualia summo pontifici et temporalia cesari, uti doctores interpretantur, subjecit, ac si diceret, duo potestates sunto..." Wolkan, *Briefwechsel*, 67: 11; Eng. tr., "Origin," 99. For more on Christian political readings of this passage, see Brian Tierney, *The Crisis of Church and State 1050–1300* (Toronto: University of Toronto Press, 1988).

125 Baldi, *Cardinale tedesco*, 119–32; Ady, *Pius II*, 82–83. Toews also argues that disenchantment with the fragmentation he had witnessed among European powers was part of his decision to join Frederick's court. See Toews, "View of Empire." See also *Reject Aeneas*, tr. Izbicki et al., 243–73 for Aeneas's official report on the reconciliation with the pope to Frederick (1447).

126 See, for example, Wolkan, *Briefwechsel*, 67: 13 and 20–21. *Genus, gens*, and *populus* will be discussed at length in Chapter 3.

127 See Patrick J. Geary, *The Myth of Nations: The Medieval Origins of Europe* (Princeton, NJ: Princeton University Press, 2002), 19, 63–64.

128 Wolkan, *Briefwechsel*, 67: 15; Eng. tr., "Origin," 103.

129 See Nederman, "Humanism and Empire," 502–03; Zippel also noted the tendency among Aeneas's critics to simplify his political views and goals, "Il mondo Germanico," 327.

130 Thomas Izbicki, "Badgering for Books: Aeneas Sylvius Piccolomini and Leonardo Bruni's Translation of Aristotle's *Politics*," in *Essays in Renaissance Thought and Letters in Honor of John Monfasani*, ed. Alison Frazier and Patrick Nold (Leiden: Brill, 2015), 12–22. Aeneas received books 1–8 of the *Politics* by late 1445, before he composed *De Ortu*, but he does not appear to have been influenced by it, preferring to rely more on Cicero.

131 Vito Giustiniani, "Gli umanisti Italiani," in *Pio II e la cultura*, ed. Tarugi, 237, believes Aeneas knew German and learned it at Basel, pointing to one of his poems in *Opera inedita*, ed. Cugnoni, 344; the poem is also found in *Renaissance Latin Verse*, ed. Alessandro Perosa and John Sparrow (Chapel Hill: University of North Carolina Press, 1979), 30–32. Robert Glendinning presents a closer look at the evidence on both sides and concludes that Aeneas knew German in "Love, Death, and the Art of Compromise: Aeneas Sylvius Piccolomini's *Tale of Two Lovers*," *Fifteenth Century Studies* 23 (1996): 101–20, see esp. 112–13. For Aeneas's denials of knowing German, see Wolkan, *Briefwechsel*. 61; 323; *Pentalogus*, ed. Schingnitz, 58.

132 Mitchell, *Laurels*, 42.

133 Hirschi, *Origins of Nationalism*, 130. On German identity, see Baldi, "Un umanista alla corte di Federico III," 161–71.

134 "Demum vero negligentibus Romam Grecis, eamque nunc barbarorum, nunc aliorum direptioni relinquentibus, populus ille Romanus, qui suo sanguine tantum pararat imperium, quique suis virtutibus monarchiam fundaverat orbis, venientem in auxilium ejus Carolum magnum, Francorum regem, natione Germanum, qui urbem... defendit, primo patricium post Augustum, concurrente summi consensu pontificis acclamavit. Talique modo in Germanos Romanum imperium constat esse translatum." Wolkan, *Briefwechsel*, 67: 13–14; Eng. tr., "Origin," tr. Izbicki and Nederman, 101, with minor changes.

135 For instance, "Here [in Italy] your name was given to you, Caesar, for you are called king of the Romans." ("Hinc tibi inditum nomen est, cesar, rex enim Romanorum diceris."); *Pentalogus*, ed. Schingnitz, 160.

136 "Sic mihi hodie de te visum est, cum in regia de studiis, que vocant humanitatis, dissertares. Nam et legistam et Theutonem superabas et Italicam redolebas oratoriam facundiamque. Sed quod fuit merori Greco, mihi letitiam prebuit. Neque enim, si Theutonia litteris claret, quas ille tradidit, Italia minus habet litterarum." Wolkan, *Briefwechsel*, 67: 79 (my translation). See also the translations in *Reject Aeneas*, tr. Izbicki et al., 293 and Baca, *Selected Letters*, 42.

137 "... quo sepulta dicendi facultate barbarorum inscitia dominabatur." Wolkan, *Briefwechsel*, 67: 80; Baca, *Selected Letters*, 42; *Reject Aeneas*, tr. Izbicki et al., 293.

138 Ady notes the glee with which Aeneas later depicted Heimburg in a diplomatic battle in Rome (with Heimburg representing German Electors and Aeneas, the emperor) as uncouth and defeated, in his unfinished *Historia Friderici*; see *Pius II*, 92; see also idem, 174–75 for her portrayal of his ungracious address to Aeneas/ Pius at the Congress of Mantua in 1459.

139 Wolkan, *Briefwechsel*, 61: 120; Ady, *Pius II*, 74.

140 Noel Brann, 'Humanism in Germany," in Rabil ed., *Renaissance Humanism*, 1: 126; Zippel, "Piccolomini e il mondo Germanico," 329 ff.

141 "At non sunt, dicis, apud te socii? Sunt utique viri boni fidelesque, sed non meum in modum litterarum amatores, nec qui oblectentur his rebus, quibus ego. Cibi

preterea magna est dissonantia, quamvis facilius est Italicum vorare Theutonice quam Theutonicum Italice lambere." Wolkan, *Briefwechsel*, 61: 543; Eng. tr., *Reject Aeneas*, tr. Izbicki et al., 226.

142 Giustiniani, "Gli umanisti Italiani," 238.

143 Zippel argues that the play is a satire on German society; "Piccolomini e il mondo Germanico," 304; Gary Grund notes prominent Germans thought to have been the models of the bumbling clerics and the allusions to its setting at Basel; *Humanist Comedies* (Cambridge, Mass.: Harvard University Press, 2005), 446, n. 1. One could also see the play as targeting the loose morals of many clergymen in general, regardless of ethnicity. For a discussion of the play's message about moral philosophy, see Emily O'Brien, Aeneas Silvius Piccolomini's *Chrysis*: Prurient pastime-or something more?" *Modern Language Notes*, 124, no. 1 (Jan., 2009): 111–36.

144 Ady, *Pius II*, 79, 109; his antipathy for Gregor Heimburg in his later unfinished work, *Historia Friderici*, takes on tones that Ady describes as "conflict between the two races—Latin and Teutonic" (ibid., 92–93), but these potshots seem limited to this individual rather than Germans as a whole. For his 1442 letter to his uncle longing for the Tuscan countryside, see Wolkan, *Briefwechsel*, 61: 38. For his letter to Piero da Noceto (1444) asking if he can find a way to turn "German Aeneas into an Italian," see Baldi, *Cardinale*, 81. See also Wolkan, *Briefwechsel*, 68: 181, for his letter to Goro Lolli on his longing for home.

145 Baldi, *Cardinale tedesco*, 78–79; Giustiniani, "Gli umanisti Italiani," 238.

146 "Veteres sunt apud me littere tue, quibus non respondi, quoniam nunc in Stiria, nunc in Carinthia, nunc in Carniola inter medios barbaros sevasque nationes constitutus, nunc apud Histriam et super oras superi maris cum Tergestinis versatus, nullum habui, cui committere litteras possem ad te perferendas." Wolkan, *Briefwechsel*, 61: 313, Eng. tr., *Reject Aeneas*, tr. Izbicki et al., 187.

147 See *Europe*, tr. Bisaha and Brown, 123, on Henry of Gorizia. This colorful portrait of Henry was not penned until 1458, however, further supporting my thesis that Aeneas did not embark on serious cultural or ethnographic writing until post 1453.

148 See Rolando Montecalvo, "The New Landesgeschichte: Aeneas Silvius Piccolomini on Austria and Bohemia," in *Pius II*, ed. Von Martels and Vanderjagt, 56–57; Howard Kaminsky, "Pius Aeneas Among the Taborites," *Church History* 28, no. 3 (1959): 281–309; Thomas A. Fudge, "Seduced by the Theologians: Aeneas Sylvius and the Hussite Heretics," in *Heresy in Transition: Transforming Ideas of Heresy in Medieval and Early Modern Europe*, ed. Ian Hunter, John C. Laursen, Cary J. Nederman (Aldershot, UK: Ashgate, 2005), 89–101.

149 Housley, *Later Crusades*, 250–51.

150 On the charges against Hus, see Thomas A. Fudge, "'O Cursed Judas': Formal Heresy Accusations against Jan Hus," in *Religion, Power, and Resistance From the Eleventh to the Sixteenth Centuries: Playing the Heresy Card*, ed. Karen Bollermann, Thomas M. Izbicki, and Cary J. Nederman (New York: Palgrave Macmillan, 2014), 55–80.

151 Kaminsky, "Pius Aeneas among the Taborites," 289–95. See Wolkan, *Briefwechsel*, 68: 22–57 for the letter to Juan Carvajal (Aug. 21, 1451).

152 "Videbatur mihi ultra Sauromathas et glacialem occeanum fuisse inter barbaros, inter antropofagos aut inter monstruosas Indie Lybieque gentes; nec sane, in omni terra, quam circuit Amphitrites, gens ulla est monstruosior Thaboritis. Ethiopas enim quosdam et Scithas et Taprobanos corporis vitio monstruosos ajunt, Thaboritas vero depravate mentis vitia et innumerabiles animi macule monstruosos efficiunt ...." Wolkan, *Briefwechsel*, 68: 56; Eng. tr., Kaminsky, "Pius Among the Taborites," 293. Reading *Amphitrite* (wife of Neptune and a metonymy for the sea) for Wolkan's *Amphitrites*; either Aeneas used the wrong form or there was a scribal error. Thanks to Rob Brown.

153 For more on concepts of monstrous races, see John Block Friedman, *The Monstrous Races in Medieval Art and Thought*, 2nd ed. (Syracuse, NY: Syracuse University Press, 2000).

154 On the preparations and negotiations for this council, see Kenneth Setton, *The Papacy and the Levant (1205–1571)* (Philadelphia: American Philosophical Society, 1978), vol. 2: 52–56. On Nicholas Cusanus's trip to Constantinople as part of a delegation from Basel, see Maarten Halff, "Did Cusanus Talk with Muslims? Revisiting Cusanus' Sources for the Cribratio Alkorani and Interfaith Dialogue," *Revista Española de Filosofia Medieval* 26, no. 1 (2019): 29–58. Aeneas's attempts to persuade the Sienese to make a strong bid to host it have already been discussed.

155 "Neque enim sine ratione moventur, scientes ducem cum Turcis, unde vetustissimam trahit originem, haereditariam habere familiaritatem, quod salva fide vituperari non potest …. Nec illud est non considerandum: Graecos fere omnes imperio Turcorum esse subjectos, curareque ne quam rebellionis suspicionem ingerant dominis, a quibus profecto impedirentur. Nec invitis Turcis deducere Graecos quisquam poterit." "Audivi," ed. Cotta-Schönberg, 76; English tr., 77, with minor modifications.

156 Cotta-Schönberg accepts "Turci" as the more likely usage in this oration. Aeneas would continue to use *Teucri* until at least 1447; "Audivi," ed. Cotta-Schönberg, 30.

157 Cotta-Schönberg, "Audivi," 27–31; Meserve, *Empires*, 14, 34–35, 99–100.

158 "Magnum est imperium Turcorum, ingentes Asiaticorum vires, et opes ipsae florentissimae, qui ex in Asia in Europam imperium prorogarunt totamque Graeciam occuparunt tamquam Troianae ultores ruinae, quos Graecia pellere non unius civitatis aut dominii, sed totius esset Christianitatis opus." "Audivi," ed. Cotta-Schönberg, 78; English tr., 79. On this oration and Aeneas's early crusade views, see Johannes Helmrath, "Pius II. und die Türken," in *Europa und die Türken in der Renaissance*, ed. Bodo Guthmüller and Wilhelm Kühlmann (Tübingen: Max Niemeyer, Verlag, 2000), 89; Meserve, *Empires*, 99.

159 Housley effectively shows how both Aeneas's conciliar views and his allegiance to Frederick shaped his negative outlook in the 1440s; see "Piccolomini, Nicholas of Cusa, and the Crusade," 649.

160 See Setton, *Papacy* 2: 74–90.

161 See Setton, *Papacy* 2: 82–91; Housley, *Later Crusades*, 83 ff.

162 Housley, *Later Crusades*, 86.

163 *Passagium* was the term Aeneas preferred for crusade, even as pope, to describe a campaign of great magnitude. This will be discussed in Chapter 4.

164 A reference to the defeat of a crusading army against the Hussites led by Cesarini in 1431.

165 "… sortitusque ad rem hanc optimum instrumentum regem Polonie, qui et ipse aliena regna invadens bonam de se prestare cupit opinionem atque ita sub colore passagii alienum Gabriel pontificatum et iste regnum tenere cupit. Harumque rerum minister est Julianus, de quo tamen dolere non debemus, quia non consuevit hic homo fortunatus esse in bellis sicut Boemia ostendit. Deus enim non opus sed finem spectat itaque deficiet ut spero in salutari suo." Wolkan, *Briefwechsel*, 61: 165; Eng. tr., *Reject Aeneas*, tr. Izbicki et al., 156, with minor alterations. This letter is undated, but Wolkan estimates that it was written in July 1443.

166 Housley, "Piccolomini, Nicholas of Cusa, and the Crusade," 649.

167 "Quantum sentio tota Christianitas Eugenii sequitur partes." Wolkan, *Briefwechsel*, 61: 324; Eng. tr., *Reject Aeneas*, tr. Izbicki et al., 191, with some modifications.

168 "… virum illum, sui splendorem seculi … bene cum eo actum puto, qui causam Christi tuebatur." Wolkan, *Briefwechsel*, 61: 499; Eng. tr., *Reject Aeneas*, tr. Izbicki et al., 216, with some modifications.

169 See *Europe*, tr. Bisaha and Brown, 84.
170 Baldi, *Cardinale*, 81, 152.
171 "Ajunt hoc magnum esse initium et spem hinc suscipi, qua Teucri ex Europa pellantur..." Wolkan, *Briefwechsel*, 61: 281–82.
172 "... homo Valachus, regionis gnarus et ingenii calidi, periculum quo ceteros irretivit, absque negotio declinavit." Wolkan, *Briefwechsel*, 67: 74; Eng. tr., *Reject Aeneas*, tr. Izbicki et al., 289, with some modifications. Aeneas presents an elaborate portrait of Hunyadi as brash and haughty before Varna in his later history, *Europe*, tr. Bisaha and Brown, 85.
173 "Contra Johannes hodie, commilitones, inquit, aut violenta Turcorum dominatione liberabimus Europam aut pro Christo cadentes martyrio coronabimur." Wolkan, *Briefwechsel*, 67:75; Eng. tr., *Reject Aeneas*, tr. Izbicki et al., 290.
174 Wolkan, *Briefwechsel*, 67: 77; *Reject Aeneas*, tr. Izbicki et al., 292.
175 See, for instance, a letter from Hunyadi to Pope Eugenius written shortly before the Second Battle of Kosovo in 1448, which states, "we shall not stop until we succeeded in expelling the enemy from Europe"; Joseph Held, *Hunyadi: Legend and Reality* (Boulder, CO: East European Monographs, 1985), 129. Around the same time, Pope Eugenius IV used "Europe" in a similar manner when he called for a meeting in Rome to discuss, among other things, the "liberation of Europe" from the Turks in a letter dated August 25, 1443; Housley, "Piccolomini, Nicholas of Cusa, and the Crusade," 653. King Bela invoked an idea of the defense of Europe in a letter to Pope Innocent IV (c. 1250) as the Mongols attacked Hungary and he sought help from western powers; *Reading the Middle Ages*, ed. Barbara H. Rosenwein (Toronto: University of Toronto Press, 2018, 3rd ed.), 387–90.
176 "Ceterum, si tertio adversus Turcorum perfidiam jam non Hungarie solius sed totius Christiane rei publice viribus bellum instauretur, facile deus ... nobis ad internetionem Turcos prosternere dabit." Sed hoc efficere, sicut et Hussitas corripere, tui muneris est et opus jubilei." Wolkan, *Briefwechsel*, 67: 77; Eng. tr., *Reject Aeneas*, tr. Izbicki et al., 92.
177 Housley, "Piccolomini, Nicholas of Cusa, and the Crusade," 654–55.
178 Regarding the Ottoman state, he asserts, "Our enterprise will be favored by their internal conflicts and enmities, which cause constant fights with the Tartars." "Moyses vir Dei" of Enea Silvio Piccolomini (24 April 1452, Rome), ed. and tr. Michael von Cotta-Schönberg: Orations of Enea Silvio Piccolomini; 14. 2014. <halshs-01064759>. Eng., tr., 71, with slight modifications.
179 Meserve also notes these conflations; see *Empires*, 97.
180 "Sed quid Graecia, litterarum mater, inventrix legum, cultrix morum, et omnium bonarum artium magistra? Quis non misereatur gentis illius afflictae, oppressae, pessumdatae, cujus imperium non sub Alexandro Macedone solum suisque successoribus, sed sub Atheniensibus, Thebanis et Lacedaemoniensibus olim et florentissimum et potentissimum fuit, nunc ubilibet effeminatis Turcis servire coacta est? "Moyses vir Dei," ed. and tr. Cotta-Schönberg, 44; Eng. tr., 45. For a discussion of early views of the Ottomans as a threat to Greek culture in the works of Ciriaco d'Ancona and Leonardo Bruni, see Nancy Bisaha, *Creating East and West: Renaissance Humanists and the Ottoman Turks* (Philadelphia: University of Pennsylvania Press, 2004), 101–03, 59–60.
181 See Bisaha, *Creating East and West*, ch. 3.
182 "Martiales enim et feroces Europae populi, nescientes quiescere .... Jam pacem ergo ut habeant Christiani, bellum in exteros est transferendum. Ad quam rem neque Germanorum illustris animus, neque cor nobile Gallicae gentis, neque mens sublimis Hispanorum, neque honesti cupidus Italorum deerit spiritus. Omnes, quod tua jubet sanctitas, constanti animo exequentur. Quis dubitet posse fieri passagium, quod Romani pontificis auctoritate decretum et imperatoris mandato fuerit convocatum?" "Moyses vir Dei," ed. and tr. Cotta-Schönberg, 64; Eng. tr., 65.

183 Cicero, *De officiis*, 1, 61.
184 "Novit majestas imperatoria: Assyriorum Aegyptiorumque gentem imbecilles, inermes, effeminatique sunt, neque animo, neque consilio martiales. Sarmacida erunt spolia sine sudore et sanguine. Quis tunicatos mitratosque Turcos aut brachatos timeat Aegyptios …. Quod si aliquando nostri exercitus ab eis victi sunt, neque viribus, neque rei militaris peritiae, sed numerositati hostium ascribendum est." "Moyses vir Dei," ed. and tr. Cotta-Schönberg, 68–9; Eng. tr., 69.
185 This subject is discussed in Chapter 4.
186 See "Moyses vir Dei," ed. and tr. Cotta-Schönberg, 48–49 where Aeneas mentions "barbarian fleets that attacks Christian shores in the Mediterranean."
187 "Cultus Christi, qui totum fere orbem oppleverat, in angulum Europae redactus est. Africam et Asiam amisimus. In Europa quoque conculcamur." "Moyses vir Dei," ed. and tr. Cotta-Schönberg, 50; Eng. tr., 51.
188 Flavio Biondo, for instance, mentions the Turks vis-à-vis Europe several times in his oration to Alfonso of Naples (August 1, 1453); See *Scritti inediti e rari*, ed. Bartolomeo Nogara (Rome: Tipografia Poliglotta Vaticana, 1927), 31–51. George of Trebizond also delivered a speech to Pope Nicholas V on crusade and "defending Europe" at the Straits of the Hellespont; it appears to date in or around October 1452, months after Aeneas delivered his oration to Nicholas; "Exhortation to Pope Nicholas V," in *Collectanea Trapezuntiana: Texts, Documents, and Bibliographies of George of Trebizond*, ed. John Monfasani (Binghamton, NY: Medieval and Renaissance Texts and Studies, 1984), 434–44.
189 Peter S. Wells, *The Barbarians Speak: How the Conquered Peoples Shaped Roman Europe* (Princeton, NJ: Princeton University Press, 1999), 122–47.
190 See Robert Bartlett, *The Making of Europe: Conquest, Colonization and Cultural Change 950–1350* (Princeton, NJ: Princeton University Press, 1993), 306–08.
191 Ohler, *Medieval Traveller*, 244.

2 1453–1455

Constantinople, "Europe vs. Asia"

In the early morning hours of May 29, 1453, a crowd of men, women, and children huddled together in the cathedral of Hagia Sophia, praying for deliverance or sanctuary as Ottoman troops poured into Constantinople. For seven weeks, a massive force of 80,000 had attacked the city by land and sea while a mere 7,000 Greek, Genoese, and Venetian fighters struggled to defend it. When reports flew through the city that the land walls had been breached, civilians dressed in their bed clothes grabbed their household members and ran toward the great church, spurred by hopes of a prophesied savior. But no solace would be granted to them on that day. Soldiers battered down the doors of the shrine, methodically seized and bound together the young, old, rich, and poor alike, then marched them back to their camp as captives. Others did not survive the assault. Some four thousand people perished on May 29 according to one contemporary, and many Greek nobles and Venetians were executed in the days following.[1] For the first time in its eleven-hundred-year history, the capital of the Eastern Roman Empire, "the God-given city" of Constantinople, had fallen into non-Christian hands. Emperor Constantine Paleologus XI (r. 1449–1453), who had spent his reign seeking aid from other Christian powers and his last days defending the walls, died when the city was captured.[2]

Sultan Mehmed II (r. 1451–1481) savored his victory. At the age of twenty-one, he accomplished a remarkable feat in taking the large and well-fortified city. Despite an enormous advantage in manpower, Mehmed faced serious challenges in overcoming the city's defenses. Surrounded by bodies of water and sea walls on two sides and massive land walls and ditches on the third, and a sea chain that blocked off the harbor, plus cisterns and orchards on the inside to sustain the inhabitants—the city was designed to withstand a siege of several months. Mehmed planned for this moment for years and plotted a strategy of speed and overwhelming force in order to capture Constantinople before a relief force could arrive.

Mehmed's path to conquest began in 1452 when he broke the longstanding Ottoman treaty with the emperor and ordered the rapid construction of the fortress of Rumeli Hisarı on the Bosphorus a few miles north of the city—easing the Ottomans' ability to safely cross from one half of their empire to the other, and enabling them to stop, seize, or sink ships coming in and out of

DOI: 10.4324/9781003315865-3

the Black Sea. After attacking nearby garrisons and Byzantine possessions in Greece to cut off local aid in early 1453, Mehmed arrived outside the city walls in April with his army, ships, artillery, and an enormous cannon crafted by a Christian engineer named Urban.[3] The Ottomans battered the landward walls each day and ingeniously evaded the sea chain by dragging ships overland past Galata and into the harbor; they even built a pontoon bridge enabling infantry to walk across the harbor and attack the sea walls. It was a brilliant operation and an epic victory for the young man who had stood in his father's shadow for almost a decade: twice Murad had tried to retire and leave Mehmed in charge with the help of viziers, and twice he was recalled—first in 1444 to face the Crusade of Varna and again in 1446 to put down a janissary revolt. With this triumph, Mehmed firmly established a new and formidable reputation as *fetih*, "the conqueror." He became the heir to the Eastern Roman Empire and gained control over a location that long held the potential to cripple communications between the two halves of the Ottoman Empire. With the city now in their hands, the Ottoman grip on their European possessions became unshakeable.

The sack of Constantinople was harsh and thorough.[4] According to Islamic law, a city that refused terms of surrender could be subjected to a three-day pillage; some studies say that Mehmed shortened it to one day.[5] Ironically, the frenzied looting gave some inhabitants and defenders the chance to flee to the harbor and set sail unimpeded after the wall was breached. Many who could not escape were captured. Some of the captives were later freed through charity or ransomed for a hefty sum; many were kept or sold, living in servitude for weeks, months, or the remainder of their lives.[6] Contemporary Ottoman accounts boast of the booty taken that day in human capital. Rape and other abuses were widely reported as well.[7] Cultural losses in the city were also substantial. Ottoman soldiers destroyed icons, stripped churches, and carried off their treasures while Mehmed claimed the illustrious sixth-century cathedral of Hagia Sophia as a mosque. Private homes and public buildings were looted and seized, and a great many books were lost or sold off by the cartload.[8] Soon after the sack, however, rebuilding began. Over the next several months, this ancient but sadly run-down city, which never recovered from the damages of the Latin conquest and rule (1204–61), would be transformed. In truth, under Mehmed, it would quickly reach a state of repair and vitality not seen in centuries.[9]

Meanwhile in Austria, oblivious to these developments, Aeneas was bored and eager for a change of pace. A year earlier he was traveling around Italy with the emperor, attending his coronation and wedding. During this time, he spoke before the pope, rubbed elbows with dignitaries, and was celebrated by the Sienese as their bishop.[10] After receiving such honors in his homeland, many of his acquaintances thought that a cardinal's cap would soon come his way. That was 1452. In 1453, he was cooling his heels up north at Frederick's newly built imperial residence in quiet Graz and wondering why he was back in practically the same position he had entered as a young layman. On July 1, 1453, he wrote plaintively to his cousin Goro Lolli,

I fear I will die in exile; I think daily of returning, but many things stand in the way …. Every day is a year to me …. I write frequently to the pope to recall me or grant me freedom to return.

He continued to stay because his presence at the imperial court was valued:

But as to my hope of gaining more from the pope by staying in Siena than lingering here, I do not deceive myself. At present, the pope and the cardinals value me a little, if not greatly, and in consideration of Caesar, not for my own worth; if I am in Siena neither the pope nor the cardinals will remember me.

The curia, he continues, "seek favor, not men. They have many men who excel me in worth, but of men dear to Caesar, they have no Italian prelate except me."[11]

At the imperial court, Aeneas was close to power yet lacked the authority to do more than observe, occasionally advise, and apply his diplomatic skills as needed. And there were long lulls between periods of excitement. As Christopher Celenza has argued, at Frederick's court, Aeneas became "the weary insider, far enough within the court environment to make distinctions between the external veneer and the internal reality." Access to information brought knowledge of "the sacking of subject cities, of kidnappings, of evil conquerors and good men slain … news which [he was] utterly powerless to do anything about."[12] But the change he craved would arrive within two weeks of penning that despondent letter to Lolli. In the years that followed, Aeneas's interests and goals would be utterly transformed by dramatic developments in Constantinople. It is no exaggeration to say that his response to the conquest gave him a purpose and a podium that would hasten his rise in both the Church and the world of letters.

Word Reaches Western Europe: Aeneas's Initial Response

It took four weeks for news of the fall of Constantinople to reach Italy, arriving first in Venice, where a stunned Senate heard the report on June 29. From there, word quickly spread to the pope in Rome, Alfonso of Naples, the republics of Genoa and Florence, and throughout Italy. Everywhere, the immediate response was shock, followed by fear and lamentation. To modern eyes, the conquest appears inevitable, but few Western Europeans seem to have expected it in 1453.[13] Aeneas, too, was taken by surprise. He knew that the Turks posed a vague threat to Constantinople and noted this in a letter dated April 6, but he seemed unaware that an active siege was underway.[14] When word of the disaster reached him in mid-July at the imperial court of Graz, Austria, he expressed his disbelief. As he wrote on July 12 to his old friend from the Council of Basel, Stefano Caccia of Novara (now living in Rome), "Here there is horrible news of the loss of Constantinople, which I hope is false!"[15] In a letter penned that same day to Pope Nicholas V, he asks,

"But what is that horrible news just reported from Constantinople? My hand trembles as I write these things, my spirit shudders, and neither indignation allows me to be quiet, nor does sadness permit me to speak. Alas, poor Christendom."[16] Not even the imperial chancery, whose business it was to keep up with current events, registered the immediacy of the threat until it was long past. All these reactions attest to the wisdom of Mehmed's plan: the speed and overwhelming force of his attack gave Westerners almost no time to stop him.

Aeneas's shock notwithstanding, he recovered enough to compose several powerful and eloquent paragraphs on the cataclysm—on the very same day (July 12) and in the same letter to the pope. This poignant and early lament to Pope Nicholas V (r. 1447–1455), a humanist and former secretary with whom Aeneas had worked, if not always cordially, merits a close reading as it encapsulates details and themes that Aeneas would revisit for years to come. First, he mourns the senseless violence and loss of life. After describing the way Mehmed II surrounded the city with a great army and took it by storm, he inaccurately claims,

> the emperor[17] of the Turks put the entire population to the sword, tore priests to pieces with diverse tortures, and spared no one, regardless of sex or age; they say that more than forty thousand people were killed there.[18]

As later reports corrected this misapprehension, Aeneas adjusted his narrative, but his initial assessment of Mehmed as a bloodthirsty villain who lacked all respect for the clergy and noncombatants would remain a near constant in his writings.

Yet, Aeneas wrote less about the loss of human life than other calamities as he immediately began to ponder the consequences from a cultural standpoint. The sack severed a vital connection to the sacred and secular past and to learning in general. Constantinople, he states, had remained in Christian hands for more than 1,100 years from its founding as the Roman Empire's second capital. Even the sack of Rome by the Visigoths in 410 was milder, he argues, because Alaric, their Arian Christian leader, forbade his troops from violating churches. In 1453 not only were churches sacked, but many were converted to mosques: "I grieve that the most famous temple in the world, Hagia Sophia, is being destroyed or polluted" and that other churches would be destroyed or "subjected to the filth of Muhammad."[19] All of this troubled Aeneas greatly, but not as much as reports about the fate of innumerable books that were lost or damaged in the fray. After an extended lament on the brutishness of this act, he penned one of his most famous quotes: "Alas, how many names of great men will now perish? This is a second death to Homer and a second loss of Plato."[20] What was surely an unintended consequence of the sack became, in Aeneas's imagination, a conscious effort to wipe out history and literature. Even the Visigoths did not sink so low.[21]

Nine days later (July 21) in a letter to Cardinal Nicholas of Cusa in Rome, Aeneas labeled the sack an act of pure barbarism. While similar in tone and structure to his letter to the pope, his discussion of Constantinople in this missive a few days later is three times the length, showing his rumination on the troubling subject. Aeneas chose his recipient carefully as Cusanus had visited the city in 1437 as part of a delegation from Basel to organize union talks with Roman Catholic clergy; Nicholas was now a cardinal, placing him at what Aeneas hoped would be the epicenter for mobilization against the Ottomans.[22] It is in this letter that Aeneas offered bold new ideas on the origins and character of the Turks.

After expounding on the exalted history of Greek learning he presents a disparaging account of Turkish origins:

> They are not, as some suppose, Trojans or Persians who are now called Turks. From the heart of the Scythians' barbaric land this race came forth, who are said to have formerly had their seat beyond the Black Sea and Pirrichean Mountains toward the northern sea, as the philosopher Aethicus believed.[23]

This is Aeneas's first reference to the theory that the Ottomans were descendants of the barbaric Scythians, not the noble Trojans, as some, including himself in his 1436 oration at Basel, had once claimed. Both theories, needless to say, were incorrect. Whatever openness or respect he harbored toward the Turks before 1453 vanished with stories of the brutal sack; it was no longer possible for him to look upon the Turks as honorable distant relations, sprung from the same illustrious Trojans whom the Romans and later Italians claimed as their ancestors. Nor could he imagine reasoned diplomacy with them. While Aeneas was not the first writer to argue that the Turks were descended from the Scythians—Flavio Biondo made the connection between the Turks and Scythians in the early 1440s—Aeneas's role in spreading this myth was likely greater due to the comparative dissemination of their works.[24]

As these letters show, a radical shift in Aeneas's view of the Turks took place in 1453. His stark portrayal of the civility, piety, and learning of the innocent victims juxtaposed to the purported barbarism, sacrilege, and inhumanity of the attackers speaks not only to the power of this moment, but to Aeneas's personal connection to it as a humanist.[25] The letter to Cusanus is the first time Aeneas used terms of barbarism in reference to the modern-day Ottomans.[26] If medieval writers previously employed "barbarians" to describe Muslims, as Andrew Holt has shown, the humanists' extensive application of the term to the Ottomans was a significant departure.[27] Other humanists like Cardinal Bessarion and Lauro Quirini responded immediately, independently, and *similarly* to the human and cultural losses at Constantinople, showing the common ideals they drew upon and the creation of a shared discourse.[28]

Despite these similarities, I contend that Aeneas stands out from other humanists not only for his sustained attention to this subject over many years, but for the early and persistent geographical bent in this thinking—specifically, his focus on "Europe." This comes through strongly in his letter to Pope Nicholas. Aeneas hints at the notion of Europe and the broader collective of Christendom (*res Christi publica*) at a few points but offers a particularly bold statement about the continent toward the end of the letter.[29] Lamenting that "one of the two eyes of Christendom" has now "been torn out," [30] he contrasts it to other Christian losses in the Crusades:

> Our ancestors lost Jerusalem, Acre, and Antioch, a great evil, I confess, but no disaster can be compared to this modern ruin. In Asia and foreign territories, our forebears lost cities, while we, in Europe, on our own soil, allow the most powerful city among Christians, the head of the eastern empire, the pinnacle of Greece, the home of letters, to be stormed by a hostile force.[31]

This rich passage contains several interlinked assumptions. First, it implies that Europeans share a common ancestry: though writing to a fellow Italian (born Tommaso Parentucelli of Sarzana), Aeneas seems to claim predominantly Frankish crusaders as "our ancestors." This squares with his description of wars between European powers as "domestic hatreds" (*domesticis odiis*) elsewhere in the letter. One might dismiss such statements as rhetorical devices, or argue that Italians, too, participated in the Crusades, but something deeper is at work: a sense of European Christians as members of one extended family by virtue of their faith, or possibly a common ethnic bond. According to Robert Bartlett, it could be both, as Christian writers had suggested a link between religion and ethnicity as early as the eleventh century.[32]

Most compelling of all in the preceding passage is the distinction between Europe and Asia—specifically losses "here" versus "there." Recall that in Aeneas's oration to Nicholas V in 1452 he had expressed equal concern for the Holy Land, islands in the Mediterranean, and Europe itself. Yet one year later, he suggests that defeats in the Holy Land were minimal or even negligible because they took place in Asia and other "foreign territories" (*in aliena possessione*), while Europeans are described as "us," and Europe is starkly portrayed as "our soil" (*nos in Europa in nostro solo*). The loss of so great a city *here*, it seems, is another matter entirely. His emphasis on location suggests a fellowship between the schismatic Greeks and the Roman Catholic Latins by virtue of their shared *continent*. Finally, he paints the Ottomans, who had ruled in Greece and other areas since the 1350s, as *trespassers* on European soil—thereby suggesting that only Christians of European descent had true sovereignty over the continent.

Yet for all his rousing rhetoric of European unity, Aeneas acknowledges the strong Ottoman presence in Eastern Europe and the weak front that squabbling Christian powers currently presented in his letter to Pope Nicholas:

> Now Muhammad[33] reigns among us, now the Turk hangs over our necks, now the Black Sea is closed to us and the River Don is made inaccessible. Now it is necessary for the Vlachs[34] to obey the Turk. Thence toward the

Hungarians and the Germans will the sword of the Turks penetrate, and meanwhile we are shaken by domestic hatreds: the kings of France and England dispute among themselves, German princes mutually wage war, rarely is Spain entirely tranquil, and our Italy, destitute of peace, competes over the rights of others. How much better would it be if we turned such abundance of arms and soldiers on the enemies of the faith?[35]

Neighboring powers, he laments, appear blind to their common interests and shared identity. Driving his frustration is his inherent belief that all these nations *should* recognize their common bonds—a notion that reflects his years of writing about the Holy Roman Empire and his earlier experiences as a traveler and secretary. His broad-ranging, first-hand knowledge of many parts of Europe enabled him to quickly envision this larger "self" identity as a foil to the aggressive Ottoman Empire. It was an aspirational rather than an actual body to be sure, but Aeneas's quest to make it real was off and running.[36] The next two years would be a period of intense intellectual and personal transformation for him.

From Shock to Action: Aeneas's Epistolary Campaign (1453–1455)

News of the fall of Constantinople spread across Europe in the summer of 1453. It was anxiously discussed in chambers of government and Church offices; reports were read in the streets; private citizens wrote about it in letters and diaries; laments were composed and publicly performed; and sermons were delivered in vernacular tongues to members of all social classes. Many of these works were later printed, giving them an even wider audience. As Agostino Pertusi, Robert Schwoebel and others have shown, the response was considerable.[37] Humanists eagerly took to the subject in a variety of forms: orations, treatises, poems, and especially letters—mostly, but not exclusively in Latin. In sum, a vast range of learned and popular works about Constantinople and the Turkish advance began to circulate in Christian Europe.

Few individuals in Europe wrote as many letters about the fall of Constantinople as Aeneas.[38] His prolific epistolary output on the conquest and proposed crusade bears witness to his preoccupation with the rising Ottoman threat and the state of Europe. Read in succession, the letters form both a narrative and map of Aeneas's shifting mindset: they enable us to date what and when he learned about key developments, his reaction to those events, and the evolution of his views over time. As such, they offer a most useful guide to this fertile period in Aeneas's conceptual development. Yet his letters from 1453 to 1455 are generally understudied or cherry-picked. The following pages seek to correct this by examining them as a group.

Over eighty of Aeneas's letters written within a twelve-month period of receiving the news contain some discussion of Constantinople, the Turks, or plans for a military response—a number that represents nearly half of his surviving private missives.[39] Compared to his letters before July 1453, this represents a sharp increase on the subject—especially when one considers that he was writing about a part of the world so distant from his own. In reality, Germany and Austria were under no direct threat from the Ottomans in 1453, but Aeneas's private letters from this time convey a different message. When added to his official letters written on behalf of Frederick III and the orations he delivered at German diets, Aeneas's commitment to this problem appears almost obsessive.

If the number of letters suggests extreme priority, the position of these subjects in individual epistles might give the opposite impression. Frequently, Aeneas placed his discussions of the Turks and related issues at the end of his letters; even the explosive early letters to Pope Nicholas V and others spend several pages discussing local news such as disagreements between bishops and princes or the activities of the troublesome bandit Peter Axamit, who was wreaking havoc in what is now Slovakia.[40] If events in the East were so disturbing to Aeneas, why did he not write entire letters on the subject? The simplest explanation is that Aeneas needed to economize in his letter writing and address several points in one missive, even if his greatest concern was only one of these topics. The process of sending letters by secure routes was neither easy nor inexpensive. It is also possible that Aeneas hoped to draw more attention to events relating to the East by placing them at the end of his letters and concluding with the subject he wished the reader to remember most vividly. One could also argue that the very structure of these letters increases their value and trustworthiness as sources. The survival of this kitchen-sink format in copies that circulated, even in printed versions, suggests that they were not heavily redacted and may offer close approximations of the original versions Aeneas wrote and sent.

One theme that unites all the letters is the thirst for news from every corner of Europe, either about the siege itself, the movements of the Turks, or Christian counteroffensives. Efforts toward peace in Italy greatly interested Aeneas as well, since a joint campaign against the Ottomans depended upon it. In a letter to Piero da Noceto in Rome on July 25, he implored "I only ask you this: if peace is being made in our Italy, attend to it with all your heart."[41] The bulk of his questions were directed to correspondents in Rome and other parts of Italy. Some were fellow secretaries like his cousin Goro Lolli and close friends Piero, Giovanni Campisio, and Stefano Caccia. These exchanges show the strength of Aeneas's international social network and its usefulness in times of crisis. He also wrote to several cardinals including his former employer Domenico Capranica, Nicholas of Cusa, and Juan Carvajal whom he came to know well at Basel. All these men were well-situated to gather and convey news to Aeneas, and he urged them to keep him abreast of any and all developments. Writing to Stefano Caccia in Rome on August 10, he implored "I therefore beg you not to be slow in writing to me about the whole situation in Italy."[42] Casting his net wider, he inquired about news from contacts in Bohemia, Poland, and even England.[43] In equal measure he shared what he had learned with most correspondents, revealing his eagerness to keep the subject alive across Europe.

The current state of Christian leadership forms a second major thread in the letters. As Aeneas gathered news, he searched for signs of a prince to rally Europeans. To many observers, Emperor Frederick III was the natural choice: his medieval predecessors Conrad III and Frederick Barbarossa led crusade armies to the Holy Land in the twelfth century, and in recent times both Sigismund and Albert II went to battle against the Turks. Who better to take up the mantle and lead a new crusade than the current occupant of the impe-rial throne? In the weeks that followed the arrival of the news, Frederick's reaction encouraged Aeneas. In a July 21 letter to Nicholas of Cusa, he described Frederick as "willing and exceedingly eager" in response to Aeneas's eloquent words on the matter at a public council.[44] And in a missive dated Aug. 10, Aeneas promised Cardinal Carvajal in Rome that he would soon hear in a separate letter (to the pope) how Frederick was thinking: "There is no reason to write much; this alone I will say, that never, after serving him for ten years, have I observed Caesar speak more frequently or listen more atten-tively about any other matter."[45] Such moments show Aeneas's keenness to convey the emperor's interest, but also his cautious phrasing: there is a con-spicuous lack of detail in all of these statements.

This is not to suggest that Aeneas's letters were purely objective, cut-and-dried affairs—even in their unedited state. Renaissance epistles often con-tained their own fictions, despite their authors' claim to spontaneity and verisimilitude. Aeneas, like Euryalus and Lucretia, the two fictitious let-ter-writing lovers in his *Tale of Two Lovers*, could be swept away by his own version of the events he attempted to portray.[46] Regarding Frederick, Aeneas initially saw only the possibilities that crusade offered his master and very few obstacles. Frederick had recently suffered a loss with the Austrian revolt that culminated in the liberation of his ward Ladislas Postumus in 1452—the boy was crowned King of Hungary and Bohemia, giving the local regents John Hunyadi and George Podiebrad greater influence than before. A crusade against an external enemy, Aeneas believed, could be the rallying point that Frederick needed to assert himself as Holy Roman Emperor in more than name. Recall that Aeneas spoke about Frederick leading an army into Italy in his *Pentalogus* (1443), or on crusade to the Holy Land in his oration to Pope Nicholas V (1452). Surely the cautious Frederick III would stir himself to action after the shocking loss of Constantinople and repair the crisis in his leadership—or so Aeneas believed.

Yet even in Frederick's letters to the pope—penned by Aeneas—the emperor carefully avoided commitment. Frederick's epistle of August 10 ech-oes the concerns and rhetorical flair of Aeneas's earlier letter to the pope with its laments on the murder and enslavement of the people of Constantinople and the destruction of sacred property and learning. But there are no con-crete offers of leadership or assistance, which the pope and cardinals would have warmly welcomed. Frederick only urges the pope to work toward peace and promote crusade, indicating his (vague) willingness to help.[47] Aeneas acknowledges the inadequacy of Frederick's stance in the personal letter he wrote to the pope the very next day:

I have spoken much with Caesar concerning this calamity of the Christian republic. I find his mind is good, yet it is impossible that a man without the means should act with distinction. But if Your Holiness, to whom princes listen, devotes his energies toward this [crusade], I have no doubt the furor of the Turks may be checked and the interests of the Christian people well served.[48]

Did Frederick truly lack the means to field even a modest army, or just the will? Less than two months after news of the fall of Constantinople reached the court, poor Aeneas was making excuses for the emperor and looking to others to help prod him forward. Five years later in his *Europe*, when he was no longer serving Frederick and could speak more freely, he would describe the emperor as being "in the conduct of affairs rather slow and easy going."[49] To be fair, Frederick was hardly alone in this inaction.

While Pope Nicholas worked toward peace in Italy to prepare for crusade, few lay rulers across the continent made any plans for a counteroffensive. The English and French, who had long been stalwart supporters of the crusades, just ended the Hundred Years War in July of 1453 and were unwilling to enter another conflict, much less as allies. In addition, the abysmal defeats of the crusades of Nicopolis (1396) and Varna (1444) appear to have dampened enthusiasm.[50] The only ruler who seemed truly eager to move forward was Duke Philip of Burgundy; an uprising in Ghent prevented him from acting sooner, but he vowed, under certain conditions, to go on crusade in February 1454 at an elaborate chivalric pageant, the Feast of the Pheasant. It was a day of jousting followed by banquets decorated with tapestries and elaborate sculptural representations, such as a beautiful woman (Constantinople) held captive by a lion (the Turk), and a three-act play that included a turbaned giant leading in a woman dressed in black and trapped in a tower (the Church), who then proceeded to beg the duke to come to her rescue. The bizarre event culminated with members of the Order of the Golden Fleece bringing a richly decorated pheasant to the duke so that he might swear an oath on it to enter the war— supposedly in accordance with ancient custom of swearing oaths on noble birds. Many men took a crusade oath that day; Philip did as well on the condition that the king of France or another great lord should also go.[51] Meanwhile, Alfonso of Naples also showed some support by sending aid to the Balkan resistance leader, George Castriot, better known as Skanderbeg of Albania.[52]

But compared to the swift preparations for crusade undertaken by Richard the Lionheart and Philip Augustus after Jerusalem fell in 1187, the response was underwhelming. Of course, the world had changed since the late twelfth century. As Housley has asserted,

> crusading lost its practicality in the face of adverse developments in Europe's political, military, and financial structures: it was outgrown rather than overthrown or discredited. This meant that while the mechanisms of crusade largely perished, beliefs and attitudes associated with it persisted.[53]

Hence, the horror and indignation in 1453 were genuine, but finding a path to address the outrage was far more complicated than it had once been.

Aeneas's growing concern and exasperation forms a recurring theme in his correspondence. While his private letters before 1453 have served as a goldmine for biographers seeking to chart his moods and movements, his letters from 1453 to 1455 have been largely overlooked as a source to explore his personal turmoil. Not only did his views and concerns change during this period, but he changed as well. After nearly two months of searching for some positive news from abroad or a hint of action on Frederick's part, Aeneas began to show both emotional and physical signs of stress. He poured out his feelings in a letter to Goro Lolli (Sept. 3, 1453), where he tells his cousin of his recent decline in health and offers a lengthy list of the diverse illnesses he suffered in different regions. Homesickness was weighing heavily on him again as well:

> Now I come to that of which you vehemently accuse me: whether I have completely forgotten homeland, parents, and friends, and that I do not wish to return home. I am not, as you think, forgetful of my own and you, Gregorio. Day and night I have the sweet soil of my country before my eyes.[54]

In this depressed state, he writes frankly on the subject of Constantinople:

> Stupidly Christian princes will have acted unless they strive to oppose the Turkish menace. The Germans were recently pacified, and if someone were to excite them toward this matter, they would be found to be not only able, but willing.[55]

Who could this "someone" be if not Frederick?

This particular letter, then, reveals more than Aeneas's frustration at the current stalemate. It demonstrates the compelling connection between the inaction of Western rulers on the crusade front and Aeneas's own well-being. The way that it literally wears on him shows that this subject was not some matter of minor interest, but a profound personal investment. The usual humor one finds in Aeneas's letters and his ability to banter amiably about other lighter topics are in short supply in this period. To use a modern expression, he appears to have been suffering from a work–life imbalance. For perhaps the first time, he lost his ability to separate himself from his job and the larger problems of the world.

Frustration hardened into cynicism in letters that followed. In three missives to recipients in Rome, all dated Sept. 18, he uses the phrase "agents of the Turks" (*Turchi procuratores*), to describe Christians who were fighting each other, such as René of Anjou, who was planning to campaign in Italy to reclaim Naples from its current ruler, the Aragonese King Alfonso. In one of these letters to his colleague, imperial secretary Heinrich Senfleben, he states, "I hear that negotiations in Italy are in turmoil, and I fear that negotiations for peace will go up in smoke. We are all agents of the Turk, and we prepare his way."[56] The words "*Turchi procuratores*" appear in one form or another in eight letters that follow and later ones as well. The precise meaning is elusive, but it speaks to Aeneas's growing expectation that all European Christians should be at peace in this moment and working side-by-side in opposition to the Turks. It evokes an ideal of a past or future continental cohort—a deeply held belief that all Western European nations needed to view the Turks as a common existential threat. Ironically, the frequency of this phrase proves that many others did not share Aeneas's view: the Turkish threat simply did not unite Christians overnight, much as it frightened many.

Aeneas's annoyance with Italy stemmed, in many ways, from Frederick's inertia. As a letter to Cardinal Carvajal (Sept. 3, 1453) states, the emperor was closely watching events in the south.[57] Peace in the peninsula, no matter how long it took to conclude, became a precondition for Frederick to make plans—and a convenient excuse to delay. No one seemed willing to take the first big step. Three weeks later (Sept. 25, 1453), Aeneas penned a long letter to his friend Leonardo Benvoglienti, the Sienese ambassador to Venice, relating how little could be expected from the imperial court. The emperor could not resist so powerful an enemy alone, nor was Christendom willing to submit to the judgment of one head: "There is no need to mention other nations. Germany barely follows its ruler. Why do I say Germany? Last year we saw Austria rebelling against its prince." Aeneas suggests that Frederick is looking for princes to join him, "but these are not even rulers who are willing to appear at the summons of Caesar, [and] I do not know how much they listen to the calls of the Roman pope."[58] Christendom was in crisis—its two universal leaders, Holy Roman Emperor and pope, appeared unable to command the loyalty of its members. Italy was also unraveling: "We are all agents of the Turks; we all prepare the way for Mehmed. While we wish to rule individually we will all lose power."[59] "On this side," he continues, "Alfonso [of Naples] and Venetians, and on that side Florentines and Milanese pursue their injuries."[60] Beyond Italy, the despot of Serbia, George Brankovic, was coming to terms with the Turks even though "it is said that nothing is lighter to him [the Turk] than keeping faith."[61] What will happen in a few months, Aeneas laments, if now, while the wound is still fresh, no one is taking serious action?[62] Meanwhile on the Eastern frontier, King Casimir of Poland was squaring off against the Teutonic Knights. Against the threat of disunity and "civil war," Aeneas uses terms that denote an expectation of unity like "Christians," "Latins," the "people of Europe" and "the face of Europe" (*Europe vultus*), but the overall message is one of disunity and cynicism.[63] Hence, his invocation of Europe at this moment arises from two concerns: first and foremost, fear of the Turks' continued advance, but also the persistent notion that Christian nations should harbor the same interests. What Aeneas did not yet know was that the pope was about to make an important announcement.

While a general peace between the major Italian powers—the Peace of Lodi—would not be finalized for several months, the pope finally made enough progress to issue a formal call for crusade. The papal bull *Etsi ecclesia*

Christi, published on Sept. 30, 1453, set a departure for March 1 the following year.[64] Aeneas, however, was skeptical that it would motivate others. He wrote on October 11 to the Bohemian nobleman Ulrich von Rosenburg, "Concerning Turkish matters, I can write these things: there is no one who devotes care to it except for the pope."[65] In addition to sending cardinals Carvajal and Capranica to gather an assembly at Rome, he reports that Nicholas had some six cardinals working on ways to restrain the Turks. Aeneas concludes the letter by holding out some hope that he and Ulrich might exhort the king of Bohemia, the young and newly crowned Ladislas, and his nobles to take some action.[66] But then, quite unexpectedly, Frederick awakened from his torpor and decided in October to call a diet to discuss crusade. Aeneas wrote of this plan in an official letter on Frederick's behalf to King Alfonso of Naples asking Alfonso to send orators and to work on peace in Italy.[67] Oddly, this news does not seem to have encouraged Aeneas, judging from his tone and complete silence on the matter in personal letters; perhaps he had learned not to take Frederick at his word and was awaiting stronger signals. Little by little, however, Aeneas regained his optimism and interest in events relating to crusade.

One unusual development at this time deserves mention, and that is Aeneas's openness to working with other Turkish leaders against the Ottomans. When envoys from Ibrahim Bey, the ruler of Karamania, and a neighboring ruler approached the imperial court to discuss possible negotiations, Aeneas was enthusiastic. In a letter of Nov. 8 to imperial councilor, Prokop von Rabenstein, he states,

> I believe that the legate of the Turks of Karaman and Karayluch came to you with apostolic and imperial letters. I wish you would take up his cause on my recommendation since it is beneficial to the faith and concerns the glory of Christ.[68]

He sent another letter to Cardinal Peter Schaumburg on the same topic ten days later.[69] The Turks of Karamania, an area in southeastern Anatolia, raised frequent opposition to the Ottomans and professed their interest in working with European powers against them; not much amounted to these talks, but Karamania did conclude a peace with Venice in February 1454.[70]

On its face, Aeneas's support for a partnership with Anatolian rivals of the Ottomans upsets the neat division he had made between Europe and Asia, but I believe it affirms it: if those Turkish allies did their part in Asia by attacking the eastern Ottoman frontier, they would never need to cross over into Europe. The temporary arrangement would be sustained by mutual interest and the comfort of considerable distance.[71] The divide, then, seemed to remain in place in Aeneas's mind. This is not to dismiss his willingness to cooperate with allies across religious lines and continental boundaries. After he became pope, he showed the same interest in an alliance with Uzun Hasan against the Ottomans. While other Christian generals and rulers had been forming pacts of this sort for centuries, for Aeneas, this was a progressive idea.

Unfortunately, this handful of examples on eastern Turkic rulers offers no firm evidence on Aeneas's cross-cultural views, but only hint at intriguing possibilities. Had the proposed alliance with Karamania in 1453 moved forward, his views of the "Turks" might have taken a different direction, even if they left his East-West, Asia-Europe boundary intact. Overall, I would argue, the letters, especially his private ones, contain more political realism and flexible thinking than his rhetorical works. It is easy to miss such moments when they occur alongside outbursts of magical thinking, sometimes in the same letter, but they point to a creative mind seeking to marry strategic planning to the art of persuasion. Informed and more objective views of the Ottomans and other Muslim powers became more common among European writers in the sixteenth century, as Meserve has argued, but moments such as these suggest that Aeneas, too, was capable of such analysis.[72]

In January of 1454, Aeneas started to shake off his depression and doubt regarding crusade. Along with other members of the chancery, he planned for the imperial diet at Regensburg, where a campaign against the Ottomans would be the main topic of discussion. At this time, he began to write about the diet to his close circle of correspondents, claiming (with a touch of self-importance) that he could not possibly return home to Italy at that point given his critical role at court. He began to speak directly to other rulers not just about crusade and Christendom, but of Europe, and perhaps for the first time, "the West." For instance, in a letter to George Podiebrad, governor of Bohemia, dated Jan. 22, 1454, he speaks of how schisms between Christians should be despised in every age, but that matters were now more desperate when

> the most powerful enemies of the life-giving cross, the Turks, prepare war against us by land and by sea, and, not content to have subjugated Constantinople, they assert that the entire West [*totum occidentem*] will be made subject to them and strive with the greatest exertion to subvert the law of Christ and the Gospels—but if we were united, we would easily blunt the pride of that people.[73]

In two letters dated January 9, 1454, to King Charles VII of France and Duke Philip of Burgundy, he describe the Turks' plan to overthrow the entire West and asks each ruler to send delegates to Regensburg.[74] Writing to Pope Nicholas on behalf of Emperor Frederick (Jan. 1, 1454), he asks the pope to support Frederick's upcoming diet so that they may all work together "to drive the foul Muslims from the borders of Europe" (*ad ... propulsandos de finibus Europe impuros Mahumeti cultores*).[75]

The choice of "Europe" and "the West," particularly in letters to foreign rulers that promoted crusade, provide unique insight into Aeneas's thought process: he was seeking new ways to find common ground (literally), in the face of an external adversary. One reason why Aeneas's rhetoric is so important to understanding modern discourse of Europe and the West is that it shows how closely he associated these terms with Christianity when he first invoked them. Over the centuries, a firm belief in Christianity became less critical, but the sense of a common history and traditions grounded in the faith never disappeared. This enduring connection can be seen in the way European Muslims are frequently treated today as outsiders.[76]

In these letters, Aeneas began to creatively promote the *idea* of greater unity among Christians, Europeans, and inhabitants of "the West." While Edward Said has argued that a confident discourse of the Western self was an outcome of political hegemony, i.e., modern colonialism, I see it instead as a precursor. As Aeneas so clearly shows, it was not power, but fear of defeat that sparked the assertion of a dominant Europe or Christendom, from himself and from other writers.[77] Randolph Starn and Linda Darling recognize the toll that this *lack* of power and feelings of loss and endangerment took upon Europeans' visions of themselves during the Renaissance—rather than admit defeat, writers like Aeneas more adamantly claimed superiority to, and separation from, their Eastern adversaries.[78] Europeans wanted to believe in a larger collective to offset the challenge of the strong and unified Ottoman Empire. And yet, as a close reading of Aeneas's letters reveals, the reality of the messy and fraught relations between European states was never far from view.

The Diet Orations and Identity: Defining the Turks, Defining the Self

Three imperial diets met to discuss a crusade against the Ottomans: the first in Regensburg (May 1454), the second in Frankfurt (October 1454), and the third in Wiener-Neustadt (February 1455).[79] Aeneas delivered orations at all of them. Called at regular intervals by the emperor, these deliberative and legislative assemblies were prone to self-interested squabbles and often ended in stalemates. Aeneas faced a daunting task in trying to persuade the diverse assembly of lay and religious representatives from across the vast empire and beyond to agree on anything, much less to contribute money, arms, and men to a war against the Ottomans. Nonetheless, envoys, princes, and bishops showed up in sizable numbers at the diets of Regensburg, Frankfurt, and Wiener-Neustadt. Duke Philip of Burgundy and Duke Ludwig IX of Bavaria-Landshut attended the first; Margrave Karl of Baden and the popular preacher Fra Giovanni Capistrano attended the second; Jakob von Sierck, archbishop of Trier attended the last two; and Margrave Albert "Achilles" of Brandenburg-Anspach, and papal legate, Bishop Giovanni Castiglione of Pavia attended all three.[80] The pope showed his support by sending Castiglione, but Aeneas viewed the gesture as half-hearted given the bishop's unimportance and lackluster oratory.[81] Albert Achilles, who loved war more than defending the faith, was particularly gung ho, but alas, Emperor Frederick was not. Making weak excuses about a recent disturbance in his homeland of Styria, he refused to come, twice. Hence, the one person who should have taken the lead at all three diets attended only the last of them.

As Aeneas wrote to a friend after Regensburg, "The new situation in Hungary, which kept the emperor at home caused great harm; it truly hindered the great meeting here, for princes are more negligent when the emperor is absent."[82] Attendees, indeed, took the opportunity to air their grievances, yet seemed surprisingly willing to move ahead, albeit slowly, with planning.[83] At the next diet in Frankfurt, delegates made tentative promises of troops, but put off firm commitments to a future diet.[84] The third diet at Wiener-Neustadt began promisingly with Frederick's actual presence, but ended with the sobering news of Pope Nicholas's death. Despite these ups and downs, and reports of the Ottomans' punishing raids and a full-scale invasion of Serbia in 1454–1455, Aeneas pushed forward.[85] His job and his personal goal throughout was to inspire as many men as possible to take meaningful action.

Aeneas produced masterful orations. Years later he described the rapt attention of the audience at Frankfurt as he spoke for two hours ("no one even cleared his throat or took his eyes off the speaker's face") while the other speakers were barely tolerated.[86] While Aeneas was no doubt exaggerating, the oration was well received. All three of his diet orations from this period, in fact, circulated extensively in his lifetime. Aeneas's contemporaries were fascinated by their rhetorical finesse and vivid content, and they eagerly sought copies. His Frankfurt oration can be found in over fifty extant manuscripts; a few decades later, the orations were printed. As a result, Aeneas's audience extended far beyond the men who gathered at the diets, just as his letters reached more people than his direct recipients.[87] However, because the diets did not lead to a major crusade, these compelling orations have received little scholarly attention in the modern era, and only recently have Aeneas's orations been edited and translated into English by Michael von Cotta-Schönberg.[88] As the following pages will show, they contain early notions of Europe, "the West," and national identity.

In form, Aeneas's speeches incorporate elements of the classical epideictic or demonstrative genres, which employ praise for the listeners as a persuasive tool, but they most closely follow the model of the classical deliberative oration which argues for or against a certain measure.[89] *Constantinople clades* from Frankfurt, an "oratorical *tour de force*," was modeled on Cicero's famous *Pro Lege Manilia*, which made the case for war against the king of Pontus. Unlike his ancient predecessors, however, Aeneas did not seek a debate or a discussion, nor did German princes and nobles have the chance to respond even to the German paraphrase at Frankfurt after sitting through the two-hour–long oration in Latin.[90] Two recent genres also made their mark on these speeches: the crusade or anti-Turk oration and the emerging model of the *Reichstag* oration.[91] As such, Aeneas's orations at these three diets were an exciting mix of old and new. While each oration was different, there is some overlap, especially between Regensburg, *Quamvis omnibus* (May 16, 1454) and Frankfurt, *Constantinopolitana clades*, (Oct. 15, 1454); their themes and language will be considered together, with a greater focus on Frankfurt.[92]

If his letters constitute Aeneas's first attempts to grapple with the fall of Constantinople, his orations represent the height of his persuasive rhetoric in this period. The emphasis on the spectacle and brutality of the sack and his emotional treatment of the city itself helped codify the way in which Aeneas and many of his readers would see Mehmed and the Turks for years to come. These addresses, as such, stand as a milestone in the creation of two myths: that of "the terrible Turk" and the equally problematic whitewashed portrait of European decency in wartime. It would take a few more years for these visions to fully crystallize in Aeneas's writings, but the speeches of 1454–55 contain the discernible outlines.

The Horror of the Sack and the Power of Repetition

The destruction and violence at Constantinople took center stage in Aeneas's diet orations—and indeed, in many of his works after 1453. Something about this siege and sack disturbed him profoundly and made it seem like no other act of war in recent history. We must get to the bottom of his second-hand trauma, I believe, in order to understand the development of his worldview. The questionable notion, shared by many contemporaries, that that the sack was beyond the pale hardened into fact in Aeneas's mind and took expressive form in his orations. At Regensburg he presents the Ottoman attack as wholly unjust and unprovoked, stating, "The Greek emperor was living peacefully at home in Constantinople …. No quarrel did he have with the Turks."[93] He then describes at length, and with varying levels of accuracy, the atrocities and damages to the city, claiming that nearly one thousand men were killed in the siege and then a general slaughter followed in which "all of the nobles" and priests were particularly targeted. He also states that,

> Virgins and matrons suffered the pleasures of the victors. Boys were killed in the arms of their parents, and an infinite number of people were carried into captivity and sent into permanent slavery. Oh, the miserable and tearful destiny of that city: everywhere you saw plunder, fire, debauchery, blood, and corpses.[94]

In addition, he laments the desecration of churches and destruction of relics and icons and the burning of sacred and secular books and libraries. The goal of this extended list of atrocities was clear: to stoke the fires of vengeance. Emperor Frederick, he asserts, "believes that these crimes and shameful acts should be revenged."[95]

Revenge may have been the immediate rhetorical goal of such disturbing images, but they had a long-term impact as well: the repetition of these stories created a lasting and unshakeable narrative of the Turks as uncivilized and wholly destructive. Something deeper than a call to arms was at work in Aeneas's mind. Recall that prior to the loss of Constantinople, Aeneas did not depict the Ottomans as particularly barbaric. His strongest insult was that of effeminacy in his 1452 oration to Pope Nicholas. After 1453, however, Aeneas presents the Ottomans as all war, all the time, and more destructive than any of their contemporaries. Along with a host of other writers, Aeneas fed the growing misapprehension of the Ottomans as "better at things that more barbaric people are better at (war) and less good at things that civilized people ... do (culture)," as Walter Andrews and Mehmet Kalpaklı aptly put it.[96] The narrative of barbarism and inhumanity builds to a crescendo in Aeneas's Frankfurt oration, *Constantinopolitana clades*, where he decries the abuses that followed the Greeks' surrender:

> I accept that many were killed in the first furious assault. But I find it horrible, revolting, and execrable that when the city had been conquered, the arms laid down, and the citizens enchained, then the worst atrocities took place ....[97]

Without underestimating the abuses and tragedies that took place on that day, we might ask if some universal law of combat had been violated in Constantinople. To hear Aeneas's words, it certainly seems that way. In his letter to Cusanus (July 21, 1453), he had described Mehmed as having "now afflicted the Christian people with disasters of such a size as I think has been previously unheard of for many centuries."[98] This statement, coupled with those in his diet orations, assumes that Aeneas's audience of European Christians held themselves to a higher standard of rights within war (*ius in bello*)—especially for civilians. This strong claim cannot be substantiated. As I have argued elsewhere, it is hard to prove that Christian warriors of this era either perceived or protected the rights of noncombatants—certainly not on a regular basis.[99] Within the previous century, Christian troops carried out two horrific sacks in Italian cities: one by papal mercenaries at Cesena in 1377, and another by Francesco Sforza of Milan's army at Piacenza in 1447. French and English armies engaged in brutal sacks of one another's cities in the Hundred Years War. Aeneas did not even have to look far for examples of senseless atrocities in warfare: Albert Achilles of Brandenburg, his ersatz crusade leader, provided them—and proudly, it seems.[100] In all these cases, Christian soldiers killed and tormented Christian civilians.[101]

Forgetful of the shocking conduct of soldiers closer to home, Aeneas and his contemporaries made repeated assertions about excessive Ottoman violence, thereby creating a false sense of European morality in warfare. Humanists' horror at the sack of 1453 may have helped pave the way for a narrative of human rights, but their notions were steeped in ethnocentrism.[102] The full intent of this concept becomes clear at the end of Aeneas's section on the justice of war, where he sums up the Turks' crimes and adds, "Ambrose says in *De officiis* that 'the use of force in a war to protect one's country from the barbarians, or the weak at home, or allies from robbers, is absolutely legitimate.'"[103] Barbarians, it would seem, can justly be attacked at will. As Margaret Meserve argues, Aeneas and other humanists believed that the savagery of the Turks in 1453 "placed them firmly outside the family of historically civilized nations."[104] The implications of such rhetoric to early notions of European identity are easy to imagine.

While both the loss in life and learning reported in 1453 troubled Aeneas, the senseless cultural attacks in the Byzantine capital seemed to wound him most deeply of all. Echoing themes from his earlier letters to the pope and Cusanus, Aeneas seeks to draw the German warrior aristocracy into the discussion at Frankfurt. It is a surprising choice, considering his complaint to a friend shortly before the diet about the princes' lack of interest in letters and the good arts.[105] Perhaps he could not resist the urge to elevate their moral standards. Before he could do that, however, he had to address the seeming oddity of this tack: "But, soldiers, here you say: "Why do you mention the losses to literature? What are letters to us? We fight with spears and swords."[106] He answers this question by invoking the universal quest for fame, as seen in a story about Alexander the Great, who purportedly envied Achilles because he had Homer to immortalize him.[107] This "arms and letters" theme was not unusual in the Renaissance, but Aeneas's attempts to connect the ancient Greeks and the modern Germans is intriguing.[108] His goal was to inspire the Germans to emulate Alexander, both in his love of literature and his mastery of Asia. Aeneas, I believe, was also trying to separate the Turks from Greece (and Europe) in a cultural sense and place them squarely back in the most primitive corner of Asia. In this way he arguably made some progress on his plan to "expel the Turks from Europe."

The Ethnography of the Turks and the Character of Mehmed II

Harsh as these characterizations may seem, they did not go far enough for Aeneas. He needed to *prove* that the Ottoman Turks were irredeemably barbaric by arguing that their distant origins destined them to be so. At Frankfurt, Aeneas describes the Turks as descendants of the barbaric ancient Scythians, elaborating on claims he first made in his letter to Cusanus (July 21, 1453). In *Constantinopolitana clades* he states,

> Many think that the Turks come from Asia Minor and call them Trojans, from whom the Romans sprung, (though the Trojans certainly did not hate letters) But this is not so: the Turks are a Scythian people from the middle of a barbarous region [*barbaria*].[109]

What is new here is Aeneas's emphasis on the connection between a people's origins and their love or hatred of literature. Whether he believed such proclivities were heritable or the result of social conditioning is unclear, but either way, they served to verify a people's ethnicity. He then rounds out the section by claiming that the modern Turks *still* indulge in barbarous manners (*barbariem*); they eat vile food and "are slaves of lust, indulge in cruelty, hate letters, and persecute the studies of humanity."[110] This, too, is a step beyond his letter to Cusanus where he was willing to admit *some* engagement with letters on the part of the Turks.[111] Over time, his insistence on this point hardened and further distorted his picture of the Ottomans, who certainly did not hate literature.

Painting the Ottomans as modern-day barbarians was a powerful trope for antiquity-loving Western Europeans, but it also opened up unwanted theoretical questions. If, according to this stereotype, the Scythians and the Turks were violent and uncultured, were they not also austere, rugged, and strong? According to the rules of classical rhetoric, a deliberative oration needed to convince its listeners that its cause was just (*iustum*), easy (*facile*), and profitable (*utile*).[112] Tales of barbaric depredations might have made the crusade cause just, but Aeneas still needed to persuade his audience that the fight would be easy. He tries to rectify this first by praising the Germans, past and present:

> But whether I consider the new state of things or ponder the old, it seems to me that among all the nations considered to be warlike, none is more ready, none is more powerful, none is more skilled, none is more daring than yours.[113]

A bit later, he adds:

> You are born to weapons, they are forced to them. You are armed, they are unarmed ... you lead nobles to war, they force servants and artisans .... Onto white hair you press the helmet, and you are content when you have fresh causes for war and live under arms. But they wear embroidered saffron and gleaming purple; sloth is their joy, and their greatest pleasure is the dance.[114]

This is a direct lift from book IX of the *Aeneid* used to insult the Anatolian Phrygians.[115]

Apart from Aeneas's obvious errors regarding the composition of both the Ottoman and Germanic armies, these assertions completely contradict his previous statements about the Turks as uncouth and warlike.[116] Even in the space of one oration, Aeneas could not decide if the Turks were hardened barbarians or effete courtiers. Each trope was too tempting to refuse, especially the classical stereotype of Eastern men as lazy and effeminate, with more interest in fine garments and court life than the rigors of the battlefield.[117]

Not only was this poor ethnography, but it did nothing to explain the Ottomans' stunning victories against European troops. Sensing the contradictions in his descriptions of the Turks, Aeneas tries to rationalize their recent successes by attributing Mehmed II's victories to his warlike character and his elite fighting force, presumably the janissaries:

> Only Mehmed and those fifteen thousand[118] ... delight in the din of weapons and their warlike spirit makes them fearless in battle. The others, as you will see, are inexperienced, timid, effeminate, and worthless. If you fight with these people, you will undoubtedly win, if only you do not turn your fight for God into a fight against God .... You yourselves are

in no way inferior to your forefathers, you have an abundance of all things considered necessary for war, you have strong soldiers and experienced leaders, lucky in war.[119]

There is a brittle logic at work here: without dismissing the gravity of Mehmed's victory, Aeneas identifies a gendered weakness in his army for the flower of Germanic chivalry to exploit. Yet, Europeans who had seen Ottoman troops at close quarters portrayed them differently. Leonard Giustiniani of Chios, an eyewitness at the fall of Constantinople, comments on the skill and strength of the janissaries without disparaging the rest of the army; he describes the Turks bravely fighting at close quarters, which led to many casualties on their side. Interestingly, Aeneas used Leonard's account, it would seem as early as the Frankfurt oration, but without accepting all its details.[120] The vacillations in Aeneas's rhetoric at Frankfurt on the Ottomans show his struggle to simplify or dismiss them. The only constant was his repeated efforts to place Europeans, specifically Germans in this case, above them.

Aeneas's portrayals of Mehmed II are sharper, but no more consistent than his characterizations of the Turks. The twenty-one-year-old military genius both frightened and fascinated Aeneas. Ever since news arrived of the fall of Constantinople, he spent a great deal of time ruminating on the sultan's character. At first, Aeneas saw Mehmed as particularly violent, owing to the grotesque—and often false—details reported by the Serbians and Venetians. In his July 21, 1453 letter to Cusanus, Aeneas vividly described the sultan as *iratum* or enraged, by turns threatening and encouraging his men to scale or penetrate the walls and commanding them to kill everyone over the age of puberty: "such an effusion of blood was shed that rivers of gore flowed through the city."[121] A few months later, Aeneas repeated a spurious story of Mehmed raping two imperial adolescents in a letter to Leonardo Benvoglienti of Siena (Sept. 25, 1453):

> they say who were present that that filthy leader of the Turks or more apt to say, that terrible beast, publicly and in full view raped a noble maiden and her adolescent brother of royal blood on the high altar of Hagia Sophia and then ordered them killed. These things are done and we are silent.[122]

This myth soon proved too outrageous even for anti-Turk propagandists, and it dropped out of most accounts of the sack, but it speaks to the credulity of many Europeans in the early days after the conquest. Aeneas, too, stopped repeating the canard but found other means to promote his narrative of Mehmed's cruelty. One year later at Frankfurt, Aeneas claimed in the first part of the oration, which seeks to establish the justice of the proposed crusade, "Mehmed himself—with fearsome face, wild eyes, terrible voice, cruel words, and horrible gestures—demands murder …. He washes his hands in the blood of Christians."[123]

But this homicidal caricature is only part of Aeneas's description of Mehmed at Frankfurt. A more complicated portrait of the sultan emerges in the section on the feasibility or ease of the proposed war. After praising the German people and contrasting them to the unwarlike, effeminate Turks, as quoted earlier, his tone becomes more serious. Lest he take the "ease" argument too far, Aeneas needed to convince the Germans that Mehmed was different from other adversaries and had to be stopped, without delay:

> I shall therefore tell you something about the habits and character of this man, as people who have spent some time with him have made them known to me.[124] Then you will better know what to hope for and what to fear. Mehmed is a young man of twenty-four years. He is fierce and desires glory, robust of body and enduring of labor, and he does not indulge in wine and banquets. Though he is given to sexual pleasure, like all his people, he does not, like his forefathers, spend his time among his wives. He avoids dancing and perfumes, and he rarely wears soft clothes. He is not fond of singing or music, he does not raise dogs or birds. He has only one pleasure: all things military .... Though he is a barbarian by nature and abhors letters, he avidly hears about the deeds of his precursors, and he puts Julius Caesar and Alexander the Great above all. He is confident that he shall be able to surpass their illustrious deeds and is striving to do so .... And since he has won Constantinople for the false prophet Muhammad, after whom he was named, he does not doubt that he shall be able to do the same with Rome, full, as he is, of barbarian audacity and Asian arrogance.[125]

Putting aside phrases like "barbarian audacity" and "Asian arrogance" for the moment, the figure of Mehmed presented here—from a mixture of eyewitness reports and classical commonplaces—is quite positive. Disciplined, strong, brave, and austere, Mehmed sounds like one of Livy's sober leaders of the Roman Republic. The entire passage curiously undermines his earlier evocations, in the same oration, of Mehmed as a bloodthirsty madman leading a nation of soft, unwarlike Easterners. Here, Mehmed stands as a respectable and worthy adversary, whose determination and leadership enabled him to conquer Constantinople, and placed Rome itself in serious danger.

When it comes to learning, however, Aeneas stands firm in his view of Mehmed: "he is a barbarian by nature and abhors letters." Aeneas concedes that Mehmed "hears" the deeds of Julius Caesar and Alexander—yet dismisses Mehmed's interest in classical authors as little more than a crude urge to compete with the scale of their conquests. But Niccolò Sagundino, whose works likely served as a source for Aeneas at Frankfurt, offers a compelling comparison and contrast. Sagundino, a Greek humanist, former Ottoman captive, and employee of the Venetian government, had the distinction of taking part in an embassy that met with Mehmed in 1453 not long after the city fell.[126] In his own oration to Alfonso of Naples several months earlier (Jan. 25, 1454), Sagundino ascribed the same seriousness and sobriety to

Mehmed that Aeneas echoed at Frankfurt some eight months later. Yet Sagundino credited Mehmed with keeping an Arab scholar of philosophy with whom he had daily meetings, as well as two doctors, one Greek, one Latin, who were helping him to learn about the Spartans, Athenians, Romans, Carthaginians, and other kings and princes, especially Alexander and Julius Caesar.[127] According to Sagundino, he was having the deeds of these ancient heroes translated into his language, as it pleased him greatly to read or to hear them.[128] Why did Aeneas repeat some aspects of Sagundino's impressions of Mehmed yet ignore the sultan's reputation as an educated man and a patron of scholarship?[129] My theory is that the scale of the sack at Constantinople, particularly the loss of books, was simply too much for Aeneas to bear; his horror led to a set of rationalizations that could not be dislodged by contrary reports. Ironically, Sagundino, who felt the loss of his homeland in a way that Aeneas never could, presented a more balanced view of the sultan and the Ottoman court.

Defining the Self: Europe, Christianity, and Civility

With Mehmed and the Turks emerging as the barbaric or effeminate "other" in the diet orations, Aeneas struggled to find one clear "self" to present to his audience. Should he appeal to most of the men gathered at the diets as "Germans"—a fraught and fledgling idea in itself, or to the larger reading audience as Christians or Europeans? He tried at different points to do all three. As noted previously, Aeneas offers generic praise for the Germans at Frankfurt, claiming that no nation was more warlike, ready, powerful, skilled, or daring than the Germans. In a special show of flattery, Aeneas reverses the trope of the conquering Roman and humbled barbarian by venerating the Germans as the only people that Julius and Augustus Caesar could not defeat—a point of pride that later German humanist Conrad Celtis would also employ in his proto-nationalist works.[130] But could such claims inspire non-Germans? Moreover, he risked alienating other nations by describing the ancient Germans' conquests as "territory ... you [the Germans] possess now"—regions that included England, Belgium, and Switzerland, not to mention Austria, Northern Italy, and Prussia.[131] One wonders what the English, French, and others who in no way considered themselves "German" made of these boasts when they later read them. If Aeneas hoped to inspire a more robust response, he would need to think bigger.

The common bond of Christianity appears in the later version of the Regensburg oration when Aeneas states, "For although [Mehmed] is a most ferocious and powerful enemy, his power will come to nothing if the Christians join forces." While Aeneas could have ended there, in the same sentence he also invokes "the united power of the Roman Empire," "the noble magnates and powerful communities of Germany," and "the Duke of Burgundy."[132] This string of larger group identities and nations suggests that one community was not enough—Aeneas had to keep shifting the lens, and in this case, did so after the oration was delivered. In the early version of this oration at

Regensburg, Aeneas focused mostly on Germans.[133] The evocation of empire had the potential to unite a large swathe of central Europe, but it was likely too problematic to utter aloud at Regensburg when Emperor Frederick was absent. Nonetheless, it is noteworthy to see the range of options Aeneas mobilizes to foster common purpose and a sense of community large enough to take on the Ottomans.

The group identity of Europe cuts across all these distinctions and appears in each oration. At Regensburg and Wiener-Neustadt, he invokes the metaphor of Christendom being driven into a corner of the world by Islam, as he had done on at least two previous occasions and as Petrarch had done before him.[134] But at Regensburg, Aeneas labeled this corner more precisely: "Of Europe we have lost a large part, and Muhammad[135] has forced us into a corner: at one end he harasses the Hungarians, and at the other the Spaniards."[136] In this same oration, he speaks of East and West, asserting that Mehmed liked to boast, "'Why should I not be able to conquer and possess the whole of the West since I am already Lord of Asia [Minor], Thrace, Macedonia, Illyria, and all of Greece? After all, Alexander … conquered [lit. "trampled under foot"] the whole East.'"[137] "Europe" and "the West," then, appear in the Regensburg oration, but mainly as defensive gestures.

At Frankfurt, Europe emerges more clearly as a place of emotional attachment. In the second paragraph of the oration he exclaims,

> but we have now been smitten and struck in Europe itself, in our fatherland, in our own home, and seat. If somebody says that it is many years since the Turks came from Asia to Greece, the Tartars settled in Europe on this side of the river Don, and the Saracens crossed the Strait of Gibraltar and occupied a part of Spain, [my answer is that] until now we have never lost a city or a place in Europe equal to Constantinople.[138]

Note how the word "Europe" appears three times in rapid succession. Aeneas does this not only to alert his listeners to the shared danger to the continent and to acknowledge similar events in the past, but ultimately to deny that anything so serious had happened before. "Europe" here is both home and fatherland. In reality, Europe was never a completely Christian continent, but Aeneas creates a vision of it as exactly that: its natural state is to be Christian; Muslims and Mongols are interlopers, no matter how many centuries they lived or ruled there.

But Aeneas raises his rhetoric to a spiritual level when he describes Constantinople as being "almost at the center of the earth that may be easily cultivated."[139] The true spiritual center for Christians had always been Jerusalem, an early idea that became enshrined in traditional crusade language. What Aeneas does here by putting Constantinople almost at the center of the world and emphasizing its location in Europe is to transform the city, Greece, and the entire continent into sacred space, akin to the Holy Land. To my knowledge, Europe had not been spoken of in these terms before.

Aeneas further reinforces his vision of Europe as a community in the Frankfurt oration when he speaks of men of different countries all fighting on the same side. He tells his audience that he was not asking the Germans to fight the Turks alone (even though he affirms that they could), but merely to lead the charge.[140]

> Here somebody may object that, 'we shall not only have to do with the Turks, but also with the Tartars, the Saracens, and all the peoples they have subjugated.' My reply is that neither will you Germans be fighting alone. Many men from Italy, France, and Spain will join you, and the Hungarians and the Bohemians, the bravest peoples, will not be missing. The Serbians, the Bulgarians, all the Illyrians, and all the Greeks will seize the moment and rise against the Turks. And finally, the neighbors [of the Turks] in Asia will come to our help...

Here he cites the Christians in Cilicia, Bithynia, Cappadocia, Pontus, Syria, Georgia, Trebizond, and Armenia.[141] Moreover,

> The Venetians and the Genoese, those mighty peoples, will help you with fleets though they are presently at peace with the Turks. But they were forced to make peace so as not to lose their Eastern cities .... The Venetians have made a sure promise to the emperor that they will act as Christians if the faithful decide on a common war against the Turks. I am quite certain, nobles, that if you take up arms then all Christianity will support you.[142]

Although Aeneas blurs the line between European and Christian when he tacks on fellow believers in Asia for good measure, the overwhelming sense is that other Europeans will naturally answer the call.

The diet of Frankfurt ended in October of 1454 with tentative promises of troops, but no firm decisions on crusade. Delegates requested more time for discussion and planned to carry the work forward at a future diet.[143] Aeneas felt a mixture of pessimism and hope: deferring to a future diet might be little more than a stalling tactic, but at least crusade was still on the table.[144] He leans toward hope in a missive to Cardinal Carvajal (Nov. 26, 1454) where he describes the substance of a letter (*hunc effectum habentes*) from governor John Hunyadi of Hungary about the massing of Ottoman troops and the imminent threat to Hungary. Hunyadi pleaded with Frederick to send aid, saying that not 200,000 or even 100,000 was necessary, but "with far fewer troops we will banish the Turks from Europe."[145] While Frederick mulled over such requests, Italian powers made progress toward a general peace. The Peace of Lodi was signed on April 21, 1454, between Milan and Venice; Florence joined on August 30, Naples on Jan. 26, 1455, and the papacy on Feb. 25.[146]

What impact might Aeneas's oratory have made amidst these maneuvers? While he could neither field armies nor raise money, he saw his role as one of active support—to persuade men who were moved by the fall of

Constantinople to seek vengeance and defend their faith. His oration at Frankfurt in Latin and its German paraphrase may have played some part in stirring those emotions. Not only did the oration circulate widely in writing, but one important listener, crusade preacher Fra Giovanni Capistrano, in a letter to Pope Nicholas, praised both Aeneas's "excellent and lengthy oration" and his advice and comportment at Frankfurt.[147] Norman Housley has described the importance of the diet of Frankfurt and the preaching of Capistrano and others to help recruit the crusaders who successfully defended Belgrade in 1456—a small, but symbolically important victory against the Ottomans, led by the charismatic Capistrano himself. Although Capistrano's role in recruitment was paramount, Aeneas's oration at this critical moment may have added some momentum as well.[148] Certainly in the long term, it was a critical means of spreading his ideas (or as Helmrath puts it, "inaugurat[ing] several discourses") on Europe and the Greeks, the Turks and Islam, and the Germans.[149]

This is not to suggest that Aeneas was blind to the rivalries and upheavals between European countries. Just a few months before Frankfurt in a letter to his friend, Leonardo Benvoglienti, he despaired of the lack of leadership and unity among the nations—it was as if he was searching in vain for a Christian who could command the loyalty and resources of so vast an area, in the way Mehmed had done:

> Christendom has no head whom all obey. Neither the supreme pontiff nor the emperor is given his due. There is no reverence, no obedience. Like characters in fiction, figures in a painting, so do we look upon the pope and the emperor. Every city-state has its own ruler. There are as many princes as houses .... What order will there be in the army? What military discipline? What obedience? Who will feed so many people? Who will understand the languages? Who will hold in check the different customs? Who will endear the English to the French? Who will get the Genoese to join with the Aragonese? Who will reconcile the Germans with the Hungarians and the Bohemians? If you lead a few men against the Turks, you are easily defeated. If you lead many, you are confounded![150]

While in other works Aeneas spoke of the nations as a tightly knit team, here he emphasizes their divisions and undercuts this notion of group identity. One is reminded of Hirschi's description of the nation as "a product of failed imperialisms."[151] Perhaps it was intentional that he did not use "Europe" in this letter, but he found the inspiration to invoke it again more positively a few months later.

A "Moment of Vision"? The Oration at the Diet of Wiener-Neustadt

Aeneas had one last diet oration to compose for the gathering at Wiener-Neustadt in February 1455—a location designed to give Frederick no excuse or escape. As Setton aptly put it, "the timid Frederick III" who resided there "had to leave his gardens and aviaries for the unpleasant deliberations of the small gatherings of nobles."[152] Agreements had already been made at Frankfurt by leaders and envoys regarding the number of troops and ships they would commit to a crusade, so there was little need on Aeneas's part to convince his listeners of the necessity.[153] This gave him the room to focus more on the planning and moral conduct of the proposed crusade, leading him deeper into religious arguments than he had ventured to this point.[154]

The oration that will be discussed here, titled *In hoc florentissimo*, is dated Feb. 25, 1455, but it is not clear that it was actually delivered, or in what form. Two other texts of the oration at Wiener-Neustadt were circulated in manuscript and in print, but this is the only version that contains a complete oration. While it is feasible that a partial text is more representative, all three have inconsistencies that make it impossible to pin down the most authoritative version. Aeneas does not even mention the oration in his *Commentaries*, unlike the first two.[155] Yet for all of its challenges, *In hoc florentissimo* is a fascinating read. It presents a stark departure from the tone of orations at Regensburg and Frankfurt, suggesting either a "moment of vision," to quote R.W. Southern regarding a later work by Aeneas, or perhaps a crisis of confidence.[156]

Despite the positive reception of his speech at Frankfurt, with its harsh portrayal of the Turks as irredeemably barbarous and their leader as successful but uncultivated, a few months later Aeneas seemed less certain of the "justice" of crusade in the diet oration at Wiener-Neustadt. Even as he continued to support calls to "banish the Turks from Europe," he seems to have doubted the disturbing methods an expulsion might entail. It was one thing to try to motivate soldiers to fight; it was another to envision the fight, especially after the enemy had been so demonized. Where Regensburg focused on vengeance and Frankfurt on the protection of European civilization, Wiener-Neustadt takes a more pious and humble approach. It captures genuine concerns about the crusade project and the spirit with which men took the cross.

Previously Aeneas had simply assumed that God would support a war against the Turks, but in the Wiener-Neustadt oration he zeroes in on the necessity of attracting God to the crusaders' cause and fighting this battle on His behalf:

> victory will not just come about because you assemble a strong army, select highly skilled leaders, get suitable weaponry, gather abundant provisions, occupy a location well suited to fighting, design an ingenious battle order, and enter the battle bravely; no, you will only be victorious if the Lord, the giver of victories, grants it to you.[157]

A few pages later, he clarifies his point:

> Let both the soldiers and the leaders of the army and the war, whom we choose, love virtue and hate vice, and let us not take wicked men into the army even though they are vigorous and skilled in fighting.[158]

Here, Aeneas calls for a much higher standard of conduct than he did at Frankfurt where he extolled the benefits of sending thieves and robbers out of Germany and on crusade.[159] One wonders if Aeneas had been criticized for that earlier claim or if hearing preachers like Capistrano, whose purity of life and ability to recruit crusaders he later praised, impacted him.[160]

Aeneas also pointedly calls for a moral leader, citing a host of victories under religious leaders like Constantine, Theodosius, and St. Germanus.[161] The rank and file must also be held to a high standard: "Above all, those who fight should be pious, and protected by the shield of innocence; thus they shall be pleasing and acceptable to God and will easily gain victory."[162] From here, Aeneas proceeds with the traditional theme that Christians suffer because of their sins, and repentance brings about reversals. One of the ironies of Aeneas's emphasis on piety and morals was that a potential leader of the crusade was Albert Achilles, who was known by this time for his violence in warfare against fellow Germans and his burning and plundering of towns and villages. Albert may have been a decisive military leader who pushed negotiations for crusade commitments forward when they were faltering at Frankfurt, but he was not an ideal Christian knight.[163] With *In hoc florentissimo*, Aeneas abandons his previous practicality and challenges Aristotle's contention in the *Politics* that it is better to choose a skilled warrior than a just man as a leader. As such, Aeneas subtly signals his discomfort with the likes of Albert. Since "all victory is from God," he argues, it is better to please him through the choice of good men.[164] Aeneas heightens his demand for piety among crusading soldiers by citing examples from the Bible, St. Augustine, and Bede.[165] He also urges listeners to repent, abandon pride, and to take as their companion "the modest and beautiful maiden whom we call humility."[166] With his praise of femininized humility, Aeneas subverts the trope of the masculine Christian warrior that appears in most of his other rhetorical works on crusade. It is a striking and unusual departure for him.

Finally, Aeneas offers a bold exhortation regarding treatment of the enemy and noncombatants. He admonishes soldiers to focus first and foremost on victory and avoid plunder "where it is inadmissible," especially of "the poor Greeks and other Christians who are forced to live under the Turks."[167] No doubt, he wished to prevent a repeat of 1204 when crusaders sacked Constantinople and attacked fellow Christians. Aeneas takes a strong stance on violence and rape as well: "In our army there should be no lustfulness and no cruelty, and no violence against women. The chastity of our female captives should be as safe as that of our own women ...."[168] Not only does he promote empathy for Muslim and Christian women alike, but Aeneas goes even further by urging restraint against Turkish soldiers and civilians:

> When victory has been achieved, the fury of weapons should cease. No one should be killed except in battle .... For though the Turks, who reject Jesus Christ, the Son of God, are worthy of every chastisement, they should not be treated rashly or cruelly. In my opinion, we should take

every care that, if we win, the Greeks should hope for freedom, and the Turks should not fear cruel death and turn desperation into bravery.[169]

The good character of the commander, he adds, is essential to ensuring fair treatment of the vanquished.

For the first time in two years, Aeneas turned the tables and imagined the Turks not as savage barbarians, but as human beings with a claim to the same protections in warfare (*ius in bello*) that the Greeks deserved in 1453. He also rejects the theme of vengeance, common to many crusade texts, including Urban II's sermon at Clermont in 1095 and his own previous works.[170] Did Aeneas, as Housley argues, "in a roundabout way, acknowledge a common humanity" with the Turks and desire an end to the cycle of violence?[171] One thing that is certain, *In hoc florentissimo* is a long way from Aeneas's call for retaliation at Regensburg in 1454. What could explain such a reversal? Judging by the authorities Aeneas cites, the inspiration seems to have come primarily from classical texts: he references Cicero and Virgil's words on restraint against the vanquished.[172] But there were contemporary Christian thinkers who called for mercy, including Capistrano, who also preached at the diet of Wiener-Neustadt and advocated for the defeat and conversion of the Turks rather than their death. The similarities between his preaching and Aeneas's words in the oration make his influence on the humanist seem likely. Juan de Segovia and Nicholas of Cusa, whom Aeneas knew from his Basel days, were also working on the question of peaceful conversion.[173]

It is hard to know how far Aeneas wanted to take these reflections, given questions about the delivery and distribution of this oration; more importantly, with the exception of one later and equally enigmatic work, his letter to Mehmed II (1461), Aeneas did not broach the subject of ethical treatment of the Turks in his other writings.[174] Nonetheless, Aeneas's words in *In hoc florentissimo* suggest a moment of religious and moral reflection—if not quite a "moment of vision."[175] It is impossible to say whether the diet of Wiener-Neustadt would have ended with a firm commitment to a joint crusade, had news of Pope Nicholas's death not arrived in early April. Scholars have been justly skeptical, but there is some evidence that Frederick tried to take steps to mobilize.[176]

Reading Aeneas's diet orations from Regensburg to Frankfurt to Wiener-Neustadt, one can see an arc of development from anger and revenge to reflection on Mehmed and the Turks' praiseworthy qualities, to full-on discomfort with holy war. Each of Aeneas's diet orations of 1454–1455 served a slightly different purpose, and each had its own tone.[177] Either Aeneas knew he could not use the same script each time, or his ideas truly evolved in this period, stimulated by conversation and interaction with the representatives at these meetings. By the end, he may have found it difficult, as a humanist and a Christian, to rouse soldiers with calls for inhumane treatment of one's adversaries. What all of the diet orations do have in common, I believe, is the desire to persuade his audience to work together as one to defend Europe.[178]

Aeneas's Reactions to 1453 in Broader Humanist Context

How do Aeneas's reactions to the fall of Constantinople compare to those of other humanist contemporaries, and was he unusual in any respect? To some extent, his rhetoric belongs to a broader discourse on the Ottomans, Islam, and the East, as my first monograph shows.[179] In his notions of Europe and the West, however, the close readings presented in this chapter show some important differences. A comparison to a group of writers on a few key points will demonstrate the broader context of Aeneas's words and ideas from 1453 to 1455 and beyond.

Contemporaries who responded immediately to news of the disaster offer the most useful starting point as they all seem to have penned their initial reactions without knowledge of each other's texts. The earliest writers include Aeneas, Leonard of Chios, Lauro Quirini, Cardinal Bessarion, and possibly Niccolò Tignosi.[180] These accounts and reactions were all written at about the same time and at considerable distance from one another. Nonetheless, they share some points of agreement. Most, if not all, express sorrow and fear for Christians or Christendom and mourning for the loss of life and destruction of religious shrines. They all depict the Turks as extremely violent, with some writers like Leonard noting that those who did not resist were spared.

Very few of these humanists immediately decried the destruction of Greek learning, as Aeneas did, with the exception of Venetian humanist Quirini, who was living in Crete at the time and wrote a plaintive letter to Pope Nicholas on July 15, 1453. He shares Aeneas's disgust over cultural losses and his fears about the impact on education, adding the detail reported to him by eyewitness Cardinal Isidore of Kiev that 120,000 volumes had been lost in the sack. At one point he states, "the language and literature of the Greeks, invented, augmented, and perfected over so long a period with such labor and industry, will certainly perish."[181] That these two men, separated by thousands of miles, reacted to the loss of books so similarly speaks to the shared cultural context or discursive field of humanism and its passionate engagement with ancient texts.[182] For both Quirini and Aeneas, Constantinople had been a beacon and a steward of ancient learning; now that repository was gone.[183] Quirini similarly thought it no accident that so many books were lost in the sack, calling the Turks, "a barbaric, uncultivated race, without established customs or laws, living a careless, vagrant, arbitrary life ...."[184]

Other humanists were less definitive about the destruction of culture. Leonard of Chios, who was present at the fall, did not comment specifically on learning, although in a speech attributed to Emperor Constantine before the final battle, he describes the Turks as "beasts" and the Greeks as men, or masters of beasts.[185] Likewise, Bessarion did not comment on books or learning in his early reaction, but he labeled the Turks "barbarians."[186] Letters by Francesco Filelfo contain mentions of barbarism as well.[187] In short, Aeneas was not the first or only humanist to draw early and serious inferences about Ottoman culture and society based on reports of the sack, but only one other contemporary, to my knowledge, immediately made extended inferences about attacks on learning.

Moving from the earliest humanist responses to a broader sample of reactions, I would like to turn now to views of Mehmed II. Here humanist opinions diverged significantly—especially on the subject of the conqueror and learning. While Aeneas insisted Mehmed was uneducated and unsupportive of scholars, better informed contemporary writers took the opposite view. Sagundino, who likely met Mehmed and spoke more highly of him, has already been discussed. Byzantines like Doukas and George of Trebizond knew Mehmed to be well educated and a patron of scholarship.[188] Doukas described Mehmed's arrival in Greece after his father's death, where he was greeted by a host of court officials, common people, and specifically, "teachers of their foul religion [and] the learned in the sciences and the arts."[189] Italian humanists like Francesco Filelfo and Lauro Quirini, who spent time in the Greek East, also saw Mehmed as an intellectual. Filelfo composed a Greek encomium to the sultan after the fall of Constantinople in the hopes of helping his in-laws find freedom; Mehmed's consent to his request shows that Filelfo had judged his appreciation of poetry correctly.[190] Quirini, who had a low opinion of the cultural attainments of Mehmed's army, was able to separate looters in the sack from their leader. He describes Mehmed as seeking to emulate Alexander and reading Arrian's account of his deeds almost daily.[191] Even Bessarion, who spent much of his life helping Byzantine refugees, securing and preserving Greek manuscripts after 1453, and tirelessly supporting crusade does not appear to have employed the unlearned Ottoman trope.[192] Similarly, the Florentine humanist Niccolò Tignosi, who did not travel east but drew on contemporary reports, describes Mehmed as studying history.[193] By way of contrast to all these examples, Aeneas implied in his Frankfurt oration that Mehmed did not, and perhaps could not, read.[194] In all this, I believe, Aeneas was an outlier. Even writers who strongly criticized Mehmed's conquest as unjust and brutal did not reduce him to the classical/ Orientalist stereotype of an ignorant barbarian. Leonard of Chios and Isidore of Kiev, who both endured the traumas of the siege and sack, describe Mehmed as wicked, but not barbarous.

If all these contemporary scholars presented a different portrait of Mehmed, why should Aeneas's erroneous one matter to us at all? The answer lies in the spread of Aeneas's works. His letters, orations, and treatises were much better known for decades, if not centuries, than most of the works noted here. Greek accounts by Doukas and Kritoboulos did not circulate widely in the West; in fact, Kritoboulos's manuscript was only discovered in Istanbul in 1865. George of Trebizond's efforts to communicate with Mehmed were kept secret.[195] The texts by Tignosi, Quirini, Sagundino, and Filelfo did not approach the distribution level of Aeneas's works. Sadly, while other writers were better informed about the Ottomans than Aeneas, he became an "authority" on them, and he remained a key source for years to come. Aeneas's characterization of the Turks as illiterate barbarians persuaded more people than it should have—even Mehmed's reputation was likely tainted in the process, and, over time, his glory diminished in the West. The irony of this false narrative is increased by modern historians' appreciation of the sophistication of the Ottoman court.[196] In recent decades, scholars have argued, for instance, that critical astronomical developments long attributed to European thinkers owed a great deal to Ottoman scholars.[197] Whether Aeneas's disparagement of Ottoman culture can be seen as a harbinger of racist thought will be discussed in Chapter 4, but I see it as an early example of Eurocentrism and erasure.

A harder question concerns Aeneas's impact upon contemporary writers. The timing of his writings versus that of other humanists is certainly suggestive. He expounded on the Ottomans in a way that most humanists would not begin to do for a year or more after news of the fall arrived in Western Europe. Given the rapid spread of his letters and orations, it is possible that Aeneas drowned out other Christian authorities and helped spread the discourse of the uncultivated Ottomans among other writers.[198] But whether this points to direct influence on Aeneas's part or a broadly shared, Foucauldian discourse is difficult to prove either way. It is safer to say that Aeneas was at the forefront of this trend and wrote more works about it than most of his contemporaries. I would note one intriguing caveat: while Aeneas was preoccupied with tropes of civility and barbarism and frequently belittled Ottoman culture, he did not use the word *barbarus* and its cognates as often as other humanists. Perhaps his current home in Austria and Germany sensitized him to the way some Italians slandered the Germans as barbarians, and he found the term distasteful.[199] Even after leaving Germany, he did not embrace it with gusto. It may also be that he took the Ottomans too seriously as a political and military threat to overuse the dismissive term; they may have behaved as brutes in his eyes, but they were formidable adversaries. As his orations show, Aeneas was not incapable of questioning his assumptions.

One final and important point concerns the language humanists employed to describe the larger Christian collective in 1453 and shortly thereafter. As noted, "Christendom" and "Christians" were the most widely used terms. Even Aeneas preferred "Christians" and sometimes "Germans" when he spoke at the diets, despite his provocative uses of "Europe" and "the West." It is also true that a handful of humanists besides Aeneas had used "Europe" in regard to the Ottomans prior to 1453 or shortly after the fall.[200] It would be misleading to claim that Aeneas was "first" or "only" in this regard. Yet most early sources and eyewitness accounts did not use "Europe" or "the West" at all; this includes Quirini, Leonard, Isidore, and Bessarion. Tignosi, who may have written his account as early as Nov. 1453 or as late as 1459 mentions Europe once.[201] And Quirini uses the term "East" when he says that "all the East" (*totus Oriens*) is in fear of Mehmed.[202]

Taken as a whole, these examples suggest that "Europe" and especially "the West" were not in common usage at this moment in time vis-à-vis the Ottoman advance. This would not change overnight, but there is a steady increase in usage, and, more importantly, a shift in what those terms came to mean in the years that followed, especially in Aeneas's writings. Other humanists like Panormita, Poggio Bracciolini, and Donato Acciauoli were employing the terms in 1454 and following.[203] This increased usage indicates a growing sense of group identity of self and other that was secular in nature, but the Christian-Muslim context is never too far outside of the frame. Suzanne Conklin Akbari has shown how the binary of East and West in many modern studies was "virtually unknown to medieval readers," but ends her study around 1450 with the recognition that a shift in thinking and terminology starts to occur at this time.[204]

Epilogue: Other Views of Ottoman Constantinople and "Europe"

Meanwhile, the Ottomans, whose society bore little or no resemblance to Aeneas's representations, were the new masters of Constantinople. At age twenty-one Mehmed II had accomplished what many commanders before him had tried and failed to do. It is hard to imagine what went through his mind as he pondered his epic victory and his next steps. Some accounts describe him as regretful of the devastation and willing, for a short time, to partner with the surviving Greek dignitaries before deciding to execute the majority.[205] Other accounts show him as wrathful and delighting in the bloodshed and suffering. All of these accounts, in the end, may only be projections of their writers' emotions, but it is interesting that Greek authors portray Mehmed as more sympathetic and self-aware than Latin or Ottoman writers.[206] We know that Mehmed did not spend long in the shattered city, but gave instructions to have it rebuilt and repopulated, with the help of Greeks who were paid for their work to earn ransom, and many Ottoman subjects who were ordered to relocate there.

Clearly, Mehmed II wanted Constantinople to become the jewel in his empire and to show a sense of continuity with its illustrious past. While it was commonly called Istanbul or "the city," a word of Greek origin, the Ottomans continued to employ "Constantinople" in official documents until the twentieth century.[207] Mehmed not only repaired the damage of the siege but erased the decay and neglect of previous centuries. Contemporary Greek historian Kritoboulos praised his energetic rebuilding program.[208] The city was no longer a Christian capital, but much of its Byzantine character would remain in the surviving churches and secular buildings, even in the shape of early mosques, which mirrored the style of Hagia Sophia. A great number of Turks from Anatolia would settle there, and their mosques, schools, bathhouses, and charitable buildings would soon outshine the churches. Many Greeks remained in or moved to the city, and Jews and other Christians, particularly Armenians, settled in the city as well. Ottoman Constantinople quickly became a vibrant, multicultural, and commercially successful urban center.[209] During his reign, Mehmed established the famous covered bazaar in Constantinople and built more than 800 shops there.[210]

Nor was Constantinople unique among Ottoman cities. As Mehrdad Kia states, "Until the arrival of the modern industrial era, the major urban centers of the Ottoman Empire were much larger, and far more prosperous, than any urban center in Europe."[211] Charitable institutions like soup kitchens (*imârets*) and dervish lodges were widespread in Ottoman Europe and catered to Christians, Jews, Muslims, poor, and rich alike.[212] And yet, European visitors, struck by the efficiency and productivity of Istanbul and other Ottoman cities, were still unable to fully convey the complexities that they saw. As Cemal Kafadar argues, "What European writers never appreciated was the presence of social institutions and practices that delineated a public sphere of political negotiation."[213] Guilds, some of them multi-confessional, *kadis*, market supervisors, Sufi orders, *sheyks*, and *waqfs* (charitable institutions) were just some of the features that provided Ottoman cities with ample opportunity for public engagement, representation, and justice. They did so in a time when Europeans with fewer institutions and little systemic effort toward religious inclusion dismissed the Ottoman government as despotic and backward.[214] Aeneas's writings on the fall of Constantinople would unfortunately continue to focus on captivity and destruction without acknowledging the repopulation and rebuilding that followed.

Eastern European neighbors quickly negotiated truces or arrangements with Mehmed, seeing no way to stop him on their own. Western European states like Venice and Genoa with possessions and significant trade interests in the Eastern Mediterranean tried to come to grips with the empire that now had full control of the straits of the Bosphorus and access to the Black Sea. Venice lamented the loss of the city and the death or capture of many of its citizens, but almost immediately sent an ambassador to Mehmed to propose a new treaty between the two powers so that free passage and trade could resume. Genoa did the same the following spring. Florence and others would soon follow suit. Such trade interests seriously complicated Venice and Genoa's ability to support a crusade. Indeed, it was difficult for any number of Italian powers to jump into the fray when they were engaged in hostilities with one or more of their peninsular neighbors; a general peace in Italy was the first step that was needed. The successful conclusion of the Peace of Lodi (1454), mentioned earlier, is a testament to the fear the Ottoman advance struck in all of them, but their conflicting interests would not make planning a crusade an easy feat—as the next several popes, especially Aeneas, would learn.[215] If a crusade were to get off the ground, these embittered peninsular neighbors would not only have to make peace, but trust each other in ways they had not done since the Roman Empire was intact. In sum, Italian governments often felt pulled in opposite directions: crusade or some form of cooperation with the Ottomans.

Finally, what, if anything, did the Ottomans think of Europe as a collective? It behooves us to remember that this growing discourse of "Europe" and "the West" was not a global phenomenon. As Gilles Veinstein, states, Europe or *Avrupa* "appeared belatedly in Turkish and was derived from the Western term. An earlier Arabic term *Urūfa* existed, but it was rarely used."[216] Terms like *Rum* (Rome) for the Byzantine Empire and the Franj for Franks were still common.[217] This is not to say that Muslims were uninterested in the peoples and countries of the region as scholars like Bernard Lewis and even

Edward Said and others have assumed.[218] A growing number of studies argue the opposite. Cemal Kafadar points to the active engagement of Ottoman merchants in areas like Venice and Ancona, among other locations.[219] As Nabil Matar has shown, there was a healthy sense of curiosity and two-way exchange between Western Africans and Europeans in the early modern period—a phenomenon that complicates the "East vs. West" dichotomy that Aeneas and others were beginning to promote.[220]

But an interest in the cities and countries that comprise Europe and a consciousness of Europe and especially "Europeans" are two separate issues. The rising usage and promotion of those terms by fifteenth- and sixteenth-century Europeans like Aeneas, and the relative absence of such terms among Muslims, underscores the fact that Europe and the West were not always there, but were very much created. Definitions of Europe and the West are never static, but a turning point, I strongly believe, was established in 1453. Given the sheer drama of that moment and its immediate publication (in Western Europe) as a tragedy, this initial definition could only be unbalanced and unfair.

Conclusion

Had Constantinople not fallen in 1453, Aeneas would still be known to modern scholars, but less so; it is unlikely that he would have become the pope or even a cardinal. His response to this event and his support of crusade helped set him apart and propel him upward through the Church hierarchy, as the next two chapters will show. Without the conquest and his strong reaction to it, he would be seen today as a talented, but lesser humanist and an able, but common functionary. What matters most in this study, however, is the way that the fall of Constantinople crystallized his vision of Christendom, Europe, and "the West," and drove him to reflect in the years to come on their identity and destiny. It is possible, of course, that Aeneas might have written about Europe without the spur of 1453; his years of traveling, political experience, and study were fundamental components of his knowledge. But as I hope to have shown, before the fall of Constantinople, Aeneas lacked the inspiration (and likely the time) to write at length on these matters; whenever he did, he was still finding his voice. Between 1453 and 1455, all of that began to change.

In many ways, the Ottoman conquest turned Aeneas's narrow political outlook away from Frederick's concerns toward the larger, more powerful imagined communities of Europe and "the West." This shift might not have been so decisive were it not also for the emperor's indecision and Aeneas's growing support of papalism.[221] Judging from Aeneas's letters, he seems to have lost confidence in Frederick by later 1453 as the prime mover of crusade. The role of "empire" had clearly declined in his view, creating space for other ideas. It is interesting that Aeneas did not simply replace it with an idea of "Christendom" with the pope at its head; while that notion was definitely present in his writings, it had to compete with Aeneas's growing vision of the continent. The remainder of this study will show how his geographic assessments of the world continued to expand and evolve—and how his view of both Christian countries in Europe and the Ottoman Empire acquired greater nuance and detail in his writings. The year 1453, then, was nothing short of transformational for Aeneas.

Aeneas's intense reaction to the Ottoman advance unfolded in the public sphere and gained many adherents. While many of his contemporaries took a more rational approach to the Ottomans and treated them as part of the European political, economic, and cultural landscape, this view could not rival the reductive, inaccurate, yet compelling discourse that Aeneas helped shape. To be fair, both he and his audience had good reason to fear the expansionist Ottoman Empire. Whereas we know that they would never conquer Vienna, though they tried twice, nor Italy, though they later conquered Otranto in the south and raided the territory near Venice, to many fifteenth-century Europeans, the Ottomans must have appeared nigh unstoppable. Furthermore, most states played a double game regarding their intentions with the Ottomans. While many Christian powers negotiated quietly with the Ottomans, few broadcast their intentions among their co-religionists. Most states, in fact, felt compelled to treat them as the "normative foe" in their public pronouncements.[222]

Finally, as Aeneas's works and activities following 1455 will clearly show, his discourse of Europe and the nations within it depended on more than just the shock of 1453. It also emerged from his efforts to broker alliances against the Ottomans and the growing realization of the divisions within "Christendom" that first had to be healed or at least addressed. If the Turks helped form an imaginary border between Europe and Asia, Aeneas still had much work ahead of him to begin to understand the peoples who made up his home continent.

Notes

1 Kritovoulos, *The History of Mehmed the Conqueror*, ed. and tr. Charles T. Riggs (Princeton: Princeton University Press, 1954), 76.
2 For details on the siege and sack see Marios Philippides and Walter K. Hanak, *The Siege and the Fall of Constantinople in 1453* (Burlington, VT: Ashgate, 2011); Kenneth Setton, *The Papacy and the Levant (1205–1571)*, vol. 2 (Philadelphia: American Philosophical Society, 1978); the most readable treatment of the siege is Steven Runciman, *The Fall of Constantinople: 1453* (Cambridge: Cambridge University Press, 1965). One of the best eyewitness accounts is that of Leonard of Chios, "History of the Capture of Constantinople by Mehmed II," in *The Siege of Constantinople 1453: Seven Contemporary Accounts*, tr. and ed. J. R. Melville Jones (Amsterdam: Adolf M. Hakkert, 1972), 11–41. See also Donald Nicol, *Immortal Emperor: The Life and Legend of Constantine Palaiologos, Last Emperor of the Romans* (Cambridge: Cambridge University Press, 1992). For a recent and more critical assessment of Constantine, see Marios Philippides, *Constantine XI Dragaš Palaeologus: The Last Emperor of Byzantium* (London: Routledge, 2019). On Constantinople as a "God-given city," see, Jonathan Harris, *Constantinople: Capital of Byzantium* (London: Hambledon Continuum, 2007).

3   The barrel was probably between twenty and twenty-six feet in length and six to eight feet in circumference, with a breach of about two feet in circumference. Contemporary estimates of the weight of the projectiles range from 11,000–18,000 pounds. The cannon required thirty wagons and sixty oxen to transport it. See Philippides and Hanak, *Siege and the Fall of Constantinople in 1453*, 418–25.

4   Contemporary chronicler Doukas recounts conversations with Ottoman soldiers who participated in the sack as saying they would have "sold [the Greeks] like sheep" had they known how few men were actually defending the city; Doukas, *Decline and Fall of Byzantium*, ed. and tr. Harry Magoulias (Detroit: Wayne State University Press, 1975), 224–25. Eyewitness Leonard of Chios, states that those who surrendered were spared, but also notes widespread seizure of inhabitants, *Siege of Constantinople*, tr. Jones, 38–39.

5   Runciman says that it was shortened to one day without noting his source; he also contends that portions of the city escaped looting and captivity by surrendering to Mehmed, in a long paragraph citing Kritoboulos, Doukas, and Lomellino; see Runciman, *Fall of Constantinople*, 148, 153. I have not been able to verify either of these claims, but they should be treated with caution given recent findings about some of Runciman's errors on the siege of Jerusalem in 1099; see Benjamin Kedar, "The Jerusalem Massacre of 1099 in Western Historiography of the Crusades," *Crusades* 3 (2004): 15–75. Runciman's rationale for his second claim is that parts of the city must have been unscathed or they could not have ransomed so many Greeks in the aftermath; again, the evidence is lacking. Doukas relates that Mehmed ordered his men on day one not to harm the buildings in the city, but he does not specifically say that he ended the sack or offered protection to the inhabitants; *Decline and Fall of Byzantium*, 231. Lomellino, commander of Genoese Galata across the harbor, describes a three-day sack; see *Siege of Constantinople*, tr. Jones, 132. Leonard of Chios, who was present at the siege, also says that it lasted three days. Thanks to Marios Philippides for his thoughts on this question.

6   Little work has been done on this subject in the early Ottoman era owing to the challenge of finding sources. A fairly recent essay collection offers useful insights into related questions; see *Ransom Slavery Along the Ottoman Borders*, eds. Géza Dávid and Pál Fodor (Leiden: Brill, 2007). Anecdotal evidence exists on some well-known cases such as Greek official George Sphrantzes, who was held captive for three months and managed to ransom himself and his wife, but not their two adolescent children who died in captivity; see Runciman, *Fall*, 145–52; Setton, *Papacy and Levant*, 2: 129–34; *The Fall of the Byzantine Empire: A Chronicle by George Sphrantzes 1401–1477*, tr. Marios Philippides (Amherst, MA: University of Massachusetts Press, 1980), 70–75; Harris, *Constantinople*, 186. On the heavy expense of redeeming prisoners, see Enikő Csukovits, "Miraculous Escapes from Ottoman Captivity," in *Ransom Slavery*, 7. John Argyropoulos was reported to have spent many months trying to secure a ransom for his family, and Francesco Filelfo used his literary skills to beg the release of his mother-in-law in a flattering letter to Mehmed II; see Nancy Bisaha, *Creating East and West: Renaissance Humanists and the Ottoman Turks* (Philadelphia: University of Pennsylvania Press, 2004), ch. 3.

7   Latin and Greek accounts report the pervasiveness of rape. Turkish sources are less direct. Tursun Beg writes "Every tent was filled with handsome boys and beautiful girls," in *History of Mehmed the Conqueror*, ed. Halil Inalcik (Minneapolis: Bibliotheca Islamica, 1978), 37. Aşıkpaşazade describes how the soldiers "enslaved the people … [and] embraced the beauties"; see Ebru Boyar and Kate Fleet, *A Social History of Ottoman Istanbul* (Cambridge: Cambridge University Press, 2010), 11. Rape was a common occurrence of warfare in Western Europe, although the shock of contemporary writers in reports of it in 1453 and their silence in other contexts would seem to suggest otherwise.

8   See Bisaha, *Creating East and West*, 64–66.

9   As Harris, states, "Mehmed ... had conquered 'a city of ruins,' with many of the great palaces, churches and monasteries already in an advanced state of dilapidation"; *Constantinople*, 187. Harris somberly adds, however, how much of the rich archaeological history of Byzantium was permanently lost in the rebuilding; ibid., 186–91.

10 Cecilia M. Ady, *Pius II: (Aeneas Silvius Piccolomini) The Humanist Pope* (London: Methuen and Co., 1913), 113–19.

11 "... timeo, ne in exilio moriar; cogito dietim redire, multa obviant ... omnis mihi dies annus est ... scribo frequenter Romano pontifici, ut me revocet aut redeundi licentiam inpartiatur ... quod autem plura me Senis manentem ex Romano pontifice consequuturum sperem, quam hic morantem, non me decipio. nunc et si non multum, tamen aliquid Romanus presul cardinalesque me existimant, intuitu cesaris non mea virtute; at cum Senis fuero, neque papa neque cardinales mei memoriam habebunt ... favorem Romana curia, non homines querit; habet multos, qui me virtute superant, at qui cesari cari sint, non habet prelatum Italum nisi me." Rudolph Wolkan, ed., *Der Briefwechsel des Eneas Silvius Piccolomini*, in *Fontes Rerum Austriacarum*, ser. 2, vol. 68 (1918), 181–82.

12 Christopher Celenza, *Renaissance Humanism and the Papal Curia: Lapo da Castiglionchio the Younger's "De curiae commodis"* (Ann Arbor, MI: University of Michigan Press, 1999), 41.

13 For reactions to the news, see Robert Schwoebel, *The Shadow of the Crescent: The Renaissance Image of the Turk (1453–1517)* (New York: St. Martin's Press, 1967), 1–4; Setton, *Papacy and Levant*, 2: 138–51. On the question of inevitability, see Setton, *Papacy*, 2: 136.

14 Letter to Cardinal Carvajal, in Wolkan, *Briefwechsel*, 68: 129. In two letters dated July 17, he stated that he had heard nothing regarding the Turks. Wolkan, *Briefwechsel*, 68: 140, 141.

15 "Hic habentur nova horribilia de perditione Constantinopolis, que utinam falsa sint!" Wolkan, *Briefwechsel*, 68: 188. Caccia appeared in Aeneas's dialogues on the authority of a council (*Libellus dialogorum de auctoritate generalium conciliorum et gestis basileensium*, 1440) as an anti-papal secretary debating the rights of the council against Nicholas of Cusa; see *Reject Aeneas, Accept Pius: Selected Letters of Aeneas Sylvius Piccolomini (Pope Pius II)*, intr. and tr. Thomas M. Izbicki, Gerald Christianson, and Philip Krey (Washington, DC: Catholic University of America Press, 2006), 25; Ady, *Pius II*, 68.

16 "Sed quid illud horribile novum modo allatum de Constantinopoli? Tremit manus, dum hec scribo, horret animus neque tacere indignatio sinit neque dolor loqui permittit. Heu miseram Christianitatem." Wolkan, *Briefwechsel*, 68: 199. See also Agostino Pertusi's edition and translation into Italian, *La caduta di Costantinopoli*. 2 vols. (Milan: Arnoldo Mondadori Editore, 1976).

17 A rare term of respect for Aeneas to apply to Mehmed, as will be discussed.

18 "Turchorum imperator ... populum omnem gladio extinxit, sacerdotes diversis tormentorum generibus excarnificavit neque sexui neque etati pepercit; quadraginta et amplius milia personarum illic occisa referuntur." Wolkan, *Briefwechsel*, 68: 199. In addition, Aeneas relates a false report of the Byzantine emperor's son escaping in the fray to Pera across the harbor, but the emperor was childless. As such, this fiction indicates how little even well-informed Western Europeans knew about Emperor Constantine and the misinformation that circulated in the first weeks after the siege. See Wolkan, *Briefwechsel*, 68: 199. Even Nestor Iskander, a Russian combatant whom Marios Philippides has shown was present at the siege of Constantinople, relates a story about the emperor's wife taking shelter in Hagia Sophia and escaping; the emperor was unmarried at the time; Philippides and Hanak, *Siege and Fall*, 132–36.

19 Doleo templum illud toto terrarum orbe famosissimum Sophie vel destrui vel pollui." Wolkan, *Briefwechsel*, 68: 200.
20 "Heu, quot nunc magnorum nomina virorum peribunt? Secunda mors ista Homero est, secundus Platoni obitus." Wolkan, *Briefwechsel*, 68: 200.
21 This is noteworthy as some humanists blamed the Goths for the loss of Roman learning. On Bruni's view of the Goths and the Ottomans vis-à-vis learning, see Bisaha, *Creating East and West*, 58–60. See also Lorenzo Valla on losses of medieval period in "The Glory of Latin Language," in *Portable Renaissance Reader*, ed. and tr. James Bruce Ross and Mary Martin McLaughlin (New York, Penguin Books, 1981; (1st ed. Viking Press, 1953), 133–34. Biondo's *Decades*, a likely source for Aeneas regarding 410, seems to take a milder view, noting the sparing of churches, for example. Aeneas repeats this in his "Epitome" of Biondo's *Decades*; see Pius II, *Opera quae extant omnia* (Basel, 1571), 147.
22 Citing Cusanus's familiarity with "matters of the East," he states, "You are not ignorant of the way Greece is related to the rest of Europe. You know the position of Thrace; you remember perfectly the size of the city of Constantinople, the mass of its walls, and the character of the adjacent sea and land." ("Quamvis res orientis satis notas et nimis, heu nimis notas dignationi vestre non dubitem… Quomodo se habeat Grecia ad reliquam Europam non ignoratis. Thracie situm scitis, Constantinopolitane urbis magnitudinem, murorum molem, adjacentis maris et terre qualitatem pulchre tenetis.") Wolkan, *Briefwechsel*, 68: 206–7; see also *Reject Aeneas*, tr. Izbicki et al., 306–18 for a translation of the letter. On Cusanus's earlier trip to Constantinople, see Maarten Halff, "Did Cusanus Talk with Muslims? Revisiting Cusanus' Sources for the Cribratio Alkorani and Interfaith Dialogue," *Revista Española de Filosofía Medieval* 26, no. 1 (2019): 29–58.
23 "Non enim ut quidam rentur, Teucri sunt neque Perse, qui nunc Turchi dicuntur. Scitharum ex media barbarie genus profectum est, quod ultra Euxinum Pirricheosque montes ad occeanum septentrionalem sedes prius habuisse traditur, ut [E]thico philosopho placet." Wolkan, *Briefwechsel*, 68: 209; Eng. tr. *Reject Aeneas*, tr. Izbick et al., 312, with some changes. The problematic Aethicus, an eighth-century writer thought to be much earlier in Aeneas's time, will be discussed in Chapter 3.
24 Meserve, *Empires of Islam*, 68–108, especially 79–81.
25 Aeneas's ability to conjure this image of barbarism so quickly and skillfully suggests a view of humanism that Baker describes as "intimately related to human, cultural, moral, political—in short, civilizational—ideals"; *Italian Renaissance Humanism*, 240. See also Kenneth Gouwens's description of the common cultural context that humanists shared in "Perceiving the Past: Renaissance Humanism after the 'Cognitive Turn'," *American Historical Review* 103, no. 1 (1998): 55–82.
26 Aeneas describes the men at Frederick's court who responded to Aeneas's exhortations of Caesar with tears and vows to fight this "impious barbarity" (*impiam barbariem*). Wolkan, *Briefwechsel*, 68: 214.
27 Holt provides a useful list of crusade chronicles and other related works where Muslims, particularly Seljuk Turks, are called barbarians. This is an important point, as I and other scholars have overlooked the frequency of this usage; see Bisaha, *Creating East and West*, 29. Still, Holt does not delve into the context in which this term is used in medieval sources, nor does he recognize the infrequency with which Urban II, for instance, employed it, as opposed to Benedetto Accolti (1415–64), who inserted the term freely into speeches he *attributed to* Urban and others in his history of the First Crusade. My sense is that it does not compare to the scale and complexity of humanist associations with the term, but I agree with Holt that more work should be done on this subject. See Andrew Holt, "Crusading against Barbarians: Muslims as Barbarians in Crusade Era

Sources," in *East Meets West in the Middle Ages and Early Modern Times*, ed. Albrecht Classen (Berlin: De Gruyter, 2013), 443–56.

28 See Bisaha, *Creating East and West*, ch. 2.

29 Aeneas also alludes to the European collective at the beginning of his lament when he states, "With Italy, Germany, France, and Spain, for the most part safe, what shame that we permit the famous city of Constantinople to be captured by the effeminate Turks." ("Italia, Germania, Gallia, et Hispania magna ex parte salva, proh pudor ab effeminatis Turcis inclitam urbem Constantinopolim capi permittimus"); Wolkan, *Briefwechsel*, 68: 199.

30 "Ecce quod timui ex duobus Christianitatis luminibus alterum jam videmus erutum ...." Wolkan, *Briefwechsel*, 68: 201

31 "Majores nostri Ierosolimam, Accaron, Anthiochiam perdiderunt, fateor, ingens malum, sed nulla clades moderne ruine comparanda est; in Asia et in aliena possessione nostri veteres urbes amisere, nos in Europa in nostro solo, inter Christianos potentissimam urbem, orientalis imperii caput, Grecie columen, litterarum domicilium ab hostili manu sinimus expugnari." Wolkan, *Briefwechsel*, 68: 201.

32 Robert Bartlett, *The Making of Europe: Conquest, Colonization and Cultural Change 950–1350* (Princeton: Princeton University Press, 1993), 250–55. More will be said on this in Chapter 3.

33 I take this to mean Muhammad the prophet, as Aeneas does not refer Mehmed II by name here, but the meaning is not fully clear. He speaks in the same letter of churches being subjected to the filth of "Maumethus," which could also mean the prophet rather than Mehmed in this context.

34 The Vlachs were inhabitants of Wallachia, a region that roughly corresponds to modern day Romania.

35 "Jam regnat inter nos Maumethus. Jam nostris cervicibus Turchus imminet, jam nobis clausus est Eusinus et Tanais inaccessibilis factus, jam Valachis Turcho parere necessum est. Inde ad Hungaros, inde ad Germanos Turchorum gladius penetrabit et nos interim domesticis quatimur odiis: reges Francie et Anglie inter se litigant, Germani principes invicem bella gerunt, raro Hispania tota quiescit, Italia nostra pacis expers de alieno jure contendit. Quanto melius tantum armorum tantumque militie in hostes fidei verteremus? Wolkan, *Briefwechsel*, 68: 201.

36 See Johannes Helmrath, "Enea Silvio Piccolomini (Pius II.)—Ein Humanist als Vater des Europagedankens?" in *Themenportal Europäische Geschichte*, 2007: 361–69. <www.europa.clio-online.de/essay/id/fdae-1327>.

37 See Pertusi, *Caduta di Costantinopoli*, vol. 2; Schwoebel, *Shadow of the Crescent*; Bisaha, *Creating East and West*, ch. 2.

38 One Western contemporary who may have come close, judging from surviving evidence, particularly his letters, is Francesco Filelfo. See Margaret Meserve, "Nestor Denied: Francesco Filelfo's Advice to Princes on the Crusade Against the Turks," *Osiris* 25, no. 1: 47–65.

39 Using Wolkan's volume of collected letters vol. 68: beginning with letter 108 (July 12, 1453) to 291 (Summer 1454).

40 His letter to Nicholas of Cusa (July 21, 1453) also has this type of structure.

41 "Solum te rogo, si de pace nostre Italie agitur, id toto pectore cures ...." Wolkan, *Briefwechsel*, 68: 216.

42 "Oro igitur te, ne pigriteris mihi de omni statu Italie scribere ...." Wolkan, *Briefwechsel*, 68: 228.

43 See Wolkan, *Briefwechsel*, 68, letters 179 and 194 to Prokop Rabstein in Prague (Oct. 8, 1453 and Dec. 12, 1453, respectively); letter 202 to Cardinal Zbigniew Olesnicki in Krakow; letter 221 to the archbishop of Canterbury, John Kempe (Jan. 17, 1454); and letter 222 to Carlo Gigli merchant in London, (also Jan. 17, 1454).

44 "Inveni mentem ejus et volentem et apprime ardentem." Wolkan, *Briefwechsel*, 68: 214; Eng. tr., *Reject Aeneas*, tr. Izbicki et al., 316.

45 "Non est, cur multa scribam; hoc solum dico: numquam de ulla re cesarem aut frequentius loqui aut attentius audire, postquam sibi annis servio decem, animadverti." Wolkan, *Briefwechsel*, 68: 225–26.

46 See the insightful and layered reading of Aeneas's popular 1444 love story, *De duobus amantibus* ("The Tale of Two Lovers") and the role of letters as literature in John Najemy, *Between Friends: Discourses of Power and Desire in the Machiavelli-Vettori Letters of 1513–1515* (Princeton, N.J.: Princeton University Press, 1993), 33–42.

47 "Nos certe pietati vestre, ut libuerit, et assistere et cooperari pro nostri officii debito minime omittemus." Wolkan, *Briefwechsel*, 68: 579 (Amtliche Schreiben, #7).

48 "Multa cum cesare de hac calamitate rei publice Christiane sum locutus. Invenio mentem ejus bonam, sed impossibile est preclare agere eum, cui desunt facultates. Quod si vestra sanctitas, cui principes auscultant, ad hoc navarit operas, non est mihi dubium, quin furor Turchorum comprimi possit et Christiano populo bene consuli." Wolkan, *Briefwechsel*, 68: 230.

49 *Europe*, tr. Bisaha and Brown, 134.

50 Colin Imber, *Crusade of Varna, 1443–1445* (Aldershot: Ashgate, 2006), 27; Jacques Paviot, "Burgundy and the Crusade," in *Crusading in the Fifteenth Century: Message and Impact* (New York: Palgrave Macmillan, 2004) 73–74. On the impact of Nicopolis on later crusades, see Kelly DeVries, "The Lack of a Western European Military Response to the Ottoman Invasions of Eastern Europe From Nicopolis (1396) to Mohacs (1526)," in *Guns and Men in Medieval Europe 1200–1500* (Aldershot: Ashgate, 2002).

51 For a full description and analysis of the event, see Schwoebel, *Shadow of the Crescent*, 85–91. See also Jacques Paviot, "Burgundy and the Crusade," 73–74.

52 See Alan Ryder, *Alfonso the Magnanimous, King of Aragon, Naples and Sicily, 1396–1458* (Oxford: Clarendon Press, 1990), 304; Setton, *Papacy*, 2: 102.

53 Norman Housley, *The Later Crusades: From Lyons to Alcazar 1274–1580* (Oxford: Oxford University Press, 1992), 454. Housley lays out the complexities and obstacles to planning a large-scale crusade in the mid fifteenth century, such as fundraising, taxation, and intensified local concerns about warfare among neighbors, making a long-term commitment to a distant campaign very difficult; see ibid., chap. 14, for a helpful overview. For a more detailed treatment, see Housley, *Crusading and the Ottoman Threat* (Oxford: Oxford University Press, 2012).

54 "Nunc ad id venio, in quo me vehementer accusas, velut patrie, parentum et amicorum penitus oblitum, qui nolim domum redire. Non sum, Gregorii, ut estimas, meorumque immemor. Dies noctesque dulce solum patrie ante oculos habeo." Wolkan, *Briefwechsel*, 68: 240.

55 "Stulte Christiani principes egerint, nisi furentibus Turchis occurrere studuerint. Germani modo pacati sunt et, si quis eos ad eam rem excitaret, non apti modo sed etiam voluntarii reperirentur." Wolkan, *Briefwechsel*, 68: 241.

56 "Intelligo illa negocia Italica turbata esse, et timeo, ne pacis negocia in fumum eant. Sumus omnes Turchi procuratores et illi viam paramus." Wolkan, *Briefwechsel*, 68: 264.

57 Wolkan, *Briefwechsel*, 68: 244.

58 "Non est, cur ceteras nationes referam. Germania suo regi minime obsequitur. Quid dico Germaniam? Anno proxime decurso Austriam vidimus suo principi rebellantem ... sed neque reges hi sunt, qui vocatu cesaris comparere velint. Nescio, quantum Romani pontificis voces audiant." Wolkan, *Briefwechsel*, 68: 279. For a letter written by Benvoglienti (Nov. 22, 1453) to the Sienese government relating his conversation with Cardinal Isidore of Kiev and his observations of Mehmed II, see Pertusi, *Caduta*, 2: 108–11.

59   "Omnes Turchi procuratores sumus, Maumetho viam omnes preparamus; dum imperare singuli volumus, omnes imperium amittemus." *Maumetho* here could also mean Muhammad the Prophet, and hence, "Islam." Wolkan, *Briefwechsel*, 68: 279.

60   "Hinc rex Alfonsus et Veneti, inde Florentini et Mediolanenses suas injurias prosequuntur." Wolkan, *Briefwechsel*, 68: 279.

61   "Nec enim quicquam levius apud illum esse quam fides traditur." Wolkan, 281.

62   Wolkan, *Briefwechsel*, 68: 282.

63   Wolkan, *Briefwechsel*, 68: 282–83. See also his letters to the Balia of Siena (25 Sept. 1453) and to Cusanus, (Oct. 3) where he worries over the fragile state of the front against the Ottomans in Hungary under the boy king Ladislas, in ibid., 272 and 294–95. He criticizes Venice's appeasement of the Ottomans in another letter to Cusanus (Sept. 30, 1453); ibid., 292. See Jacques Le Goff's insightful comments on some of these letters in *The Birth of Europe*, tr. Janet Lloyd. (Malden, MA: Blackwell, 2005), 186.

64   See Housley, *Later Crusades*, 100–01; Paviot, "Burgundy and the Crusade," 74.

65   "De rebus Turchorum hec scribere possum: nemo est, qui curam ejus rei gerat nisi Romanus pontifex." Wolkan, *Briefwechsel*, 68: 296.

66   Wolkan, *Briefwechsel*, 68: 297.

67   (Late October 1453) Wolkan, *Briefwechsel*, 68: 593–95.

68   "Credo venisse ad vos legatum Caramanni et Carayluchi Turchorum cum litteris apostolicis et imperialibus. Causam illius ut commendatam suscipias opto, quoniam fidei est et Christi gloriam respicit." Wolkan, *Briefwechsel*, 68: 348–49. "Karayluch" is likely Qara Yoluq Osman; see Pius II, *Commentaries*, ed. Margaret Meserve (Cambridge, MA: Harvard University Press, 2018), 3: 487, n. 53.

69   Wolkan, *Briefwechsel*, 68: 359.

70   Franz Babinger, *Mehmed the Conqueror and this Time* (1953; Rev. ed., Princeton: Princeton University Press, 1978), 110.

71   For Meserve's reading of this phenomenon, see *Empires*, 224–29.

72   Meserve, *Empires*, 240–41.

73   "… nunc potissimum divisiones sunt fugiende ac abhominande, quando potentissimi vivifice crucis inimici terra marique bellum adversus nos instruunt Turchi nec contenti subegisse Constantinopolim totum sibi subjiciendum auctumant occidentem summoque conatu nituntur, ut legem Christi evangeliumque subvertant, quod si nos uniti essemus facile superbiam gentis retunderemus illius." Wolkan, *Briefwechsel*, 68: 427.

74   Wolkan, *Briefwechsel*, 68: 603 and 608.

75   Wolkan presents two versions of this letter, which differ in some specifics and in length. *Briefwechsel*, 68: 601.

76   Talal Asad, *Formations of the Secular: Christianity, Islam, Modernity* (Stanford, CA: Stanford University Press, 2003); Nora Fisher Onar, "Turkey in the Post-Ottoman Mediterranean: Transcending the 'West'/'Islam' Binary," in *Mediterranean Frontiers: Borders, Conflict and Memory in a Transnational World*, ed. Dimitar Bechev and Kalypso Nicolaidis (London: I.B. Tauris, 2010), 57–68.

77   See Bisaha, *Creating East and West*, introduction.

78   Randolph Starn, "The European Renaissance," in *Companion to the Worlds of the Renaissance*, ed. Guido Ruggiero (Oxford: Blackwell Publishing, 2002); Linda Darling, "The Renaissance and the Middle East," in *Companion*, ed. Ruggiero.

79   For a recent treatment of these diet orations, particularly that of Frankfurt, see Johannes Helmrath, "Political-Assembly Speeches, German Diets, and Aeneas Sylvius Piccolomini," in *Beyond Reception: Renaissance Humanism and the Transformation of Classical Antiquity*, ed. Patrick Baker, Johannes Helmrath, and Craig Kallendorf (Berlin: De Gruyter, 2019), 71–94.

80 Setton, *Papacy*, 2: 151–57.

81 Pope Nicholas, who was working to promote crusade among Italian powers, was leery of "anything resembling a council"; Setton, *Papacy*, 2: 151. Sending a bishop rather than a cardinal as papal legate was likely a calculated move on Nicholas's part. See "Constantinopolitana clades" of Enea Silvio Piccolomini (15 October 1454, Frankfurt). Edited and translated by Michael von Cotta-Schönberg. 3rd ed.: (Orations of Enea Silvio Piccolomini/Pius II; 19). Ed. and transl. by Michael von Cotta-Schönberg. 2nd ed. 2015. <hal-01097147v3>, 7.

82 Letter to Heinrich Senfleben (May 19, 1454): "Multum nocuit ea novitas Hungarie, que cesarem domi retinuit; magnum enim hic conventum impedivit; nam principes absente imperatore negligentiores sunt." Wolkan, *Briefwechsel*, 68: 480.

83 For a sense of Aeneas's frustrations following the diet of Regensburg, see his letter to Benvoglienti (July 5, 1454), discussed earlier in this chapter.

84 On those tentative plans, see Aeneas's letter to Carvajal, describing agreements, troops, and so on, made at Frankfurt, in *Aeneae Silvii Piccolomini Senensis qui postea fuit Pius II Pont. Max., Opera inedita*, ed. Giuseppe Cugnoni (Rome: Salviucci, 1883), 105–8; see also Setton, *Papacy*, 2: 153.

85 See his letter to the archbishop of Cologne (May 21, 1454), Wolkan, *Briefwechsel*, 68: 488. On the invasion of Serbia, see John V.A. Fine, *Late Medieval Balkans* (Ann Arbor: University of Michigan Press, 1987), 568–69.

86 *Commentaries*, ed. Meserve and Simonetta, 1: 135.

87 On dissemination, see Housley, *Crusading and the Ottoman Threat*, 159–60; Johannes Helmrath, "The German *Reichstage* and the Crusade," in *Crusading in the Fifteenth Century, Message and Impact*, ed. Norman Housley (New York: Palgrave Macmillan, 2004), 62; Meserve, *Empires*, 292, n. 129. Cotta-Schönberg calls Frankfurt "one of the most important and one of the best-known examples of humanist oratory"; "Constantinopolitana clades," 3.

88 Cotta-Schönberg has edited most of Aeneas's orations and provided elegant and faithful English translations via Open Access. Aeneas's diet orations have also been edited in the *Deutsche Reichstagsakten* series.

89 Helmrath, "German Reichstage," 54. Parts of the orations appear judicial in nature with efforts to prosecute the Turks. On genres of rhetorical speeches see Laurent Pernot, *Rhetoric in Antiquity*, tr. W.E. Higgins (Washington, DC: Catholic University of America Press, 2005), 220–21. On deliberative rhetoric, see Heinrich Lausberg, *Handbook of Literary Rhetoric: A Foundation for Literary Study*, ed. David E. Orton and R. Dean Anderson; tr Matthew T. Bliss, Annemiek Jansen, David E. Orton (Leiden: Brill, 1998), 97–102. Caspar Hirschi also notes how deliberative orations often served an epideictic function; see *The Origins of Nationalism: An Alternative History from Ancient Rome to Modern Germany* (Cambridge: Cambridge University Press, 2012), 138.

90 Hirschi, *Origins of Nationalism*, 138; see also Helmrath, "German *Reichstage*," 58, 60.

91 Helmrath, "German *Reichstage*," 54–59. See also Cotta-Schönberg, "Quamvis omnibus" of Enea Silvio Piccolomini (16 May 1454, Regensburg). Ed. and transl. by Michael von Cotta-Schönberg: Orations of Enea Silvio Piccolomini (Pius II) before the pontificate; 16. 2014. <hal-01086738>, 8.

92 It should be noted that earlier and later versions of the same oration contained occasional differences. I note major differences between these versions where it is relevant. (Passages labeled OV = original version, or EV = early version, were written closer to the date of delivery; FV = final version, reflect a later, presumably more edited version.)

93 "Quiescebat Graecorum imperator domi suae apud Constantinopolim .... Nulla ei cum Turchis lis erat." Cotta-Schönberg, "Quamvis omnibus," 28; English tr., 29 [OV].

94 "Virgines ac matronae ea perpetiuntur, quae sunt libita victoribus. Filii in amplexu parentum enecantur, infinitus animarum numerus in captivitatem ac perpetuam servitutem arripitur. Miseram ac lacrimabilem urbis fortunam, omnia plena rapinis, flammis, libidinibus, cruore, cadaveribus vidissetis." Cotta-Schönberg, "Quamvis omnibus," 30; English tr., 31 [OV].

95 "... digna haec scelera suae majestati videntur, digna flagitia, quae vindicemus..." "Quamvis omnibus," ed. Cotta-Schönberg, 34; Eng. Tr., 35 [OV].

96 Walter G. Andrews and Mehmet Kalpaklı, *The Age of Beloveds: Love and the Beloved in Early-Modern Ottoman and European Culture and Society* (Durham: Duke University Press, 2005), 10.

97 "Nec ego hoc magni duco in ipso furore primi introitus trucidatos esse quamplurimos; illud horreo, illud abhominor, illud omnino detestor, capta civitate, depositis armis, conjectis in vincula civibus, tum maxime saevitum est ...." "Constantinopolitana clades," ed. Cotta-Schönberg, 36; Eng. tr. 37 [EV].

98 "... tantisque nunc cladibus Christianum populum affecit, quantis ante hac multis seculis inauditum arbitror." Wolkan, *Briefwechsel*, 68: 212; Eng. tr., *Reject Aeneas*, tr. Izbicki et al., 315, with some changes.

99 See Bisaha, "Reactions to the Fall of Constantinople and the Concept of Human Rights," in *Reconfiguring the Fifteenth-Century Crusade*, ed. Norman Housley (London: Palgrave Macmillan, 2017), 285–324. For a discussion of Ottoman views, see A. Nuri Yurdusev, "Ottoman Concepts of War and Peace in the Classical World," in *Just Wars, Holy Wars, and Jihads: Christian, Jewish, and Muslim Encounters and Exchanges*, ed. Sohail H. Hashmi (Oxford: Oxford University Press, 2012), 190–218.

100 On Albert's brutality toward civilians and clergy, see Thomas A. Brady, *German Histories in Age of Reformations, 1400–1650* (Cambridge: Cambridge University Press, 2009), 95.

101 Bisaha, "Constantinople and the Concept of Human Rights," 293–94; 302. On the Hundred Years War, see contemporary historian Jean Froissart's moving accounts, especially concerning the sack of Limoges (1370). *Chronicles*, tr. and ed. Geoffrey Brererton (London: Penguin Press, 1978), 178–79.

102 Erasmus, writing decades later, was one of the few Europeans who strongly criticized the harshness of warfare among Christians rather than point the finger at the Ottomans; see Bisaha, *Creating East and West*, 174–75.

103 "Fortitudo, inquit Ambrosius in Officiis, quae bello tuetur a barbaris patriam, vel domi defendit infirmos, vel a latronibus socios, plena justitia est." "Constantinopolitana clades," ed. Cotta-Schönberg, 50, Eng. tr., 51 [EV].

104 Meserve, *Empires*, 65.

105 *Opera quae extant omnia* (Basel, 1571), epistle cxxvii, 656–57 (July 5, 1454); See also *Portable Renaissance Reader*, ed. Ross and McLaughlin, 74–78 for a fuller version and freer translation of his letter to Benvoglienti.

106 "Sed dicitis, milites: Quid tu nobis litterarum detrimenta commemoras? Quid nobis et[sic] litteris? Nos hastas gladiosque versamus." "Constantinopolitana clades," ed. Cotta-Schönberg, Latin, 46; Eng. tr., 47 [EV].

107 The source for this story was Cicero, *Pro Archia*, 9, 26; "Constantinopolitana clades," ed, Cotta-Schönberg, 46–49.

108 For a discussion of the relationship and tensions between arms and letters in Renaissance Italy, see John M. Najemy, "Arms and Letters: The Crisis of Courtly Culture in the Wars of Italy," in *Italy and the European Powers: The Impact of War, 1500–1530*, ed. Christine Shaw (Leiden: Brill, 2006), 207–38.

109 "Neque enim, ut plerique arbitrantur, Asiani sunt ab origine Turci, quos vocant Teucros, ex quibus est Romanorum origo, et quibus litterae non essent odio. Scytharum genus est ex media barbaria profectum ...." "Constantinopolitana clades," ed. Cotta-Schönberg, 44, Eng tr., 45. [EV mentions Roman origins; FV does not].

110 "... [gens] libidini servit, crudelitati succumbit, litteras odit, humanitatis studia persequitur." "Constantinopolitana clades," ed. Cotta-Schönberg, 44, Eng. tr., 45 [EV].

111 In the letter to Cusanus, rather than claim the Turks have no learning whatsoever, he states that "they little value the study of letters" and recognizes that they indeed have books, but they are "inept." "... litterarum studia parvi faciunt." Wolkan, *Briefwechsel*, 68: 209; "ut suis ineptiis locum faciant ...." Wolkan, *Briefwechsel*, 68: 210; Eng. tr., *Reject Aeneas*, tr. Izbicki et al., 312, with some changes.

112 *Pro lege Manilia* helped structure Aeneas's oration by providing these three rubrics. See Housley, *Crusading and the Ottoman Threat*, 159–60; Helmrath, "German *Reichstage*," 62; "Constantinopolitana clades," ed. Cotta-Schönberg, 8, 32 [EV]; Pernot, *Rhetoric*, 225.

113 "At mihi seu nova consideranti, seu vetera mente repetenti inter omnes nationes, quas bello idoneas judicant, nulla expeditior, nulla fortior, nulla peritior, nulla audatior quam vestra videtur." "Constantinopolitana clades," ed. Cotta-Schönberg, 82, Eng., tr., 83 [EV]. On the importance of Aeneas's praise of the nobles in his audience as "Germans" years before Conrad Celtis, see Helmrath, "Political-Assembly Speeches," 93.

114 "Vos nati ad arma, illi tracti. Vos armati, illi inermes .... Vos nobiles in bellum ducitis, illi servos aut artifices cogunt .... Canitiem galea premitis, semperque recentes bellorum habere causas cupitis et vivere in armis. Illis picta croco et fulgenti murice vestis desidiaeque cordi sunt; summa voluptas est indulgere choreis." "Constantinopolitana clades," ed. Cotta-Schönberg, 90; Eng., 91 [EV].

115 *Aeneid*, 9, 606–616; "Constantinopolitana clades," ed. Cotta-Schönberg, 91.

116 In reality, both armies included men of all ranks. Peasants and artisans, indeed, comprised much of the Ottoman army, but Aeneas disregards the level of training they received and the discipline for which they were famed. German armies drew fighters from all classes, but the myth of noble dominance in the ranks was probably still strong.

117 See, for example, Erich S. Gruen, "Herodotus and Persia," in *Cultural Identity in the Ancient Mediterranean*, ed. Erich S. Gruen, (Los Angeles: Getty Research Institute, 2011), 71–2.

118 Leonard of Chios, whose report Aeneas read and used, cited the specific number of 15,000 janissaries at Constantinople; *Siege of Constantinople*, tr. Jones, 15. See Marios Philippides, "The Fall of Constantinople 1453: Bishop Leonardo Giustiniani and His Italian Followers," *Viator* 29 (1998): 189–225.

119 "Solus Mahumetus et quos dixi quindecim milia expediti sunt, quos sonus delectat armorum, et animus in bella paratus exhibet audaces. Ceteros inexpertos, timidos, effeminatos nullius pretii judicetis. Quod si manus cum illis conferatis, nihil est, quod de victoria dubitetis, si modo, quam gesturi estis pro Deo pugnam, adversus Deum non convertatis ... cum vos ipsi nihilo minores vestris progenitoribus sitis, cum omnibus his rebus abundetis, quas bello necessarias putant, cum vobis fortissimi milites, peritissimi duces ac satis fortunati sint ...." "Constantinopolitana clades," ed. Cotta-Schönberg, 92; English tr., 93 [EV – same as FV].

120 See *Siege of Constantinople*, tr. Jones, 25. Leonardo's account was written in August of 1453; see Marios Philippides, "*Urbs Capta*: Early 'Sources' on the Fall of Constantinople (1453)," in *Peace and War in Byzantium" Essays in Honor of George T. Dennis, S.J.*, ed. Timothy S. Miller, and John Nesbitt (Washington DC: Catholic University of America Press, 1995), 221–24. Aeneas clearly used Leonardo's account in 1458 when he wrote *Europe*, but the similarities in "Clades," suggest he read it at a much earlier date.

121 "Tanta sanguinis effusio facta, ut rivi cruoris per urbem currerent." Wolkan, *Briefwechsel*, 68: 207. This usage is similar to that of Niccolò Barbaro, a Venetian surgeon who was present at the siege and escaped on a ship fleeing the city; see

Diary of the Siege of Constantinople, ed. and tr. J.R. Jones (New York: Exposition Press, 1969). It also echoes Latin accounts of the crusader conquest of Jerusalem in 1099.

122   "Ajunt, qui presentes fuere, spurcissimum illum Turchorum ducem, sive ut aptius loquar, teterrimam bestiam apud summam aram sancte Sophie propalam videntibus omnibus nobilissimam virginem ac fratrem ejus adolescentem regalis sanguinis constuprasse ac deinde necari jussisse. Hec fiunt et silemus." Wolkan, *Briefwechsel*, 68: 280. The source of such reports was likely Venetian as Aeneas was responding to a letter from Benvoglienti who served as orator for the Sienese Republic in Venice at this time; see also Philippides, *Mehmed II*, 39, and Meserve, *Empires*, 37.

123   "Mahumetus ipse, terribili facie, taetris oculis, horribili voce, crudelibus verbis, nefandis nutibus homicidia mandat … manus in sanguine Christianorum lavat …." "Constantinopolitana clades," ed. Cotta-Schönberg, 38, Eng. tr., 39 [EV]. For other contemporary sources describing Mehmed's violent nature, see Marios Philippides and Walter Hanak, *Cardinal Isidore, c. 1390–1462* (New York: Routledge, 2018), 255–57.

124   One of these people was probably Niccolò Sagundino, discussed below.

125   "… reserabo vobis aliqua de consuetudine et natura hujus hominis, quae mihi per eos nota sunt, qui secum aliquando conversati fuere, ut quid sperandum, quidve timendum sit eo certius habeatis. Est autem Mahumetus adolescens annos natus XXIV, animo truci et gloriae cupido, robusto corpore ac laboris patiente, neque vino neque cenis indulget, et quamvis more gentis libidinosus, non tamen inter uxores ritu paterno languescit, choreas fugitat, unguenta devitat, raro induitur mollibus: non cantu, non sono delinitur, non canes alit, non aves nutrit. Una ei voluptas est arma tractare …. Et quamvis est natura barbarus abhorretque litteras, gesta tamen majorum cupide audit ac Julium Caesarem et Alexandrum magnum omnibus anteponit, quorum illustria facta superare posse confidit atque contendit …. Et quoniam falso prophetae suo Mahumeto, ex quo nomen habet, Constantinopolim subjecit, non dubitat, quin et Romam submittere possit, barbara temeritate et Asiana superbia plenus." "Constantinopolitana clades," ed. Cotta-Schönberg, 106, 108; Eng. tr., 107, 109 [EV].

126   See Andrei Pippidi, *Visions of the Ottoman World in Renaissance Europe* (London: Hurst and Co., 2012), 36–37. Cotta-Schönberg also notes Sagundino as a source for Aeneas's description of Mehmed in the Frankfurt oration; *Constantinopolitana clades*, 107. Philippides agrees that it is "not unreasonable to suppose that Aeneas Sylvius discussed the siege and fall of Constantinople in 1453 with Sekoundinos"; *Mehmed II*, 17. Babinger also notes Sagundino's presence in Alfonso's court in Jan. 1454 and what he reported about his mission to Mehmed; see *Mehmed II*, 494.

127   Giacomo Languschi (writing after April 1454) tells a similar story, but adds that Mehmed was proficient in three languages: Turkish, Greek, and Slavic; see Agostino Pertusi, *Testi inediti e poco noti sulla caduta di Costantinopoli* (Bologna: Pàtron Editore, 1983), 173.

128   Pertusi, *La caduta*, 2: 130–32.

129   To a lesser extent, I also underestimated Mehmed's ability to focus intently on both war and cultural projects. See *Creating East and West*, 73–74.

130   "Constantinopolitana clades," ed. Cotta-Schönberg, 86–87. See Chapter 3 for more expansive views of Aeneas's views of ancient Germans and Romans in his *Germania*.

131   "Constantinopolitana clades," ed. Cotta-Schönberg, 82, 84.

132   "Etenim quamvis est ille, ut ante dixi, ferocissimus et potentissimus hostis, nihil erit inde sua potentia, si Christianorum vires coeant, si Romani potestas imperii concors arma capessat, si nobilissimi Germanorum proceres, potentissimae communitates unanimes cum gloriosissimo principe duce Burgundiae, qui adest,

ad defensionem fidei consurrexerint." "Quamvis omnibus," ed. Cotta-Schönberg, 52; English tr., 53. [FV].

133 It is an imaginative list that includes Charlemagne, who never visited the Holy Land, although some later traditions claimed he had; he also credits emperors like Conrad III and Frederick I and II who did not win substantial victories in the Holy Land.

134 Letter to Cusanus, in *Reject Aeneas*, tr. Izbicki et al., 313; "Moyses vir Dei" of Enea Silvio Piccolomini (24 April 1452, Rome). Ed. and transl. by Michael von Cotta-Schönberg: Orations of Enea Silvio Piccolomini; 14. 2014. <halshs-01064759> "Moyses vir Dei" of Enea Silvio Piccolomini (24 April 1452, Rome), ed. and tr. Michael von Cotta-Schönberg: Orations of Enea Silvio Piccolomini; 14. 2014. <halshs-01064759>, 51. On Petrarch's usage of "Europe" see Bisaha, "Petrarch's Vision of the Muslim and Byzantine East," *Speculum* 76, no. 2 (2001): 289 and 297. Aeneas also mentions this idea in "In hoc florentissimo" (25 February 1455, Wiener Neustadt). Orations of Enea Silvio Piccolomini before the pontificate; 18. Ed. and transl. by Michael von Cotta-Schönberg. 2015. <halshs-01141255v2>, 61.

135 Cotta-Schönberg translated this as "Mehmet," which may be correct. I interpret it here, however, as the prophet Muhammad because of the reference to Spain.

136 "Europae maximam partem amisimus; in angulum nos Maumethus coarctavit: Hinc Hungaros, inde Hispanos premit." "Quamvis omnibus," ed. Cotta-Schönberg, 48; Eng. tr., 49 [OV].

137 "'Cur non ego mihi totum occidentem armis acquiram atque submittam, qui sum Asiae, Thraciae, Macedoniae atque Illyrici dominus et totius Graeciae, quando Alexander ... totum calcavit orientem ... ?'" "Quamvis omnibus," ed. Cotta-Schönberg, 42; Eng. tr., 43 [FV is the same as OV except that FV inserts "atque Illyrici"].

138 "... nunc vero in Europa, id est in patria, in domo propria, in sede nostra per-cussi caesique sumus. Et licet dicat aliquis ante plurimos annos ex Asia Turcos in Graeciam transivisse, Tartaros citra Tanaim in Europa consedisse, Saracenos Herculeo mari trajecto Hispaniae portionem occupasse; numquam tamen aut urbem aut locum amisimus in Europa, qui Constantinopoli possit aequari." "Constantinopolitana clades," ed. Cotta-Schönberg, 22, Eng., tr. 23 [EV], with minor modifications. For a good reading of the Frankfurt oration in relation to the concept of Europe, see Isabella Walser-Bürgler, *Europe and Europeanness in Early Modern Latin Literature: Fuitne Europa tunc unita?* (Leiden: Brilll, 2021), 43–45.

139 "... totius terrae, quae commode colitur, paene centrum ...." "Constanti-nopolitana clades," ed. Cotta-Schönberg, 22; Eng. tr., 23 [EV].

140 In claiming the Germans could fight alone, he refers to the First Crusade leader Godfrey of Bouillon, Duke of Lorraine, whose ethnicity the French could claim as well. "Constantinopolitana clades," ed. Cotta-Schönberg, 97. See also ibid., 95.

141 "Dicat hic fortasse quispiam rem non esse cum Turcis tantum, sed cum Tartaris simul ac Saracenis cumque omnibus gentibus, quas illi subjectas habent. Huic ego contra insto: nec vos soli, Theutones, inquam, pugnabitis. Ex Italia, ex Gallia, ex Hispania multi concurrent, nec Hungari deerunt, nec Bohemi, fortis-simae gentes. Rasciani, Bulgari, omnes Illyrienses, omnes Graeci sumpta occa-sione consurgent. Vicini quoque in Asia dabunt manus. Nolite existimare, principes, ita omnem Asiam Mahumeto parere, ut non multi sint Christo servi-entes: multi in Cilicia, Bithynia, Cappadocia, Ponto, Syria Christiani sunt, qua-mvis jugo servitutis oppressi. Hiberi, qui et Georgiani vocantur, Trapezuntii, Armeni Christum colunt, nec cunctabuntur arma sumere, si vos viderint audentes." "Constantinopolitana clades," ed. Cotta-Schönberg, 94; Eng., tr., 95 [EV].

142 "Veneti quoque et Januenses, potentes populi, quamvis pacem cum Turcis habent, partes tamen vestras classibus adjuvabunt. Coacti namque, ne civitates orientis amitterent, pacem fecere .... Veneti certe fidem imperatori dedere facturos se, quod deceat Christianos, si bellum communi fidelium consilio contra Turcos decernatur. Ego, etsi certe scio, proceres, vobis arma sumentibus ex tota Christianitate affutura praesidia ..."; "Constantinopolitana clades," ed. Cotta-Schönberg, 96; Eng. tr., 97 [EV].

143 On those tentative plans, see Aeneas's letter to Carvajal describing agreements, troops, etc. made at Frankfurt, in Cugnoni, ed. *Opera inedita*, 105–8; see also Setton, *Papacy*, 2: 153.

144 Setton, *Papacy*, 2: 154. Housley calls these deferrals one of the envoys' two "cleverest tricks" at such diets, in *Crusading and the Ottoman Threat*, 79. Regarding Aeneas's pessimism, see his letters to Carvajal, Cusanus, and Goro Lolli, in Cugnoni, *Opera inedita*, 105–116; Housley, *Crusading and the Ottoman Threat*, 160.

145 Cugnoni, *Opera inedita*, 116. Hunyadi's frequent use of the expression of "expelling the Turks from Europe," makes it likely that Aeneas is quoting him here. As stated in Chapter 1, Aeneas seems to have developed an association of this expression with the Hungarians. Preacher and crusade leader Giovanni Capistrano also spoke of Hunyadi expelling the Turks from Europe in a letter to Pope Nicholas V from the Hungarian assembly at Raab (June 21, 1455), in *Annales Minorum*: 12: 292–4, cited in Housley, *Crusading and the Ottoman Threat*, 108.

146 Setton, *Papacy*, 2: 156–57.

147 Setton, *Papacy*, 2: 154.

148 Housley, *Crusading and the Ottoman Threat*, 107–08. It is also important to note that Aeneas urged Capistrano to attend Frankfurt where the preacher spoke as well; ibid., 107. For more on Capistrano's popularity as a preacher in Italy and in the North and Aeneas's role in bringing him to imperial domains, see Ludwig Pastor, *History of the Popes from the Close of the Middle Ages* (London: Kegan Paul, Trench, Trübner, and Co., 1899), 2: 125–30. Cardinal Juan Carvajal also played a central role at the diet of Buda in February, 1456; Setton *Papacy*, 2: 173.

149 Helmrath, "Political-Assembly Speeches," 92–93.

150 "Christianitas nullum habet caput, cui parere omnes velint. Neque summo sacerdoti. Neque Imperatori quae sua sunt dantur. Nulla reverentia, nulla obedientia est. Tanquam ficta nomina, picta capita sint, ita Papam Imperatoremque respicimus. Suum quaeque civitas Regem habet. Tot sunt principes quot domus .... Quis ordo in exercitu erit? Quae disciplina militaris? Quae obedientia? Quis pascet tantum populum? Quis intelliget varias linguas? Quis reget diversos mores? Quis Anglicos amicabit Gallicis? Quis Ianuenses coniunget Arragonensibus? Quis Theutones Ungaris, Bohemisque conciliabit? Si paucos contra Turcos ducis, facile succumbis. Si multos, confundetis." *Opera omnia* (1571), Epistle cxxvii (July 5, 1454), 656–57; Eng. tr., Setton, *Papacy*, 2: 153. See also *Portable Renaissance Reader*, 74–78; and O'Brien, *Commentaries*, 18, for a discussion of the letter.

151 Hirschi, *Origins of Nationalism*, 40–44.

152 Setton, *Papacy*, 2: 157.

153 "In hoc florentissimo" of Enea Silvio Piccolomini (25 February1455, Wiener Neustadt). Orations of Enea Silvio Piccolomini before the pontificate; 18, ed. and tr. Michael von Cotta-Schönberg. 2015. <halshs-01141255v2> Cotta-Schönberg, 11. Aeneas begins the oration by listing these promises, ibid., 23–29.

154 At Frankfurt, religion was discussed lightly and not traditionally, see for example, "Constantinopolitana clades," ed. Cotta-Schönberg, 123–25. Religious motivations did not easily fit with classical *utilitas* arguments.

155 In his *Commentaries*, Aeneas only mentions a different speech made in response to the Hungarian envoys at this diet. In addition, surviving versions do not match the summary that was written by envoys of Nuremberg who attended the diet. Among the internal textual difficulties with the texts, in "In hoc florentissimo" Aeneas refers to audience members like Hunyadi, who was not at the diet—an error he did not later correct. There is also a confusion of the location of the oration in different versions. See "In hoc florentissimo," ed. Cotta-Schönberg, 14–15.

156 R.W. Southern, *Western Views of Islam in the Middle Ages* (Cambridge, MA: Harvard University Press, 1962), 98–103.

157 "Neque enim congregato forti exercitu, delectis peritissimis ducibus, quaesitis utilibus armis, provisis abunde commeatibus, occupato loco pugnandi idoneo, structis prudenter aciebus, commisso viriliter proelio mox victoria datur, nisi victoriarum distributor dominus hoc nos munere donet." "In hoc florentissimo," ed. Cotta-Schönberg, 38; Eng. tr., 39. (Only one version of this oration is cited here).

158 "Et milites igitur vel exercitus et belli duces, quos eligimus, virtutis amatores, osores vitii sint, neque scelerati, quamvis manu prompti et rei militaris periti, ad pugnam recipiantur." "In hoc florentissimo," ed. Cotta-Schönberg, 44, Eng. tr. 45.

159 "Constantinopolitana clades," ed. Cotta-Schönberg, 102–03.

160 For Aeneas's later views of Capistrano, see *Commentaries*, eds. Meserve and Simonetta, 1: 137 where he praises the friar's sermons at Wiener-Neustadt, but not other speakers. His praise in *Europe* was more qualified: "… he got together no small army of crusaders, not from the rich or the nobly born but the penurious and simple common people. The ears of the rich were deaf to the Gospel, and the leaders failed to hear the word of God"; *Europe*, tr. Bisaha and Brown, 101. For a more critical view Capistrano's weakness for vainglory after Belgrade, see ibid., 103.

161 "In hoc florentissimo," ed. Cotta-Schönberg, 46–51.

162 "Expedit ergo pugnantes in primis pios esse atque innocentiae scuto munitos; sic enim Deo grati atque accepti facile victoriam consequentur." "In hoc florentissimo," ed. Cotta-Schönberg, 54; Eng. tr., 55.

163 Setton, *Papacy*, 2: 153.

164 "In hoc florentissimo," ed. Cotta-Schönberg, 46, 47. On Albert Achilles, see Aeneas's *Europe*, tr. Bisaha and Brown, 189–90; Brady, *German Histories*, 95.

165 "In hoc florentissimo," ed. Cotta-Schönberg, 56–63. See also 71 where Aeneas addresses some of the contradictions inherent in his call for humility and bravery at the same time. "Quamvis omnibus" also briefly noted the importance of atoning for past sins; 46–49.

166 "… illa modestissima et pulcherrima virgo, quam vocamus humilitatem …." "In hoc florentissimo," ed. Cotta-Schönberg, 68; Eng. tr., 69.

167 "Cavendum tamen est, ne rapiamus, unde non decet, ne pauperes Graecos atque alios Christianos, qui coacti sub Turcho degunt, suis bonis spoliemus." "In hoc florentissimo," ed. Cotta-Schönberg, 72, Eng. tr., 73.

168 Here again, Aeneas assumes that Christian soldiers treated female noncombatants better than the Ottomans did.

169 "Absit ex nostro exercitu [reading exercitu for exercito] omnis libido, omnis crudelitas, nulli feminae vis inferatur. Pudicitia non modo nostrarum, sed etiam captivarum salva sit. Parta victoria furor armorum cesset. Nemo nisi in acie occidatur. Etenim quamvis sunt Turchi omni malo digni, qui filium Dei abnegant, Jesum Christum, nihil tamen in eos temere ac crudeliter agendum est. Illud curandum omnino existimo, ut Graeci, si vincimus, libertatem sperent, Turchi crudelitatem mortis non timeant, ne desperationem in virtutem vertant." "In hoc florentissimo," ed. Cotta-Schönberg, 76; Eng. tr., 77.

114   *1453–1455*

170 Urban's calls for a violent "cleansing" of the Holy Land, according to some
     accounts of Clermont, may have incited behavior that bordered on genocide in
     the conquest of Jerusalem.
171 Housley, *Crusading and the Ottoman Threat*, 20.
172 Cicero, *Pro lege Manilia*, 14, 42; Virgil, *Aeneid*, 2, 354; Cotta-Schönberg, "In hoc
     florentissimo," 76–77.
173 Housley, *Crusading and the Ottoman Threat*, 20. On Segovia and Cusanus, see
     Southern, *Western Views*, 83–104.
174 The letter to Mehmed II will be discussed in Chapter 4.
175 Southern, *Western Views*, 67.
176 Setton notes Frederick's lack of enthusiasm in *Papacy and Levant* 2: 157;
     Housley aptly describes the two means of escape from actually fielding a cru-
     sade. The first was to "seize on changes in the political landscape as excuses";
     Nicholas's death offered an easy excuse. The second, as mentioned above, was to
     defer to a later diet or council; see *Crusading and the Ottoman Threat*, 79. As a
     counterweight to this, Claudius Sieber-Lehmann cites archival evidence of
     Frederick writing to Swiss confederates in January 1455, requesting specific mil-
     itary contributions to his campaign against the Ottomans. See "An Obscure but
     Powerful Pattern: Crusading, Nationalism and the Swiss Confederation in the
     Late Middle Ages," in Housley, ed., *Crusading in the Fifteenth Century*, 86.
177 Sometimes Aeneas worked several angles in one tract, in an effort to inspire as
     many audience members as possible. Meserve describes his "protean attempts to
     make the crusade seem a compelling endeavor to the wide variety of audiences
     he addressed … embracing the rhetorical principle of *amplificatio*, he could leave
     no argument untried"; *Empires*, 97.
178 In the Wiener-Neustadt oration, he laments the faith being driven into a corner
     of Europe and later states, "The whole of Egypt is ignorant of Christ. The whole
     of Libya is estranged from us. The whole Orient reviles the cross of Christ. This
     we could bear with, if we did not see our own Europe [*nostram Europam*] falling
     into the abyss"; "In hoc florentissimo," ed. Cotta-Schönberg, 118–19.
179 See Bisaha, *Creating East and West*.
180 Tignosi's treatise has not been conclusively dated. Mario Sensi places it between
     1455–1459; see "Niccolò Tignosi dal Foligno, l'opera e il pensiero," *Annali della
     facoltà di lettere e filosofia della Università degli Studi di Perugia* 9 (1971–72):
     378–79. Pertusi dates it before Nov. 1453 without explanation; *Testi inediti e
     poco noti*, 101. It could be either early or very late.
181 Bisaha, *Creating East and West*, 67; Pertusi, *Testi inediti*, 74.
182 Gouwens, "Perceiving the Past," 80.
183 Kritoboulos and Doukas also lament the loss of many books; see Bisaha,
     Creating East and West, 66.
184 "Gens barbara, gens inculta, nullis certis moribus, nullis legibus, sed fusa, vaga,
     arbitraria vivens …." Pertusi, *Testi inediti*, 76; Bisaha, *Creating East and West*, 67.
185 Leonard of Chios, *Siege of Constantinople*, tr. Jones, 34. For the Latin text, see
     Patrologia Graeca 159: 923–41.
186 Henri Vast, ed. *Le Cardinal Bessarion* (Paris: Librairie Hachette et Companie,
     1878), 454.
187 Francesco Filelfo's letters have recently been edited in an excellent 4 volume set
     by Jeroen de Keyser; Filelfo comments briefly on Constantinople and the
     Ottomans, but he does so in several letters, creating a recurring theme. His first
     surviving letter that mentions the siege was written rather late, December 15,
     1453, asking his correspondent, Pietro Tommasi, for news and lamenting the
     "savage barbarism" (*efferata barbaria*) of the Turks. *Collected Letters,
     Epistolarum Libri XLVIII*, ed. Jeroen De Keyser (Alessandria: Edizioni
     dell'Orso: 2015–2017): 2: 570–71. Other letters written after this also seek news

or recommend Greek refugees, bleakly referencing their loss of property, family, and in some cases, freedom; they seem to have found an advocate in him.

188 George of Trebizond tried for years to obtain an audience with Mehmed in the hopes of converting him, using their mutual interest in Aristotelian philosophy as an enticement. See John Monfasani, *George of Trebizond: A Biography and a Study of his Rhetoric and Logic* (Leiden: E.J. Brill, 1976).

189 Doukas, *Decline and Fall*, 187–88.

190 This fascinating letter, dated March 11, 1454 can be found in DeKeyser, *Collected Letters*, 2: 587–89.

191 Quirini, Letter to Nicholas V (July 15, 1453) in "Epistole storiche," ed. Agostino Pertusi, *Lauro Quirini umanista*, eds. Konrad Krautter, Paul Oskar Kristeller, Agostino Pertusi, Giorgio Ravegnani. Helmut Roob, Carlo Seno (Florence: Leo S. Olschki Editore, 1977), 229.

192 Bisaha, "European Cross-Cultural Contexts Before Copernicus," in *Before Copernicus: The Cultures and Contexts of Scientific Learning in the Fifteenth Century*, ed. Rivka Feldhay and F. Jamil Ragep (Montreal: McGill University Press, 2017), 40–41.

193 "... moribusque dicatur antiquorum studet historiis et illorum facinora cum admiratur se Alexandrum macedonem superaturum extimat et Cesarem, Octaviumque imitaturus firmissimum credit se posse toto orbe potiri." Sensi, "Niccolo Tignosi," 426. See also Philippides and Hanak, *Cardinal Isidore*, 256–57.

194 This may be too strong an interpretation, but Isidore describes Mehmed as both reading and being read to; Philippides and Hanak, *Cardinal Isidore*, 207, 253. Sagundino portrays him as a reader, as does Quirini.

195 See Kritovoulos, *History of Mehmed*, tr. Riggs, ix; Monfasani, *George of Trebizond*.

196 More broadly, one should note the crucial role Islamic scholars played in the preservation of ancient Greek texts and their return to Western Europe by way of Muslim Spain and Sicily. It is hard to imagine the medieval university without this essential body of work and the learned commentaries these scholars provided.

197 See Sally Ragep and Jamil Ragep's articles in *Beyond Copernicus*.

198 See for instance Antonio Beccadelli (Panormita) writing to Alfonso of Naples on April 1, 1454, in James Hankins, "Renaissance Crusaders: Humanist Crusade Literature in the Age of Mehmed II," *Dumbarton Oaks Papers* 49 (1995): 179–80; and Donato Acciaiuoli writing to Greek refugee and scholar John Argyropoulos on August 6, 1454; Bisaha, *Creating East and West*, 72.

199 As will be discussed in Chapters 3 and 4, Pius more freely applied "barbarian" and "barbaric" to other Europeans.

200 Filelfo, Biondo, and Cretan humanist George of Trebizond used the term in this context before 1453. See Bisaha, *Creating East and West*, 78–87, on uses of "Europe" in 1453 and following. Leonardo Benvoglienti, for example, wrote a missive to Siena from Venice (Nov. 22, 1453) mentioning hopes of driving them from Europe as expressed by Isidore of Kiev; see Pertusi, *Caduta*, vol. 2: 111.

201 Sensi, "Niccolò Tignosi," 424.

202 Letter to Nicholas V, in *Lauro Quirini umanista*, 229.

203 Bisaha, *Creating East and West*, 85–86; Hankins, "Renaissance Crusaders," 179–86.

204 Suzanne Conklin Akbari, *Idols in the East: European Representations of Islam and the Orient, 1100–1450* (Ithaca: Cornell University Press, 2009), 3, 19.

205 See Kritovoulos, *History of Mehmed*, 82; Doukas, *Decline and Fall*, 231. Andrews and Kalpaklı, *Age of Beloveds*. 1–9, provide interesting insights into this question and how we choose to read the sources.

206 For a discussion of the many views of Mehmed, see John Freely, *The Grand Turk: Sultan Mehmet II—Conqueror of Constantinople and Master of an Empire* (New York: Overlook Press, 2009).

207 Thank you to Bogac Ergene for his help with this question. See also Harris, *Constantinople*, 194.

208 Kritovoulos, *History of Mehmed*, 93–94, 104–05. For numbers and other information on the swift repopulation of the city, see Niccola dell Tuccia's account in Pertusi, *Testi inediti*, 98–99; Gilles Veinstein, "The Great Turk and Europe," in *Europe and the Islamic World: A History*, ed. John Tolan, Gilles Veinstein, and Henry Laurens (Princeton: Princeton University Press, 2013), 132.

209 Mehrdad Kia, *Daily Life in the Ottoman Empire* (Santa Barbara: Greenwood Press, 2011), 77–78; Boyar and Fleet, *Social History of Ottoman Istanbul*, 26 ff. On the settlement of different religious groups into quarters or *mahalles*, see Kia, *Daily Life*, 71–73.

210 Kia, *Daily Life*, 80.

211 Kia, *Daily Life*, 71.

212 Heath W. Lowry, "The 'Soup Muslims' of the Ottoman Balkans: Was There a 'Western' and 'Eastern' Ottoman Empire?" in *Beyond Dominant Paradigms in Ottoman and Middle Eastern/North African Studies: A Tribute to Rifa'at Abou-El-Haj*, eds. Donald Quataert and Baki Tezcan (Istanbul: ISAM, 2010), 97–133.

213 Cemal Kafadar, "The Ottomans and Europe," in *Handbook of European History 1400–1600*, vol. 1, eds. Thomas A. Brady, Jr., Heiko A. Oberman, James D. Tracy (Leiden: Brill, 1994), 616.

214 Kafadar, "Ottomans and Europe," 598–600, 615–16.

215 Bisaha, "Reactions to the Fall of Constantinople," in *Routledge Handbook of Christian-Muslim Relations*, ed. David Thomas (New York: Routledge, 2017) 219–26. An older, but still useful summary of Italian reactions to 1453 is Nicolai Rubenstein's essay, "Italy," in *The Fall of Constantinople*, ed. Steven Runciman et al. (London: School of Oriental and African Studies, 1955), 25–32.

216 Veinstein, "The Great Turk and Europe,"184.

217 Veinstein, "The Great Turk and Europe," 184–85.

218 Mohamad Tavakoli-Targhi, "Orientalism's Genesis Amnesia," *Comparative Studies of South Asia, Africa and the Middle East* vol. XVI, no. 1 (1996): 1.

219 Cemal Kafadar, "A Death in Venice (1575): Anatolian Muslim Merchants Trading in the Serenissima," in *Merchant Networks in the Early Modern World*, ed. Sanjay Subrahmanyam (Aldershot: Variorum, 1996), 97–124.

220 Nabil Matar, *Europe Through Arab Eyes, 1578–1727* (New York: Columbia University Press, 2009). Tavakoli-Targhi argues this as well for the early modern period in Persia; see "Orientalism's Genesis Amnesia."

221 This attitude can be seen in Aeneas's *Dialogus de somnio* (1453–1457). Rolando Montecalvo dates it to December 1453 and sees it as decisively marking Aeneas's embrace of papalism. The fall of Constantinople does not factor into Montecalvo's equation, but I see it as instrumental; see "Between Empire and Papacy: Aeneas Silvius and German Regional Historiography (PhD diss., University of California, Berkeley, 2000), 18; and 94 ff.

222 Norman Housley, *Religious Warfare in Europe, 1400–1536* (Oxford: Oxford University Press, 2002), 131.

3 "The German Cardinal" at the Roman Curia

In December 1456, after two decades of service as an underappreciated secretary in the cold, gray North, Aeneas achieved his dream of returning to Italy and winning a cardinal's cap. Over the years he had written to friends and family about his longing to see them and his homeland (*patria*) with its beautiful countryside, speaking at times of his life in Germany as "exile."[1] And yet, despite being comfortably ensconced in Rome as a prominent member of the papal court, he felt a little out of sorts. When Aeneas shared the news of his elevation with Emperor Frederick, he wrote,

> So long as there is breath in my body, I will try to conduct myself in such a way that all may know this honor came from your favor and your court, and that I am a German rather than an Italian cardinal.[2]

Clearly, his time in Germany and Austria had changed Aeneas; after some sixteen months in his homeland, broadly speaking, he still did not feel like an Italian cleric.[3] It suggests a view of his own cultural identity as both fluid and measurable. His claim to be a German rather than an Italian, and his implied expertise in both cultures, offer a telling glimpse into his mindset just before a period of intense intellectual activity that would produce three lengthy works dealing with ethnicity, nationhood, and continental community.

The speed with which Aeneas wrote these three works is astonishing. The *Germania* was produced in late 1457 or early 1458; *Europe* and *The History of Bohemia* appeared a few months later. For once, his gout served him well as two separate attacks in 1458 forced him to retire first to bed in Rome and then to the baths of Viterbo to recuperate—and to write. Aeneas's unwillingness to simply rest is a further testament to the thoughts that swirled in his brain. In the dedication letter of *Europe*, he joked,

> It would have been worthwhile, I confess, to compose a history of events from the beginning of our era up until the present, as I have often intended. But that project would have required more than a single attack of gout ....[4]

DOI: 10.4324/9781003315865-4

These periods of extended convalescence enabled him to address the questions that had haunted him since 1453. Hence, this was no mere interlude before his papacy, as many scholars have treated it. It was a critical phase in which his concerns about the Ottoman advance, divisions within Christendom, and his recent reading on geography and territoriality all coalesced to form a more coherent vision of Europe and its nation states.

Aeneas's First Weeks in Rome

The death of Pope Nicholas V (March 24, 1455) may have halted Aeneas's mounting hopes of crusade, but it gave him a much-needed break from the imperial court. Although Aeneas believed in early 1453 that being in Germany made him more useful to the papal curia, by mid-1455 it was clear that nothing could compel the phlegmatic Frederick to take meaningful action. As seen in his missives to the pope, the emperor repeatedly looked to the holy father to take the lead and was likely relieved by the excuse for yet another delay.[5] In the words of Cecilia Ady, "Sad, weary, and disappointed, [Aeneas] realized, perhaps for the first time, the limitations of that 'goddess of persuasion' in whom he had put his trust."[6] When Cardinal Alfonso Borja (or Borgia) was elected pope, taking the name Calixtus III, Aeneas was appointed imperial ambassador, and his fortunes began to change. The future with Calixtus, a reclusive Spanish prelate whom Aeneas barely knew, was uncertain, but it provided a change of scenery. As it turned out, Aeneas would never cross the Alps again.[7]

Life in Rome in the mid fifteenth century must have been jarring to Aeneas after years in more modern cities of the North and witnessing the splendors of Siena and Florence. Once the seat of the glorious Roman Empire, the city had changed tremendously since ancient times owing to wars, fires, depopulation, and neglect. The vast area contained many open spaces and unexcavated ruins. Its broken monuments still lay partially buried under layers of soil and vegetation, with names that revealed nothing of their glorious past: the Roman Forum was called "Campo Vaccino" (cow field) and the Tarpeian Rock on the Capitoline Hill was known as "Monte Caprino" for the goats that roamed there. Only one ancient aqueduct still functioned, and not consistently.[8] Antiquarians like Flavio Biondo and Leon Battista Alberti called for the preservation of ancient buildings, but even kindred spirits like popes Nicholas and, later, Pius, despoiled their marble for new projects.[9] Meanwhile, humanists from Petrarch onward contemplated what remained visible and tried to map the city; Biondo's efforts to catalogue its ruins in his *Roma instaurata* (1446) was especially important to Aeneas and many others.[10] It must have provoked both wonder and unspeakable sadness for humanists to be surrounded by such sights and history.

Much of the damage to Rome was more recent than the sacks of the fifth century and the changes that followed. The territory around the city suffered greatly during the papacy's move to Avignon, the Schism, and the wars that took place during this period. Local barons did nothing to support agriculture and the livelihood of farmers—their rivalries and recent wars had ruined farmland. Both barons and popes turned to cattle and sheep raising, and the region was marshy, unhealthy, underdeveloped, underpopulated, and prone to brigandage. Within the city, feudal families (especially the Colonna and Orsini) wielded great power and influence while others engaged in general lawlessness and conspiracies.[11] The humbler city dwellers, moreover, had little or no political representation or sense of civic unity; the local economy was largely based on catering to the curia and pilgrims. The most profitable businesses, such as banking, were dominated by foreigners like the Florentines.[12]

In addition, the city badly needed some modern planning and fresh building. In 1455, most of the palaces, fountains, and squares that one associates with Renaissance Rome had not yet been constructed. These changes would have to wait until the reigns of Sixtus IV (1471–84) and sixteenth-century popes. As Charles Stinger notes, while other cities in Northern and Central Italy had built strong governments and taken steps to centralize urban planning, improve the water supply, and regulate buildings, Rome was "two centuries behind."[13] Some parts of Rome, however, were undergoing a transition when Aeneas arrived. Pope Nicholas had made the important decision to move the papacy's headquarters from St. John Lateran to the Vatican and proceeded to add new buildings and wings to that area.[14] He also laid the groundwork for the massive Vatican library collection, if not the building itself. In any case, Aeneas does not appear to have spent much time assessing recent building plans; his mind was more focused on war.

The election of Calixtus (April 8, 1455) brought new energy to the crusade front.[15] With a record of promoting church unity and a strong relationship with Alfonso of Aragon and Naples, Calixtus seemed poised to coordinate crusade resources and designate the king as its commander. His number one goal as pope was to turn back the Ottoman advance.[16] When Aeneas arrived in Rome on August 10, 1456, with fellow ambassador Johann Hinderbach, he received a warm reception from Calixtus—even though he ignored Aeneas's requests from Frederick regarding tithes, nominations of bishops, and clerical taxes. The power dynamic had clearly changed since 1447, when Aeneas last negotiated with a pontiff on the emperor's behalf. The Council of Basel was now over, and Frederick had recently endured a revolt; given the circumstances, Aeneas thought it best to offer the emperor's obedience without delay.[17] Whether Aeneas made any effort at all to carry out these wishes is unclear, as later sources suggest he was already a papalist.[18] Either way, Aeneas's failure on the German agenda gravely disappointed a significant faction in the empire, led by Archbishop Jakob von Sierck of Trier, who hoped for fulfillment of their pacts with Eugenius and greater independence from Rome.[19] It is hard to imagine anyone from this camp in the Holy Roman Empire calling Aeneas "the German bishop" at this juncture.

The public speech Aeneas delivered to Calixtus was far more successful than his private negotiations. Delivered on August 13, 1455, *Solent plerique* became one of his most popular orations.[20] It strikes many of the same rhetorical notes as the diet speeches and addresses the role that both emperor and pope should play to promote crusade and bring needed order to Europe. The emphasis, as expected, is on the pope: "All peoples are willing and ready to take up arms for the Christian faith. But they have all turned their eyes onto you; and they all expect that order and planning should come from you."[21] While Aeneas expounds enthusiastically on the excellence of the Roman Empire, the virtues and resources of the German people, and the House of Austria, Frederick all but fades into the background. When he does speak of the emperor, Aeneas does not lie: no great warrior appears, but rather a man of peace, justice, and piety. His greatest qualification for Calixtus's crusade seems to be his Portuguese wife, who offers a link to the pope and King Alfonso.[22] Finally, rather than boast of Frederick's potential contribution, Aeneas disposes of him by stating that he would privately apprise the pope of Frederick's activities and reveal "by what maneuvers the expedition against the Turks has been held up this year." Aeneas makes no public effort to defend his inaction.[23]

Aeneas likely reveled in the opportunity to show his expertise and advise the pope; more than half of the oration focuses directly on crusade and the Ottomans. He made two specific recommendations: the first was to fulfill Nicholas's promise of a fleet, without which there could be no hope of raising ground troops in Germany.[24] The second was to boldly suggest that the pope "stand up [and] open the coffers of the Church," in addition to offering the usual spiritual rewards to participants.[25] In terms of regional focus, Aeneas urges Calixtus to attend to Hungary. The Hungarians alone had been fighting the Turks who threatened all of Christendom for many years. They were the wall, bulwark, and shield of the Christian religion (*murus; antemurale; clipeus*), but they desperately needed help.

Unlike the diet orations, his focus in *Solent plerique* is geopolitical, with arguments that are surprisingly subtle. The greatest threat that the Turks posed, according to this oration, was not suffering and annihilation, but the assurance of a reasonable surrender—especially in Hungary. Aeneas relates how Hungarian legates at the diets of Frankfurt and Wiener-Neustadt had warned the Germans,

> if they [the Hungarians] are deserted by us, they will accept the conditions which the Turks might offer. If they can have no hope of victory, then they do not intend to commit their cities and fields to the fire, their wives and daughters to the brothel, and their own and their sons' heads to the sword of the enemies.[26]

Here, Aeneas shows surprising empathy for rulers who capitulated to the Turks when fellow Christians would not come to their aid—even though such actions put Central Europe in great peril.

A few paragraphs later, Aeneas considers the plight of the common people even more closely:

> Moreover, many taxes, much extortion of money, many robberies burden the Christian people, and many are the abuses carried out by our princes, not to say tyrants, against their subjects. Therefore, I greatly fear that

when the Turk comes and lightens the burdens on our peoples, they will willingly submit, especially if he grants freedom of faith—for he is a clever enemy.[27]

This is an unusual example of Aeneas placing the Turks in a positive light, arguing that they could be fairer rulers than Christian princes. The Ottoman practice of allowing freedom of worship, moreover, complicates the classic "enemies of the faith" characterization. It shows that Aeneas was familiar with the Ottomans' style of rule and aware that much of their success resulted from strategic accommodations and varying degrees of suzerainty and autonomy—not simply unrelenting war and intimidation.[28] It is a striking portrait of peace and productivity.

This brief moment of nuance, however, soon gives way to the black and white rhetoric of "Europe," "Christianity," and "the West" that one expects from Aeneas:

> The Gospel of the Savior which he proclaimed to the whole world now is heard by Europe alone, and not by all of it. In the West we are under pressure from the Saracens; a large part of the North has been invaded by blind pagans; the Turks have thrown us out from the East that stretches into Greece. Unless we are vigilant, unless we stand up, unless God helps us, unless your Holiness bravely confronts him, as you have begun to, Mehmed will soon occupy your throne and whatever remains of Christianity for he seems already and without any resistance to be lord of sea and land.[29]

With a rough sketch of the continent, Aeneas portrays the Europeans, the only true adherents to the Gospel, being threatened on every front by non-Christians. He reinforces this image later when he urges the pope on Frederick's behalf to "endeavor to make the Christian powers keep peace between themselves, turn their weapons against the infidels, and chase the common enemy out of Europe."[30] As in his diet orations, Aeneas strives to portray the Turks as an alien force to be ejected from a continent that should belong only to indigenous Christians.

And yet, in his effort to motivate European Christians to stand together, Aeneas is forced to reveal the fragility, if not the outright fantasy, of that bond. Echoing his July 1454 letter to Benvoglienti and harking back to some imagined sense of prior unity that might be recovered, he laments:

> Everybody is his own emperor and pope. *Many heads, many minds* [Cicero]. *The wavering crowd is torn into opposing factions* [Virgil]. Germany is disturbed by a thousand conflicts. Between France and England the old hate is still fresh. Ambition sows enmity among the kings in Spain. Italy that had been brought to peace with great effort is now shaken by new turmoil, and in Siena new fires are flaring up. So, how can we hope? Our own ways make us the agents of Muhammad.[31]

Aeneas's awareness of the tensions between the local agendas of burgeoning nation states and the centralized Church is acute, but so is his desire to downplay those divisions as a temporary aberration.[32]

This oration is, indeed, more complicated than others. It undermines the images of the Turks as a threat to Christianity and the embodiment of barbarism by showing their effective government and hands-off policies. In fact, Aeneas altogether avoids the term "barbarian" in this oration. The Ottomans appear as both a danger and an example of successful coexistence. Without intending to, Aeneas comes close to portraying the Turks as a legitimate European power, while clinging to the notion that they were *not* part of Europe and could be excised and ejected. Like today's staunch critics of Muslim immigration in Europe and the United States, Aeneas does not define the exact source of his fears: whether the Ottoman threat was more political, cultural, or religious in nature remains deliberately vague. The geographical boundary between the Ottomans and Europe that Aeneas began to draw in 1453 stays intact, but he appears less convinced of its solidity.

Calixtus's Crusade and Aeneas's Elevation to the Cardinalate

Calixtus was already at work on crusade by the time Aeneas arrived in Rome. The pope published a crusade bull on May 15 and was sending preachers across Europe to enlist recruits, sell indulgences, and collect tithes to help fund the campaign. With the eastern Mediterranean and Hungary at risk, time was of the essence. In September 1455, at his own expense, Calixtus placed Archbishop Pietro Urrea of Tarragona, Antonio Olzina, and Antonio de Frescobaldi in charge of a small fleet of ships to assist Christian islands in the Aegean Sea. In December he appointed Cardinal Lodovico Scarampo as captain general of the fleet and ordered the construction of sixteen vessels on the shores of the Tiber.[33] Calixtus also worked to raise an army and funds to defend Hungary, sending Cardinal Juan Carvajal as his legate to Austria and Buda in the fall of 1455 to help arrange a Hungarian diet for the purpose of planning a crusade.[34] Furthermore, unlike Nicholas V, who spent large sums on the arts and learning, Calixtus channeled money toward this pious undertaking by selling off papal jewels, gold salt cellars, and precious book bindings to help fund his fleet.[35] Aeneas learned much about the difficulties and expense of crusade by watching efforts to collect tithes around Europe and extract promises from Christian rulers and governments, not to mention the processions and prayers that Calixtus required of the faithful.[36] Despite Calixtus's willingness to liquidate papal treasures, he could not fund a fleet or army large enough to do more than temporarily slow the Ottoman advance.[37] A much larger effort was needed, and one imagines Calixtus was pleased by Aeneas's oration and his very presence in Rome.

After all of Frederick's postponements and excuses, it must have been exhilarating for Aeneas to witness such decisive action. Despite Calixtus's advanced age of seventy-seven and his frequent bouts of illness, Aeneas described him in both his *Europe* and *Commentaries* as declaring war and making preparations without delay: "No sooner had he risen to the summit of the papacy than he turned his mind toward destroying the religion and race of the Turks and made a solemn vow to that effect."[38] Aeneas, for his part, shared the pope's firm commitment to crusade and stood out as one of the rare individuals who comprehended the logistics and had connections with rulers throughout Europe.[39] In addition, Aeneas and Calixtus both struggled with illnesses that frequently laid them up—in some ways, they were kindred spirits.[40]

In this environment, so different from that of the imperial court, Aeneas thought he would soon be named a cardinal. But Calixtus dashed these hopes in December of 1455 when he elevated three men in their twenties instead—a prince of Portugal and two nephews, one of whom, Rodrigo Borgia, would go on to become the scandalous Pope Alexander VI.[41] Scholars have differing views of the extent of Calixtus's nepotism and preference for Spaniards at the papal court, but it clearly bothered Aeneas.[42] Between his delay in entering the clergy and his declining health, he must have felt that the window was closing each time new cardinals were created and he was not among them.

Luckily for Aeneas, an opportunity to prove his worth arose in early 1456 just as he was preparing to return to Germany. While visiting his episcopal see in Siena, the government asked him to negotiate a peace with the condottiere Niccolò Piccinino, who was threatening their territory with the tacit support of King Alfonso. After securing the pope's permission, Aeneas traveled to Naples, where Alfonso—whom he had previously met during Frederick's journey to Italy—warmly received him. Aeneas spent several months in Naples, enjoying the company of humanists and artists at the glittering court and traveling to local sites of interest including the ruins of Baiae, Cumae, and Nola as well as the cities of Salerno and Amalfi—adding to his arsenal of geographical knowledge.[43] Negotiating with Alfonso was delicate work, but Aeneas's success in orchestrating a peace greatly increased his value with the pope.

The mood in Rome was brighter when Aeneas returned in late 1456. In addition to the peace he just brokered in Italy, news had arrived that a small Christian army at Belgrade led by Hunyadi, Carvajal, and Capistrano had triumphed over a large Ottoman force commanded by Mehmed himself on July 22.[44] Calixtus, elated by reports about Belgrade, and pleased with Aeneas's role in restoring peace in central Italy, rewarded him a few months later with the cardinal's cap on Dec. 18, 1456.[45] As the newly appointed Cardinal of Santa Sabina, Aeneas achieved a long-cherished dream. He quickly dispatched a host of letters to his connections across Europe, informing them of his elevation and his hope that they would continue to work together for their mutual benefit and for the good of Christendom.[46] Among the recipients and senders were Emperor Frederick and his wife Eleanora, Alfonso of Naples, Cardinal Nicholas of Cusa, Archbishop Dietrich of Mainz, and chancellor of Florence Poggio Bracciolini. That Aeneas took the time to write to each of these individuals and many more, within days of his elevation, demonstrates the continued importance of these connections; it was in one of these letters (to Frederick) that he called himself "a German cardinal."[47] He sought to maintain his friendships with less powerful men, too, often in touching personal ways, as is seen in his consolation letter to Henry Rožmberk on the death of his son and in his letters to other humanists.[48] One thing is certain: Aeneas's new position in Rome did not lessen the worth of his international ties.

In the twenty months that he was a cardinal, Aeneas had three main concerns. One was to consolidate his position among the other cardinals, who had the power to elect him pope at a future date. Whereas most cardinals used their wealth to offer favors and gifts among their cohort and to position themselves as generous patrons, Aeneas relied on his charm and wit. He befriended many of the cardinals, including Rodrigo, the talented but impetuous nephew of the pope.[49] A second area of pressing concern was the growing tension between German prelates and the papacy over papal tithes, taxes, and the reservation of local benefices for papal secretaries and cardinals (Aeneas received three such German churches). These matters were discussed at the diet at Frankfurt in March 1457, and many in Rome feared the situation might explode into another Pragmatic Sanction of Bourges.[50] Aeneas did not go to Germany at this time, but he instructed papal legate Lorenzo Roverella on the matter. He also drafted Calixtus's brief on this issue, strongly defending Rome's prerogatives and emphasizing the dire need for crusade against the Ottomans.[51] The "German cardinal" certainly worked to keep the peace, but he did little to advocate for his adopted countrymen. Aeneas's third goal, crusade, outweighed all other concerns and diminished his patience for German complaints.

From his vantage point in Rome, Aeneas helped coordinate Calixtus's plans to build a coalition grounded in trust between the participants. For a time, the prospect of a crusade was very bright. Between Calixtus's concerted efforts and the victory at Belgrade, anything seemed possible. But general John Hunyadi's death of plague shortly after the battle left the future of the movement in the balance; Capistrano, too, succumbed to plague after Belgrade, creating a vacuum in both spiritual and military leadership. Nonetheless, Calixtus continued the fight by supporting the efforts of Balkan rulers like Skanderbeg of Albania and Stephen of Bosnia; he also allowed Castilians to receive remission of sins for their battles against the Moors, seeing it as part of the larger struggle and a means to encourage those fighting the Turks.[52] The results of these initiatives were mixed. In Burgundy, phony preachers collected tithe money for themselves, and Calixtus was pressured to lower their expected contribution from a tenth of their annual income to a hundredth while dealing with the problem; this would happen under Pius's pontificate as well. The curia also faced ongoing problems managing finances, the misbehavior of their captains and legates, and the expectations of central actors in the leagues. The failure of fifteenth-century crusading, as Housley and Weber have shown, owed less to apathy or insincerity than a host of complicated dynamics such as these.[53]

A key objective for Calixtus and his new cardinal after Hunyadi's death was to find someone willing to lead the crusade. On March 8, 1457, Aeneas wrote to Emperor Frederick III about the plans for an expedition against the Turks, arguing that there was nothing more suitable to his name and authority as emperor than to fight in defense of the Catholic faith.[54] He wrote a similar letter to Alfonso of Naples on March 27, noting the preparations against the Turks in Hungary, which had stalled after the death of both Hunyadi and Capistrano. While the pope continued to urge the Germans and Hungarians in letters and messages, Aeneas tried to entice Alfonso to step forward:

> I will have no great hope unless I see your Highness with a furnished fleet, on the stern of that great and memorable ship, armed and giving the signal of departure against the Turks. For the remaining princes of the world, even if they have the will, they lack the means to invade Greece. If your Highness has the will, nothing will be lacking ....[55]

Clearly for Aeneas, getting a crusade off the ground mattered far more than the question of its leadership—almost anyone would do—but it was hard to find leaders whose enthusiasm matched that of lower-born volunteers.[56] From where Aeneas and Calixtus sat in Rome, they could not understand why so few leaders wished to build on the victory at Belgrade.[57] Perhaps to these Christian rulers, the Turks posed a lesser threat than their own subjects or neighboring Christians who might seize the opportunity to attack in their absence.

Importantly, while leaders made excuses to delay a campaign, none of them rejected the notion that they were part of the same common fabric—be it Christendom, Europe, the West or all three. The Peace of Lodi (1454), while imperfect, had some long-term unforeseen benefits such as the increase in embassies and the cultivation of diplomacy in Italy and beyond—crusade was one of many factors fostering cooperation.[58] Contributions toward crusade in the form of tithes indicate a widespread concern and commitment to the protection of Christendom.[59] Hence, in some measurable ways, the Ottoman threat was being used to promote a set of common goals, even an embryonic notion of unity among European states. But the parameters of that community still needed definition. That is where Aeneas was so important.

Through his rhetoric, Aeneas drew geographical borders around notions of Christian community and clarified who was included or excluded. A good example from this period can be found in his letter to Alfonso of Naples (Apr. 7, 1457), where he reports rumors of a great Muslim alliance with the Soldan of Egypt, the Karaman of Cilicia, and the Tartars of Scythia heading toward Hungary and Belgrade. He nonetheless believed that the Christian people (*Christiani populi*) could prepare a strong defense and calls upon Alfonso to inspire the other princes of Europe (*Europae principes*).[60] This rumor is not repeated in other letters, but it echoes earlier ones from mid-1453, showing Aeneas's tendency to view the Ottoman advance as part of a larger clash of religions and possibly "civilizations." The reality, of course, was much messier, but Aeneas's simplistic evocation had a powerful clarity.[61] Similarly, Antonio Beccadelli (Panormita), a humanist from Palermo serving as Alfonso's secretary, also found this rhetoric to be useful, making references to the princes of Europe, Europe and Asia, the West, and various terms for Christendom in his letters from 1455–1458—possibly echoing Aeneas's usages.[62]

Just as he did in Basel and Austria, Aeneas continued to use letters as a vehicle for news. But he did not just convey the news; he filtered and revised it—affecting not only the way many of his contemporaries viewed current events, but which stories received attention. Sometimes the assortment of news was random, but as Aeneas became more attached to the project of crusade, his comments tended to revolve around two things: tensions between Christians and the movements of the Ottoman Turks. Hence, his selective reports of the news created a sharply focused picture of his concerns while maintaining a façade of secretarial objectivity.[63] The prominence of these themes in his letters show that Aeneas's fears and obsession with the Ottoman advance had not abated. Yet he repeatedly rose above his cynicism and looked for ways to motivate fellow Christians, especially their leaders. Indeed, interest in crusade was widespread, with recruits and money being raised as far away as Denmark during the reigns of Nicholas, Calixtus, and Pius.[64] Despite the vacuum in leadership after Belgrade, contemporaries report that a great many peasants and nobles in central Europe and beyond were moved to take the cross by local preachers and papal exhortations, swelling young Ladislas Postumus's army to 44,000. These troops assembled at Belgrade in early 1457, but they were disbanded after the murder of Ulrich, Count of Cilli by Hunyadi's son, Laszlo.[65] What all this shows is that, even after Hunyadi's death, recruiting rank and file crusaders was easier than finding consensus among the leaders.

Despite these setbacks, the teenaged Ladislas Postumus was a beacon of hope for both Calixtus and Aeneas; with him lay the future of a united Central and Eastern Europe. Descended from two generations of crusaders, Ladislas stood at the epicenter of the Turkish advance and was finally coming of age to take the reins of power.[66] After years of struggles that began with his father's death before he was born, Ladislas inherited the crowns of both Hungary and Bohemia, and the duchy of Austria. He reached the age of seventeen in February 1457, enabling him to rule these lands more directly. During this time, Aeneas, the pope, and other crusade advocates sought to persuade him to face the Ottoman threat head on. A handful of letters were written by Aeneas in Calixtus's name.[67] One such missive from Calixtus to Ladislas (Oct. 20, 1457), which was later printed in Aeneas's *Opera omnia*, urges the young king to join with other Christian princes and the pope to fight the Ottomans.

Tellingly, this letter mentions "Europe" three times. Twice, Aeneas uses it to evoke an ominous, existential threat, depicting "Christian Europe" in danger of being overrun by the Turks and lamenting the atrocities and losses to religion and learning that have already been sustained. He then warns that the Turks threaten to subject "all of Europe" to themselves and to destroy their law and the Gospels. But Aeneas offers a hopeful vision of the continent as well, affirming that if Christian princes work together, they will "soon expel the Turks from Greece and snatch all of Europe from their jaws."[68] They could even go on to reclaim the Holy Land. This letter, which may be an embellished later version, reflects Aeneas's usual rhetoric on the Ottomans and crusade, but in one respect it is weightier: it becomes a geopolitical defense of European territory and a reclamation of what had been seized by the Ottomans.[69] The fragile position of Hungary made Aeneas's anxiety and hopes about borders more pronounced. It was both the frontier that had to be protected at all costs and the staging ground from which a crusade army might break the Ottoman hold in Europe. Given Hunyadi's penchant for "Europe" in his letters and speeches, Aeneas likely chose words that would move a Hungarian audience.

Yet both Calixtus and Aeneas knew the hurdles Ladislas faced in bringing unity to Central and Eastern Europe: internal rivalries in Hungary and Austria; disagreements with Emperor Frederick, Ladislas's former guardian; and the Hussite heresy in Bohemia. Another letter dictated by Calixtus and addressed to Cardinal Carvajal (Oct. 1, 1457) shows the pope's consternation over unresolved tensions regarding the inheritance of Ulrich of Cilli, the powerful feudal overlord whose domain included parts of Austria and Slovenia. It also conveys the pope's regrets about the "internal wars" waged between princes in the "Christian Republic" when external wars against the Turks threatened (*intestina bella; externa* [*bella*]).[70] He takes comfort, however, in the knowledge that Ladislas would soon marry the daughter of King Charles VII of France and urged Carvajal to use the occasion of the wedding to speak to the illustrious guests, including the dukes of Bavaria and Saxony and the king of Poland, about the "defense of our religion against the attacks of the Turks."[71] Aeneas penned his own letter to Carvajal on the same day, urging him to hasten the wedding arrangements in order to stabilize defenses. With an alliance between Hungary and France—two kingdoms with honorable crusading traditions—Aeneas was optimistic that they would work together to fight the Turks.[72] Sadly for Calixtus and Aeneas, none of this came to pass as Ladislas died before his wedding on Nov. 23, 1457.[73]

New Approaches to Identity, History, and Geography: *Germania, De Europa*, and *Historia Bohemica*

Despite the calamities of late 1457 to early 1458—the death of Ladislas, rising German hostility toward the papacy, and two serious bouts of personal illness—Aeneas entered a period of remarkable productivity as a writer. A confluence of events that would have thrown others into despair mysteriously energized him. In the span of nine months, he appears to have written nonstop, producing three lengthy tracts that innovatively explored both the identities and histories of European peoples and their relationship to place. With his *Germania, Europe*, and *History of Bohemia*, Aeneas helped transform the scale on which Renaissance (and later) thinkers wrote history: from this point on, histories of a people, a country, or a continent would become increasingly common.

In some ways, this shift in Aeneas's conception of history began in 1453 with the fall of Constantinople. After this date, he could no longer imagine individuals in isolation from their broader context or homeland. His struggles between 1455 and 1458 to write a history of Frederick III—with three attempted versions, which ultimately morphed into a history of Austria before he abandoned the unfinished work—bear witness to this changed worldview.[74] His new life as a cardinal also enabled him to write history in a whole new way. First, his very position in Rome—a hub for news, petitions, and plans that affected all of Christian Europe—gave him both a better view of all of Europe and critical distance from Germany, Austria, and Bohemia. Second, it was also in Rome in this period that Aeneas gained full access for the first time to influential ancient ethnographic and geographic works by Tacitus, Strabo, and Ptolemy. I contend that these aspects of his cardinalate and the ideas he had been ruminating on since 1453 all coalesced to inspire Aeneas's trifecta of bold new texts.

Most monographs on Aeneas comment briefly on these works in their hurry to get to his election as pope in August of 1458—a serious oversight in my opinion, given the way that this period shaped Aeneas's geopolitical views.[75] These three works reflect both years of personal observations and his recent study of ancient ethnography, but more importantly, they offer a mature commentary on individual states and cultural-linguistic groups, i.e., "nations," and their relation to Europe and Christendom. The remainder of this chapter will explore major themes that mark the three works—discussing the works in tandem so that the connections will be clear. Other scholars have treated these works separately, which is reasonable for biographies, articles, or editions, but this study seeks to understand the powerful vision that was taking shape in Aeneas's mind. To set the stage for this discussion, each work requires a brief introduction.

Aeneas's extraordinary and complex *Germania* was first conceived with a very simple goal: to respond to complaints about Rome's disregard for Germanic ecclesiastical prerogatives—particularly a letter from an old friend, Martin Mayer, chancellor of the Archbishop of Mainz, dated September 1, 1457.[76] Some of Mayer's criticisms directly targeted Aeneas. Mayer accused the Roman curia of stealing church offices and income from the Germans after Aeneas received three major benefices from Calixtus in the dioceses of Trier, Cologne, and Mainz: "Our once great [German] nation," Mayer laments, is "… now reduced to poverty, become a handmaiden and tributary, and lying in squalor." German leaders, he adds, "have resolved to regain their ancient liberty."[77] Provoked by this letter and rising discontent in the empire, Aeneas decided to educate the Germans on the history and current state of their nation in his influential *De ritu, situ, moribus et conditione Germaniae descriptione*, or more simply, the *Germania*.[78] The work begins in antiquity and ends in his day, showing the Germans' trajectory and present greatness.

Written in late 1457 to early 1458 (book 3 ends with the date February 1, 1458), it represents Aeneas's first major effort to grapple with a nation's origins and current circumstances. In the long run, it produced the opposite of Aeneas's intended effect: instead of inspiring humility, gratitude to the Roman Church, and unreserved support for crusade among the Germans, his work fed burgeoning nationalist sentiments.[79]

While earlier writers in the Holy Roman Empire had evoked a sense of a "German" cultural, and even political identity, Aeneas's repeated and pointed use of "German nation" is unusual among texts in this period.[80] He appears to be one of the earliest thinkers to speak so powerfully to the Germans about their shared identity. Within decades, the *Germania* was printed and read by Conrad Celtis, Jakob Wimpfeling, and Martin Luther among others.[81] Hence, what began, at least in part, as a response to an ecclesiastical complaint became much more in the end. As Johannes Helmrath states, Aeneas "became the foremost foreign expert on Germany of his time."[82]

No sooner had he finished writing *Germania* than Aeneas began to think bigger. During the season of Lent in 1458, bedridden with gout pains, he drafted *De Europa* or *Europe*. According to his dedication letter to Cardinal Antonio de la Cerda, the project offered a way to pass the time and an opportunity to expand on a brief (now lost) account of the deeds of recent Holy Roman Emperors. The result, he states, was an expansive look at "the many great achievements within the Christian world from the time when Frederick received power to this day."[83] But while the beginning of Frederick's reign (1440) provides a rough starting point, this is neither a history of Frederick, the empire, nor even Christendom, which extended well into Africa and Asia. Aeneas's intention, he notes in his preface, was to record "the most memorable deeds accomplished among *the Europeans* [emphasis mine] and islanders who are counted as Christian during the reign of Emperor Frederick III" with some material from earlier periods when it suits.[84] Early manuscripts and print versions use the designation *Deeds during the reign of Frederick III* (*De gestis sub Federico III*), but *Europe* soon became the preferred title, one assumes, because it was more accurate.[85] Perhaps one of the attractions of the title "Europe" for copyists, printers, and readers was its relative neutrality: it offered a collective without a clear secular or religious leader.[86] Despite its popularity, *Europe* defies categorization. It cannot be grouped with medieval universal histories, chronicles of towns or events, or ancient geographical treatises, although it has elements of each genre.[87] It was a unique examination of the recent history of the continent and an effort to capture the spirit of contemporary European society.

Three months later, Aeneas found yet another block of time to write while convalescing from his chronic illness. Few diseases say "Renaissance" quite like the gout—at least among elite men of the period. Cardinal de la Cerda suffered from the same ailment: it provided one man the time to read and the other, the time to compose. Aeneas joked with him in his dedication: "The gout loves my residence[88] and no sooner departs than it happily returns." Perhaps when it did, he mused, he would expand on his *Europe*.[89] But when this next attack came in June of that year, Aeneas started a brand-new project in between his curative baths at Viterbo to the north of Rome.

Bohemia and its new king were very much on his mind. His hopes for cooperation between Rome and George Podiebrad, elected in 1458 to succeed Ladislas Postumus, had all but evaporated. As Aeneas was still adding finishing touches to *Europe*, he decided to put his expertise on Bohemia and the Hussites to use by writing his lengthy *Historia Bohemica*, or *History of Bohemia*.[90] Drawing on his years of experience with Bohemia among other sources, he composed the work in a matter of weeks and dedicated it to his friend and celebrated patron of the arts, King Alfonso of Naples.[91] Far more ambitious than his *Germania*, it seeks to tell the story of the Bohemians from their mythical founder, Czechius, to their present day and draws heavily on Czech authors like Papousek of Sobeslav.[92] The speed of this composition came at a price, however: scholars have found countless errors in the work. However, as Montecalvo has argued, the very concept of the *History of Bohemia* changed the way contemporaries wrote about the past: it represents the first humanist territorial or regional history (a *Landesgeschichte*) outside of Italy, and it would influence trends in historical writing that focused on a large region over time and attempted tell the story of its "people."[93] Having introduced these three works, the following sections will address central themes they all share.

Ethnicity and the Concept of Nation

The city of Rome brought many new associates and friends into Aeneas's orbit. It also offered an introduction or deeper acquaintance of a different kind: the writings of three ancient authors whose world views would affect his own: Tacitus, Strabo, and Ptolemy. Their texts were, indeed, only just beginning to circulate in Western Europe again. After lying dormant and forgotten in a monastic library for centuries, Tacitus's now famous *Germania* (98 CE) was rediscovered and came to Rome in 1455 thanks to manuscript hunters who scoured neglected and disordered collections in the days before card catalogs, descriptive titles on spines, or tables of contents.[94] Two works by Strabo (63 BCE–23 CE) and Ptolemy (100–170 CE), both titled *Geography*, also recently became accessible to scholars like Aeneas with little or no knowledge of Greek—Strabo through the translations of Guarino da Verona and Gregorio Tifernate, and Ptolemy, through the work of Jacopo d'Angelo. All of these Latin works were available to Aeneas in Rome, and he took full advantage of that access.[95]

Tacitus is, in some ways, the most surprising of all these inspirations. What value could this first-century writer who never set foot in Germany offer to a man who lived there some fourteen centuries later? Tacitus's information was either second or third hand or gleaned from written texts. His "Germany," moreover, predated both the Holy Roman Empire and the arrival of Christianity in the region—it was nothing like the fifteenth-century version Aeneas knew so well. Ironically, these factors may have only increased

Tacitus's value to Aeneas as an ancient, respected author: they lent Tacitus's text simplicity, clarity of vision, and a veneer of objectivity. For Aeneas, Tacitus not only swept away the dizzying variety of regional differences and layers of complicated history, but in doing so, he reduced the Germans to their "essence" as a people.

Of critical importance here, is Aeneas's belief that this essence transcended many centuries and linked ancient Germanic tribes to modern-day inhabitants of Germany; in other words, he believed that they were the *same people*. This was an interpretive leap that no one seems to have made before Aeneas, but others, especially German thinkers, would thereafter accept.[96] Aeneas's insistence on ethnic continuity provided a detour around the intense rivalries that divided the empire along provincial lines and turned urban centers against princely control. It also enabled Aeneas to seamlessly fold all Germans into "Christendom" and downplay the strong resistance that many individuals in the empire posed to the papacy. In short, Tacitus's *Germania* provided an almost blank slate on which Aeneas could inscribe his hopes and desires.

In terms of methodology, what Aeneas lacked until that point and found in Tacitus, Strabo, and Pliny were the language and concepts of ancient ethnography and geography. To appreciate the impact of these ancient works on Aeneas's worldview, one need only compare his cardinalate writings to his earlier ones. His previous attempts at history were narrow and topical, focusing on an event, like the Council of Basel in his two histories (1440 and 1450), or on individuals divorced from their regional context, like the short entries of his *On Famous Men* (1445–50).[97] Both of these approaches were typical of their time—chroniclers and historians in the medieval and Renaissance periods, with very few exceptions, described a moment, a city, a ruler, illustrious men, or, conversely, the world, in so-called universal histories that began with Adam and Eve and continued up to the writer or compiler's day.[98] Aeneas's earlier remarks on countries or regions followed similar lines. His claims about the honor of the German "nation" in his *Pentalogus* (1443) and his praise of German bravery and martial prowess in his oration at Frankfurt (1454) suggest an early, if passing and undeveloped, curiosity about ethnic identity. By contrast, in 1457–1458, with the help of ancient authors, Aeneas turned his lens on the "people" of Germany and Bohemia and the "peoples" who made up the continent of Europe.

Book II of Aeneas's *Germania* was his first attempt to apply the tools of ancient ethnography. In the hope of persuading Germans that their connection to the Church and Rome improved rather than impoverished them, he describes the region's fertile landscape and thriving cities and the accomplishments of its brave and industrious inhabitants. Present-day Germany, he asserts, far surpasses the land of their ancient ancestors in size, power, beauty, and prosperity. With little regard for current provincial borders, he moves from city to city, describing magnificent churches and palaces, comfortable homes, impressive bridges, and spotless streets. The canal city of Strasbourg is healthier and more pleasant than Venice; Prague is the equal of Florence in size and beauty.[99] At one point, he opines,

... if you compare nation to nation, there is no reason to place Italian cities before German ones. The appearance of Germany has a certain freshness, and its cities seem as if they were put together and built just days ago.[100]

Speaking of Nuremberg, he praises its splendor and elegance, adding for good measure that "the kings of Scotland would desire to live as well as the middling citizens of Nuremberg."[101]

What is perhaps most striking is the assumption that all of these cities, despite their differences, are distinctly "German," and that they contain some essential quality that enables them to be lumped together as one. The entire region flourishes, it seems, without exception: "it is clear that your nation is not destitute, for paupers cannot build magnificently."[102] The producers of this wealth are the bustling businessmen and merchants of these cities as well as the gold and silver mines in the region, like Rammelsberg and Meissen. Metals are so abundant, he adds, that every inn uses metal plates and cups.[103] Compared to his description of Italian cities, Germans are more industrious and progressive in their pursuit of wealth. But in contrast to this picture of urban sophistication and productivity is Aeneas's more traditional portrait of German princes and citizens as inherently warlike:

> Boys who are born in Germany learn to ride before they learn to speak; they cling, affixed, to the saddles of galloping horses, carrying the longer lances of lords. Hardened by heat and cold, they are not overcome by any labor.[104]

Despite the stereotypical and exaggerated quality of this claim, it is interesting that Aeneas does not oversimplify "Germans" as having only one sort of character, skill, or set of interests. Perhaps he envied their facility with arms and combat and compared it to his own lack of training in this area and the declining military interests of his countrymen.

The rapid pace and colorful descriptions of Aeneas's sweeping narrative, however, have overshadowed the most innovative aspect of this work: its very premise. In order to convince the Saxons, Bavarians, Austrians, and others that all "Germans" were better off than ever before, he had to persuade at least some of them to *think of themselves as Germans*. He does this not only by repeated use of the words Germany (*Germania*) and Germanic (*Germanica*) in the work, but a through host of subtler terms that connote their relationship to one another as a collective.[105] While setting forth the extent of German accomplishments and control over Europe, he states:

> Your nation [*natio*] is larger than it ever was and so great that it is inferior to no people, and it can rightly claim that there is no race [*gens*] so lofty as to have gods waiting upon it as closely as our Lord God stands by the German people [*populo*].[106]

As *natio, gens,* and *populus* suggest above, Latin terms (and their interpretations by ancient ethnographers) offered an array of choices to convey ideas of a people, a nation, or a state.

Natio, meaning "people, race, nation, or nationality,"[107] did not generally signify a "state" as it does today, but rather a group of people with common cultural traits and usually one shared language. *Natio* in the European Middle Ages could denote collective origins of foreign students at universities, but at times it also took on a political meaning. Patrick Geary and Caspar Hirschi have analyzed such usages and the messages behind them in early Greek and Roman ethnographic works and found that Romans generally referred to themselves as a *populus,* connoting a constitutional state bound by laws, whereas *gens* and *natio,* when applied to foreign peoples, suggest a "natural" people, connected by common ancestry, language, and customs—a society they inhabit by accident of birth rather than choice or effort. To the Romans, members of the *gens* and *natio* were often peoples without history.[108] These are not unwavering distinctions, and all of these terms could be interchanged.[109] Certain patterns do emerge, however, with the term "nation" having a more negative connation for ancient Roman and early Christian writers. St. Jerome helped set this trend in the Christian era by using terms like *populus Christianus* versus pagan *nationes* in his translation of the Bible into Latin.[110]

Yet, in Aeneas's *Germania* there is little sense of *natio* as derogatory. In addition to Tacitus's positive outlook on the German nation, Aeneas was also exposed to "nations" as representative groups at the Council of Basel and nations at universities.[111] In any case, the term *natio* was useful as it enabled Aeneas to speak of "Germans" as a broad, geographically imprecise group who inhabited an expanse of Europe that was at times larger or smaller than the Holy Roman Empire; the common denominators were language and culture, although he sometimes included peoples like the Bohemians, because they were part of the empire, or Dutch and Flemish towns like Ghent and others, which, he states, "appear to be under Gallic rule, [but] their speech and ways are Germanic."[112] Between Aeneas's articulations of "German nation" and "Germany," and the spread of Tacitus's text, these terms started to rise in usage among Germans themselves.[113]

Aeneas's use of *natio* to describe other groups in *Europe* is also instructive. For example, when discussing the history of Hungary, he moves quickly over previous inhabitants of the region, in order to come to its most decisive moment: "Finally the nation [*natio*] of Hungarians flooded in from the farthest reaches of Scythia. They have held sway until this day and exercise sovereignty far and wide on both sides of the Danube."[114] Used here, the word seems to connote both a people and a legitimate state. For Aeneas and other fifteenth-century thinkers, "nation" had become a more productive concept.[115]

The situation is less clear for Aeneas's use of *gens,* generally translated as "race" or "people." I believe that Aeneas often gravitated toward this term when he wished to avoid describing a collective group as a legitimate state.[116] For example, in *Europe* when discussing Transylvania, he asserts,

> The region of Transylvania is situated beyond the Danube and was once inhabited by the Dacians—a fierce people (*populi*) famous for many defeats inflicted on the Romans. It is inhabited in our time by three races (*gentes*): the Germans, the Székelys, and Vlachs.[117]

None of these "races" rise to the level of a *populus*, but perhaps, when combined, they did. But if Aeneas occasionally referred to a European people as a *gens*, when it came to the Ottoman Turks, his use of *gens* rarely wavers, making it seem a deliberate choice.[118] Was he reluctant to accept the Ottomans as a *populus* like the Roman Empire? To most modern observers, the parallels between these two powerful, multiethnic empires are clear, but for Aeneas, it appears unthinkable. Calling Mehmed emperor (*imperator*) on rare occasions was as far has he seemed willing to venture. Even the troublesome Bohemians, whose heretical embrace of Hussitism put them in tension with the rest of Latin Christendom, were described by Aeneas in an oration to Calixtus as both *gens* and *populus*, and their land was a kingdom (*regnum*).[119]

I want to be clear that there is no hard and fast rule that applies in all cases to Aeneas's usage of *populus, natio, or gens*, but it was a tendency that suggests comparison and ranking of the societies he describes along a continuum: sophistication and legality on one end and haphazard raw power on the other. Regardless of his word choice, Aeneas's attraction to the ancient Romans' division of the world into "us" and "them," with the latter camp being the barbarians, is clear.[120] He may have shifted the boundaries of the broader self to welcome in many of the ancient barbarians, but he, like other humanists, still needed a modern version to exist on some level. As Constantine Cavafy aptly put it in his famous 1904 poem, "Waiting for the Barbarians," "They were, those people, a kind of solution."[121]

While Aeneas took inspiration from ancient writers on concepts of identity and ethnography, the way he applied these notions to the past was rather more innovative. By focusing on *groups* rather than individuals or dynasties, Aeneas gave these peoples, and not just their rulers, a history. Few writers before him viewed nations or peoples as having a valid and chartable historical past in the way that Aeneas did. It was one thing to briefly praise the "race of Franks" while calling for crusade or to note a people as the subjects of a king (as in Rex Anglorum), but it was another to focus one's lens on a people and their history over a period of time.[122] The implications of such usages, of course, are rarely neutral. Discussions of a people, especially a "race," have led to troubling biological and exclusionary constructs. Tacitus's works have been blamed for influencing dangerous racial theories, particularly Nazi views on the supposed "purity" of Germanic blood.[123] Did Tacitus have a similar impact on Aeneas?

At times, Aeneas seems to hint at a biological notion of race: his previouslymentioned description in *Europe* of the inhabitants of Transylvania, the Germans, the Székelys, and Vlachs, as three presumably distinct races (*gentes*) comes to mind.[124] Also in *Europe*, Aeneas describes a riot in the Hungarian city of Székesfehervár that erupted after a German-born judge (*iudex natione*

Theutonicus) condemned a Hungarian man to death, which led to the indiscriminate slaughter of many Germans in the city; this was on account, Aeneas asserts, of the hatred the Hungarians bore toward "the German race" (*theutonicum nomen*).[125] Given the feeling of separation and occasional enmity between some of these groups, one might infer a belief that distinct ethnic groups did not intermix.

Aeneas's stance is a bit more complicated. While he tends to describe modern peoples as the descendants of ancient folk by the same name, he makes none of Tacitus's claims about purity of blood. In fact, he only explicitly evokes bloodline in regard to dynasties.[126] Oftentimes, his application of a group name to a region is generally to show which group "holds sway"—or dominates the region politically, linguistically, and culturally—without suggesting that they in any way eradicated the people who lived there before them. A passage from *Germania* on the growth of German territories conveys the ambiguity of the meaning of "race" (*gens*):

> Therefore, let us compare the old with the new and first speak of size. The Danube and the Rhine, which formerly enclosed the boundaries of Germany, now glide through the middle of German lands. The region of Belgium, which previously comprised a third of Gaul, has now for the most part yielded to Germany, being Teutonic in language and customs. And also the Swiss, once a Gallic race [*gens*], have been transformed into Germans.[127]

"A Gallic race … transformed into Germans" is a fascinating phrase. In fairness, I cannot say what exact meaning Aeneas had in mind: did these regions become "German" by accepting German rule, or were they were already Germanic in character, thereby facilitating the shift in suzerainty? Either way, the quote strongly suggests that he defined "race" by characteristics that could be learned or acquired rather than a set of biologically inherent markers.

Perhaps most telling of all is where Aeneas situates himself and his own identity. When describing "Italy"—as illusory a concept as "Germany" at this time—he most often uses the term *patria* or homeland/fatherland; when describing Germany, he uses *natio*, suggesting a comparative sense of personal distance from the region. Yet, when in Rome, his sense of belonging to Germany was palpable; recall how he described himself on several occasions as "German" or "the German cardinal."[128] Similarly, in his letter to Martin Mayer that preceded the *Germania*, he wrote "We came to Germany in the flower of our youth; we were at the council of Basel for many years and we did not conduct ourselves otherwise than if we had been born and brought up in that province."[129] Had Aeneas come to identify so strongly with German culture and society, or was this simply a rhetorical move on his part to highlight his expertise in an area few cardinals possessed? To some extent, I would imagine both held true, but his descriptions of himself as alternately German or Italian suggest a fluid concept of ethnicity or even "race." Importantly, his use of the term *gerere* (to conduct oneself) implies action and choice as components of identity.

This Land Is My Land. That Land Is Your Land: Ethnicity, Territory, and Sovereignty

Aeneas's encounters with Strabo and Ptolemy were just as important as his reading of Tacitus. Their geographies of Europe described natural borders, topography, and human settlements, enabling Aeneas to imagine the size, shape, and location of states and to ponder how these variables shaped their fortunes and relations with neighbors. Both Strabo and Ptolemy's works, of course, offered little guidance on fifteenth-century political boundaries, but for Aeneas, they presented a host of possibilities. They enabled him to explore the connection between land, human society, and the customs and values that transcended the reign of any king or dynasty. With their help, he sketched the topography of the Holy Roman Empire in *Germania* and that of Bohemia in his history of the nation, but the geographical component was especially pronounced in *Europe*. Aeneas introduces nearly every region and country in *Europe* by its natural borders and features; the approach only falls away toward the end, especially in his lengthy section on Italy—either because that section originated as a separate piece, or as because he drew more heavily on a different set of sources as he hurried to finish the text.[130]

The dominance of geography in *Europe*, however, was not just an exercise in imitation; it emanated from Aeneas's newfound desire to comprehend the extent of each state's political reach. Where did one polity end and another begin? Were the boundaries firm or contested? As one would expect, this recent focus on geography created a domino effect. His reflections on any given nation or state prompted musings on others, as well as the larger problem of how they all somehow fit together as "Europe" or "Christendom." Hirschi's "external design principle" again proves useful in explaining Aeneas's thought process: in order to construct the idea of one nation, its neighbors needed to be simultaneously constructed as well, leading to the creation of "not only one, but of several nations." In other words, constant juxtaposition was (and is) necessary to create a self-image in a world of nation-states.[131]

The ultimate border for Aeneas, of course, was the imaginary line that separated Europe from Asia—a subject of intense interest to him after July 1453. Some portions of this line were easier to draw than others: Constantinople and everything west of the Bosphorus and the Hellespont were clearly European, as Aeneas strongly claimed in 1453 and following—as if Anatolia, for centuries a seamless part of the Roman Empire and Byzantium, were an ocean away from Thrace instead of less than one mile in some places. Still, there was a certain logic to the use of waterways as dividers between continents or countries, not to mention mountain ranges and deserts; for centuries, natural boundaries made for easy demarcations. The line between Europe and Asia became less clear north of the Black Sea. For reasons that will be discussed in the next section, Aeneas did not view Russia in any way as part of Europe; it is not even mentioned in *Europe*. Hence, he drew his borders in this case according to his own definitions of religious and political affiliation rather than an imaginary line between North and South or a set of natural boundaries. His rationale on the northern borders, while persuasive to many, was less influential than his insistence on the otherworldliness of Asia Minor.

If the eastern borders of Christian Europe looked vulnerable to outside threats in 1453, by late 1457, both Eastern and Central Europe looked ready to implode from internal stresses resulting from the death of Ladislas Postumus, the king of Hungary and Bohemia. While his brief reign offered a possible counterweight to both the Ottoman advance from without and the Hussite challenge from within, his premature death unleashed new insecurities. Would the internal borders between Central and Eastern European countries hold? This confluence of modern geopolitical change and ancient geographical knowledge made these questions seem urgent in 1457–1458.

This leads to the question of territory and sovereignty: how did Aeneas conceive and define a given area, and how was it connected to the people who ruled or lived there? A look at Aeneas's varied terms for place offers a useful beginning. The words that Aeneas employs most often in *Europe* for a geographical area or territory were *terra* (land or country), *regio* (region), *provincia* (province), *patria* (native land or fatherland), and sometimes *regnum*, (kingdom). But in a way that appears to extend the usage of ancient writers, Aeneas sometimes blurred the distinction between people and land, using *gens* or *natio* to connote place. For example, in *Europe*, he describes the central Balkans as "the Illyrian races/nations, which look toward the west and the north."[132] This usage (*illirice gentes*) is interesting because it conveys both a people and settled territory within set coordinates. Similarly, in *Germania*, in an effort to show how much Rome improved the Germans' fortunes, he uses *natio* to designate both a people and their territory:

> Such was your Germany until emperor Hadrian ... under that emperor, however, the entire German nation [*Germanica natio*] came under the rule of the Romans .... Then, having become milder, it accepted a refined culture. And then it was much narrower and shorter than it is now, since the whole of Germany was closed in on all sides, stretching from west to east between the Rhine and the Elbe ... and from the Danube in the south to the Britannic Ocean and the so-called Baltic Sea in the north...[133]

So much is contained in the word *natio* here: it is a people who, in his eyes, go from barbarism to civility, and a stretch of land or state that grows from "narrow and small" to the bulk of central Europe. For a number of possible reasons, he less frequently applied *natio* to Italy.[134] Regardless of the terms he used, one sees a strong link between history and geography in Aeneas's imagination.

So, Aeneas sees a connection between land and people somewhat similar to the model of national thought that would become popular in France.[135] One cannot, of course, describe Aeneas's loosely formed, premodern views as "nationalism." Aeneas's world lacked several of the distinctly modern components of nationalism, among them industrialization, criticism of monarchy, and the circulation of media such as newspapers and novels. These conditions, as Benedict Anderson put it, enable the nation to claim a sense of "deep, horizontal comradeship."[136] Other hallmarks of nationalism like increased travel and the rise of vernacular languages may apply in lesser degrees to premodern eras like the Renaissance in Europe, but forcing aspects of Aeneas's world into the mold of nationalism obscures the richness of the fifteenth-century context and Aeneas's way of describing it. Nonetheless, with a slight adjustment to Hirschi's terminology, one can find more than a hint of "nationalist thought" in Aeneas's works.[137]

Medievalist Patrick Geary has examined nations with an eye toward the differences and similarities between premodern eras and our own. He describes two broadly defined theories of national identity: 1) as a fluid concept, in which the state is a product of multiple migrations, influences, and changes over time; or 2) as a static notion of a founding and "true" origin, described as "primary acquisition." Primary acquisition suggests that an area became the state that is today through one crucial period of migration or conquest, rendering any subsequent migrations, invasions, or political absorptions by external powers illegitimate.[138] Both of these concepts are hotly debated today as modern states face questions about immigration, multiculturalism, and ethnic and religious identity. It is no accident that nationalists and nativists largely favor the "primary acquisition" theory, as it allows them to argue for an exclusive definition of citizenship and a justification for annexation or separation.[139] Aeneas, at any rate, seems to have a foot in each of these conceptual camps, viewing the nation as fluid or static at different times.

Some moments in Aeneas's works from this period suggest a static notion of nationhood. In his histories of Bohemia and Austria, as Montecalvo has argued, Aeneas projects a belief that territorial history "ought to begin ... with the point in time when it was first occupied by the ethnic group that inhabited it in the author's present."[140] In his *History of Bohemia, when* Aeneas describes the arrival of the legendary ancestral leader of the Czechs, a man known as Czechius, he states that Germans had previously settled in the area and were presumably displaced by the Slavic newcomers. Far from condemning this displacement, he describes the Bohemians cultivating the harsh land, unlike the pastoralist Germans, which, by settler-colonialist logic, gave the Bohemians a greater claim to it.[141]

Like his previously mentioned view of the Hungarians, the arrival of the Bohemians and their development of the area made them its new rulers; centuries of habitation and shifts in language and culture seemingly transformed it even more into their homeland. Given this connection, Aeneas's language about the Hungarian plain in *Europe* deserves a second look. He describes the ancient peoples who successively inhabited Pannonia like the Gepids and the Dacians, the Romans, the Huns, and the Lombards. But the key moment that seems like "primary acquisition" occurs when "finally the race/nation [*natio*] of Hungarians flooded in from the farthest reaches of Scythia. They have held sway until this day and exercise sovereignty far and wide on both sides of the Danube."[142]

Most striking about this passage is what Aeneas does *not* say: he shows no consternation at the loss of Roman power in the region nor is the arrival of Hungarians—from Scythia, no less—portrayed as a barbaric incursion, unless one reads into his use of the word "flooded." Moreover, Aeneas rejects the classical name Pannonia for modern Hungary because the rule of the Hungarians extends well beyond this region, and presumably, because the Hungarian people's dominance over the region gives them the right to name it.[143] Then there is his chapter on "the Illyrian nations" (*illirice gentes*) in *Europe*. While Aeneas uses the classical term Illyria to describe this broad swathe of the Northwestern Balkans, he is well aware that the population had changed and was now more Slavic—a result of migrations beginning in the sixth century CE: "In our time," he states, "we refer to this race of people [*genus hominum*] as Slavs. Some are called Bosnians, some Dalmatians, others Croatians, Istrians, and Carnians."[144] Such rhetoric bears a resemblance to imperialist narratives in modern times that erase the ongoing participation and impact of indigenous peoples.

While these pronouncements on Bohemia, Hungary, Illyria, and other places suggest that Aeneas subscribed to the "primary acquisition" view of national identity, other aspects of his works from 1457–1458 demonstrate a more fluid definition. For one thing, he does not profess strong views about ethnic purity within regions and states in Europe. Several of the areas Aeneas describes—without condemnation or praise—show mixed populations and languages. Recall his statement in *Europe* on Transylvania: "The region of Transylvania is ... inhabited in our time by three races (*gentes*): the Germans, the Székelys, and Vlachs."[145] He goes on to relate the myth of the Székelys' ancient origins, which entitled them to special privileges and the name "nobles," yet there is no sense that any of these three races or peoples has a stronger claim on the land than the others. In Aeneas's narrative, they all dwell together. All this suggests that for him, a territory could be politically united despite the presence of different languages and, presumably, different ethnic groups.

Indeed, when it comes to the question of shared language and ethnic or political identity, Aeneas shows considerable flexibility. Despite his emphasis on the widespread use of German as a unifying factor in *Germania*, he seems less sure about the role of language in other parts of the continent. In *Europe* he acknowledges that a similar language does not indicate a shared faith or state. Regarding the Slavs, Aeneas states,

> The national language [of Lithuania] is Slavic, for this tongue is wide-spread and divided into many branches. Some of the Slavs follow the Roman Church, like the Dalmatians, Croatians, Carnians, and Poles. Others follow the false beliefs of the Greeks, like the Bulgarians, Ruthenians, and many of the Lithuanians. Others have invented their own heresies—like the Bohemians, Moravians, and Bosnians .... Others remain trapped in heathen blindness, like many of the Lithuanians who worship idols.[146]

The Slavs (or Slavic speakers) were clearly harder to shove into an imaginary mold of seamless unity for Aeneas than "the Germans" had been. Where most Germans fell within the Holy Roman Empire and were adherents of the Roman Catholic Church, the Slavs had no emperor and followed a variety of faiths. The Lithuanians alone practiced three different religions: Roman Catholicism, Orthodoxy, and paganism. Aeneas's knowledge of the recent history of Lithuania, acquired from the missionary John Jerome of Prague at Basel and during his years at the imperial court, likely enabled him to see how diverse one *gens* or *natio* could be. While Aeneas may have contributed to early expressions of German nationalism, he was no advocate of pan-Slavism. It is easy to imagine how later thinkers might mine *Germania*, the *History of Bohemia*, and *Europe* to support later nationalistic views that one tightly knit ethnic group had exclusive rights to a piece of territory, or that all the citizens of a state needed to speak one language or follow one faith. But, as the preceding examples in other works show, Aeneas shatters those myths by repeatedly exposing the messier realities of the countries he describes.

How did Aeneas's views of habitation apply to the Ottomans? On balance, Aeneas articulated a fluid definition of ethnicity, religious faith, and even borders—*within Christian Europe*. This is a crucial caveat. Christian countries could change Christian rulers, and it did not seem to trouble Aeneas in most cases, as seen in his treatment of the Spanish monarch, Alfonso of Aragon, fighting for his claim to Naples in *Europe*.[147] Adjustments to borders, moreover, were a natural by-product of dynastic changes, wars, and settlements. At several points Aeneas confesses his inability to pinpoint the exact borders of a people because they had changed so much over time. Regarding Saxony, he states: "I will admit, however, that the boundaries of Saxony contracted and expanded at different times. For, as with empires, the boundaries of countries also shift in the course of time."[148]

Yet, as his reactions to 1453 show, Aeneas could not allow the same plasticity when it came to Ottoman conquests: their rule in Europe could never be legitimate. Consider his fascinating language about whether to include a detailed discussion of the Ottoman dynasty in his *Europe*. After mentioning the Turks more than ten times in the text, he prefaces a section devoted to them (book 4) with an apology:

> Although I may seem to be digressing from my plan, I think it not irrelevant to describe their origin and expansion. For in our era, this race of people [*genus hominum*] has grown so great that it controls Asia [Minor] and Greece and instills terror throughout Latin Christendom.[149]

Is the persistent urge by many today to depict Muslims as "not European" a lingering effect of Aeneas's first framing of their position? To him, a century after settling in Greece and Bulgaria, they were in Europe, but not of it.[150]

This ambivalence regarding the Ottoman presence in Europe informs Aeneas's word choice in the subtlest of ways. He uses *patria* only to describe their perceived origins in central Asia rather than their dominion within

Europe—a place that for many Turks had been their homeland/fatherland for generations.[151] When describing incursions into Ottoman territory by the king of Hungary and John Hunyadi in 1443, he does not use any term that smacks of state, kingdom, or nation, but rather uses "lands" or even "fields" (*agros Turcorum*). This stands in contrast to his use of the term *natio* for the Vlachs who became tributaries of the Ottomans in 1417, and other uses of *natio* and *populus*. In his chapter on the Turks, he uses *regnum* (kingdom or rule) twice: once to refer to the Ottomans' Asian kingdom and once to refer to Mehmed coming to power—but importantly, not in regard to their exercise of power in Europe. His preferred term for the Ottomans, as noted, was the less organized sounding *gens*. One vivid example appears in his description of the practice of Ottoman dynastic fratricide as *more gentis*, the custom of the people.[152] The practice of executing other male heirs to the throne when one succeeded was considered a necessary evil to protect the heir apparent and prevent civil war, but it was a recent political policy rather than an ancient ethnic custom.[153]

This pronounced tendency to use humbler and simpler terms for the Turks and their states than for their Christian European counterparts may have been a subconscious choice for Aeneas, but it is significant.[154] It shows a comfort in speaking of European states and peoples in one way—as established, legitimate, sovereign collectives—and a general avoidance of using those terms for the Turks, making their rule seem haphazard and impermanent. He largely avoids naming the Ottomans as anything but *Turci* or, on occasion, *barbari*.[155]

In Search of a Common European Culture I: The Ties and Tensions in Christianity

When Aeneas spoke of states and peoples, he often defined their sense of belonging by shared cultural experiences. There was no greater common bond among most Europeans than the Christian faith. Even as Aeneas began to invoke a more secular notion of "Europe" and "Europeans," the terms "Christians," "Christendom," and "Christian republic" still held primacy of place in his works.[156] It should come as no surprise then, that the Catholic Church is a constant theme in his three works of 1457–1458, whether the subject was the deep past or the present-day. A primary goal in each text was to promote the faith—from the work of popes, bishops, and cardinals (like himself), to humbler local religious practices of laypeople and priests, such as the yearly Lenten tradition in Halberstadt described in *Europe*, where a sinful member of the populace was selected, named Adam, and forced to go through a series of penitential acts for forty days until he was absolved of all sin at the end.[157] Despite local variations he describes, there were countless common threads that his Christian readers would have found utterly familiar, creating a broad sense of community. And the pope, at least in theory, offered independent and growing nations a focal point and source of stability that often proved helpful.

A people's triumphal conversion to Christianity forms a recurring theme in all three works, marking the break with a barbarous and violent past in many cases. In the *Germania*, after praising the region's present-day wealth and prosperity, he reminds them of their darker, pre-Christian history:

> [The ancient Germans] worshipped empty images, burning their children as offerings to demons and, taking pleasure in rapine and slaughter, they counted it praiseworthy to injure their neighbors and despoil them of their goods. But now, the true rites of our Lord have been brought to you, and you worship Christ, the one and only true God, together with the holy Roman church.[158]

This is a brief, but clear reminder to Martin Mayer and his countrymen of the Germans' debt to Rome for their civility as well as their faith.[159] A similar thread runs through *Europe* where he describes the conversions of Clovis, the pagan king of the Franks, and the Saxons of Northern Germany as part of the march toward civilization—in both examples, these former opponents of the faith became its champions.[160]

Closer to his own time, he celebrates the conversion of Eastern European pagans from Lithuania, including Duke Wladyslaw Jogaila who accepted baptism in 1386 in order to marry the heir to the crown of Poland, Jadwiga, and become king of that country:

> Wladyslaw had been a heathen and a worshipper of idols, but he agreed to accept baptism along with the kingdom. After his conversion to Christ, he proved himself a pious leader, attracting many Lithuanians to the Gospel, founding several pontifical churches, and treating the bishops with considerable honor. While he was out riding, he took off his cap and lowered his head whenever he saw church towers, in homage to the God who was worshipped within.[161]

Aeneas paints a vivid picture of transformation from paganism to Christian devotion that (seemingly) went beyond political expediency. Wladyslaw not only became a pious Christian, but he supported the high clergy, and, as Aeneas goes on to report, defended Poland against the Tartars and the Prussians.

Inspiring though this story was, Aeneas does not hide the fact that many Lithuanians still clung to paganism, despite the bold efforts of John Jerome of Prague in the 1390s to burn the snakes they worshipped and to cut down their sacred groves of trees. Prince Vytautus, who had initially supported Jerome's proselytizing, eventually heeded the complaints of his people who resented Jerome's tactics and ordered him to leave the country: "fearing a popular uprising, [Vytautus] preferred that the people should desert Christ rather than him."[162] Conversion of an entire people could take a long time, but Aeneas seemed confident that the true faith would win out in the end.

This positive narrative of Christianity, however, cannot be sustained at all times in the cardinalate texts. Countless moments reveal the fragility and disunity of "Christendom" as a concept. After all, the resistance of German prelates to papal directives is the main subject of book 1 of *Germania*, and the *History of Bohemia* is haunted by the divisions caused by the Hussites and Rome's refusal to engage in a dialogue with them. Tensions appear in *Europe* as well regarding the relationship between Eastern Orthodox and Latin Christians. Indeed, the Greeks presented a unique challenge to Aeneas's aim of promoting unity: the vast majority of them were still in schism with the Latin Church despite the proclamation of union in 1439 at the Council of Florence. The same author who described the fall of Constantinople with unalloyed grief in 1453 shows more ambivalence five years later. He describes the city in *Europe* as divinely appointed, the site of many councils that condemned heresies, but also the origin point of new "heresies."[163] After blaming the Greeks alone for the schism that divided the Church, he uncharitably says of the last emperor, Constantine XI, "whether as the result of others' deception or his own madness, [he] seemed in no way favorable to union."[164] This is perhaps softened later when Aeneas also holds the Latins responsible for the fall of the city in 1453: "For shame! The ears of our leaders were deaf [to calls for aid], their eyes blind. They failed to see that if Greece fell, *the rest of Christendom* would collapse [emphasis mine]."[165] Despite the schism, the Greeks were still part of Christendom to Aeneas.

The Greeks were also clearly a part of Europe. As his many statements on 1453 show, the loss of this buffer for Western Europeans troubled him as much as the Greeks' sad fate; in any case, his focus on heresy in *Europe* shows the perils of religious division to continental security in Aeneas's mind. By way of contrast, Aeneas does not include the Russians in *Europe*—a choice that speaks volumes. Condemned and rejected by Pope Honorius III as schismatics in 1222, the Russians' relationship to the rest of the continent hovered between uncertain and non-existent.[166] For Aeneas, Russia lay firmly outside of both Christendom and the continent, while Catholic Ruthenia (modern day Ukraine) and Lithuania were deemed part of both. The schismatic Greeks, however, were still eagerly claimed by Aeneas, perhaps because of their willingness to consider union over the centuries and their value as a link to ancient learning. Nevertheless, their position was tenuous. As the Russians and Greeks both learned, religious disunity brought a political price. But as Aeneas was perhaps coming to appreciate, nations often became strong and found passionate support from their citizens through religious differences with their neighbors.

Central Europe was a more concerning site of religious division with the Hussite heresy holding strong in this period. For as long as the Catholic Ladislas Postumus reigned as Bohemia's king (1453–57), Aeneas believed that a peaceful solution could be found. The Bohemians, he thought, were crucial to both the balance of power in Europe and security against the Ottomans. Perhaps for this reason, Aeneas initially favored compromise and supported granting the compacts, which included the privilege of Utraquism or communion in both kinds. He made this point a few years earlier in an oration to Calixtus in 1455 (*Res Bohemicas*) when he argued in favor of ratifying the Compacts of Basel:[167]

> If we grant their [the Utraquists'] demands, we call a powerful people, a large kingdom, and the most warlike peoples of Europe into the obedience of the Holy Roman Church, we unite the divided peoples of Bohemia, we give King Ladislas a tranquil region, we give the neighboring peoples peace, we become reconciled with strongly armed people whom we can mobilize against the Turks. Above all, we open the gates of Paradise to an infinite number of souls ....[168]

Perhaps Aeneas hoped to turn the Hussites' fighting spirit, even the ferocity of men like John Zizka, whose exploits will shortly be discussed, against the Turks.[169]

But by 1458, these hopes were tempered by Ladislas's death, Pope Calixtus's decision to take a harder line, and the resistance of the current king, George Podiebrad. In *Europe* he describes how the heresy, this "deadly taint" (*pestifera labe*), had reached into northern Hungary/modern-day Slovakia and Moravia, with the bandit leader Axamit and Moravian nobles among its followers. He was especially concerned about Bohemia, the birthplace of Hussitism, where the heresy's popularity plagued the reign of four kings who tried unsuccessfully to suppress it.[170] Podiebrad still occupied an uncertain position in regard to the heresy and obedience to Rome. In *Europe*, Aeneas conveys the mixture of suspicion and hope the king inspired: "he is thought to be tainted with the Hussite stain, though in other respects he is a great man."[171] Such repeated references to Hussitism in *Europe* demonstrate the anxiety it provoked in Aeneas, setting the stage for a fuller exploration in his *History of Bohemia*.

By the time Aeneas set about to write the *History of Bohemia* there was no clear path forward for Bohemia, making an examination of its history all the more compelling for him. Perhaps he thought it would help contemporary readers to understand how the present stalemate arose and wished to offer suggestions on seemingly insoluble problems. Presenting an objective and verifiable account, it seems, was not among his priorities. For Aeneas and many humanist historians, accuracy was often sublimated to the illustration of ethical conduct and good values. Exposing heretics and refuting their beliefs was of the highest value and utility to Aeneas.[172] He is no fairer to the Hussites in the *History* than he was to the Ottomans in some ways, but as in *Europe*, he tries not to stray too far from the basic facts. Unfortunately, Aeneas lacked a firm grasp of the nuances of Hussitism and its various forms.

One of the *History of Bohemia*'s biggest flaws is the way it lumps different expressions of Hussite belief into one group. The result is a pessimistic portrait heavily influenced by his observations of the radical sect at Tabor in 1451. There, he claims, they not only took communion in both species, but believed it to be merely a representation of Christ and not his true presence;

they spurned fasting, did not baptize with holy water or bury their dead in consecrated ground, and were hostile to clergy.[173] Moreover they venerated the memory of the harsh general Zizka, whose armies in the 1420s killed Roman Catholics, burned cities, destroyed monasteries, set fire to churches, prostituted nuns, and killed priests.[174] Not all of his observations were negative, though; Aeneas commended the Hussites' deep love of learning—a virtue he refused to ascribe to the Turks.[175] For the most part, however, his depiction of the Hussites was biased and one sided. Unfortunately for this sect of Christian believers or anyone seeking to understand them, Aeneas's *History of Bohemia* not only validated the papacy's firm rejection of Hussites and the Compacts, but as a resource, it was largely unchallenged until the eighteenth century.[176]

Perhaps the clearest convergence between the *History of Bohemia* and this study is the way Aeneas uses it to explore the national goals and character of this people—particularly the influence of Jan Hus (1369–1415). As Thomas Fudge argues, "Aeneas clearly sees the religious dissent practiced by Hussite heretics as linked to the national question, and indeed he alleges heretical poison is spread through nationalist sentiment, and, conversely, nationalism promotes heresy."[177] Recall how in *Germania*, Aeneas emphasized Bohemia's rightful place as part of the Holy Roman Empire; its king was, after all, one of the seven electors.[178] Indeed, Hus and his followers initially fell in line with Aeneas's view of this relationship and trusted in their position as subjects of the emperor. Hoping to clear his name, Hus attended the Council of Constance under assurances of safe conduct from Emperor Sigismund, who summoned it to end the prolonged papal schism. But when the emperor failed to prevent the reformer's arrest, or to ensure a fair hearing and block his torture and execution in 1415, Sigismund's Hussite subjects lost faith in him. In his *History of Bohemia*, however, Aeneas lays all the blame on Hus and his disciple Jerome of Prague for coming to Constance "prepared not to listen modestly to the ideas of others, but brazenly to impose their own, desiring to teach rather than to learn and infatuated with popular favor."[179] Apparently, the Council's refusal to listen to Hus did not trouble Aeneas.

By 1419 the Hussites were in open rebellion. Aeneas never blames Sigismund for breaking his word to Hus in the *History of Bohemia*, but he does criticize him for raising troops to fight the Turks when Queen Sophia of Bohemia, the widow of King Wenceslaus, implored him to aid her against the revolting Hussites. Had Sigismund intervened at this moment, the movement might have been extinguished:

Sigismund, having taken bad advice regarding the Turks, who for a long time had been depriving him of fortresses, conceived a desire to move his soldiers away before attacking Bohemia. Whereas if he had quickly led his army to Prague before the forces of the heretics had coalesced, those fires, which we later saw, would never have consumed Germany. But while he prepared to provoke the Turks, he lost Bohemia and did not defend Hungary.[180]

Precious few dangers loomed larger to Aeneas than the Turkish advance, but looking back at the 1420s, the Hussite revolt was one of them. His historical analysis of this moment is telling. It sheds light on his broader perspective of the security of Europe and Christendom. If the center of Europe was unstable and the Bohemians continually drew Christian forces away from the Ottoman front, then the continent as a whole would be significantly weakened. Anxiety about European unity arose from both of these sources for Aeneas; they each needed to be addressed.[181] Is it possible that Aeneas hoped Alfonso, the work's dedicatee, would use the temporal sword to bring the Hussites under control for the good of all Christian Europe? Or did he hope the king of Naples would use his influence to attract Podiebrad to a suitable alliance of some sort? Alfonso's successful negotiations with the inscrutable Filippo Maria Visconti in 1435 might have entered his mind.[182]

Either way, more than any other European country, Bohemia laid bare Aeneas's ambivalence about nation-building. He admired strong nations but was critical when they became too isolated and combative and threatened the fabric of Christian unity. One sees this in Aeneas's language contrasting Zizka to Emperor Sigismund. Zizka was blind and low born, but he was a proud Bohemian who energized his people to stand against the interests of empire and Church—to the point where the glorious Emperor Sigismund, whose name was "venerated in Italy, France, Germany, and *all of Europe* [emphasis mine]" was preparing to pay him off with gold and the promise of a share in government. Sigismund could not break the national movement the humble Zizka helped inspire; only his death by plague stopped him.[183]

Christian unity seemed within reach during Ladislas's impending nuptials to the king of France's daughter Madeleine, which Aeneas discusses with all their pomp and ceremony. Amidst these preparations,

> a third delegation to Calixtus had been decided upon to end the controversies concerning religion and to join the kingdom of Bohemia to the Roman Church. Beside these things, a fourth concern weighed upon the spirit of the king: to raise a mighty army against the Turks, by which at last, in our time, the wicked Muhammadan superstition could be expelled from Europe.[184]

As king of both Hungary and Bohemia, young Ladislas had inherited the burden of liberating the continent. Such assertions echo Aeneas's letters when Ladislas was still alive. Had all of this been achieved, the Bohemian nation might have fostered unity in central Europe, and even helped form the vanguard against the Ottomans, in conjunction with Hungarian military might. But alas, it all ended abruptly with Ladislas's death and George's rise as king. Even after Ladislas's death, it would seem, Aeneas still looked on him with unrealistic longing for what might have been.

Nor were the Bohemians the only flashpoint of concern in this regard. George Brankovic, the despot of Serbia, provides one of the strongest examples of the link between local religious preferences and nation-building in

Europe. Aeneas laments his stubborn refusal to forsake his national church and accept Roman Catholicism, repeating a story told to him by Franciscan friar Giovanni Capistrano about his efforts to convert Brankovic:

> Through an interpreter he discussed the Scriptures with him at length and ardently exhorted him to abandon the error of his people [*gentis*]. Finally, George gave the following response: 'I have lived for ninety years and know no other religion than the one I received from my forefathers [*patribus*]. Up until now, my countrymen [*cives*] have considered me wise, though unlucky. But now, as people often do, you want to make an old man lose his mind. I would rather end my life with a noose than abandon the traditions of my ancestors.'[185]

This fascinating exchange may reflect some of the substance of George's feelings, watered down as they were by both translation and second-hand reporting, but the word choices here are those of Aeneas. He employs both *gens* and *cives*, distinguishing between a more natural, social, or ethnic grouping of people and legally bound subjects or citizens. George may have inherited his religion from the former, but his control over the latter depended upon his decision to remain a member of their collective faith.

Common religion, then, could join peoples together across country lines and forge a united front, as Capistrano and the pope hoped to do, but a sudden change in religion was risky on the local and national level; it could alienate rulers from their people and create divisions between citizens. What Brankovic believed, and what Aeneas was trying to articulate, is the way that a shared, ancient religion could make nations stronger and more self-identified—a notion that nineteenth-century nationalists regarded as self-evident. Emperor Constantine XI (even if he was not ultimately successful) knew this as well when he refused to abandon Orthodoxy. Conversely, John Zizka and George Podiebrad forged a wave of national unity based on a "new" or reformed religion.

Above all this religious instability sit the popes, who were not only spiritual leaders of the faith, but also territorial princes in central Italy.[186] Aeneas captures both of these aspects, but focuses more on the latter in *Europe*, foreshadowing his princely portrait of himself in his *Commentaries*. In *Europe*, he leaves behind past criticisms of Pope Eugenius IV and praises his defeat of the schismatic forces at Basel. Eugenius, he asserts, brought stability to the church by crowning Emperor Sigismund, convening the Council of Florence to restore unity with the Greeks and Armenians, recovering the Church's lost cities in central Italy, and bringing calm to Rome.[187] The same writer who dismissed the pope as "Gabriel" in his letters from Basel now claims, "Eugenius was without doubt a great and distinguished pope."[188]

Aeneas's portrait of Nicholas V (who failed to promote Aeneas to the cardinalate) was more ambivalent. Despite his magnificent patronage of the liberal arts, building projects in Rome, and other deeds, Aeneas ends his description by noting two things that "diminished his glory to no small extent": the loss of Constantinople and his slow progress on the Peace of Lodi. With the latter, he nearly squandered a golden opportunity:

> After being chosen unanimously by the various parties to initiate and arbitrate a peace settlement in Italy, which was then being ravaged by sword and flame, he dragged out the deliberations day after day and came to be suspected by Francesco Sforza, now lord of the Milanese, and by the Venetians of being unwilling to pronounce a decision that seemed to bring peace to others but war to the church.[189]

Nonetheless, Aeneas shows that the agency of the pope was critical to achieving peace in Italy. Because Nicholas could not accomplish this personally, he called upon talented agents like the humble monk Simonetto da Camerino, "who was insignificant and completely unknown before this, but a man of unimpeachable integrity."[190] Aeneas took pleasure, it seems, in revealing that it was Simonetto more than Nicholas who brought the Venetians and Milanese to a successful peace.

Aeneas's confidence in the see of St. Peter was clearly diminished by the human occupants of this position and their inability to tame the divisions of growing national agendas. All three of his cardinalate texts reveal these concerns—even *Europe*, which Baldi views as an affirmation of the pope's authority and his critical role as a stabilizing force in the Italian peninsula.[191] While Aeneas never questions the theory of papal supremacy, a closer reading of *Europe* shows the leadership of recent popes to be less decisive and impactful than the heroes of the early Church and high Middle Ages. In Aeneas's text, the recent vicars of Christ are all too human and limited; he offers no hagiographical rendering of miraculous achievements, but rather worldly stories of papal struggles and too many failures.

Rather than pinning all his hopes on Rome in *Europe*, Aeneas spends a good deal of time searching for a strong secular leader to unite Christians— especially one to fill the vacuum that Hunyadi and Ladislas Postumus had left on the Ottoman front. Indeed, the prominence of secular rulers in *Europe* offers a sharp contrast to his later *Commentaries*, where Aeneas as pope is the protagonist. Just a few months before he rose to the see of Peter, he was much more willing to share the stage. Alfonso of Naples receives special attention; the text closes with Aeneas singing his praises as a triumphant scion of the Goths, who not only subdued Southern Italy, but "has become the keeper of peace in Italy and also seems to be the guide and arbiter of affairs in Spain."[192] Ultimately, however, there is no single leader, ecclesiastical or secular, who dominates *Europe*. Perhaps that is Aeneas's goal. He acknowledges the shortcomings of both empire and papacy in *Europe* more than ever before, and yet he does not give up on the idea of something greater tying all these regions together—a sense of unity that transcended country and even "Christendom." Perhaps Aeneas was inspired by the feeling of unity he saw in the ancient Roman Empire and longed for something in his own time to take its place.[193]

Was crusade or the threat of the Ottoman "outsiders" enough to forge a sense of European unity? If this was, indeed, Aeneas's intention, his works from this period promote common ground not by erasing national and local differences, but by emphasizing and celebrating them—as diverse members of a talented, resourceful team. This is an idea Aeneas first hinted at in his oration to Nicholas V in 1452 and repeated in his July 21, 1453, letter to Nicholas of Cusa; in some ways, *Europe* can be viewed as a much lengthier version of that idea. Importantly, *Europe* asks no one to surrender their love of city or country in order to embrace their crucial role as part of the larger collective—the two went hand in hand. If this was one of Aeneas's goals, it was a fine line to walk, as *Europe* reveals many moments where the interests of a kingdom or city-state clashed with the goals of crusade or the defense of neighboring Christians.

Indeed, instead of ignoring the obstacles to cooperation—an acceptable rhetorical move in an oration or exhortatory letter—Aeneas acknowledges other uncomfortable truths in *Europe*. He describes rich and powerful leaders who were "deaf to the Gospel" when Cardinal Carvajal tried to recruit crusaders for the relief of Belgrade and criticized several participants for the selfish errors that led to the defeat at Varna, as will shortly be discussed.[194] Yet, as clunky and ill functioning as "Christendom" often appears in *Europe*, a common bond emerges when juxtaposed to the one group who could not be a part of that community: the Muslim Turks. The stark contrast provided some sense of definition when it felt like Christian differences were spiraling out of control. But was it enough? As the previous examples have shown, common religion, though an important theme in all three works of 1457–58, did not erase the divisions and rivalries among European Christians, not even for Roman Catholic nations. Fortunately for Aeneas, there were other qualities that bound most of the inhabitants of Europe together. A city or a country might throw off their subordination to the pope, but they could not change their location as many tribes did in the ancient and early medieval periods. Aeneas continued to seek ways to help the inhabitants of "Europe" recognize and hold dear their shared part of the globe.

In Search of a Common European Culture II: Learning and Local Customs

Beyond a culture of Christianity, other shared experiences loom large in the cardinalate works, namely education and higher learning, local customs, values, and general comportment. But Aeneas does more than simply describe these attributes. A loose ranking system pervades the three works whereby Aeneas evaluates societies and conveys a sense of their national or civic characters. This was not the first time he undertook such examinations, as his early epistolary descriptions of cities like Genoa, Basel, and Vienna show— works that echo the influence of Leonardo Bruni's *Laudatio* on the city of Florence. But Aeneas's observations in his cardinalate writings reflect a more conscious agenda. While other humanists wrote about their birth cities or adopted homes and praised or denigrated the areas they visited, Aeneas went much further in these ambitious works. For him, something larger was a stake than civic or national pride. Aeneas, I believe, was consciously positioning himself as an authority on Europe and its diverse peoples in the hopes of protecting, elevating, and celebrating its culture.

Of all these categories, education was the most prominent. If learning was the measure of a truly civilized society, Italy ranked first in Aeneas's estimation. In *Europe*, for nearly every Italian town or capital that he mentions, and there are many, he names at least one of its illustrious (humanist) scholars by name. Of Florence, he states, "The wisdom of the Florentines is to be commended in many respects, above all because in selecting their chancellors they focus not on legal skill, like most cities, but on oratory and what they call the humanities."[195] He goes on to name Leonardo Bruni, Carlo Marsuppini, and Poggio Bracciolini, whom he knew, and the illustrious Coluccio Salutati as ornaments of the city. In Milan he commends Leodrisio Crivelli and Francesco Filelfo; in Venice, Francesco Barbaro; and in Ferrara, Ugo Benzi, Giovanni Aurispa, and Guarino da Verona. The list goes on. No other area can match the density of scholars per square mile that prevailed in Italy, yet Aeneas recognizes learning in other regions and seems encouraged by the spread of the liberal arts.

In the *Germania* he notes the erudition of theologians and the overall commitment to learning with the following statement:

> Letters and studies of all the good arts flourish among you. Many cities in Germany have schools in which the law, medicine, and the liberal arts are taught, such as Cologne, Louvain, Heidelberg, Prague, Erfurt, Leipzig, Vienna, and Rostock, where the most learned men have won renown, and men of equal stature are renowned in our own age.[196]

He does not name scholars as he moves from town to town in Germany, either from ignorance or a lack of interest, but he is aware of major centers of scholarship. He calls attention to learning in other parts of the continent with his mention of the career of Italian humanist Pier Paolo Vergerio in Hungary and the accomplishments there of locals John Vitez and Janus Pannonius. Regarding Poland, he praises the "flourishing school of the liberal arts" in the capital city of Kraków and the wit and refinement of its bishop, Cardinal Zbigniew Olesnicki, who corresponded with Aeneas and even sent a fur coat to thank Aeneas for sending him a copy of his collected letters.[197] The rest of Poland is described as rough and rugged with "less than elegant" cities and the cultivation of beer over wine, but Kraków is highlighted, perhaps as a beacon for the future.

In addition to education, one finds subtler commentaries on the polish or roughness of a given people regarding anything from dress to architecture to manners to speech. Fancying himself the knowledgeable and balanced ethnographer, Aeneas often praised a region for one attribute and criticized it for another. In the *Germania*, for instance, he touts the Germans' excellent hospitality, a universal sign of civility and good manners, but goes on to insult their language:

You live courteously with all people, and there is such elegance in your men and your affairs, that no barbarism seems to remain among you, except for your ancestral tongue. But if any persists in calling you barbarians, they should be judged more truly so themselves, whether Greek or Latin.[198]

He goes on to say that areas of Greece and Southern Italy [Magna Graecia] would be lucky to be less "barbarous" than the Germans. This is a fascinating mix of high praise and haughty denigration. With one hand he swipes at the German language, to which he apparently never warmed, and with the other, he denounces ignorant non-Germans who have no understanding of his former home's sophistication. While Aeneas himself never described the modern Germans as "barbarians," as some Italians were wont to do, he could be faulted for repeating the slur and thereby drawing attention to it. Perhaps he felt unable to describe German learning as equal to that of Italy, at least in terms of the humanities. As such, he offered encouragement while implying that Germans had much to gain from continued close interaction with the smooth-talking Italians and their superior Latin eloquence.[199] What sounds like cultural insensitivity to modern ears may have been intended as historical objectivity.

For the most part, Aeneas shows little sense of smug superiority as he surveys the rougher parts of Europe, but on a few occasions, he blends secular and religious ideas of progress with his use of "barbarian" and "barbarous." His description of the conversion of Livonia offers a rich example. The North, he states, was a region little known by Italians and Greeks, but "the Christian religion opened up this part of the world to our generation, cleansed it of its barbarism, and revealed a gentler way of life to its ferocious tribes."[200] Both the word choice and silences here are striking: Aeneas removes all traces of political actors and pressure that appear in other conversion narratives in *Europe*, making it seem as if the clergy acted alone, without inflicting any pain or discomfort; the willingness of the inhabitants to receive this "gentler way of life," and which parties its introduction most benefited, is left to the imagination. In his own day, areas of Northern Europe were still in the process of converting, with large pockets of resistance in areas like Lithuania—it was a process he seemed confident would continue. Conversion in this very direct sense was a gateway to the European community and "civilization."

For some countries, the achievement of cultural refinement took place in the deep past, as he described in the *Germania*, but for some Christian peoples, the civilizing process was not yet complete. In *Europe*, he describes the Ruthenians as "a rough and barbarous race" (*gens barbara, incompta*), and on a few occasions he uses "barbarian" to refer to Christian foreigners.[201] Such comments on rugged and underdeveloped areas are perhaps balanced by Aeneas's persistent narrative thread about the growth of scholarship across Europe and a general sense of progress as some areas "catch up" while contributing strengths that more developed regions lacked. Without drawing a direct line to the rhetoric of cultural imperialism in the Americas and Africa in later centuries, one can perceive similarities and wonder what Aeneas would have made of modern justifications that echo his own.

Importantly, Aeneas likely developed this sense of Christianity as a cultural unifier from more than just reading Church fathers and saints' lives: this notion owed a great deal to memories of his own journeys as a younger man. No amount of reading could replicate the impact of seeing so many parts of Christian Europe firsthand. He found differences in language and customs, to be sure, but also strong continuities. Every town had at least one church, if not several; local saints and some rituals might vary, but every region under the Roman Church adhered to the same liturgical calendar, venerated many of the same saints, and followed the same canon of the mass.[202] In addition, the learned and administrative language in all or most of these areas was Latin. Finally, the basic political and economic structures were similar everywhere Aeneas visited, following a pattern Bartlett calls the "knightly-clerical-mercantile consortium."[203] Control over the reins of government differed from place to place among these classes, with one group or another or perhaps the king having more direct sway over local affairs, but the players were generally the same. Towns, villages, churches, and estates tended to follow much the same model. As such, Bartlett argues: "Travellers in later Middle Ages going from Magdeburg to Berlin and on to Wroclaw, or from Burgos to Toledo and on to Seville, would not be aware of crossing any decisive social or cultural frontier."[204] All of these memories worked in synergy as Aeneas read new sources and reflected on the state of Europe and its countries.

This link between Christianity, civility, and belonging in Europe thrust the Bohemians into an uncertain position. Compared to the Germans, whom Aeneas describes as barbaric at the time of Christ, but sophisticated and accomplished a few centuries later, the Bohemians are still less polished in their habits and interests. In his dedicatory preface of the *History of Bohemia* to Alfonso, where he describes his sources, he notes that part of his information comes from what he saw among "the barbarians." In some contexts, this word choice signifies foreigners, but his meaning becomes clearer when he later describes the present-day Bohemians with classical barbarian tropes, like fondness for drinking and gluttony. They are bold and contemptuous of danger, but also rash in speech, cunning, and changeable in nature, not to mention avid for robbery. Such behavior is true, he argues, for all social classes of Bohemia.[205] In essence, he establishes a narrative of a troublesome, untrustworthy, impetuous people in the guise of the dispassionate language of ethnography and geography, particularly in book I, but they are a coherent nation, nonetheless.[206] Apart from his descriptions of atrocities of war and shifty heretical leaders, some of whom he grudgingly admires, the story of the Bohemians is not that different from those of other European nations.[207] While Aeneas may have been frustrated by the Hussites, he did not treat them as utter outcasts; they were as European as the Bosnian Manichean "heretics."[208] There was always the chance that they could all return to the larger community.

Ottoman Culture and Society in Europe: The Insufficiency of "Self and Other"

While Aeneas arranged the peoples of Europe on a continuum between civilization, tolerable backwardness, and malleable paganism, the Turks were the one group who seemingly had no place on this spectrum. They obviously failed the religious admissions test and showed little interest in conversion: any Muslim who did convert risked capital punishment for apostasy unless they lived in a Christian-ruled state. Meanwhile in Ottoman Europe, Islam was making slow but steady inroads among the nobility in areas like Bulgaria, even if the majority of the population remained Christian.[209]

Pius's disdain for the Ottomans, however, went beyond religion; it was coupled with his distorted view of their broader culture. Even in his cardinalate years, with good access to reports and travelers' accounts that must have been making their way to Rome, Aeneas continued to deny the Ottomans' devotion to scholarship and the arts. While he does not repeat the canard that they hated learning and books in *Europe*, he completely ignores their cultural attainments, their impressive urban planning throughout the Balkans, their rebuilding of Constantinople, and their stimulation of trade and industry. Ottoman cities are not granted the same lush descriptions of their Christian counterparts. It was of little interest to Aeneas that the Ottomans created a system in their European dominions where members of different faiths could participate and thrive—not on equal terms, but with access to justice and clear social guidelines to help smooth interactions.

But Aeneas's treatment of the Turks was not as two-dimensional as one might expect. From the earliest pages set in Eastern Europe, they are key players: as adversaries, allies of Christian leaders, and rulers of vast regions. And yet, as mentioned, he couches his description of the Ottoman dynasty in *Europe* as a "digression." To Aeneas, the Ottomans were in Europe, but not of it. His attention to the Ottomans' origins was complicated, but also deliberate and consequential: he could not describe the recent history of Europe without them. This unresolved tension haunts the pages on the Ottomans in *Europe*. Even in his works on Bohemia and Germany the Turks make appearances; they were impossible to ignore.

Ethnic origins play a key role in his discussion of the Ottomans, much more so than religion. Aeneas repeats the same basic narrative that he established about Turkish origins in 1453, but the framing and emphasis of certain points in *Europe* adhere to a different standard. Just before the explanation for his long discussion of the Turks, he states,

> I note that many writers of our time, not only orators or poets, but even historians, are ensnared in the error of referring to the Turks as 'Trojans.' I believe they are influenced by the fact that the Turks occupy Troy, which was inhabited by the Trojans. But the Trojans originated in Crete and Italy. The Turkish race is Scythian and uncivilized.[210]

Not only does Aeneas deny the Turks an ancestry his readers would find distinguished, but he separates the Trojans from their Asian roots—by invoking a line in Book 3 of the *Aeneid* which places Trojan origins in Europe.[211] Although he had used the form *Teucri* until about 1448 and invoked the theory that the Turks were descended from the Trojans in his 1436 oration at Basel, after 1453, he discarded it and vigorously promoted the equally false Scythian theory. It was as though Aeneas had become convinced that nothing good could come from Asia—excepting the Holy Land, of course.

Aethicus, the early medieval writer (believed in the Renaissance to be an ancient philosopher) makes a more expansive appearance than in Aeneas's letter to Cusanus or his oration at Frankfurt.[212] Among the new mentions here are diet, sexual mores, a sinister future path for their descendants, and a reference to a more recent authority Otto of Freising (1114–1158):

> [The Scythians] were a ferocious and shameless race, given to fornication with whores and every kind of illicit intercourse. They ate what other people abominate—the flesh of beasts of burden, wolves, and vultures— and even partook of human fetuses .... This race, according to Otto of Freising ... emerged from the Caspian Gates during Pepin's reign over the Franks and clashed in a fierce battle with the Avars .... Then after crossing Pontus and Cappadocia, they gradually infiltrated the other adjoining populations and built up their strength through clandestine raids in the manner of brigands ... occupying strategic mountains and passes from which they could easily launch assaults when opportunity offered.[213]

This persistent use of Aethicus (and Otto) rather than Herodotus, who offered a more accurate and positive account of the Scythians, allowed Aeneas to depict the Turks' supposed ancestors as sexually shameless and devoid of religion except for the observance of Saturnalia. Even their diet was savage. Centuries later, Aeneas claims, they crossed into Anatolia and supported themselves through cowardly surprise raids.[214] His recent foray into ethnography, it seems, led Aeneas to pay more attention to such details than he did a few years before, questionable though they were. From such ignoble beginnings, Aeneas continues, the Turks acquired enough wealth and power that they were able to rise up under Osman in the early 1300s.

Aeneas is obviously mistaken in equating the Scythians with the Turks, who only arrived in Western Asia in the tenth century CE. The errors build with a lack of differentiation between the Seljuk and Ottoman periods and an omission of the impact of the thirteenth-century Mongol conquest and successive Turkic migrations. He also depicts the early Ottomans as rootless warriors rather than a heterogeneous society that included pastoralists, farmers, craftsmen, merchants, engineers, and scholars.[215] As Meserve has shown, medieval sources were available to historians seeking to construct a more balanced picture, but Aeneas avoided most of them as they did not suit his purpose.[216] His reliance on flawed and inappropriate ancient texts to

investigate the origins of the Turks and other peoples would be less noteworthy had these texts and their assumptions not factored so heavily into his view
of their supposed modern descendants.

The trope of backwardness briefly falters in *Europe* when Aeneas describes
the military genius of the siege of Constantinople. He represents the
Ottomans at a much higher level of organization, discipline, and military
accomplishment than their supposed forebears, conceding that, "Mehmed
meanwhile mustered forces from all quarters and attacked the imperial city
by land and sea with impressive armaments and formidable vigor."[217] But
when he turns to the sack that followed, he portrays the Ottomans at their
barbaric worst:

> As soon as they had captured the city and killed everyone who dared to
> resist, they took to pillaging. The victors, whose numbers were beyond
> count showed utter depravity in their lust and cruelty: neither rank nor
> age nor sex protected anyone. Rape was mixed with butchery, and butch-
> ery with rape. Old men of advanced age and women worthless as booty
> were dragged off just for sport .... And since this immense and ill-as-
> sorted army, comprised of fellow countrymen, allies, and foreigners, held
> such a diversity of languages, customs, and desires, and each man dif-
> fered in his sense of right and wrong, for three full days there was noth-
> ing in Constantinople that was not permitted.[218]

There is little new in this now rote list of atrocities, but Aeneas's language
about the Ottomans and the rule of law is, indeed, different. His use of the
term *cives* (subjects or citizens) alongside allies (*socii*) and foreigners (*externi*)
serves as a rare admission of the complexity of the vast, multinational
Ottoman army. This is one of the few times Aeneas has not flattened the
diverse Ottomans into one *gens* of "Turks." While Aeneas does not use
"Ottoman" in this passage or almost anywhere in his works, at least here, he
seems to comprehend the sense of it.

Whether European readers of this well-circulated work apprehended the
subtlety of Aeneas's word choice is questionable. The predominant message
of the passage is brutality, which is reinforced as he continues with descriptions of the stripping of Hagia Sophia, the desecration of other churches and
icons, and the execution of Greek nobles, Venetians, and Genoese who
defended the city. As in his letters and orations from five years earlier, he
constructs a horrifying scene of lawlessness and depravity in terms that had
become familiar to his readers.

The Turkish threat to civilization forms a steady refrain throughout
Aeneas's discussion of Greece in *Europe*. As Aeneas describes each region, he
emphasizes the ancient period, noting illustrious rulers or important battles,
then abruptly shifts to recent decades of doom and gloom, creating a back-
beat of encroaching barbarism in tandem with the Ottoman advance. Missing
from this portrait are the Byzantine centuries, enabling Aeneas to overleap
any discussion of the region as the seat of the Eastern Roman Empire.[219]

A few examples help illustrate this selective view of Greek history; starting with the region bordering on Bulgaria, he states:

> Next to them, the maritime region extending south to the Hellespont is *Romania*—a Greek nation, though once it was barbarian, and it is returning to barbarism in our own time, now that the empire of the Greeks has been destroyed and the Turks hold sway.[220]

Similarly, after relating some of the ancient glories of Macedonia, which extended its rule over Greece and Central Asia, he states,

> This is the same country which has now fallen subject to the filthy race of the Turks and is forced to pay them tribute and bear their most miserable yoke. The armies of the Turks also invaded Magnesia and Thessaly within our time.[221]

A little later he mournfully recalls the ancient Greek victory at Thermopylae: "Here are the narrows of Thermopylae, renowned for the slaughter of the Persians. Although they once withstood the attack of Xerxes, they failed completely to obstruct the passage of the Turkish army."[222] Finally, on Boeotia he states:

> Here is the birthplace of the Muses in the grove of Helicon, here the glades of Cithaeron .... This city, which was once the homeland of Father Liber [Dionysus] and Hercules and which produced the brave Epaminondas—a city not inferior to Athens in fame—is in our time the insignificant stronghold of Thebes, which in recent years has been occupied by the Turks together with the rest of Boeotia.[223]

There is much to ponder and tease out in all of these passages.

First are the repeated assertions that the (barbaric) Ottoman conquest, rather than the passing of centuries, brought about the end of classical Greece—as if time should have stood still in the region. This misleading narrative, moreover, conjures an image of Muslims as destroyers of culture and erases centuries of Islamic scholarship that preserved and added to the Greek corpus.[224] Second is the sense that Greece was still regarded as a perpetual bulwark against eastern invaders, an unbroken association since the Persian Wars. Finally, by saying Boeotia was "occupied" by the Turks (*occupatum*), Aeneas affirms the notion that they were not the newest wave of legitimate rulers, but merely interlopers.

Equally striking is Aeneas's silence on centers of Byzantine culture that also lay in the path of the Ottoman advance—including vibrant medieval towns like Thessalonica and Mistra, which overshadowed Athens, Thebes, and other ancient sites at that time. Aeneas's romantic lament for the destruction of ancient Greek sites largely ignores contemporary Greeks and their voices.[225] To some extent this may be attributed to Aeneas's sources for this region, which were primarily ancient, but it also shows an utter disregard for the medieval centuries that followed Rome's fall in the West. Aeneas simultaneously elevates Greece as part of the broader European cultural landscape, while minimizing its more recent cultural achievements. If the Byzantines' greatest contribution was to preserve the ancient heritage, now even that role was being taken away. This is an unfair portrait of the Greeks to be sure, but the Ottoman (and Islamic) narrative is even more reductive.

While many of these claims may sound familiar to readers who followed Aeneas's writings since 1453, *Europe* goes much further in one important aspect: it adds a stark geographical component to the destruction of learning and high culture—one that extends beyond the loss of a single city or collection of books. Reading Aeneas's narrative of loss of so many historic Greek sites, one can envision the Ottoman advance superimposed on a map of Greece like a suffocating wave of darkness over everything humanist readers idealized about the region. There is no mention of the positive changes taking place under energetic Ottoman administrators, only the ruin of Greece as a nation. This became so powerful a trope that even later travelers to the region who marveled at the wonders of Ottoman cities penned conflicted descriptions of what they saw.[226] They could not displace the expectations that Aeneas's texts and others had planted in them or recognize and work through the resulting cognitive dissonance.

Clearly, Aeneas found it unnatural, to say the least, that Eastern "barbarians" could dominate this classical Greek paradise, and he was determined to provoke other educated Europeans to share in his outrage. His *Europe* presents a subtle and skilled use of the *ubi sunt* paradigm to persuade readers to see ancient Greece as their own heritage and to take action to save it. Aeneas's ideas about ancient Greece and its relationship to contemporary Europe constitute an early, often overlooked, articulation of "Western Civilization"—an idea designed to foster a sense of coherence among diverse European cultures and to firmly push the Ottomans *outside* of that tradition.[227] While this concept took on new layers of meaning and deployment in the nineteenth and twentieth centuries, modern scholars have rarely considered what sparked the earliest uses of these terms and how a palpable fear of conquest fed into this mythical construct.[228] Aeneas, importantly, was not the only writer of his generation to consider the loss of the ancient Greek heritage as a collective blow to Europeans; Ciriaco of Ancona who traveled the region a decade earlier expressed similar ideas in his letters and diary, and other humanists like Bessarion and Ficino lamented the loss of Greek learning.[229] Hence, Aeneas engaged in a poignant narrative that was recognizable to learned contemporaries; others evoked similar sentiments, but he helped shape and publicize the message to a broader readership.

Was this the sum total of Aeneas's views of the Ottomans in this period, or could he imagine a way for them to become legitimately "European"? In order for this to happen, theoretically speaking, the Ottomans would have needed to transform, just as early European peoples did and some were still doing. An important question is, which aspect of the Turks constituted the greatest challenge in his mind: their religion or their purported barbarism? His writings as pope offer more insights into that question, but the complexities and contradictions within the pages of *Europe* suggest that Aeneas was less fixed in his opinions of the Turks than meets the eye.

The theoretical construct of self and other may have helped many scholars, including myself, to navigate Christian views of Muslims in the past, but the limits of this model and its polar opposite, peaceful coexistence or *convivencia*, have been receiving increasing attention.[230] A number of studies on Christians, Muslims, and Jews in Europe have presented a more nuanced model of tense coexistence, or "fear and conversation," to quote Palmira Brummett.[231] While *Europe* contains many examples of the Turks as dangerous adversaries whose presence in the continent was disruptive, a closer reading of the text reveals a counter narrative that upends the notion of the Ottomans as consistently "other."

Aeneas's repeated references to bargaining, diplomacy, alliances, and other exchanges prove how easily the Ottomans fit into the political landscape of Europe and behaved in much the same ways as their Christian counterparts. The moment when the Ottomans first entered the continent by way of Greece in the 1350s is particularly instructive:

> Murad[232] was the first of the Turks to cross into Greece, at a time when two men were disputing the Greek empire, and one of them, who feared defeat, called him in for assistance. Once there, he deliberately protracted the war, and, having observed that the strength of the two had been sapped and squandered, leaving both men in a weakened and exhausted state, he changed course, as the saying goes, and turned his arms upon them indiscriminately, as opportunity offered.[233]

While neither a flattering nor fully accurate portrait of the Greco-Ottoman alliance, Aeneas's telling still admits that the Greeks *invited* the Ottomans as allies against other Christians. This is an embarrassing fact that Aeneas could have omitted but did not.[234]

Other passages reveal the Ottomans' tumultuous alliances with Serbian rulers:

> [Murad] ravaged the lands of the Illyrians, took many towns by force, and sacked and burned them. Following the custom of his race, he entered into marriage with a great many wives, including [Mara Brankovic] the daughter of George, despot of Serbia. Not long afterward, he led an army against George, heedless of their familial bond.[235]

But this is not a simple case of villain versus guileless victim. As other portions of *Europe* show, Aeneas had little respect for George or his sons.[236] After George's death, Aeneas describes the struggle over succession within the family: "Then Lazarus [George's son and heir] died, and no small quarrel arose over his succession. Gregory [his brother] strove to win back his father's kingdom with the aid of the Turks"—this despite the fact that Murad had previously blinded Gregory for treason.[237] These passages show Murad, George, and his sons to have been equally loose with their word and unconcerned with Christian, Muslim, or domestic unity. Murad's marriage to Mara is also fascinating. Although dynastic marriage alliances between Muslims and Christians appear to have been rare at this time, her case shows they were motivated by the same political desires as Christian ruling houses.[238]

The Albanian and Greek despots in *Europe* had similar relationships with the Ottomans. When the Albanians of the Peloponnese wanted to throw off Greek despots Thomas and Demetrius Paleologus after 1453, "Both sides begged for the help of Mehmed, to whom the nobler side seemed more deserving; he therefore supplied Demetrius and his brother with reinforcements to use against the Albanians."[239] This partnership would soon sour when Mehmed demanded an exorbitant sum of tribute money, which the Greek despots could not pay. Within a few years, Thomas would flee Greece and become an exile in Italy.[240] Such stories served as warnings about the dangers of trusting the Ottomans, but they also reveal an undeniable fact pattern: many princes treated with the Turks, despite religious or cultural differences, whenever it suited them.

Looking beyond alliances, other examples muddy the self-other dynamic, like Aeneas's portrayal of the Crusade of Varna. First, after incredible gains in early 1444 against the Ottomans, the Hungarians willingly considered a truce:

> The Hungarians, who had no illusions about their strength and ascribed their victory more to chance than to their own power, thought it dangerous to try their luck further and accepted the terms of peace which the Turks proposed on their own initiative. A truce of ten years was declared.[241]

Yet soon after this peace treaty was declared, Wladyslaw consented to the pope's wishes to launch a campaign, thereby breaking it. This in and of itself raised ethical questions even for Christian contemporaries. Fourteen years after Varna, Aeneas persisted in seeing Wladyslaw's final battle as a diversionary tactic. As he states in *Europe*: "Wladyslaw, who had invaded a foreign kingdom [Hungary], thought it would serve his interests for the inhabitants to be preoccupied with war."[242] Second, worse than the confusion and disunity surrounding the battle of Varna was the role the Genoese played: at a critical moment, Aeneas describes how they ferried an Ottoman force led by Murad across the Bosphorus for "one gold coin per head,"[243] helping them reach the battle in time to make a decisive impact. Clearly, the Genoese valued their century-old alliance with the Ottomans and monetary gain more than some notion of a united Christian cause. If they had simply done nothing to aid the Ottomans at that juncture, they might have delayed the large relief army long enough to force young Mehmed to surrender. Here too, Aeneas could have left this detail about the Genoese out of his history, but instead he chose to report their role.

All these passages show how readily local Christians turned away from one another—and some vague notion of Christian or "European" unity—and toward the Ottomans for alliances or profit. This was not the safest choice in the long term given the way the Ottomans soon became masters of each area they "helped," but it was a choice that Christian rulers made freely. Aeneas's moments of straightforward reporting of such developments, in contrast to his typical language of "us versus them," deserve more attention than they have been given. For all the rhetorical liberties he so often took regarding the Ottomans, he relates these developments with surprising evenhandedness.

Finally, Aeneas includes instances of grudging praise in *Europe* for the Ottomans, or at least Sultan Murad II, the father of Mehmed the Conqueror, who was often portrayed as more moderate than his hawkish son: "This was a great man in peace and war, as beloved by his own people as he was hated by ours."[244] Describing Murad's victory at Varna and his abdication soon after, Aeneas states:

> The victor Murad did not pursue the fleeing enemy, nor did he swagger and speak boastfully among his men or hold a cheerful expression, as he had in the past. When asked why he was so dejected and not reveling in the enemy's defeat, he said: 'I would prefer not to win more victories like this.' ... he returned to Adrianople and fulfilled the vows for victory which he had made to his god .... Choosing instead a private life, he himself set out for Asia with a few companions to share his retirement and devoted himself to some solitary form of religious observance.[245]

Murad's reputed restraint in battle and his desire for contemplation and study after an active life of governance and war make him the perfect balance of arms and letters in one man. Petrarch regretted that Cicero did not embrace such a quiet life in his retirement.[246] Had Aeneas made an effort to learn about the interests of other sultans off the battlefield, he might have painted a very different picture of the "dreaded" Turks.

Taken all together, the passages in *Europe* on the Ottomans reveal more nuance on the subject than Aeneas had shown in the past five years. This complexity seems to have two sources. In part, it may derive from his growing knowledge of the Ottomans, as when he described their reputation for fair and tolerant rule in his 1455 oration to Calixtus, *Solent plerique*. Second, the genre of this work as a history required Aeneas to alter his usual approach; simply put, he could not ignore reliable reports of successful Ottoman diplomacy or Christian betrayals in order to craft a compelling rhetorical scenario. He indicates this in the previously cited quote: "I note that many writers of our time, *not only orators or poets, but even historians*, are ensnared in the error of referring to the Turks as "Trojans" [emphasis mine].[247] "Even historians" (*veram etiam historicos*) is a telling phrase, showing Aeneas's distinction between their work and that of poets and orators. Historians may fall prey to their own fictions and personal leanings, as seen in Aeneas's use of the dubious Aethicus, but his words show that he expected historians to strive for a higher standard of objectivity. For recent events, at least, he appears to have largely adhered to that directive.

Aeneas's thinking on the Ottomans, then, is less binary than many scholars, myself included, have claimed.[248] This does not mean that Aeneas felt no attachment to the barbarian model he evoked elsewhere on so many occasions. There is reason to believe that Aeneas's rhetoric worked on his own emotions as well as those of his audience, creating tensions in his view of the Ottomans that he may have never reconciled. Either way, it is my assertion that the Renaissance reader found two visions of the Ottomans in Aeneas's *Europe*: the cruel barbarian, intent on destroying Christian culture and autonomy, and a sophisticated, agile political power much like the others on the continent. Whichever version they chose to believe, perhaps a mixture of both, it constituted a reality of its own.

Conclusion: Many Nations, One Europe: Relationships Between the Parts and the Whole

Aeneas's time in Rome from 1455–1458 was critical to his conception of identity and belonging within the Christian nations of Europe and the continent as a whole. During these years, ideas that surfaced in 1453 and earlier memories of his travels took fuller shape with the aid of ancient ethnographic and geographical works. Aeneas's new position as a papal supporter and, from late 1456, a cardinal, also colored his view of the world, but importantly, it did not lessen his attention to Europe and secular matters. While his attachment to Christendom and his use of Christian terms were pronounced, his vision of Europe as a cultural and political entity continued to strengthen.

Some points should be highlighted about Aeneas's methodology. First is his selective use of ancient sources. Like most humanists, Aeneas venerated ancient writers without repeating all they had to say; there was always a negotiation between the source and the goals of the Renaissance writer.[249] The clearest example of this is Aeneas's use of Tacitus on the Germans. While Tacitus can be criticized for indulging in negative classical stereotypes of barbarians, he was also quick to praise German liberty, valor, honesty in public life, and their private morality. Aeneas, looking to prove how much Rome and the Church had elevated the Germans, left these positives out of his portrait of the ancient Germans, casting them instead as crude, backward, and brutal. By contrast, German nationalist thinkers would mine Tacitus for the flattering qualities while ignoring the negative ones.[250] Yet if Aeneas ignored Tacitus's positive points on the ancient Germans, I contend that he fully grasped the subtext. If Tacitus's treatise was a warning to Roman contemporaries not to underestimate the Germans of his day, implying how far they could go with a little more (Roman) industry and organization, fifteen centuries later Aeneas showed that the Germans had attained that full potential. In some ways, Aeneas's *Germania* was also an answer to Tacitus.

In a similar vein, Aeneas's decision to ignore stronger ancient sources on the supposed ancestors of the Turks in favor of less credible polemicists reveals a fast and loose use of the ancient past for present-day goals. What is perhaps most arresting about Aeneas's portraits of ancient Germans and (supposed) Turkish ancestors are his biased interpretations of history and progress: the Germans, he conceded, "overcame" their barbarous past and matured into a gloriously advanced society; the Turks, however, were prisoners of their purported ancient origins, unable to rise above them in any significant way.

This inconsistent view of ancient origins and growth or stagnation feeds into Aeneas's view of the progress of European civilization. The Greeks and the Romans achieved a high level of civility very early on, and Aeneas believed that most other peoples—*within Europe*—had either caught up with them by his day or were well on their way. Cultures beyond Europe did not fare so well in his estimation. This view is dishonest and Eurocentric. More objective observers from the time described Ottoman areas as refined, well organized, economically thriving, and stable—characteristics that correspond to notions of progress—but Aeneas would have very little of it. This may be one of the earliest efforts to claim the mantle of modernity for Europeans or Westerners alone.

Aeneas's perception of nations in this period deserves some comment as well. What the three major works of his cardinalate share is a growing sense that nation states—not just their rulers—merited attention and were the way of the future. Whereas in 1446 in *De ortu*, Aeneas spoke almost exclusively of Central Europe as "empire," in 1457–1458, he repeatedly described the "German nation"—a people and sometimes a region that superseded the bounds of any province or city-state and had a character of its own, independent of the Holy Roman Empire. Aeneas's decision to write the expansive *History of Bohemia* shows his awareness that nation-states had unique stories that went beyond any given dynasty or period; this same spirit is reflected in his *Germania* and gives shape to his *Europe*. There is more than a hint of Benedict Anderson's "imagined community" at work in all three of these texts, but whether Aeneas saw nations as grounded in "the right of soil" like the later French model, or "the right of blood" like the later German model, is far from clear.[251] He may well have been responding to a growing sense among the Germans, for instance, that they were part of a political unit that did not depend upon the structures of empire.[252]

Importantly, though Aeneas found it easy to describe other areas as coherent nations, he was less inclined to apply this simplistic framework to the region where he was born and raised. The men and women of Saxony, Franconia, and other areas may have balked at the notion of being packaged as one indistinguishable people (i.e., "Germans"), but to an outsider, it seemed more natural. "Italy," by contrast, is rarely treated in this way by Aeneas—at least until his papacy. In this, he was not unlike ancient Roman and Greek writers who constructed notions of coherent "peoplehood" (or nations) for foreign groups but saw themselves as much more diverse and heterogeneous.[253]

Even more significant, I believe, is the positive spin that Aeneas put on the concept of "nation." Nationalism would not fully take shape for a few centuries, but Aeneas should be credited for an early vision of nationhood as more pleasing than the ancients believed. This is not to say that everything about nation-states was congenial to Aeneas. On the one hand, he admired their "manly" protection of their liberty and local agendas, but he anxiously watched their impact on the unity of the Church and as they pushed for national prerogatives on appointment of high-ranking clerics, the payment of burdensome tithes, and the Church's irksome claims to hold all their property tax free. The Hussites of Bohemia demanded even more. He watched troublesome wars across Europe over territory and dynastic rights and popular revolts, while contrasting this worrisome bickering to the powerful unity of the Ottoman Empire. As nations became stronger and more self-conscious, Aeneas mourned the loss of a united Christendom that never really was. He sought to promote the *res publica Christiana* while repeatedly offering the alternative of "Europe" as an overarching, conveniently neutral, group identity. One could theoretically quit the collective that was Catholicism, but these nations could never pick up and leave the continent. If previous generations could conceive of whole nations migrating to new territory, for Aeneas, their place on the continent was much more permanent.

Indeed, a major attraction of "Europe" for Aeneas was its solidity. The boundaries (as he saw them) never altered. While at times he notes his inability to pin down the borders of a specific province or state (like Saxony) given all the changes it had seen over time, he seems untroubled by most regime shifts in Europe—so long as they were done by other European Christians. He was trying, it seems, to craft a permanent notion of what Europe meant amid constant change within its boundaries, and the one main component was that Muslim and Asian rulers were not welcome. For Aeneas, they simply did not fit the picture.

This is not to say that he believed a people's character and culture could never change; he includes many examples of regions shifting due to the arrival of new ethnic groups and presumably blending over time. Some areas remained heterogenous like Transylvania, while in other areas, one culture, or at least a language, achieved dominance—recall Aeneas's assertions that some areas "became" German. Whereas nationalist ideology depends on dangerous notions of blood and biology, Aeneas presents a more open-ended view of belonging and group affinity within Europe, and his notions of ethnicity seem fairly flexible. There is no evidence that he saw groups as distinct and unmixing, apart from the Ottomans, but even they are often described as an integral part of the European political scene. Some of what he wrote about various peoples drew from his past experiences, colored by time, the impact of 1453, and ancient ethnography. Some of it came second hand, likely from reading, evoking the "discursive practice" Elizabeth Spiller has described in regard to race.[254]

This chapter has shown just how developed Aeneas's concepts of Europe, its nations, and the Ottomans became during this period in Rome. He was still putting the finishing touches on two of his major works when Pope Calixtus was on his death bed. How well these writings prepared him to take his place on the throne of St. Peter is debatable, but they certainly hardened his perspective of the regions over which he would assume spiritual leadership.

Notes

1 See, for example, Aeneas's letter to his uncle, Giovanni Tolomei in 1442, where he praises the beauty of the Tuscan countryside; *Reject Aeneas, Accept Pius: Selected Letters of Aeneas Sylvius Piccolomini (Pope Pius II)*. ed. and tr., Thomas M. Izbicki, Gerald Christianson, and Philip Krey (Washington, DC: Catholic University of America Press, 2006), 131–32; Rudolph Wolkan, ed., *Der Briefwechsel des Eneas Silvius Piccolomini*, in *Fontes Rerum Austriacarum*, ser. 2, vol. 61 (1909): 114–16. See also Aeneas's letter to Goro Lolli, July 1, 1453, for his mentions of his homeland and fear of dying "in exile" (*in exilio*). Wolkan, *Briefwechsel*, 68: 181–82.

2 "Conabor tamen dum spiritus hos regit artus, ita me gerere ut omnes intelligant ad hanc me dignitatem tuo favore et ex tua curia provenisse, meque Theutonicum magis quam Italicum Cardinalem esse." Letter to Frederick III (Dec. 22, 1456) in *Opera quae extant omnia* (Basel, 1571), 763.

3 This is not to minimize the diversity of the regions of Italy at this time. More will be said on the subject of "Italians" in Chapter 4.

4 *Europe (c. 1400–1458)*, tr. and ed. Robert Brown and Nancy Bisaha (Washington D.C.: Catholic University of America Press, 2013), 50.

5 R.J. Mitchell, *The Laurels and the Tiara* (New York: Doubleday and Co., 1962), 102–03.

6 Cecilia M. Ady, *Pius II: (Aeneas Silvius Piccolomini) The Humanist Pope* (London: Methuen and Co., 1913), 130.

7 On Calixtus's quiet years in Rome as a cardinal, see Michael E. Mallet, *The Borgias: The Rise and Fall of a Renaissance Dynasty* (New York: Barnes & Noble: 1969), 67.

8 Charles L. Stinger, *The Renaissance in Rome* (Bloomington: Indiana University Press, 1985), 21–24; Arthur White, *Plague and Pleasure: The Renaissance World of Pius II* (Washington DC: Catholic University of America Press, 2014), 94–95.

9 White, *Plague and Pleasure*, 277–78. For more on Alberti's research on St. Peters and its restoration, supported by Pius during his papacy, see Anthony Grafton, "The Winged Eye at Work: Leon Battista Alberti Surveys Old Saint Peter's," *Renaissance Quarterly*, vol. 73, no. 4 (2020 [2021]): 1137–1178.

10 Aeneas remarks on Biondo's work in *Europe* (1458). On Biondo and Rome, see Angelo Mazzocco, "Rome and the Humanists: The Case of Biondo Flavio," in *Rome in the Renaissance: The City and the Myth*, ed. P.A. Ramsey (Binghamton, NY: Center for Medieval and Early Renaissance Studies, 1982), 185–95.

11 See Stinger, *Renaissance in Rome*, 14–21.

12 Stinger, *Renaissance in Rome*, 282–86; 26–32.

13 Stinger, *Renaissance in Rome*, 26. See also Elizabeth McCahill on the disrepair Pope Martin V found in Rome after the resolution of the Schism; *Reviving the Eternal City: Rome and the Papal Court, 1420–1447* (Cambridge, Mass.: Harvard University Press, 2013), 2–10.

14 White, *Plague and Pleasure*, 95.

15 Contemporaries like Capistrano and Aeneas had found Nicholas V's crusade efforts wanting; Capistrano in particular criticized Nicholas's use of papal funds on building projects instead of crusades; see Norman Housley, *Crusading and the Ottoman Threat, 1453–1505* (Oxford: Oxford University Press, 2012), 73.

16 Mallett, *Borgias*, 62–70.

17 Ludwig Pastor, *History of the Popes from the Close of the Middle Ages* (London: Kegan Paul, Trench, Trübner, and Co., 1899), 2: 342–3; Ady, *Pius II*, 133.

18 Years later in his *Commentaries* and in Bartolomeo Platina's biography, there is an assertion that Aeneas counseled the emperor not to side with the people on this issue as the people were less trustworthy than another prince, but these statements may reflect later views. Rolando Montecalvo argues that Aeneas's shift

toward papalism can be seen as early as late 1453 in his *Dialogus*; see "Between Empire and Papacy: Aeneas Silvius and German Regional Historiography (PhD diss., University of California, Berkeley, 2000), 18, 123–24. Regardless, it is clear he did not argue strenuously for the rights of the German church in 1455.

19 See *Commentaries*, ed. Margaret Meserve and Marcello Simonetta (Cambridge, Mass.: Harvard University Press, 2003), 1: 142–47; see also Michael Cotta-Schönberg. Oration "Solent plerique" of Enea Silvio Piccolomini (13 August1455, Rome). Ed. and transl. by Michael v. Cotta-Schönberg: (Orations of Enea Silvio Piccolomini/Pope Pius II; 21). 2015. <hal-01176055>, 7.

20 The oration circulated widely. Cotta-Schönberg lists sixteen manuscripts of the early version and six manuscripts of the later version, "Solent plerique," 8, 12–14. It was later printed several times, including in the two sixteenth-century Basel *Opera omnia* editions.

21 "Voluntarii sunt et prompti omnes populi pro Christi fide arma suscipere. Sed omnes in te oculos direxere; omnes ex te modum atque ordinem expectant." Cotta-Schönberg, "Solent plerique," 74, Eng. tr., 75.

22 "Solent plerique," ed. Cotta-Schönberg, 30–39.

23 "Solent plerique," ed. Cotta-Schönberg, 54–55.

24 "Solent plerique," ed. Cotta-Schönberg, 56–57.

25 "Exurge igitur, aperi ecclesiae thesauros, aperi caeli portas ...," "Solent plerique," ed. Cotta-Schönberg, 76; Eng. tr., 77.

26 "... sin reliquantur a nobis, leges accepturos, quas Turci dederint. Neque enim consilium eorum est sine spe victoriae urbes et agros igni, uxores et filias lupanari, sua et liberorum capita hostili ferro committere." "Solent plerique," ed. Cotta-Schönberg, 58; Eng. tr., 59.

27 "Tot deinde sunt in Christiano populo vectigalia, tot pecuniarum extorsiones, tot rapinae, tot principum, ne dicam tyrannorum nostrorum in subditos contumeliae, ut magnopere verear, ne venienti Turco et onera relaxanti, plebes nostrae libenti animo colla submittant, maxime vero, si ut est callidus hostis, libertatem de fide fecerit." "Solent plerique," ed. Cotta-Schönberg, 64; Eng. tr., 65.

28 On the development of the system that came to be known as the *millet*, whereby the Ottomans organized non-Muslims according to their religious groups and gave them some autonomy, see Daniel Goffman, *The Ottoman Empire in Early Modern Europe* (Cambridge, U.K.: Cambridge University Press, 2002), 169–72; Mehrdad Kia, *Daily Life in the Ottoman Empire* (Santa Barbara: Greenwood Press, 2011), 111–128. For a useful overview of the different strategies and "circles of domination" that the Ottomans used in Europe, ranging from direct rule and ownership of much of the land by Ottoman elites in the center, to a lighter tributary relationship on the peripheries, see Gilles Veinstein, "Ottoman Europe: An Ancient Fracture," in *Europe and the Islamic World: A History*, ed. John Tolan, Gilles Veinstein, and Henry Laurens (Princeton: Princeton University Press, 2013), 149–52.

29 "Evangelium salvatoris, quod in omnem terram intonuit, sola jam audit Europa, nec ipsa quidem omnis. In occidenti Sarracenis premimur, septentrionis magnam partem caeca gentilitas invasit; ex orienti, qua Graecia protenditur, Turci nos pepulere; prope est, nisi vigilamus, nisi consurgimus, nisi Deus adjuvat, nisi tua sanctitas, ut coepit, animose occurrat, ut et hunc tuum thronum et quidquid restat Christiani nominis Mahumethus occupet, qui jam sine resistentia terrae dominus ac maris esse videtur." Cotta-Schönberg, "Solent plerique," 66; Eng. tr., 67.

30 "Sed quoniam propulsare Turcos et illatam Christianae plebi contumeliam ulcisci commune opus est omnium fidelium, magnoque sumptu et magnis viribus indiget, supplex orat tuam beatitudinem Caesar, quae Christi vicarium gerit, ut antequam hostis appropinquet magis, una secum ad ea intendas animum, per quae Christiani potentatus inter se pacem tenentes, adversus infideles arma convertant et communem hostem ex Europa deturbent." "Solent plerique," ed. Cotta-Schönberg, 68; Eng. tr., 69.

31 "Rex quisque sibi et pontifex esse videtur. Quot capita, tot sententiae. [Cicero: *De finibus bonorum et malorum*, 1, 4, 15] Scinditur incertum studia in contraria vulgus [Virgil: *Aeneid*, 2, 39]. Illic Germaniam mille conturbant lites; inter Galliam et Angliam vetus odium viget; Hispaniae reges inimicat ambitio; Italiam magno labore pacatam novus jam turbo concutit; nova exurgunt apud Senas incendia. Quid speremus? His moribus procuratores Maumethi sumus." "Solent plerique," ed. Cotta-Schönberg, 62; Eng. tr., 63.

32 For more on this tension in crusade planning and papal policy, see Benjamin Weber, *Lutter contre les Turcs: Les formes nouvelles de la croisade pontificale au XVe siècle* (Rome: École Française de Rome, 2013), 195 and 201–02.

33 Pastor, *History of the Popes*, 2: 349, 365, 368–69; Norman Housley, *The Later Crusades: From Lyons to Alcazar 1274–1580* (Oxford: Oxford University Press, 1992), 102–03.

34 Pastor, *History of the Popes*, 2: 391–92.

35 Ady, *Pius II*, 132–33; Pastor, *History of the Popes*, 2: 355–56; Mallett, *Borgias*, 79–80; Housley, *Crusading and the Ottoman Threat*, 73.

36 Mallett, *Borgias*, 70–73.

37 See Weber, *Lutter*, for a breakdown of expenses on crusading and the methods of funding. See also, D.S. Chambers, *Popes, Cardinals and War* (London: I.B. Tauris & Co., 2006), 48–49.

38 "Is ut primum pontificatus apicem adeptus est, mox animum ad delendam Turcorum et legem et gentem convertit votumque vovit ad eam rem sollemne." *De Europa*, ed. Van Heck, 249; Eng. tr., *Europe*, tr. Bisaha and Brown, 269–70; *Commentaries*, ed. Meserve and Simonetta, 1: 142–43.

39 As Ady puts it, "Common enthusiasm for the Crusade at once created a strong bond of union between Aeneas and the Pope: *Pius II*, 133.

40 Calixtus suffered from gout, with symptoms similar to Aeneas's ailments; Mallett, *Borgias*, 70. On the impact of illness in Aeneas's life, see Antonia Whitley, "Mind over matter. Living with ill health: the case of Pius II," in *Pio II Piccolomini: Il Papa del Rinascimento a Siena*, ed. Fabrizio Nevola (Siena: Protagon Editore, 2009), 269–79.

41 Pastor describes Calixtus's nepotism as "the only blot on his otherwise blameless character," *History of the Popes*, 2: 447. See Mallett, *Borgias*, 67–81 for a more sympathetic reading of Calixtus's attachment to his nephews and the support they offered a foreign and isolated cardinal and pope in Rome.

42 Mallett, *Borgias*, 78; Pastor, *History of the Popes*, 2: 347. Aeneas later expressed his disapproval; see *Commentaries*, ed. Meserve and Simonetta, 1: 151. His disappointment at the time can be seen in a long, philosophical letter dated May 7, 1456 to his close friend Pietro da Noceto, *Opera omnia* (Basel, 1571), 756–63.

43 Ady, *Pius II*, 134; White, *Plague and Pleasure*, 105.

44 For more on the Crusade and Battle of Belgrade, see Setton, *Papacy*, 2: 173–83; Housley, *Later Crusades*, 103–04.

45 *Commentaries*, ed. Meserve and Simonetta, 1: 154–55; Pastor, *History of the Popes*, 2: 399–400. For a useful collection of essays on the cardinalate in this period, see *A Companion to the Early Modern Cardinal*, ed. Mary Hollingworth, Miles Pattenden, and Arnold Witte (Leiden: Brill, 2020).

46 Either Aeneas's letter writing sharply increased after becoming cardinal or, more likely, he and his associates chose to preserve and edit more examples from this important period. See his *Opera omnia* (Basel: 1571), 763 ff. and *Lettere scritte durante il cardinalato*, ed. Ettore Malnati e Ilaria Romanzin (Brescia: M. Serra Tarantola, 2007); a facsimile of *Enee Siluii Piccolominei qui et Pius Secu[n]dus fuit Epistole in cardinalatu* (Rome, 1475). These collections contain many letters where Aeneas informs friends and colleagues of his elevation and accepts their felicitations. For more on Aeneas's letters in this period, see Fabio Forner, "Enea Silvio Piccolomini e le epistole del cardinalato. Alcune considerazioni," in *Pio II*

nell'epistolografia del Rinascimento, ed. Luisa Secchi Tarugi (Florence: Franco Cesati Editore, 2015), 223–236.

47 *Opera omnia*, 763 (Letter to Frederick III, Dec. 22, 1456).

48 *Opera omnia*, 834.

49 An early letter to Borgia, who was overseeing the papal states in the Marches, bears witness to his tact: "Since I have not received any of your letters for a long time, I judge the cause to be your vast and weighty duties and the dangers of those lands. I nevertheless rejoice that in adverse and difficult circumstances your excellence shines forth, for those who come from the territory of the Marches, say that the province has been saved from the gravest danger by your care, diligence, zeal, and most singular ability." ("Quod nihil tuarum literarum iampridem acceperim, causam esse arbitror ingentes ac gravissimas occupationes tuas, et illarum terrarum pericula. Ego tamen gaudeo quod in adversis et arduis rebus tua virtus elucet, nam qui ex agro Piceno veniunt, tua cura, diligentia, studio, et singularissimo ingenio ex gravissimo discrimine servatam provinciam aiunt.") (April 1, 1457) *Opera omnia*, 787. The tone is positive, but Aeneas's message regarding Rodrigo's faux pas is also clear—a delicate balance to strike with the pope's nephew. He appears to have had a genuine affection for his young colleague from the start and hoped to guide him toward more mature behavior; Mallet, *Borgias*, 77.

50 The Pragmatic Sanction of Bourges was issued by Charles VII of France in 1438 in an effort to take direct control of a host of issues pertaining to the French church.

51 Pastor, *History of the Popes*, 2: 414–21; Barbara Baldi, *Pio II e la trasformazione dell'Europa cristiana, 1457–1464* (Milan: Unicopli, 2006), 30.

52 Housley, *Later Crusades*, 102–05; 293–94; Setton, *Papacy and the Levant*, 2: 173–195.

53 See Housley, *Later Crusades*, 412–13, 426, and also his "Pope Pius II and Crusading," *Crusades* 11 (2012); Weber, *Lutter*.

54 *Opera omnia*, 780.

55 "Mihi non magna spes fuerit, nisi viderim Celsitudinem tuam classe instructa in magnae illius memorandae navis puppe, armatam, signum profectionis contra Turcos dare. Nam reliquis orbis principibus, etsi voluntas est, non adest facultas qua Graeciam invadere possint. Tuae Sublimitati si voluntas affuerit, nihil deerit...." *Opera omnia*, 785.

56 Even Capistrano was disgusted by the inactivity of lords and kings leading up to the crusade of Belgrade. See Housley, *Religious Warfare in Europe, 1400–1536* (Oxford: Oxford University Press, 2002), 65–66.

57 See his letter of March 8, 1457, where he confesses his despair to the papal legate Cardinal Juan Carvajal in Hungary about the stalemate in crusade planning and the vacuum in leadership; *Opera omnia*, 780.

58 Garrett Mattingly, *Renaissance Diplomacy* (1955. Reprint. New York: Dover Publications, 1988), 75–76; Joycelyne G. Russell, *Diplomats at Work: Three Renaissance Studies* (Wolfeboro Falls, NH: Alan Sutton Publishing Inc., 1992).

59 Setton, *Papacy*, 2: 159; Setton believes that at least until the reign of Sixtus IV, most crusade tithes actually found their way to the crusade in some form.

60 *Opera omnia*, 791.

61 See, for example, his use of "universae reipublicae Christianae" in his letter to Procop Rabenstein of Bohemia (July 3, 1457), *Opera omnia*, 794.

62 See James Hankins, "Renaissance Crusaders: Humanist Crusade Literature in the Age of Mehmed II," *Dumbarton Oaks Papers* 49 (1995): 179–86; Alan Ryder, *Alfonso the Magnanimous, King of Aragon, Naples and Sicily, 1396–1458* (Oxford: Clarendon Press, 1990), 306–07.

63 For example, a letter to Frederick III on Sept. 11, 1457 (*Opera omnia*, 797); see also *Opera omnia*, 788 ff. to Cardinal Carvajal and others.

64 Janus Møller Jensen, *Denmark and the Crusades 1400–1650* (Leiden: Brill, 2007), 70–97.

65 Housley, *Religious Warfare*, 65–67; Pastor, *History of the Popes*, 2: 409–12.

66 His father Emperor Albert II (d. 1439) died of disease while returning from a campaign against the Ottomans, and Emperor Sigismund (d. 1437) fought them on several occasions, most notably at Nicopolis in 1396. For more on the relationship and correspondence of Ladislas Postumus and Aeneas, see Klara Pajorin, "La pietà di Pio. Ladislao Postumo nella corrispondenza di Enea Silvio Piccolomini," in *Pio II nell'epistolografia*, ed. Tarugi, 23–32.

67 The letters close with the words "dictated to Aeneas" (*dictata per Aeneam Cardinalem Senensem*), and in his *Europe*, Aeneas remarks on Calixtus's habit of dictating letters, sowing doubt as to Aeneas's authorial role; *Europe*, tr. Bisaha and Brown, 273. However, these epistles ended up in Aeneas's letter collections and *Opera*, which suggests that either he claimed them as his own or that later editors recognized Aeneas's authorial stamp. They certainly match his style and phrasing. As a group, they reflect Calixtus's wishes, which corresponded closely to those of Aeneas. Letters concerning or directed to Ladislas Postumus stand out in this group, showing Aeneas's pride in crafting them.

68 "... Turcos ipsos brevi e Grecia pelleremus, omnemque prorsus Europam ab eorum faucibus eriperemus." Giuseppe Cugnoni, ed. *Aeneae Silvii Piccolomini Senensis qui postea fuit Pius II Pont. Max., Opera inedita* (Rome: Salviucci, 1883), 132.

69 "Europe," is prevalent in this letter, but not every missive of this sort features it so strongly. Another letter written around same time in Calixtus's name to Cardinal Carvajal uses only Christian terms; *Opera omnia*, 819–20 (1457).

70 *Opera omnia*, 825. See Pastor, *History of the Popes*, 2: 440.

71 "... religio nostra contra Turcorum impetus defendatur ...." *Opera omnia*, 825.

72 *Opera omnia*, 825–26.

73 Aeneas writes of his tearful reaction in a letter to Johann Roth, dated Dec. 20, 1457; *Opera omnia*, 815–16. Thanks to Tom Izbicki and Thomas Fudge for help with the identification of Roth.

74 Montecalvo discusses other reasons for the changes that influenced his views of Frederick and his shift toward papalism, but he also notes that "Aeneas wrote at least half of the second redaction in Rome, between 1455 and 1458, after he had left Frederick's service"; "Between Empire and Papacy," 38. This freed him to be more critical of Frederick as Montecalvo notes, but I suspect it also helped broaden Aeneas's view of the history beyond Frederick to Austria itself.

75 Barbara Baldi is an important exception. See *Il "cardinale tedesco": Enea Silvio Piccolomini fra impero, papato, Europa (1442–1455)* (Milan: Edizioni Unicopoli, 2012); Baldi, *Pio II*. Ady also notes the significance of this period and his leisure time writing; *Pope Pius II*, ch.13.

76 Some have claimed Aeneas was the actual author of Mayer's supposed letter. Mayer's letter is dated September 1, 1457. Fadiga finds the timing unusual. If Mayer truly wrote it in September, he was congratulating Aeneas some eight months after his elevation; see *Germania*, ed. Maria Giovanna Fadiga (Florence: SISMEL, 2009), 135, n. 1. Thomas Mauro describes this letter as "fictive" without elaboration; "Praeceptor Austriae: Aeneas Sylvius Piccolomini (Pius II) and the Transalpine Diffusion of Italian Humanism before Erasmus" (PhD diss., University of Chicago, 2003), 131. Some argue that a letter from Mayer existed, but does not survive and that Aeneas summarized it; see Gerald Strauss, *Manifestations of Discontent in Germany on the Eve of the Reformation* (Bloomington, IN: Indiana University Press, 1985), 36. One aspect of the letter that may, in my view, support the theory of Aeneas as coauthor is the use of word "nation" and the accusation of Germanic barbarism—a term and a notion about which Aeneas wrote freely from this period onward. "German nation," does not appear to have become a popular usage north of the Alps until a few

decades later. See Peter H. Wilson, *Heart of Europe: A History of the Holy Roman Empire* (Cambridge: Belknap Press, 2016), 255.

77 "Ob quas res natio nostra quondam inclita ... nunc ad inopiam redacta, ancilla et tributaria facta est et in squalore iacens .... Nunc vero ... optimates nostri se in pristinam vendicare libertatem decreverunt." *Germania*, ed. Fadiga, 136–37. Mayer's main concern about these benefices is that Aeneas had obtained them for future use, under the right of reservation—a formula that was unusual and unheard of; ibid., 135. For further discussion of the context of Mayer's complaints, see Fadiga's introduction, ibid., 6–11.

78 I have used Fadiga's edition of Aeneas's text and Martin Mayer's letter, noted above. For an English translation of book 2 of the *Germania*, along with information on the printing and transmission of the text, see Mauro, "Praeceptor Austriae."

79 Kurt Statwald, *Roman Popes and German Patriots* (Geneva: Librairie Droz, 1996), 44. For Jakob Wimpfeling's annoyed response to Aeneas in 1515, see Strauss, *Manifestations of Discontent*, 40–48. Aeneas also responded in other ways to Mayer and enlisted the support of friends in Germany to help resolve this crisis; see his *Opera omnia*, letters 320, 331, 335, 337. On the growing mistrust between German reformers and the papacy and efforts to address it, see Emily O'Brien, *Commentaries of Pope Pius II (1458–1464) and the Crisis of the Fifteenth-Century Papacy* (Toronto: University of Toronto Press, 2015), 75–76; Ady, *Pius II*, 139–40.

80 On earlier notions of Germany, see Len Scales, "Late medieval Germany: an under-Stated nation?" in *Power and the Nation in European History*, ed. Len Scales and Oliver Zimmer (Cambridge: Cambridge University Press, 2005), 166–91. See also Duncan Hardy's argument that the empire was "both a monarchical kingdom and a community of elites" in this period. Hardy states, however, that it is only in the later fifteenth century (post 1486) that we begin to see German 'nation' evoked in a political sense in official documents; *Associative Political Culture in the Holy Roman Empire: Upper Germany, 1346–1521* (Oxford: Oxford University Press, 2018), 11, 153–54. More will be said on this subject in Chapter 4, but it appears that Aeneas was one of the early voices on the idea of a German nation.

81 Aeneas's text does not appear to have been well known north of the Alps before it was printed in 1496 in Leipzig, but readership grew after that point; Mauro, "Praeceptor," 17, 343 ff; Fadiga, *Germania*, xiii. Fadiga discusses the impact of the work on German audiences in ibid., 58–71.

82 Johannes Helmrath, "Political-Assembly Speeches, German Diets, and Aeneas Sylvius Piccolomini" in *Beyond Reception: Renaissance Humanism and the Transformation of Classical Antiquity*, ed. Patrick Baker, Johannes Helmrath, and Craig Kallendorf (Berlin: De Gruyter, 2019), 82. See also his assertion that Aeneas "was the first to cheer on the German princes in Frankfurt as *Germani*," showing the earlier manifestations of such views in his rhetoric; ibid., 93.

83 "... multa et magna inter christianos gesta ... ab eo tempore, quo Fridericus imperium accepit, usque in hanc diem ...." *De Europa*, ed. Van Heck, 25; Eng. tr., *Europe*, tr. Bisaha and Brown, 50.

84 "Que sub Friderico, tertio eius nominis imperatore, apud Europeos et, qui nomine christiano censentur, insulares homines gesta feruntur memoratu digna mihique cognita ...." *De Europa*, ed. Van Heck, 27; Eng. tr., *Europe*, tr. Bisaha and Brown, 51.

85 Nicola Casella, "Pio II tra geografia e storia: la Cosmographia," *Archivio della Società romana di storia patria*, 95 (1972): 35–112.

86 On Aeneas's changing views of imperial power in Europe, see O'Brien. *Commentaries*, 104; Casella, "Pio II," 43.

87 See *Europe*, ed. and tr. Bisaha and Brown, introduction, 16–17, 51; Casella, "Pio II tra geografia e storia," 106–12. For the importance of territoriality in Aeneas's

evolving historical vision see Rolando Montecalvo, "The New *Landesgeschichte*: Aeneas Silvius Piccolomini on Austria and Bohemia," in *Pius II, 'El Più Expeditivo Pontifice': Selected Studies on Aeneas Silvius Piccolomini*, ed. Zweder Von Martels and Arjo Vanderjagt (Leiden: Brill, 2003), 66–67.

88 Or possibly "our residence" (*edes nostras*), to signal their common bond. It is difficult to say as Aeneas refers to himself in the singular in this letter, but it was common to use the plural as well, which he often does in other works.

89 "Amat edes nostras ipsa podagra nec tam recedit quam revertitur libens." *De Europa*, ed. Van Heck, 25; Eng. tr., *Europe*, tr. Bisaha and Brown, 50.

90 Aeneas's knowledge of the kingdom was patchy and flawed, but to non-Bohemi-ans, he was seen as an expert and advised Pope Calixtus on these issues. As dis-cussed in Chapter 1, this education began at Basel and continued during his time at the imperial court, culminating in a visit to Bohemia in 1451. The following year (1452), Pope Nicholas V named Aeneas apostolic legate for Bohemia. In 1455, sometime after arriving in Rome, he delivered a second oration to Pope Calixtus titled "Res Bohemicas," which will be discussed later.

91 On Alfonso's patronage, see Patrick Baker, *Italian Renaissance Humanism in the Mirror* (Cambridge: Cambridge University Press, 2015), 76–77.

92 Thomas A. Fudge, "Seduced by the Theologians: Aeneas Sylvius and the Hussite Heretics," in *Heresy in Transition: Transforming Ideas of Heresy in Medieval and Early Modern Europe*, ed. Ian Hunter, John C. Laursen, Cary J. Nederman (Aldershot, UK: Ashgate, 2005), 92. On Aeneas's likely sources, see Howard Kaminsky, "Pius Aeneas among the Taborites," *Church History* 28, no. 3 (1959): 283.

93 Montecalvo, "New *Landesgeschichte*," 57–58.

94 Pier Candido Decembrio describes a manuscript of Tacitus's *Germania* that he saw in Rome in 1455, which appears to have been brought from Germany that year by Enoch of Ascoli. See Paul Oskar Kristeller and L.D. Reynolds, "Tacitus," in *Texts and Transmission: A Survey of Latin Classics*, ed. L.D. Reynolds et al. (Oxford: Clarendon Press, 1983), 410. On Aeneas's access to the manuscript, see Montecalvo, "Between Empire and Papacy," 72; Caspar Hirschi, *The Origins of Nationalism: An Alternative History from Ancient Rome to Modern Germany* (Cambridge: Cambridge University Press, 2012), 168.

95 On the Strabo translations, see Nicola Casella, "Enea Silvio a difesa dell' Occidente cristiano," in *Eneas Silvio Picccolomini*, ed. Maria Antonietta Terzoli (Basel: Schwab Verlag, 2006), 55–68. Aeneas does not appear to have used Strabo until he penned *Germania*; see Baldi, *Pio II*, 41, n. and 45. On Strabo and Aeneas's use of him, see Patrick Gautier Dalché, "Strabo's reception in the West (fifteenth–sixteenth centuries)," in *The Routledge Companion to Strabo*, ed. Daniela Dueck (London: Routledge, 2017), 369–70.

96 For instance, ninth-century scholar Rudolf of Fulda used Tacitus to discuss the Saxons, but only as a historical people; Christopher B. Krebs, *A Most Dangerous Book: Tacitus's Germania from the Roman Empire to the Third Reich* (New York: W.W. Norton & Co., 2011), 63, 81.

97 We can compare *On Famous Men* to similar compilations by Jerome and Petrarch. Vespasiano da Bisticci, writing a few decades later, took a similar approach; see Eric Cochrane, *Historians and Historiography in the Italian Renaissance* (Chicago: University of Chicago Press, 1981), 45.

98 Aeneas may have been influenced by Flavio Biondo's work, especially his *Italia illustrata* (completed in 1453, but continually revised by Biondo thereafter). Aeneas used *Italia illustrata* in the *Commentaries*, but it is unclear if he had access to it when he wrote *Europe*, although he does mention Biondo's work there. In my view, one point that argues against his use of *Italia illustrata* in writing *Europe* is that Aeneas describes Italy with little reference to geography and topography—unlike Biondo's heavy treatment of both.

99 *Germania*, ed. Fadiga, 189; 194.
100 At si nationem nationi conferas, non est, quod urbes Italie Germanicis ante-
    ponas. Nova quodammodo Germanie facies et urbes ipse veluti nudiusquartus
    constructe atque erecte videntur." *Germania*, ed. Fadiga, 199.
101 "Cuperent tam egregie Scotorum reges quam mediocres Norimberge cives habi-
    tare." *Germania*, ed. Fadiga, 199.
102 "... constat nationem tuam non esse inopem, neque enim pauperes edificare
    magnifice possunt." *Germania*, ed. Fadiga, 199.
103 *Germania*, ed. Fadiga, 201.
104 "Nati in Germania pueri prius equitare quam loqui discunt: currentibus equis
    immobiles herent sellis, lanceas dominorum longiores ferunt, frigore ac sole
    durati nullo labore vincuntur." *Germania*, ed. Fadiga, 208–09.
105 Other German thinkers before Aeneas had written about the "Germans" as a
    political identity, which he may well have absorbed during his time in the empire.
    See Scales, "Late medieval Germany." Arguably, the scope and nature of
    Germania was more ambitious than these precedents.
106 "... amplior est vestra natio quam unquam fuerit atque adeo magna est, ut nulli
    genti cedat, meritoque illud affirmare possit, quia non est gens tam grandis, que
    habeat deos appropinquantes sibi sicut adest Germanico populo dominus Deus
    noster." *Germania*, ed. Fadiga, 187.
107 According to the *Oxford Latin Dictionary*.
108 Patrick J. Geary, *The Myth of Nations: The Medieval Origins of Europe*
    (Princeton: Princeton University Press, 2002), 49–50; Hirschi, *Origins*, 78–79.
    Romans used *gens* to refer (proudly) to their ancestors, evoking a social, rather
    than a political unit. Robert Bartlett also notes the distinction sources often
    made between *populus* and *gens*, the latter implied ethnicity or race, but not the
    former; "Medieval and Modern Concepts of Race," *Journal of Medieval and
    Early Modern Studies* vol. 31, no. 1 (Winter 2001): 42.
109 Susan Reynolds cautions against investing too much meaning in specific words
    and losing sight of the context and meaning; see "The idea of nation as a polit-
    ical community," in *Power and the Nation in European History*, ed. Scales and
    Zimmer, 55. This is a fair point, but as I will explain, Aeneas's wording shows
    some identifiable patterns.
110 Hirschi, *Origins*, 79.
111 On the role of the Council of Constance and nations, see Hirschi, *Origins*,
    81–88. Wilson also describes how during the thirteenth century the term acquired
    a more positive association; see *Heart of Europe*, 236.
112 "Que licet gallici iuris esse videantur, theutonico tamen sermone et moribus ves-
    tris utuntur." *Germania*, ed. Fadiga, 188; see also ibid., 194. Aeneas's sense of
    "German territory" is complicated and shifting, as his oration at Frankfurt in
    1454 shows. On the questions of borders of Germany at this time, see Thomas
    A. Brady, *German Histories in Age of Reformations, 1400–1650* (Cambridge:
    Cambridge University Press, 2009), 12–14. Interestingly, by putting his focus on
    "Germany" or "the Germans," Aeneas avoids the question of Northern Italy's
    relationship to the empire.
113 Wilson dates the first use of "German Nation" to 1474, with an increased fre-
    quency after 1512 and notes that only 1 in 9 documents used "Germany" after
    1560. Terms to denote empire were much more common. See *Heart of Europe*,
    255.
114 "Postremo Hungarorum natio ex ultimis Scytharum finibus inundavit, que
    usque in hanc diem regno potitur et ultra citraque Histrum late dominatur." *De
    Europa*, ed. Van Heck, 28; Eng. tr., *Europe*, tr. Bisaha and Brown, 52. In *Europe*,
    Rob Brown and I translated *natio* as "race," which is also an acceptable reading.
    I render it here as "nation" as I suspect the choice may have been more subtle
    and deliberate.

115 Hirschi, *Origins*, 78. Wilson, *Heart of Europe*, 236.

116 For a discussion of an earlier author's use of the term (Gerald of Wales, who also drew on Roman texts for inspiration), see Robert Bartlett, *Gerald of Wales, 1146–1223* (Oxford: Oxford University Press, 1982), 187–94.

117 "Transilvana regio est ultra Danubium sita, quam Daci quondam incoluere, feroces populi et multis Romanorum cladibus insignes. Nostra etate tres incolunt gentes: Theutones, Siculi et Valachi." *De Europa*, ed. Van Heck, 54; Eng. tr., *Europe*, tr. Bisaha and Brown, 64, with slight modifications.

118 There may be more instances, but I have only noted one use of *populus* for the Turks, and that is in his 'Letter to Mehmed' (1461), a unique text that will be discussed in Chapter 4.

119 "If we grant their demands, we call a powerful people, a large kingdom, and the most warlike peoples of Europe into the obedience of the Holy Roman Church, we unite the divided peoples of Bohemia, we give King Ladislas a tranquil region, we give the neighboring peoples peace, we become reconciled with strongly armed people whom we can mobilize against the Turks. Above all, we open the gates of Paradise to an infinite number of souls …." ("Si concedimus, quae petuntur, potentissimum populum, amplissimum regnum, ferocissimas Europae gentes ad oboedientiam sanctae Romanae ecclesiae convocamus; discordes inter se Bohemiae plebes unimus; Ladislao regi provinciam quietam reddimus; Theutonibus in circuitu pacem praebemus; militiam fortissimam, quam contra Turcos armare possimus, nobis conciliamus; et quod rebus omnibus praestat, infinitis animabus paradisi portas aperiemus.") "Res Bohemicas" of Enea Silvio Piccolomini (1455, Rome), ed. and tr., Michael von Cotta-Schönberg. Preliminary edition, 2nd version. (Orations of Enea Silvio Piccolomini / Pope Pius II; 28). 2015. <hal-01180832>, 102; Eng. tr., 103.

120 Geary, *Myth of Nations*, 52.

121 C.P. Cavafy, "Waiting for the Barbarians," in *Collected Poems*, tr. Edmund Keeley and Philip Sherrard, ed. George Savidis, rev. ed. (Princeton, NJ: Princeton University Press, 1992), 19.

122 Important medieval precedents were the descriptions of the Welsh and Irish by Gerald of Wales (c. 1146–c. 1223), but it is unclear if Aeneas read them. The Venerable Bede's eighth century *Historia ecclesiastica gentis Anglorum* is also noteworthy, but his focus was on the Church in England. Jordanes's sixth-century *History of the Goths* may also have influenced some of Aeneas's ideas.

123 Krebs, *A Most Dangerous Book*.

124 *De Europa*, ed. Van Heck, 54; *Europe*, tr. Bisaha and Brown, 64.

125 *De Europa*, ed. Van Heck, 37; *Europe*, tr. Bisaha and Brown, 55.

126 See, for instance, his claim in the final paragraph of *Europe* that Alfonso of Aragon and Naples was a "true scion of the Goths, from whom the royal family of Spain into which he was born is undoubtedly descended." *Europe*, 307.

127 Comparemus ergo cum veteri novam, et primum de amplitudine dicamus. Danubius ac Rhenus, qui quondam Germanie limites clausere, nunc per medios Germanorum dilabuntur agros. Belgica regio, que Gallie prius portio tertia fuit, nunc maiori ex parte Germanie cessit, lingua et moribus theutonica. Helvetii quoque gens antea gallica, in Germanos transivere," *Germania*, ed. Fadiga, 185.

128 See for example, *Opera omnia*, 763 (Letter to Frederick III, Dec. 22, 1456).

129 Nos in ipso iuvente nostre flore Germaniam intravimus; fuimus in concilio Basiliensi pluribus annis neque aliter nos gessimus quam si nati educatique in ea provincia fuissemus." *Germania*, ed. Fadiga, 170.

130 Casella, "Pio II," 40–43; for Aeneas's direct use of Bartolomeo Facio's history of Alfonso of Naples for portions on Italy, see *Europe*, tr. Bisaha and Brown, 20–22.

131 Hirschi, *Origins*, 36, 39.

132 "Post Albaniam illirice sequuntur gentes ad occidentem septentrionemque verse." *De Europa*, ed. Van Heck, 93; Eng. tr., *Europe*, tr. Bisaha and Brown, 115.

133 Talis tua Germania fuit ad Adrianum Cesarem. Sub illo autem imperatore, tota Germanica natio in potestatem Romanorum facta est .... Exinde mitior facta civilem cultum accepit. Eratque tunc longe angustior breviorque, quam modo sit siquidem Germania universa inter Rhenum et Albim ... ab occidenti ad orientem protensa solem, ab austro Danubii flumine, a septentrione britannico oceano et mari quod Balteum vocant, undique claudebatur. *Germania*, ed. Fadiga, 185.

134 Aeneas opens his section on Italy in *Europe* using the word *"patria."* His entire treatment of the peninsula in this work is different from most other areas. He does almost nothing with founding stories in Italy, except to note ancient ruins, perhaps thinking that the Romans needed no introduction and his focus was, indeed, on recent history. As mentioned, Aeneas loses the geographical thread by the time he reaches Italy. He tends to describe people by towns and cities— Milanese, Venetians, Florentines, etc., and sometimes as citizens or townsmen (*cives*).

135 Adrian Hastings, *The Construction of Nationhood: Ethnicity, Religion, and Nationalism* (Cambridge University Press, 1997), 13.

136 Hirschi, *Origins*, 21. See ibid., 20–33 for a summary of ideas of Anderson, Ernest Gellner, and Eric Hobsbawm and Hirschi's critiques of their views as presentist.

137 Here, I use Paschalis Kitromilides's insightful wording in his review of Hirschi's book in *Nations and Nationalism* 20, issue 1 (January 2014): 173–75.

138 Geary, *Myth of Nations*, 12, 156, 174.

139 On the misuse of the Middle Ages, see David Perry's introduction to *Whose Middle Ages: Teachable Moments for an Ill-Used Past*, ed. Andrew Albin et al. (New York: Fordham University Press, 2019), 4. See also Geary, *Myth of Nations*, 15–16.

140 Montecalvo, "Between Empire," 73.

141 *Historia Bohemica*, ed. Joseph Hejnic and Hans Rothe (Cologne: Bohlau Verlag, 2005), 1: 34–36. These notions are somewhat similar to the Lockean labor theory of property.

142 "Postremo Hungarorum natio ex ultimis Scytharum finibus inundavit, que usque in hanc diem regno potitur et ultra citraque Histrum late dominatur." *De Europa*, ed. Van Heck, 28; Eng., tr., *Europe*, tr. Bisaha and Brown, 52.

143 *Europe*, 51. See Montecalvo "New *Landesgeschichte*," 74 for similar points.

144 "Hoc genus hominum nostra etas Sclavos appellat, et alii Bosnenses, alii Dalmate, alii Croati, Histri Carnique nuncupantur." *De Europa*, ed. Van Heck, 93; Eng., tr., *Europe*, tr. Bisaha and Brown, 115.

145 *Europe*, tr. Bisaha and Brown, 64.

146 "Sermo gentis sclavonicus est; latissimi est enim hec lingua et in varias divisa sectas. Ex Sclavis enim alii romanam ecclesiam sequuntur ut Dalmate, Croatini, Carni ac Poloni; alii Grecorum sequuntur errores ut Bulgari, Rutheni et multi ex Lituanis; alii proprias hereses invenere ut Bohemi, Moravi et Bosnenses ... alii gentili adhuc cecitate tenentur, quemadmodum multi ex Lituanis idola colentes." *De Europa*, ed. Van Heck, 115; Eng., tr., *Europe*, tr. Bisaha and Brown, 143.

147 An important exception was Wladyslaw of Poland's acceptance of kingship over Hungary, at the expense of the infant heir of Albert II, Ladislas Postumus. Aeneas was highly critical of this move. Regarding Naples, Aeneas celebrates the conquest by Alfonso of Aragon in chapter 65. Alfonso claimed the throne after Joanna of Naples (briefly) designated him her heir and withdrew the offer; *Europe*, tr. Bisaha and Brown, 305–06. By contrast, Ottoman sultans in Europe, who were invited as allies in a civil war were expected to depart.

148 "Fatebor tamen Saxonie limites aliquando minores fuisse, aliquando maiores. Nam sicut imperia, ita et provinciarum limites ex tempore variantur." *De Europa*, ed. Van Heck, 127; Eng. tr., *Europe*, tr. Bisaha and Brown, 157.

149 "De cuius origine atque progressu, quamvis propositum egredi videar, dicere haud alienum existimo, quando sub evo nostro in tantum hoc genus hominum auctum est, ut Asiam Greciamque tenens latinum christianumque nomen late perterreat," *De Europa*, ed. Van Heck, 62; Eng. tr., *Europe*, tr. Bisaha and Brown, 72.

150 Talal Asad, "Muslims and European Identity," in *The Idea of Europe From Antiquity to the European Union*, ed. Anthony Pagden (Cambridge: Cambridge University Press, 2002), 209; see also Asad, *Formations of the Secular: Christianity, Islam, Modernity* (Stanford, CA: Stanford University Press, 2003).

151 *De Europa*, ed. Van Heck, 63.

152 For *Turcorum agros* see *De Europa*, ed. Van Heck, 71; for *natio*, 66; *regnum*, 77, and 78; *more gentis*, 76.

153 Colin Imber, *Ottoman Empire, 1300–1650: The Structure of Power* (Hampshire: Palgrave Macmillan, 2002), 26–27.

154 This is not to say he never uses *gens* for Europeans (as previous examples have already shown), but it is not as consistent as his application of the term to the Ottomans.

155 On at least one occasion he uses *cives* (citizens, or as we translated it contextually, native Turks) for Turkish soldiers sacking Constantinople. He also has George Brankovic use it to describe his own people; *De Europa*, ed. Van Heck, 67. Also, in *Europe* and many other works, Aeneas tends to call Mehmed *Maomethes* rather than king, leader, or emperor, unlike his treatment of European rulers. The only time I have specifically noted Aeneas using the term "Ottoman" is in his *Asia* (1461), in order to differentiate the Ottomans from other Turkish ruling powers in Asia Minor; see *Descripción de Asia*, ed. and tr. Domingo F. Sanz (Madrid: Consejo Superior de Investigaciones Científicas, 2010), 422, 424.

156 See Denys Hay, *Europe: The Emergence of an Idea* (Edinburgh: Edinburgh University Press, 1957), 96, on the fluid use of either term to denote the larger community in works by Aeneas and others.

157 *Europe*, tr. Bisaha and Brown, 160.

158 "… qui et vana simulacra colebant, liberos suos demoniis immolantes et rapinis cedisbusque gaudentes iniuriari vicinis eosque bonis spoliare in laudem trahebant. Nunc vero ad vos legitima Dei nostri sacra deducta sunt et unum cum sancta Romana ecclesia verum et unicum Deum Christum colitis." *Germania*, ed. Fadiga, 211.

159 Aeneas focuses more intently on the necessity for unity under Rome and the papacy in book 3 of *Germania*.

160 *Europe*, tr. Bisaha and Brown, 182–83. Regarding the Saxons, he states that "the three Ottos," tenth-century Roman Emperors, "thoroughly earned the gratitude of the Roman Church"; ibid, 157.

161 "Gentilis fuerat Vladislaus et ydola coluerat, sed baptismum cum regno suscipere non recusavit. Conversus ad Christum religiosum principem gessit. Multos ex Lituanis ad evangelium traxit, pontificales ecclesias nonnullas erexit, episcopos magno honore prosecutus est. Inter equitandum, quotienscumque turres ecclesiarum inspexit, detracto pileo caput inclinavit Deum, qui coleretur in ecclesia, veneratus." *De Europa*, ed. Van Heck, 112; Eng. tr., *Europe*, tr. Bisaha and Brown, 139.

162 "Motus ea re Vitoldus veritusque populorum tumultum Christo potius quam sibi deesse plebem voluit…" *De Europa*, ed. Van Heck, 117–18; Eng. tr., *Europe*, tr. Bisaha and Brown, 146.

163 *Europe*, tr. Bisaha and Brown, 70.

164 "… sive deceptus, sive sponte sua insaniens haudquaquam unioni consentiens videbatur …." *De Europa*, ed. Van Heck, 61; *Europe*, tr. Bisaha and Brown, 71.

165 "Surde (pro pudor!) nostrorum principum aures fuere, ceci oculi, qui cadente Grecia ruituram christiane religionis reliquam partem non viderunt ...." *De Europa*, ed. Van Heck, 78; Eng. tr., *Europe*, tr. Bisaha and Brown, 94.

166 See Robert Bartlett, *The Making of Europe: Conquest, Colonization and Cultural Change 950–1350* (Princeton, NJ: Princeton University Press, 1993), 255.

167 Kaminsky, "Taborites," 297. For more on Aeneas's views of compromise and complicated politics in Rome, see Baldi, *Cardinale tedesco*, 179–85; Montecalvo, "New *Landesgeschichte*," 57; Fudge, "Seduced by Theologians." See also Izbicki, *Protector of the Faith*, 21.

168 "Si concedimus, quae petuntur, potentissimum populum, amplissimum regnum, ferocissimas Europae gentes ad oboedientiam sanctae Romanae ecclesiae convocamus; discordes inter se Bohemiae plebes unimus; Ladislao regi provinciam quietam reddimus; Theutonibus in circuitu pacem praebemus; militiam fortissimam, quam contra Turcos armare possimus, nobis conciliamus; et quod rebus omnibus praestat, infinitis animabus paradisi portas aperiemus." "Res Bohemicas" of Enea Silvio Piccolomini (1455, Rome). Edited and translated by Michael von Cotta-Schönberg. Preliminary edition, 2nd version. (Orations of Enea Silvio Piccolomini / Pope Pius II; 28). 2015. <hal-01180832>, 102; Eng. tr., 103.

169 Kaminsky, "Taborites," 301; and 309, n. 92.

170 *Europe*, tr. Bisaha and Brown, 63, 135, 171.

171 "... qui Hussitarum labe infectus putatur, magnus vir alioquin et rebus bellicis clarus." *De Europa*, ed. Van Heck, 136; Eng. tr., *Europe*, tr. Bisaha and Brown, 171.

172 Aeneas addresses the great utility of a history of this region in his preface to Alfonso, *Historia Bohemica*, ed. Hejnic and Rothe, 1: 12–14. See also Maria Fadiga, "L'*Hist Bohemica*: la genesi di un'idea?" in *Il Ritorna dei classici nell'umanesimo: Studi in memoria di Gianvito Resta*, ed. Gabriella Albanese, Claudio Ciociola, Mariarosa Cortesi, and Claudia Villa (Florence: Sismel, 2015), 246; Fudge, "Seduced by Theologians," 91–92; Montecalvo, "Between Empire and Papacy," 66–67.

173 Letter to Juan Carvajal (21 Aug. 1451), Wolkan, *Briefwechsel*, 68: 24–25.

174 Wolkan, *Briefwechsel*, 68: 23–24; Fudge, "Seduced by Theologians," 98–99.

175 Wolkan, *Briefwechsel*, 68: 36–37.

176 Fudge, "Seduced by Theologians," 100–01.

177 Fudge, "Seduced by Theologians," 99. See also Kaminsky on Aeneas's observation of the way resentment of German domination in the university and the royal court helped feed the religious movement; "Taborites," 285.

178 That sense of belonging presented in *Germania* is complicated in *Historia Bohemica* when Aeneas describes the Poles and Bohemians as natural allies because of their shared language and common origin, adding that they had nothing in common with the Germans; *Historia Bohemica*, ed. Hejnic and Rothe, 1: 442.

179 "Venerunt ambo non tam verecunde aliena discere, quam sua impudenter ingerere parati, docendi quippe quam discendi cupidiores et popularis amantes aure.") *Historia Bohemica*, ed. Hejnic and Rothe, 1: 246.

180 "Sigismundum malo usum consilio in Turcos, qui se iampridem castris exuerant, arma prius movere quam Bohemiam petere libido incessit. Quod si mox exercitum Pragam duxisset, antequam vires hereticorum coaluissent, nunquam ea incendia, que postea vidimus, Germaniam exussissent. At ille dum Turcos lacessere parat, Bohemiam amisit et Hungariam non defendit." *Historia Bohemica*, ed. Hejnic and Rothe, 1: 272; see also Montecalvo, "The New *Landesgeschichte*," 83.

181 See Fadiga, "L'*Historica Bohemica*," 253; Fudge, "Seduced by Theologians," 98.

182 See *Europe*, tr. Bisaha and Brown, 220.

183 "... cuius nomen Italia, Gallia, Germania et omnis Europa venerata est ...."
Historia Bohemica, ed. Hejnic and Rothe, 1: 338. Aeneas's inflated estimation of
Sigismund, moreover, echoes in the words he attributes to Cardinal Cesarini at
Basel in the presence of the Hussite delegation, when he praises the Roman
Catholic Church as "mother of all the faithful." ("Ecclesiam ... omnium fidelium
matrem ...") *Historia Bohemica*, ed. Hejnic and Rothe, 1: 372.

184 "Tertia quoque legatio ad Callistum, pontificem maximum, decreta erat, que
controversias de religione dirimeret regnumque Bohemorum Romane ecclesie
coniungeret. Super his quarta cura regis urgebat animum, comparandi contra
Thurcos validi exercitus, quo tandem nostra etate scelerata Maumethis supersti-
tio pelli ab Europa posset." *Historia Bohemica*, ed. Hejnic and Rothe, 1: 602,
604.

185 "Diu secum per interpretem de sacris eloquiis disputavit; ut errorem sue gentis
relinqueret, magnopere cohortatus est. Ille hoc denique responsum dedit: 'Annis
nonaginta vitam produxi nec aliam religionem, quam suscepi a patribus, novi.
Sapientem me cives mei, quamvis infelicem, hactenus putavere. Tu nunc, quod
sepe agitant, senem delyrum efficere cupis. Laqueo vitam finire malim quam
patrum traditiones relinquere.'" *De Europa*, ed. Van Heck, 67–68 (reading *senem*
for *senes*); Eng. tr., *Europe*, tr. Bisaha and Brown, 80.

186 For an overview of studies on the relationship between the high clergy and the
Christian faith as it was lived and practiced in fifteenth-century Italy, see David
S. Peterson, "Out of the Margins: Religion and the Church in Renaissance
Italy," *Renaissance Quarterly* 53: 3 (Autumn 2000), 835–79.

187 *Europe*, tr. Bisaha and Brown, 262.

188 "Magnus profecto et clarus pontifex fuit Eugenius." *De Europa*, ed. Van Heck,
234; Eng. tr., *Europe*, tr. Bisaha and Brown, 261.

189 "... quod non parum eius gloriam imminuit. Nam cum pacis Italie, que tum
vehementer ferro vastabatur et igne, ipse repertor et arbiter concordi partium
voto delectus esset, dum diem ex die in deliberationem ducit, suspectus esse
Francisco Sfortie, iam Mediolanensium principi, ac Venetis cepit, tam quam
eam sententiam promere nollet, que aliis pacem, Ecclesie bellum allatura videretur." *De Europa*, ed. Van Heck, 247; Eng. tr., *Europe*, tr. Bisaha and Brown, 268.

190 "... obscuri antea nominis et prorsus ignoti, sed vite integritate probato ...." *De
Europa*, ed. Van Heck, 247; Eng. tr., *Europe*, tr. Bisaha and Brown, 268.

191 Baldi, *Pio II*, 54–55; 59.

192 "... magister italice pacis factus, hispanicarum quoque rerum moderator et arbiter esse videtur." *De Europa*, ed. Van Heck, 275; Eng. tr., *Europe*, tr. Bisaha and
Brown, 307.

193 For a sense of what "Roman" conjured, see Geary, *Myth of Nations*, particularly
63–64.

194 "Surde opulentum aures evangelio..." *De Europa*, ed. Van Heck, 82; Eng. tr.,
Europe, tr. Bisaha and Brown, 101. Yet, Aeneas also finds inspiration in the
trustful poor recruits who answer that call and "readily submit to the word of
preachers. Over forty thousand received the sign of the cross—an army protected more by faith than the sword." *Europe*, tr. Bisaha and Brown, 102.

195 "Commendanda est multis in rebus Florentinorum prudentia tum maxime,
quod in legendis cancellariis non iuris scientiam, ut plereque civitates, sed oratoriam spectant et que vocant humanititatis studia ...." *De Europa*, ed. Van Heck,
221; Eng. tr., *Europe*, tr. Bisaha and Brown, 248–49.

196 "Littere quoque et omnium bonarum artium studia apud vos florent. Scolas
quoque in quibus et iura et medicina et liberales traduntur artes, in Germania
plures urbes habent, ut Colonia Agrippina, Lovanium, Hedelberga, Praga,
Herfordia, Lipztia, Vienna, Rostavia, in quibus doctissimi viri claruerunt et nostra quoque etate non inferiores clarent." *Germania*, ed. Fadiga, 212. See also
ibid., 203 for his earlier praise.

197 See *Europe*, tr. Bisaha and Brown, 65–66; 138. For more on Aeneas's correspondence with Olesnicki, see "'Discourses of Power and Desire': The Letters of Aeneas Silvius Piccolomini (1453)," in *Florence and Beyond: Culture, Society, and Politics in Renaissance Italy*, ed. David Peterson and Daniel Bornstein (Toronto: Centre for Reformation and Renaissance Studies, 2008), 121–34.

198 "Convivitis humanissime omnibus gentibus, tantusque hodie et hominibus vestris et rebus nitor impositus est, ut preter sermonem patrium nihil inter vos barbarum remansisse videatur. Quod siqui vos amplius barbaros appellaverint, ipsi verius barbarissimi censendi fuerint, sive Greci, sive Latini." *Germania*, ed. Fadiga, 212.

199 On Aeneas's views of German learning, particularly the humanities, see ch. 1 on his letter to Heimberg. See also Noel Brann, 'Humanism in Germany," in *Renaissance Humanism: Foundations, Forms and Legacy*, ed. Albert Rabil (Philadelphia: University of Pennsylvania Press, 1988), 2: 123–55; Eckhard Bernstein, *German Humanism* (Boston: Tayne, Publishers), 1983; Paul Joachimsen, "Humanism and the Development of the German Mind," in *Pre-Reformation Germany*, ed. Gerald Strauss (Palgrave Macmillan, 1972), 162–224.

200 "Christiana religio hanc orbis partem nostro generi aperuit, que ferocissimis gentibus detersa barbarie mitioris vite cultum ostendit." *De Europa*, ed. Van Heck, 118–19; Eng. tr., *Europe*, tr. Bisaha and Brown, 148.

201 *De Europa*, ed. Van Heck, 118; Eng. tr., *Europe*, tr. Bisaha and Brown, 147; see also *De Europa*, 54, *Europe*, 66.

202 For a recent discussion of the spread of rituals in the early Church, see Nathan J. Ristuccia, *Christianization and Commonwealth in Early Medieval Europe* (Oxford: Oxford University Press, 2018).

203 Bartlett, *Making of Europe*, 308.

204 Bartlett, *Making of Europe*, 306.

205 For examples of "barbarian," see *Historia Bohemica*, ed. Hejne and Rothe, 1: 12 and 18; on cultural stereotypes of the Bohemians, see ibid., 28–30.

206 On Aeneas's view of "a geographic and ethnographic basis for national identity" as seen in the *History of Bohemia* and other works, see Montecalvo, "The New *Landesgeschichte*," 73.

207 Fudge finds some admiration even of heretical leaders for their resolve and toughness, like Zizka. See "Seduced by Theologians," 94.

208 *Europe*, tr. Bisaha and Brown, 115.

209 In the period after Pius's death, more conversions would take place in Albania, Bosnia, Macedonia, and Crete. For numbers based on census records, see Gilles Veinstein, "The Great Turk and Europe," in *Europe and the Islamic World: A History*, ed. John Tolan, Gilles Veinstein, and Henry Laurens (Princeton: Princeton University Press, 2013), 159–60.

210 "Video complures etatis nostre non oratores aut poetas dumtaxat, verum etiam historicos, eo errore teneri, ut Teucrorum nomine Turcos appellent. Credo eos idcirco motos, quoniam Turci Troiam possident, quam Teucri coluere. Sed illorum origo ex Chreta atque Italia fuit; Turcorum gens scythica et barbara est." *De Europa*, ed. Van Heck, 62; Eng. tr., *Europe*, tr. Bisaha and Brown, 72. For theories about the origins of the Turks, See Meserve, *Empires*, ch. 1; Bisaha, *Creating East and West*, ch. 2.

211 *Aeneid*, Bk III: lines 94–105; 129. See also Nicholas Horsfall, *Virgil, Aeneid 3: A Commentary* (Leiden: Brill, 2006). 110–11.

212 Discussed in Chapter 2.

213 "... gens truculenta, ignominiosa et in cunctis stupris ac lupanaribus fornicaria. Comedit que ceteri abominantur: iumentorum, luporum et vulturum carnes, nec abortivis hominum abstinuit .... Hec gens teste Othone, historico ... regnante apud Francos Pipino a Caspiis Portis egressa cum Avaribus ... Exin Pontum Capadociamque transgressa, ad reliquas inde finitimas gentes sensim dilapsa,

more latronum clandestinis quibusdam excursionibus vires sibi vendicans, occupatis quibusdam montibus et claustris opportunis, unde per occasiones facile irruptiones fieri possent ...." *De Europa*, ed. Van Heck, 63; Eng. tr., *Europe*, tr. Bisaha and Brown, 73.

214 *Europe*, tr. Bisaha and Brown, 73–74.

215 On the Turks in Anatolia prior to the Ottoman dynasty, see Imber, *Ottoman Empire*, 4–8; Claude Cahen, *Pre-Ottoman Turkey: A General Survey of the Material and Spiritual Culture and History, c. 1071–1330*, tr. J. Jones-Williams (New York: Taplinger Publishing Co., 1968).

216 On Aeneas's attitude toward medieval sources, see Meserve, *Empires*, ch. 3.

217 "Maomethes interea coactis undique copiis mirabili apparatu, formidando animi impetu terra marique regiam urbem aggressus ...." *De Europa*, ed. Van Heck, 78; Eng. tr., *Europe*, tr. Bisaha and Brown, 94.

218 "Tum subito capta urbe cesis omnibus, qui resistere ausi sunt, in rapinas est itum. Erat victorum infinitus numerus in libidinem ac sevitiam corruptior: non dignitas, non etas, non sexus quemquam protegebat; stupra cedibus, cedes stupris miscebantur. Senes exacta etate, feminas viles ad predam in ludibrium trahebant .... Cumque in exercitu maximo ac dissono, ex civibus, sociis atque externis conflato, diverse lingue, varii mores atque cupidines essent et aliud cuique fas, nihil illicitum toto triduo in Constantinopoli fuit." *De Europa*, ed. Van Heck, 80–81; Eng. tr., *Europe*, tr. Bisaha and Brown, 98.

219 Most Byzantines were still calling themselves "Romans" at this point, but Aeneas reflects a common Latin (and humanist) usage of "Greek." See Bisaha, *Creating East and West*, ch. 3.

220 "Post quos maritima loca versus meridiem ad Hellespontum usque Romania est, natio greca, quamvis olim barbara fuerit, et iterum nostro tempore deleto Grecorum imperio dominantibus Turcis in barbariam redit." *De Europa*, ed. Van Heck, 59; Eng., tr., *Europe*, tr. Bisaha and Brown, 69.

221 "Hec eadem nostra etate spurcissime Turcorum genti subiecta tributum pendere et iugum ferre miserrimum cogitur. Magnesiam quoque ac Thessaliam nostro tempore Turcorum arma invaserunt." *De Europa*, ed. Van Heck, 86; Eng. tr., *Europe*, tr. Bisaha and Brown, 105.

222 "Hic Termopilarum angustie Persarum cede insignes; que licet olim Xerxis impetum tenuere, Turcorum tamen armis claudere transitum minime potuere." *De Europa*, ed. Van Heck, 87; Eng. tr., *Europe*, tr. Bisaha and Brown, 106.

223 "Hic Musis natale in Eliconis nemore, hic saltus Cytheron .... Que patria quondam Liberi patris atque Herculis fuit, que fortem produxit Epaminundam, non cedens Athenis claritate. Civitas ea nostra etate exiguum castellum Thebarum est et a Turcis proximis annis cum reliqua Boetia occupatum." *De Europa*, ed. Van Heck, 87; Eng. tr., *Europe*, tr. Bisaha and Brown, 106.

224 Aeneas does allow some indication of decline over time in the above passage on Thebes and in his mention of Athens, which "once enjoyed great distinction .... In our time, the same place looks like a small town." *Europe*, tr. Bisaha and Brown, 107. On Islam and Greek learning, see William Montgomery Watt, *The Influence of Islam on Medieval Europe* (Edinburgh: Edinburgh University Press, 1994); Juan Cole, *Muhammad, Prophet of Peace Amid the Clash of Empires* (New York: Nation Books, 2018).

225 This imaginative view of Greece as somehow timeless and unchanging from the ancient period is an important subject on its own. For a fuller discussion of how Latins portrayed the Greeks in this period, the ways in which Greek refugees responded to this portrayal, and its possible impact on the later nationalist movement in Greece, see Bisaha, *Creating East and West*, chapter 3. See also Isabella Walser-Bürgler on how Aeneas treats Greek culture as a critical part of European culture; *Europe and Europeanness in Early Modern Latin Literature: Fuitne Europa tunc unita?* (Leiden: Brilll, 2021), 96.

226 Bisaha, *Creating East and West*, epilogue.
227 See Linda Darling's description of the "thickening wall" that European thinkers began to construct against the Ottoman Empire: "The Renaissance and the Middle East," in *A Companion to the Worlds of the Renaissance*, ed. Guido Ruggiero (Oxford: Blackwell Publishing, 2002), 65.
228 Lynn Hunt ascribes this othering process to Hegel and others in the modern era; see *History: Why It Matters* (Cambridge: Polity Press, 2018), 56–58. Kwame Anthony Appiah similarly sees the myth of the West as a nineteenth-century creation; see "There is no such thing as western civilization." *The Guardian*, Nov. 9, 2016.(https://www.theguardian.com/world/2016/nov/09/western-civilisation-appiah-reith-lecture); Peter Burke, too, emphasizes the modern era as the point of origin for an awareness of "Europe," but recognizes the parallels between two moments of invasion as creating heightened awareness of the continent; "Did Europe Exist Before 1700?" *History of European Ideas* 1, no. 1 (1980): 21–29, especially 25.
229 On Ciriaco and others, see Bisaha, *Creating East and West*, ch. 3.
230 See, for instance Brummett, *Mapping*; Jonathan M. Elukin, *Living Together, Living Apart: Rethinking Jewish-Christian Relations in the Middle Ages* (Princeton, NJ: Princeton University Press, 2007); Paul Freedman, "The Medieval Other" in Timothy S. Jones and David Sprunger, eds. *Marvels, Monsters, and Miracles* (Kalamazoo, MI: Medieval Institute Publications, 2002), 1–24; Eric Dursteler, *Renegade Women: Gender, Identity and Boundaries in the Early Modern Mediterranean* (Baltimore: Johns Hopkins University Press, 2011); E. Nathalie Rothman, *Brokering Empire: trans-imperial subjects between Venice and Istanbul* (Ithaca, NY: Cornell University Press, 2012).
231 Palmira Brummett, "The Lepanto Paradigm Revisited: Knowing the Ottomans in the Sixteenth Century," in *The Renaissance and the Ottoman World*, ed. Anna Contadini and Claire Norton (Burlington, VT: Ashgate, 2013), 71.
232 Aeneas mistakenly names Murad here, but Orhan was the first.
233 "Qui duobus de Grecorum imperio disceptantibus ab altero, qui superari timeret, in auxilium accersitus Turcorum primus transivit in Greciam, ubi consulto bellum protrahens, postquam ambos enervatis consumptisque viribus fractos ac defessos animadvertit, versis ut aiunt, proris arma in eos sine ullo discrimine per occasionem convertit ...." *De Europa*, ed. Van Heck, 64; Eng. tr., *Europe*, tr. Bisaha and Brown, 75.
234 Emperor John VI Cantacuzenus formed this alliance with Orhan against his rival, John V Paleologus in 1352; see Bisaha, *Creating East and West*, 97; Housley, *Later Crusades*, 65; John V.A. Fine, *Late Medieval Balkans* (Ann Arbor, MI: University of Michigan Press, 1987), 305; Imber, *Ottoman Empire*, 9–10.
235 "Illiriorum agros vastavit, oppida multa vi cepit, diripuit atque incendit. Uxoribus more gentis quamplurimis iunctus est, inter quas Georgii, Servie despoti, filiam duxit; nec diu post immemor affinitatis adversus eum duxit exercitum." *De Europa*, ed. Van Heck, 66; Eng. tr. *Europe*, tr. Bisaha and Brown, 78.
236 See *Europe*, tr. Bisaha and Brown, 78–79.
237 "Obiit deinde Lazarus, de cuius hereditate non parva contentio exorta est. Gregorius Turcorum auxilio paternum regnum vendicare nititur." *De Europa*, ed. Van Heck, 68; Eng. tr., *Europe*, tr. Bisaha and Brown, 81.
238 Cantacuzenus also gave his daughter, Theodora, to Orhan in marriage in 1345, although Fine does not see it as a formal marriage; *Late Medieval Balkans*, 305. For a recent study that examines some interfaith marriages in the sixteenth century, see Dursteler, *Renegade Women*. Ibn Battuta describes a fourteenth-century dynastic marriage between the daughter of the Byzantine emperor and a Turkish emir; see *Travels of Ibn Battuta, A.D. 1325–1354*, ed. H.A.R. Gibb, (Cambridge: Cambridge University Press, 1962), 2: 488–504. On Mara, see Donald Nicol, *The Byzantine Lady: Ten Portraits 1250–1500* (Cambridge: Cambridge University Press, 1994), 110–119.

239 "Utraque pars Maometis auxilium imploravit; illi nobilior pars visa iustior: auxilia adversus Albanos Demetrio fratrique tradita." *De Europa*, ed. Van Heck, 89; Eng. tr., *Europe*, tr. Bisaha and Brown, 109.

240 Fine, *Late Medieval Balkans*, 565.

241 "Hungari, qui suas vires non ignorarent nec tam potentie sue quam casui victoriam imputarent, periculosum existimantes sepius tentare fortunam, oblatas ultro conditiones pacis non recusarunt. Inducie belli in decem annos dicte." *De Europa*, ed. Van Heck, 69; Eng. tr., *Europe*, tr. Bisaha and Brown, 83.

242 "Vladislao, qui alienum regnum invasisset, e re sua visum est solicitudinem belli provincialibus non deese." *De Europa*, ed. Van Heck, 71; Eng. tr., *Europe*, tr. Bisaha and Brown, 84.

243 See *Europe*, tr. Bisaha and Brown, 84.

244 "Magnus hic vir fuit, domi bellique tam suis amatus quam nostris odiosus." *De Europa*, ed. Van Heck, 68; Eng. tr., *Europe*, tr. Bisaha and Brown, 81–82.

245 "Victor Amurates neque fugientes hostes insecutus est neque gloriabundus inter suos magnifica verba iactavit neque, ut ante assueverat, hilarem vultum ostendit. Interrogatus quidnam tristior esset et cur non victis hostibus exultaret, 'Nollem' inquit 'hoc modo sepius vincere' …. Ipse Adrianopolim reversus deo suo, que pro victoria fecerat, vota persolvit …. Ipse privatam deligens vitam in Asiam profectus cum paucis ocii sui comitibus religioni cuidam solitarie sese addixit." *De Europa*, ed. Van Heck, 75; Eng. tr., *Europe*, tr. Bisaha and Brown, 89.

246 See Petrarch's famous letter to Cicero, dated June 16, 1345 (*Fam.*, XXIV, 3).

247 "Video complures etatis nostre non oratores aut poetas dumtaxat, verum etiam historicos, eo errore teneri, ut Teucrorum nomine Turcos appellent." *De Europa*, ed. Van Heck, 62; Eng. tr., *Europe*, tr. Bisaha and Brown, 72.

248 Bisaha, *Creating East and West*, 147–52.

249 Helmrath has fruitfully explored Aeneas's "transformative" use of ancient sources. See "Political-Assembly Speeches," 89–94.

250 Ronald Martin, *Tacitus* (London: Batsford Academic and Educational Ltd., 1981), 49–59. Christopher Krebs also points out that Romans in general did not have just one way of looking at Germans; "Borealism: Caesar, Seneca, Tacitus, and the Roman Discourse about the Germanic North," in *Cultural Identity in the Ancient Mediterranean*, ed. Erich S. Gruen (Los Angeles: Getty Research Institute, 2011), 202–221. On German readings of Tacitus, see Hirschi, *Origins*, 129.

251 Benedict Anderson, *Imagined Communities: Reflections on the Origin and Spread of Nationalism* (London: Verso, 1983). On right of soil and blood, see Hastings, *Construction of Nationhood*, 13–14; 107–09.

252 Scales, "Late medieval Germany," 167.

253 Geary, *Myth of Nations*, 155–56.

254 Elizabeth Spiller, *Reading and the History of Race in the Renaissance* (Cambridge: Cambridge University Press, 2011), 7–11.

4 Papacy and Crusade (1458–1464)

August of 1458 found Aeneas once again at Viterbo taking curative baths for his gout and adding the finishing touches to his *Europe* and *History of Bohemia* when news arrived that abruptly ended his respite: Pope Calixtus III had died in Rome on August 6, and cardinals within a hundred miles of Rome would meet to elect one of their number as his successor. Aeneas and his servants cut short their sojourn and hastened to the Vatican. There he paid his last respects to the pope and joined with seventeen other cardinals to begin their solemn task. The papal conclave was designed to be the most secretive, secure, and intimate of elections: as its Latin name (*conclave, -is*) suggests, participating cardinals were literally locked in together. Two chapels in the papal palace were set aside for this purpose. As Aeneas himself writes, "In the larger chapel [the old Capella Magna] they constructed cells where the cardinals would eat and sleep; the smaller, called the chapel of St. Nicholas, was reserved for deliberation and voting."[1] For however many days or weeks it took to reach a decision, they spent every waking and sleeping hour beside one another in an effort to block outside influence. They could walk about the halls, but the latrines were one of the few places where they might privately scheme—a sordid detail Aeneas delights in revealing.[2] The cardinals met to agree on capitulations—promises which they agreed in advance to uphold if elected—and to vote, again and again, until a candidate emerged with a two-thirds majority. Amidst the lobbying, jockeying for position, and even a scuffle at the end, if the account in the *Commentaries* is to be believed, Aeneas eventually prevailed.

On August 19, 1458, Aeneas was elected pope, taking the name of Pius II. Both a nod to his new role as the Holy Father and an obvious reference to "pius Aeneas," the hero of Virgil's *Aeneid*, Pius's papal name symbolized his desire to embrace the radical transformation while retaining core aspects of his persona.[3] The poor country boy from Corsignano would finally enjoy luxuries, pomp, and privileges he had so often only observed from a distance. As head of all Latin Christians, he would be waited on and ensconced in the lush surroundings of the Vatican and other papal residences. The Sistine Chapel and the current gargantuan church of St. Peter still lay in the future, but Pope Nicholas V had begun to beautify the Vatican and make it a worthy home for the head of the Church, after decades of neglect. Among Nicholas's

DOI: 10.4324/9781003315865-5

improvements to the papal palace were the rebuilding of the north and west walls of the palace, and the refurbishment and redecoration of public rooms in the papal apartments. The architects Leon Battista Alberti and Bernardo Rossellino helped design the buildings, and the artist Fra Angelico painted fresco cycles in the chapel of St. Nicholas. Pope Nicholas also hired scores of copyists and scholars to fill the papal collection with priceless books. Though in 1458 it was far from its present-day magnificence, the Vatican was beginning to resemble other Italian courts, and Pius was its newest prince.[4]

A few years later in his *Commentaries*, Pius attributed his election to his eloquence and keen understanding of the desires and weaknesses of several key cardinals—an intriguing assertion which cannot be independently verified due to a lack of sources; it goes without saying that participants in a conclave were expected to maintain strict confidentiality.[5] Additional factors clearly weighed in Aeneas's favor, including his first-rate knowledge of European politics and the Ottoman advance, his connections with rulers throughout Europe, and his diplomatic aplomb, acquired from twenty-six years of service to secular and ecclesiastical princes. These distinctions helped Aeneas rise above the other candidates, but so did a major asset that he omits from his self-flattering account: the behind-the-scenes support of Duke Francesco Sforza of Milan and King Ferrante of Naples. Their backing, it should be noted, came only after the death of the favored candidate, Domenico Capranica, less than a month before Calixtus passed.[6] Whatever the forces may have been that brought Aeneas to the papal throne, it was expected that crusade against the Turks would become the focal point of his papacy and that he would further this cause in any way possible.

Knowing that Pius II's crusade ended before it could depart from Italy, modern scholars often describe his papal reign in ominous terms, characterizing the aborted campaign as the predictable end to a nostalgic quest, or worse, as an opportunistic power grab. Whether they blame Pius's overreaching, the apathy of secular leaders, or both, they portray his crusade and, by extension, his reign, as idealistic and unsuccessful.[7] Others assess Pius's plans and actions on crusade as sincere and even inherently reasonable: Barbara Baldi, for instance, sees his plans as grounded not in quixotic idealism, but a profound knowledge of the political and historical realities of Europe.[8] Putting aside the soundness of his plan, as stated at the opening of this book, I take a different view of its outcome. Pius's failed campaign was not the end of his legacy; on the contrary, his influence was only beginning. The forceful language he used to evoke his crusade was far more consequential than its immediate strategic results.[9]

The stirring rhetoric Pius crafted regarding the identity of Christendom, Europe, and nation states—all in the service of crusade—would take on a life of its own and make a profound impression upon readers for many years after his death. This chapter will trace the development of these ideas in his papal bulls, his oration at Mantua, a treatise on Asia, a controversial letter to Mehmed II, and his autobiographical *Commentaries*. In many ways, Pius's papal writings reflect decades of thought and offer a continuation and capstone to his ideas. But would Pius, now the theoretical head of all Christendom, maintain his focus on Europe, or envision a community of believers on a much grander global scale?

Pius's First Call to Crusade

It is hard to imagine what went through Pius's mind when, after decades of advising emperors, princes, and popes on how to wield their power more effectively, he now found himself in a position of enormous authority. His biographer, Giovanni Antonio Campano, reports that when his friends congratulated him, Pius said, "Those who rejoice over so exalted a position do not think of the toils and the dangers. Now I must show to others all that I have so often demanded of them."[10] Clearly, Pius appreciated the irony. His top priority as pope was to call a large-scale crusade against the Ottomans in order to protect Christian territory in Europe and possibly recoup some of losses of the past century. Urgent matters in Italy often diverted his attention—namely rival claims to Naples in the wake of Alfonso's death (Jun 27, 1458) and Jacopo Piccinino's invasion of papal territories. Indeed, the majority of fifteenth-century popes faced the dual challenge of solidifying their leadership over Christians from within and securing European borders from without.[11] But to any student of Pius's writings from 1453 forward, his dedication to crusading should be clear. Pius's papacy began and ended in pursuit of a campaign against the Turks.

The best way to do this, to Pius's mind, was to start with a meeting of Christian rulers and delegates to discuss and plan a large-scale crusade—a gathering he had dreamed of since he first learned of the fall of Constantinople. If only the sitting pope could convene such a meeting, he thought, anything could be accomplished. His famous 1453 letter to Cardinal Nicholas of Cusa ended with a rush of optimism on the prospect: "I do not doubt, if a fitting place is named for these matters, that either the kings will come, or they will send envoys; and with good souls, they will embrace this business of the faith." After describing the emperor and German nobles' eagerness to take action, he praised the attributes of different European nations and warmly added:

> It will, believe me, the crusade will be launched with the common consent of all Christians, if the authority of the Roman pontiff rises up at this moment and [if] the faithful and eloquent voices of preachers, among whom the common judgment holds Your Piety to belong, resound to the ends of the earth.[12]

This passage underscores Aeneas's belief—years before he became pope—that "persuasion" and "eloquent voices" were the keys to building a spirit of common enterprise. This view of the diverse nation-states coalescing into a massive team with distinct, yet complementary talents only grew in strength, as his writings of 1457–1458 attest. After all his years of imagining this moment, as pope, Pius could finally call European Christians together and put his celebrated oratorical skills to the test. He would spend much of his papacy trying to forge a powerful collective identity among his diverse flock.

The first step was to convince rulers and governments to commit to a meeting. On October 13, 1458, Pius issued the bull *Vocavit nos Pius*, which summoned rulers and legates to attend a congress to plan the crusade in the north of Italy with an opening date of June 1, 1459.[13] In composing his first major bull, Pius faced some rhetorical choices: should he address all of Christendom in traditional papal language? Should he describe crusade in strictly religious terms or use medieval chivalric language? Should he simply try to sound more like his humanist self? In the end, he seems to have opted for all of the above. The bull employs some of Pius's most recognizable rhetoric, describing Mehmed II as a "dragon" (*draco*), an "abominable monster rather than a king" (*taetra potius bellua quam rex*), and an "enemy of the human race" (*hostis humani generis*). He singles out the Turks from other Muslims as "a barbarous race" (*barbara Turcorum gens*) and "the cruelest nation" (*crudelissima natio*).[14] Interestingly, this was the first time he referred to the Turks as a "nation," but the intent, of course, was not flattering. He offers no depiction of an organized state, nor does he refer to Mehmed as "king" or "emperor" as he had occasionally done in the past; the last thing he wished to do in this bull was to confer any legitimacy on the Ottomans.

Yet *Vocavit nos Pius* departs in several ways from Pius's pre-papal style and shows his new role as the Roman pontiff seeking to unite and lead his Christian audience. First, it places threats to the faith above the security or culture of the continent. "Europe" appears only once and in passing,[15] while the language of Christ, Christians, and Catholicism dominates. Second, Islam and the Holy Land feature more prominently than in his previous writings. Rather than focus on Constantinople, Pius launches into a lament about the way the faith has been driven into a corner, dating back to the rise of the "pseudo-prophet" Muhammad, whose followers invaded the site where Jesus was laid to rest, as well as Asia, Libya, Spain, and eventually, Greece. Beautiful churches that once invoked Christ's name, he exclaims, now implore the abominable name of Muhammad.[16] With this evocation of the Holy Land tarnished by Muslim rule, Pius echoes a tradition of papal crusade rhetoric beginning with Urban II's first call in 1095. Finally, instead of emphasizing contemporary geopolitical concerns, he spends at least as much time discussing the sins of the Christians and the necessity of putting one's trust in God, as did Moses, David, and Judith—themes that were, again, very much at home in traditional crusade rhetoric. Citing St. Paul, he states, "Evils have befallen us because of our sins .... Those whom God loves, he corrects and chastens."[17] Writing now as pope, Pius addresses all Christians, regardless of their location.

More surprising are the words Pius does not use in this bull: namely, "crusade." Many scholars, myself included, have translated Pius's words describing war against the Turks as crusade. But as Norman Housley has demonstrated, the term *cruciata* was "just entering its heyday." It was favored by Pope Calixtus III, who may have been drawing on its Iberian coinage, but it did not appeal to

Pius. If the term was too recent for his liking, other powerful, medieval terms could be deployed, such as "pilgrimage" or "soldiers of the cross"; yet Pius rejects these as well. Instead, he employs more classical and secular terms like war, expedition, or undertaking (*bellum, expeditio,* or *profectio*) against the Turks (*in, adversus,* or *contra Turcos*). The non-classical word *passagium* was also often used by Pius, at least initially, to denote "an exceptionally large military expedition against unbelievers by Christians," who were entitled to a plenary remission of sins if they were signed with the cross.[18]

Pius's preference for these classical terms shows his interest in defending and expanding borders—a goal that often overshadowed the spiritual aspects of crusade. His conscious use of the language of Roman imperialism heralded ideas that would take fuller shape in his *Commentaries.* Even the name of the meeting itself departed from the usual script. The gathering that eventually assembled at Mantua was a "congress" (*conventio*) and not a "council" (*concilium*), although Pius tries to blur the distinction by using both terms in the bull and in his *Commentaries.*[19] *Vocavit nos Pius,* then, uses traditional crusade language while incorporating new ideas deriving from his humanist training and the current political climate. The overall effect was something of a mash-up. It would take a little time for Pius to find his own style on this subject as pope.

Indeed, the mix of themes in Pius's bull echoes the changing perceptions and realities of crusading. While the First Crusade was conceived and called by Urban as an armed pilgrimage under papal control, by the fifteenth century, battles against the Ottomans regularly took place without the benefit (or hindrance) of papal leadership; these secular affairs only became crusades when the pope was involved—like the successful "long campaign" of 1443 led by John Hunyadi and King Wladyslaw that morphed into the unsuccessful Crusade of Varna.[20] As such, the nature of Renaissance crusades was relatively fluid. At the same time, popes were still expected to work toward the larger goal of union with all Christians and the recovery of Jerusalem to help prepare for the second coming of Christ.[21] In addition to all these ideological complexities, Pius faced an enormous task in coordinating forces and raising funds for this vast undertaking.[22]

Despite these considerable challenges, Pius was optimistic—at least at first. One reason, I contend, is that his goals were smaller in scale and more attainable than is often understood. If one puts aside his grand rhetoric about battling Islam and liberating the Holy Land, a much narrower target appears again and again in his writings: the defense of Hungary.[23] Moreover, while critics have portrayed Pius's crusade as an idealistic power grab, they fail to explain his willingness to delegate military leadership and decision-making to others. A point here that has gone largely unnoticed is that Pius was not picky as to whom the crusade leader should be; he had been pleading with a long list of rulers since 1453 to take up the mantle and seemed, even as pope, to be willing to accept any of them. He only sought to raise all the resources and men he could possibly mobilize. With this fairly limited set of goals, Pius was determined to make his case at Mantua where he hoped to build a coalition against the Ottomans. He had been thinking hard about these issues for years and had acquired firsthand experience in the politics of crusade in Austria and in Rome. In these settings, he observed the complicated German diets and the relative success of the Italian League of 1455 and hoped to find a balance. What Pius was less prepared to confront were concerns that European rulers harbored toward each other—namely that one's departure for crusade would render his lands vulnerable to attacks by Christian neighbors. At the same time, however, Christian rulers feared to empower a rival to lead the crusade. This made it hard for princes to either volunteer or to support another leader.[24]

The Congress of Mantua: Crafting the Message

Pius's journey from Rome to the congress was a long and showy affair. A trip that might have taken a few days by horse became a four-month tour, punctuated by lengthy sojourns in Perugia, Siena, and Corsignano, and shorter stays in Florence, Bologna, and Ferrara.[25] The *Commentaries* contain elaborate descriptions of his progress through Italy and the celebrations and pageantry that greeted him along the way—the pope's pleasure in his own importance is unconcealed. But the attention did more than inflate his ego; it helped him to promote an image of papal leadership over the peninsula at a time when it was shaky. On the downside, it did little to reassure the Romans, who would come to complain of Pius's frequent and long absences from the city.[26] He arrived in Mantua on May 27, in a grand procession comprised of cardinals, local clergy, and riderless white horses with golden saddles and bridles. He was welcomed by the marquis of Mantua, Ludovico III Gonzaga, and his wife, Barbara of Brandenburg, as well as the Duchess of Milan, Bianca Maria Sforza. The following day, Sforza's fourteen-year-old daughter, Ippolita, delivered an accomplished Latin oration, which Pius warmly praised.[27] The celebrated humanist Francesco Filelfo would later deliver one as well.

Mantua in 1459 was a convenient, if not comfortable setting for a large papal congress. Its location in Northern Italy near the Po River made it easier for transalpine delegates to reach, but the city was crowded, swampy, and distinctly unpleasant in the summer. Ludovico Gonzaga was making plans for the city's beautification and would employ the master painter Andrea Mantegna and the architect Leon Battista Alberti to help achieve his vision, but none of this had been brought to fruition when Pius arrived in the city.[28] According to the *Commentaries*, Pius's critics carped,

> The place was a swamp and a hazard to health; it was too hot; the wine was terrible and so was the food; everyone was getting sick and many were catching their death of fever; all you could hear was the frogs.[29]

Pius's own faint praise for the city's charms suggests that he shared such views to at least some extent. He was not ungrateful, however, for the Gonzagas' and the Mantuans' hospitality. Mindful of the costs and logistical challenges the marquis incurred in hosting the large six-month gathering, Pius created his seventeen-year-old son Francesco cardinal in 1461.

Conspicuously missing from Pius's reception at Mantua were the crowds of foreign dignitaries he expected to find. The delegates summoned from across Christian Europe took even longer than he did to arrive, signaling problems for the negotiations ahead. Not only did Emperor Frederick fail to appear and support his longtime servant, but he insulted Pius by sending ambassadors of low rank. Pius refused them and waited five months for the Margrave of Baden and two bishops to arrive. Other representatives gladly traveled to Mantua, like envoys from Albania, Bosnia, Ragusa, Cyprus, Rhodes, Lesbos, and the Morea who sought to procure rather than offer aid.[30] Eventually Pius's patience was rewarded with the splendid arrival in September of Duke Francesco Sforza of Milan with a fleet of forty-seven vessels along the river Mincio; his presence buoyed Pius's spirits and encouraged other Italian powers to quickly send their own legates.[31] Soon thereafter, enough representatives and rulers trickled in for the first formal session to take place on September 26.[32]

After mass was said in the cathedral and attendees squabbled over their seating order, the pope addressed the crowd from his throne, delivering what would become his best-known oration, *Cum bellum hodie*.[33] Dispensing with any false modesty, Pius boldly claims in his *Commentaries* that he "commanded silence and spoke for three hours amid such rapt attention that not a single word went unremarked."[34] While, yet again, he may have exaggerated the ability of all his listeners to fully comprehend a Latin oration, his audience would expand over time. The text circulated widely in manuscript and print, carrying this powerful message far and wide for decades to come; it was also one of the handful of orations printed in the sixteenth-century editions of his *Opera omnia*. As Helmrath states, "profiting fully from papal authority and surviving in more than 110 manuscripts, [*Cum bellum hodie*] appears to be the most widely diffused speech of the century."[35]

In some ways, Pius takes a traditional approach in his first major papal oration. With its prayer to God to help expel the Turks from the "lands of the Christians" (*de Christianorum finibus*), *Cum bellum hodie* invokes the same shared religious identity employed in Pius's bull. His intended audience is broad and undifferentiated, and he addresses them as an all-embracing collective with terms like "Christian republic" (*respublica Christiana*), "Christians," or simply "we" and "us." In these respects, Pius echoes the sermons of previous popes, who called for a defense of the faith as a whole.[36] Turning to the question of the justice of the war, he answers with a lament for the losses of the Holy Land and other key areas in the Christian East, then builds up to a description of recent atrocities of 1453.[37] The implication is that the universal fabric of Christendom has been torn but can be repaired and restored to its former unity—a golden age in which the Christian faith filled "almost the whole world" (*universum ferme orbem*).[38] The obstacle to such unity, of course, is Islam. Midway through the oration, he speaks at length about the rival faith, aided by a recent tract on Islamic errors by

Cardinal Juan de Torquemada, who accompanied Pius to Mantua.[39] In short, Pius sought to emphasize Christian solidarity and history to condemn the powerful rival faith.[40]

Less expected is Pius's renewed emphasis on the protection of Europe and the importance of ethnicity and cultural identity—notions that complicate the seamless world of "Christendom" that he sought to portray in his bull. First, he emphasizes a tension between Greeks and Romans, in both past and present, at several points in the oration. Erasing the role that Greeks played in the spread of early Christianity, he highlights the reign of the Roman Emperor Constantine as the pinnacle of Christian unity:

> For at the time of Constantine the Great both the Indians and the Spaniards worshipped the boy born of Mary, and the North and the South knew Christ. The voice of the Roman Bishop, as Vicar of Christ, reached over the seas and across the countries …. The Christians were held to be a holy people, an elected people, a chosen people, they received tributes from the gentiles and were placed above all other peoples. Such, o Christians, was once the glory, the empire, and the authority of our forefathers.[41]

Then, with no mention of the fall of Rome in the West and the preservation of the Eastern empire by the Greeks, he discusses the rise of Islam and the descent of Eastern Christians into religious error.

But his omissions about the Greeks soon give way to insults. The disastrous turning point, Pius claims, began under (Greek) Emperor Heraclius, during whose reign Islam began to arise:

> At that time, the empire had already become enfeebled in the hands of the Greeks, and Roman strength [*virtus*] had grown weak under another sky. This gradually eroded the strong Christian position. Still, there remained many Christians in Asia until the time of King Pepin of the Franks, who reigned famously over the Germans and the Gauls about 600 [actually 700] years ago.[42]

After this point, the Turks began to occupy Anatolia and other areas. As Meserve has noted, Pius likely drew on Andrea Biglia's view of a loss of Roman *virtus* as the cause of the rise of the Arabs—an argument that suited Pius's penchant for masculinist rhetoric.[43]

Other historians have taken a different view of Heraclius (r. 610–41), an emperor who inherited a protracted war against the Persians but emerged victorious and reformed the Byzantine military system in the process. The war left both sides weakened, however—precisely as Islam was starting to spread from the south, easing the path of Arab conquests in both Byzantine and Sassanid areas. But this later outcome does not change the fact that Heraclius and the Greeks fought the war effectively; with a few more years to recover from the conflict, the aftermath might have been quite different. Pius casts such complexities aside, just as he does with his silence, here and in other texts, about the collapse of Roman rule in the West. He also ignores the complexity of the relationship between Arabia and the Roman Empire in this period. There were indeed more interactions and shared traditions than conflicts between Romans and Arabs, but Pius had even less interest in crediting the Arabs than he did the Greeks.[44] A distinctly Latin-centric view of the diverse Roman Empire and its relations with its neighbors and allies begins to emerge in this call for crusade.

The trope of Greek weakness was, in many ways, a device to prove the feasibility of the war. By arguing that the Greeks' passivity led to their easy defeat, he seeks to reassure his audience that they, as Western Europeans, could handily dispatch the Turks:

> … the Greeks, although once courageous and brave, have not kept their former vigor. Almost all who are subject to the Turks have become weak and lost their former spirit with regard to military matters and letters. All went into decline when they lost power. Courage and servitude do not mix. All the strong men in the Turkish army come from the Christians.[45]

Here Pius's ethnic slurs start to collapse under their own weight.

Did the Greeks become weak by Heraclius's day, or as a result of their domination by the Turks? Who were these strong Christians (or former Christians) fighting in the Ottoman ranks if not, at least partly, drawn from Greek areas? Finally, why does he say here that the Greeks have lost their spirit in letters after his anguish at the cultural losses in Constantinople—of learned men and schools as much as books? None of this makes particular sense, but it is consistent with his inexplicable, recent desire to diminish the Greeks of his own period. His earlier letters were filled with empathy and laments for the loss of "outstanding Greece" in 1453.[46] But in both his oration to Calixtus (*Solent plerique*, 1455) and *Europe* (1458), he began to criticize the Greeks' faith and their emperor for their schismatic beliefs; finally, in *Cum bellum hodie*, he blatantly asserts the ethnic inferiority of the Greeks and blames the spread of Islam on their supposed inaction in the seventh century.[47]

Having painted the Greeks as weak, he builds a case for the masculine faith of Western European Christians. He lays the groundwork with centuries-old polemic about Islam as a cunning invention, in contrast to the true Christian faith, "proven" by Christ's miracles, the Gospels, and the repeated witness of martyrs.[48] Pius then ties these points to observations on the personality and cultural traits of each religion's followers, arguing that the superior judgment and temperament of the men who embraced Christianity verifies its worth:

> The authority of the Romans is quite important: being the wise and powerful lords of the world, they would never have submitted to the Gospel unless they had been convinced by reasons or miracles. And who can believe that those strong and wise men, the Spaniards, the French, and

the Germans would have accepted the Gospel unless they had been persuaded by very strong arguments. Indeed, since the law of the pagans is
lax while the law of the Christians is exacting, no one would have
accepted the harder law unless he had learnt that its author was God
himself.[49]

This striking assertion undermines centuries of conversion stories grounded
in suffering, revelation, and piety with a pivot toward reason, concrete proof,
and most fascinating of all, national character or mettle. Pius's argument that
only strong men have chosen such a demanding faith seems a far cry from the
spirit of Christ's Sermon on the Mount, his outreach to the poor and margin-
alized members of society, and the example of humble missionaries and
saints.

This passage brings the oration full circle from his earlier comments about
Romans and Greeks. The Greeks may have embraced Christianity earlier and
more fully than the Romans, but Pius marginalizes them. As for Asian
Christians, he barely mentions them at all; even the Armenians, one of the
earliest Christian nations, are noted for their "error" rather than their tena-
cious belief.[50] Apart from a brief nod to Ethiopia, there is no consideration
of Christian Africa, which produced many saints and Church leaders like
Augustine of Hippo. With his focus on the Romans, but also Spaniards,
Gauls, and Germans, Pius suggests that the best and firmest of all Christians
were and are European—*Western European*, to be precise. To most observers
of the time these nations had little in common culturally, but Pius groups
them all as "strong and wise men," characterizations that exist almost independent of their religious beliefs. As such, listeners and readers of this popular, highly circulated oration witnessed an early evocation of "Europeanness."
While Meserve has argued that this oration and other post-1453 humanist
texts do not suggest "a Herodotean antithesis between a monolithic East and
West," a close look at *Cum bellum hodie* alone shows a conviction that Asia
was not only different, but vastly inferior.[51]

Bound up with Pius's discussions of ethnicity is a notion of territory, ownership, and a bold characterization of "Europe." After criticizing the Greeks
for not halting the rise of Islam, he lumps in the (much later) movement of
Turks westward with the migrations of non-Christians from every direction,
with little sense of chronology: Berbers from the South on the coasts of Italy,
pagans from the North (Lithuania and "half-wild men" in northern
Scandinavia[52]), Moors from the West in Spain, and Tartars and non-Christian Hungarians in the East.[53] These movements happened over the course of
centuries, but Pius places them in one group to create a sense of ongoing
threat:

These are your boundaries, oh Christians, this is how you are surrounded
on all sides, this is how you are pressed into one corner, you who were
once the lords and masters of the Earth. It is indeed a great empire that
you have lost, with many noble cities, and many rich provinces. Among

them you have even forgotten about Judea, the noble land, the holy land, the land overflowing with milk and honey, the land where the first flowers of our Faith appeared. Oh, what shame! Oh, what grief![54]

This image of a vast expanse of territory once ruled by the "manly" Roman Christians and lost, piece by piece (by the effeminate Greeks), to non-Christians is provocative enough on its own. Without yet uttering the word "Europe," Pius has drawn a map of its boundaries, sounded the alarm on external threats, and portrayed Christendom being choked off and driven into a "corner." But "Europe" will, indeed, make a bold appearance.

This brings us at last to the most shocking statement in the oration. Rather than pitch his crusade call to all Christians and press his audience to liberate the Holy Land, he turns his focus sharply on the continent:

> But let us put aside, if you please, the ancient infamy and the losses of old, and let us not be concerned about things which did not bother your forefathers. *Let all of Asia and Africa pass away,*[55] *and let us look only to Europe* and take account of the present [emphasis mine]. Is it maybe a small loss that we have suffered in our own age and because of our own fault? [No]. It is Constantinople, the capital of the Eastern Empire and the backbone of all of Greece, that has been lost, and not by our forefathers, but by ourselves.[56]

"Let all of Asia and Africa pass away, and let us look only to Europe," is a remarkable statement from anyone at this time, but especially the pope. It strongly suggests that, even now, Pius's primary concern was not the universal community of Christians, but the borders of his continent.[57] If he was hoping to get his audience's attention (and that of his readers), he likely succeeded.

One hopes Pius affected a different tone when he was approached shortly after the Congress ended by emissaries from Georgia and Armenia, who pleaded for assistance against the Turks. Indeed, it is hard to reconcile such brash language with papal efforts initiated by Eugenius IV and continued by his successors to send embassies to Christian rulers in the eastern Mediterranean. Pius himself supported the mission of Franciscan friar Ludovico da Bologna in areas that bordered the Ottoman Empire.[58] But the preceding passage, paired with his use of "West" a few pages later where he warns that the young, strong, and ambitious Turkish sultan will not rest "until he has defeated all the Western kings,"[59] makes the pope seem less committed to his Eastern brethren than he probably was. For him, Europe and "the West" had to be protected, namely by shoring up defenses in Hungary:

> Only the faithful Hungarians persevere, but they cannot hold out long unless they are given help. They have, indeed, been a bulwark for you towards the East, and if that bulwark is destroyed, neither the Germans, nor the Bohemians, nor the Poles will be safe. Neither craggy mountains

nor deep rivers will be a barrier. If Hungary is defeated, nothing stands in the way of the Turks, nothing is insuperable, in their quest for world empire.[60]

The domino metaphor in his language of borders interweaves the destinies of each country.

After vigorously arguing the dangers that the Turks posed to continental security, Pius tries to reassure his audience that their cause is "easy." Arguing that the Turks are not as fearsome as many presume, he claims that their resources were no greater than those of

> rich Italy, noble France, strong Spain, warlike and populous Germany .... Even if they stretch themselves to the limit, they cannot mobilize more than 200,000 men. And what kind of men? Unwarlike, unarmed, and mixed with Asians and Greeks! You know what Virgil's Remus thinks of the Asians. He says: 'Phrygian women, indeed!—for Phrygian men you are not.' (*Aeneid*, 9, 618–620)[61]

Without directly calling the Turks effeminate here, as he did in his Frankfurt oration and early letters, Pius paints all Asians and Easterners in general as weak and womanly.

If gender and ethnic stereotypes were long considered fair game in crusade orations, Pius brought them to a new level at Mantua, where adherence to either Christianity or Islam was less a matter of belief than a cultural barometer of the men who practiced them.[62] Ironically, some of the same notions would recur under a different premise in Pius's Letter to Mehmed (1461)—a tract supposedly written to convert the sultan. For now, it is important to highlight the instability of Pius's gendered categories, and the fear and insecurity that his swaggering rhetoric barely masks. He tries to dismiss the Turks as weak Asians, but rather half-heartedly. Indeed, he finds himself in a logistical trap: if they are Eastern, they must be weak according to the classical stereotype, and yet their military strength and vigor were undeniable. Without questioning the Turks' masculinity here, Pius skirts the issue with blanket slurs of Asians by asserting, for instance, that both (the Roman) Julius Caesar and (the Frankish) crusader Godfrey of Bouillon easily defeated the men of Asia and regarded their enemy with contempt.[63] In short, Pius's ethnic views are intense, yet murky. They rest on fallacies of positional superiority, and his criteria continually shift and inevitably contradict each other. He has shown this in his statements on the Greeks. Were they weaker than Latins by nature, or as a result of their servitude under the Turks? Pius tries to have it both ways.

From Mantua to *De Asia*

The response to Pius's speech was less forceful than he had hoped. As he himself states in the *Commentaries*, there were no resounding shouts of "Deus vult" (God wills it) as Urban II elicited at Clermont in 1095. Pius managed to secure a unanimous vote for war against the Turks immediately afterward, but in the long run, few states honored their promises of troops, money, and ships.[64] As Housley has shown, the difference between a council and a congress was more than semantic, and Pius misjudged the risk he took in trying to find a middle ground. Church councils, where several crusades had been called by past popes, brought solemnity to the vows and decisions that were made in regard crusade. A congress simply did not have the same juridical foundation or framework, and the promises given there were less binding.[65]

Lay rulers, deprived of a council where they could air legitimate grievances, were equally disappointed by Mantua. Given Pius's fraught past with conciliarism and concerns that religious and secular leaders would derail the work of the council with their demands, he calculated that it was better to avoid such a forum. Despite the religious rhetoric that infused his sprawling oration, it did not provoke the fervor of past summonses to crusade. To be fair, some of the causes of failure lay beyond Pius's control. While the presence of arms on these pilgrimages was always problematic, in the minds of early crusaders, the sacred aspect was inseparable from the military.[66] But the foundation of crusade as a devout pilgrimage had fallen away over the centuries. By the fifteenth century, the secular goals of these campaigns largely overshadowed its penitential origins, with some participants focusing more on chivalric glory and others on their own narrow political aims.

Unfortunately for conciliarists, the frustrations of Mantua drove Pius to take an even stronger measure than dodging the issue. Just before he left Mantua, he published the bull *Execrabilis* (Jan. 17, 1460), condemning the practice of appealing to a future council against a pope's decisions. Some have seen this as a cynical power play, but Housley has argued that Pius's primary motivation was to protect the crusade; he feared that if it were left under the control of a council or the emperor that it would never materialize. Similarly, Baldi contends that Pius viewed his role in crusade as inextricably tied to his view of papal leadership.[67] Pius's use of papal power to promote crusade was indeed complex, but I have found no clear evidence that Pius used crusade as a tool; since 1453, it was always his end goal. In fact, it speaks to Pius's determination that the Congress of Mantua took place at all in the face of so many roadblocks. The congress shows his vision to bring centralized leadership to European Christians and to forge common bonds.[68]

Regardless of Mantua's shortcomings, with *Cum bellum hodie* the idea of "Europe" and even "the West" gained greater traction. If nothing else, the gathering shows Pius's boundless confidence in the power of rhetoric to persuade and unite—especially with his own silver tongue. His words continued to circulate to a larger audience long after 1459. Over one hundred manuscript copies and at least sixteen early printed versions of his oration exist.[69] Modern scholars disagree as to whether this speech was one of Pius's best, but his contemporaries clearly admired it.[70]

Meanwhile, peace in Italy faltered in the autumn of 1459 when a fleet commanded by René of Anjou landed in the South to assert his claim to the throne of Naples. Ferrante of Naples, the Aragonese heir to the throne and Alfonso's illegitimate son, had the support of both the pope and the duke of Milan, who sought to prevent the French (who recently took over Genoa) from gaining more ground in Italy. The powerful French crown backed René, leaving Florence and others caught between their loyalty to France and their commitment to other Italian powers as part of the Peace of Lodi (1454). Others, looking to profit, like condottiere Jacopo Piccinino and Neapolitan princes of Rossano and Taranto threw their lot in with René. The war continued for two years until René gave up his claims in late 1462. During that time, King Louis XI of France and Pius played a tense game of diplomacy in which Louis offered to end the Pragmatic Sanction of Bourges against the papacy and to field an enormous crusade army in exchange for Pius's support of René.[71] Pius refused to budge, but attempted to placate Louis by creating two French cardinals in December 1461. The war in Naples, in Baldi's words took on a "European character" and prevented Pius from his urgent work on crusade for months to come.[72]

Unable to plan his crusade during this period, Pius began to ponder the East in a less confrontational manner. In 1461, he composed two works that looked eastward in radically different ways: his geographical-historical treatise on *Asia* and his controversial letter to Sultan Mehmed II. In his *Commentaries*, Pius attributes the inspiration for *Asia* to a lively conversation about the Trojan War with the well-read commander of the papal troops, Federigo da Montefeltro of Urbino, as he journeyed from Rome to Tivoli in July 1461 to escape the oppressive heat.[73] As Pius states,

> Since the topic of Asia Minor had come up and there was some disagreement about its boundaries, the pope later composed a description of Asia itself in his spare time at Tivoli, drawing on passages from Ptolemy, Strabo, Pliny, Quintus Curtius, Julius Solinus, Pomponius Mela, and other ancient sources that seemed relevant to an understanding of the subject.[74]

Some recent sources factored in as well, including reports from the Ottoman frontier, the account of Venetian traveler Niccolò de Conti, Niccolò Sagundino's short history of the early Ottomans, and most likely the recent world map of Fra Mauro.[75] Like many other periods of "rest," Pius's sojourn in Tivoli—where he could admire the ruins of Hadrian's Villa and sit with his cardinals in the shade of olive trees or beside the banks of the Aniene— became a time to write.[76]

Divided into six books, *Asia* opens with a broad geographical discussion of the continents, then moves through Asia from east to west, beginning with China and ending in Asia Minor.[77] Unique for its time and highly esteemed, Pius's *Asia* possessed an unrivaled air of geographical authority and thorough "coverage" for several decades until other sixteenth-century works superseded it; Christopher Colombus was among its many readers.[78] It was translated into Italian and printed as late as 1707, showing its continued popularity.[79]

It was a flawed work, nonetheless. With so many possible sources to explore, a willing staff to assist him, and the leisure time to write, other scholars in Pius's position might have seized the opportunity to test their previous assumptions and take a fresh look at Asia. But Pius seemed less interested in finding accurate information than confirming his preexisting views. His choice of sources, as Meserve has shown, is telling. Rejecting more reliable medieval texts at his disposal by Marco Polo, Odorico da Pordenone, and others, Pius relied mostly upon the words of ancient scholars. Among the works he heavily consulted were two Latin translations of Strabo by Gregorio Tifernate and Guarino da Verona, recently presented to him in beautifully produced manuscripts.[80] The resulting treatise is a mixture of geography and history—most of it ancient. As such, Pius's *Asia* was the inverse of *Europe*, which focused almost entirely on recent history with some gestures to the deeper past. A printer later packaged the two texts as one and named it *Cosmographia*, but as Nicola Casella has shown, they were conceived as two very different works.[81]

Pius's focus on the ancient period conveniently dovetails with one of his favorite topics: the Scythians. One can imagine Pius's reaction when he discovered a more complicated portrait of the Scythians in Greek and Roman sources than he likely anticipated. Diodorus Siculus and Pompeius Trogus presented the Scythians as hardy, peaceful, and uncorrupted, but as Meserve has noted, "[Pius] omits all the positive comments Diodorus and Trogus make about their bravery, virtue, or abstemiousness, repeating only the passages that present them in a poor light."[82] He discredits reports of Scythian military might as the exaggerations of the Greeks, insisting that "The nation of the Scythians is barbarous, heeding neither justice nor rectitude; their life is utterly ignoble," and they are steeped in idolatry, luxury, and greed.[83] Perhaps his use of "nation" here indicates some hint of newfound respect for the Scythians, but Pius still goes out of his way to both denigrate them and associate them with the Turks. The Goths, for instance—whom he oddly admired despite their sack of Rome in 410—were not from Scythia, as some presumed, but were "European" (*Europaeos*).[84] Here he cites Jordanes for support, yet the sixth-century author was far more specific—pointing to the region of Scandinavia as the homeland of the early Goths. For Pius, however, it was enough to distinguish them as European, not Asian. Hence, Pius's assessment of the Scythians does not appear to have altered since 1453, even in the face of contradictory evidence from ancient sources. To support his predetermined views, he invokes the dubious Aethicus once again in the very next paragraph along with all his revolting claims about diet and sexuality.[85] Pius, as we saw with his use of Tacitus, was often selective with ancient sources.

In an intriguing move, however, Pius was willing to accept stories of Scythian descent for one important, Catholic, and civilized group of contemporary Europeans: the Hungarians.[86] The place of the Hungarians is noteworthy because it breaks down his anti-Asian and anti-Scythian bias, softening the boundaries that hold firm in so many other aspects of his world view. Importantly, it also suggests that Pius did not subscribe to some "purity of blood" notion in regard to ethnicity. But his flexibility on the evolution of the Hungarians beyond their Scythian roots did not extend to the Turks—at least for the time being. Pius would reconsider this question, however, in his letter to Mehmed in light of possible conversion.

Pius's views on the ancient Trojans were less flexible. When speaking of the region believed to be ancient Troy, he notes how many peoples, including the French, English, and ancient Romans, have boasted of Trojan descent in order to "appear very noble." Amused by these harmless beliefs, he neither accepts nor rejects them, yet he strongly affirms only a few pages later that the Turks are definitely *not* descended from the Trojans as many claimed in his day in order to "appear learned" (*docti*).[87] Pius's obstinacy on this issue is intriguing in light of his equivocal view of such questions for "European" peoples discussed in the previous chapter. The reason in this particular case seems political: Pius wished to deprive the Turks of just cause for attacking Greece above all. But he equally wished to deprive them of the honor of a distinguished, refined ancestry. Did he believe that bloodline shaped character more than environment and upbringing? More will be said on questions of race and racism later in this chapter.

Whatever the reason for Pius's choice of sources, it produced a distorted view of Asia. Unlike the vibrant, up to the minute, at times gossipy feel of *Europe*, this is an antiquarian's vision of Asia, largely limited to the Greco-Roman imperialistic context. It is this lost "classical" heritage, at least as much as the doomed Christian faith in these regions, that Pius mourns.[88] He makes little effort to research and report on the Byzantine centuries and the Middle Ages apart from a few references to the Crusades. As for the Mongols who dominated and shaped the area in the thirteenth and fourteenth centuries, there is no mention at all.[89] In fact, there is little sense of Asians themselves as having built anything of value: almost everything Pius celebrates about the continent came by way of European hegemony. Whether or not this was Pius's conscious intent, when read alongside *Europe*, the text conjures a vision of fifteenth-century Asia, at least the northern and westernmost part, as broken and backward—while all the urban growth, economic energy, and advances in learning of his day occurred only in Europe. Even in a work titled "Asia," Pius centers Europe through his focal points and his stunning silences; as Michel-Rolph Trouillot has argued, such one-sided narratives have the veneer of revealed historical truth, but they are merely productions of historical knowledge.[90] Modern readers may spot the yawning gaps in Pius's account, but contemporaries and generations of later readers had fewer tools at their disposal to question his lofty position.

The only Asians who seem to feature prominently in this work are the Turks. The Ottomans, in fact, receive more attention than any other group in his discussions of recent events. As in *Europe*, he mixes the past and present as the narrative moves from region to region. As a result, the text leaps back and forth between the glittering European-inflected distant past and the bleak present day under Turkish rule. Like his passages on Greece in *Europe*, there is a recurring theme of loss—of both Greco-Roman culture and

Christian influence, especially in Asia Minor. But at times in *Asia*, he seems to be coming to grips with the changes that have taken place. He concedes, for instance, that "Turkish power has grown so much that what was once called Asia, today they call Turkey" (*Turcia*).[91] Similarly, in at least one other passage, Pius refers to Mehmed as "the emperor of the Turks" (*Turcorum imperator*).[92] Whether or not this denotes growing respect for Mehmed and the Ottoman Empire's power and legitimacy, is hard to say, but I would argue that there is a grudging acceptance in *Asia* and the Letter to Mehmed of a reality he fervently denied a decade earlier.

When it came to the Christians of Asia who lived under the Turks, Pius was not optimistic. While he declares without criticism that Armenian followers of Christ mixed among the Muslims in Pontus and Cappadocia,[93] his concerns emerge in the last section of the work when he compares the piety and devotion of early Christian Anatolia to the current state of the faith under the Turks. Only a few slaves in Anatolia, he claims, adhere to the faith, but they are not Christians in the truest sense of Gospel teachings.[94] *Asia* remained unfinished, so it is difficult to know how Pius intended to conclude the text. Whole regions, like the Indian subcontinent, are missing. As the text stands, the culminating chapter on the Turks—which rehashes many of his earlier views—creates a somber final note.[95] While he concedes that the Turks' Scythian-rooted barbarity has been somewhat softened by centuries of living in Asia and in Greece, he still laments the utter loss of learning and the downfall of the faith in Asia Minor. The land of St. Paul, Homer, Hippocrates, and the Colossus of Rhodes was, for Pius, forever altered.[96]

But as Pius was generally an optimist, it is hard to imagine he would leave European readers without some glimmer of hope. Several potential allies are mentioned, like the Armenians, who, despite their "errors" once aided the crusaders, and the Georgians, who sent a legation to him in Rome and adore Christ, although they, too, follow a faith that is not completely orthodox.[97] Interestingly, two of these would-be allies were Muslims: Ismail, the ruler of Sinope on the Black Sea had sent an embassy to the pope promising many things and asking for aid against the Ottomans. Perhaps, he posits, it would be more expedient to join forces with them, given the challenges of composing a crusade army:

> But it takes a long time for Christians not only to arm, but to meet for the purpose of deliberating whether they should take up arms. We should not wonder if imminent danger rather than distant and dubious hope carries more weight with a prince under attack.[98]

Ismail unfortunately had recently surrendered to Mehmed, but the other leaders, "The Grand Caraman" (or Karaman, Ibrahim Beg) and Uzun Hasan, were still viable prospects:

> But not all the Turks are subject to the supremacy of the Ottomans, for Caraman, the lord of Cilicia, who possesses a great part of Cappadocia,

and Uzun Hasan, who rules the area near the Euphrates, and several other chieftains of Turkish origin have been fighting for a long time with the descendants of Osman over the possession of their kingdoms.[99]

Caraman, he adds, fights both the Ottomans and the Soldan of Egypt and is a "friend of the Christians" (*amicus Christianorum*).[100] Noteworthy here is Pius's use of the term "Ottomans" (*Ottumani*) twice in this section. Context matters, though, as it is only used to differentiate the Ottomans from the other Turkish powers he is discussing.[101] Still, it may be the only incidence of Pius's use of the term the Ottomans used to describe themselves, rather than his preferred, more dismissive "Turks."

Uzun Hasan's situation was a bit more complicated. On the one hand, Pius describes him as permitting little rest to the Ottomans and notes his bond with the emperor of Trebizond, John IV Comnenus, through his marriage to John's daughter Theodora. Yet Pius questions the strength of this alliance because the Turks, he argues, regard marriage with little importance and take as many wives as they please.[102] Marital affection aside, Uzun was prevented from honoring his vow to aid Trebizond when he himself was attacked by Mehmed and forced to turn his energies to self-defense. Just as Mehmed had masterfully isolated Constantinople before besieging it in 1453, he used the same tactic here. Trebizond surrendered to Mehmed in 1461. Despite the outcome, Pius's willingness to partner with a Muslim ruler against a mutual enemy is highly significant; the time and resources he gave to the Franciscan friar Ludovico da Bologna to promote such alliances is telling. Had Mehmed not circumvented these plans, the outcome might have tempered Pius's rhetoric regarding Asia and Islam.[103] Three decades later, Hartmann Schedel wrote favorably of Hasan in the *Nuremberg Chronicle*, describing him as "a great man," highly learned, a friend of popes, and a scourge of infidels.[104] Uzun's would-be partnership with Pius, whom Schedel admired, clearly elevated the Turkish leader's status.

Examples of stalwart Christian defense are found in descriptions of the Knights of St. John, or the Hospitallers, in Rhodes and the small fleet built by Calixtus as helping to defend "all the East" (*omni oriente*) against the Ottomans in the eastern Mediterranean.[105] Calixtus's fleet no longer operated during Pius's reign, and the knights were ever vulnerable, but Pius may have included these passages to suggest that a few pockets of bold activity could accomplish much. Or perhaps he intended such examples as cautionary tales: Europeans should be vigilant lest they are overrun, bit by bit, like the peoples of Asia.

A more intriguing illustration of resistance in *Asia* appears in the story of a heroic, unnamed woman of Lesbos "who, dressed in the armor of men, marvelous to tell, saved her country" against invading Turks by helping her townspeople hold them back until the papal fleet assembled by Calixtus arrived; regretful that her name was not known, he praises the girl as no less worthy of memory than Sappho.[106] Pius's uncharitable view of Greek men as weak plus the anonymity of this woman might suggest this story was his own fabrication, but he takes the trouble of naming his source, the bishop of Caffa who delivered the account to the pope and senate in Rome, lending it greater credibility. This description, in fact, matches the story of Orietta Doria, a widow of Genoese extraction who had been married to the ruler of Lesbos and helped defend the island against an attack by Murad in 1450.[107] An extended study of Pius's praise of strong women leaders deserves more attention than this study can provide, but *Europe* and the *Commentaries* contain similar instances.

Despite its scholarly deficiencies, *Asia* was greeted by contemporary readers as a breakthrough. Not only did it offer detailed geographical information on an area that was little known to Europeans, but it rose above the myths and fables that marred many of its predecessors. Compared to texts with legends of monstrous peoples or apocalyptic interpretations of the Turks as precursors to Antichrist, Pius's focus on human history appears modern and rational.[108] Many turned to it as a geographical guide when few such works existed. I have not attempted here to parse its geographical passages, but they are extensive. Yet, as the preceding passages show, landscapes were not all that this work contained. Mixed with topographical information, readers found a host of cultural, ethnic, and political judgements. Pius removed the monsters, but he also erased many of the human inhabitants of Asia, and his skewed cultural portraits of its peoples were uncritically absorbed by many contemporaries as they sought to learn about geography.[109] One wonders if Columbus, who copiously annotated Pius's *Asia*, supported crusade, and viewed his mission as divine, equated the indigenous people he met in the Caribbean with Pius's surreal, strange, and fictionalized Asiatic peoples. More broadly, did Pius's narrative of Asia, curiously bereft of modern cities, impact early modern notions of the Americas as uninhabited, open "frontiers"—waiting for more "civilized" men to settle there?[110] Regardless, Pius's authoritative vision of Asia may well have influenced many European travelers and writers' responses to their eastern neighbors, which is as significant as it was unfortunate.

Pius's Letter to Mehmed II: A Moment Where East Meets West?

While Pius generally portrayed the Turks as radically other, having little in common with Christian Europeans, in reality the borders that separated Europe and Asia were much more permeable. Diplomacy, trade, and pilgrimage brought Western Europeans into frequent contact with the diverse peoples and regions of the Ottoman Empire. Many humanists and other writers emphasized a sense of separation and antagonism, but other writers evinced greater curiosity and appreciation, and traces of material culture and trade goods suggest a lively exchange between East and West. Just how tense or positive those interactions were, and how those parties viewed each other, however, are difficult to pin down. No one pattern spoke for every interaction, which ranged from military conflict to the fluid transnational world of commerce and social relations. The Mediterranean, as Claire Norton and others have argued, was "a zone of [both] diffusion and difference."[111] Evidence of Ottoman material goods, especially luxury items, in Christian Europe studied by Anna Contadini, and "appeals to the Turk" by Western Christians seeking alliance, friendship, or mutual benefit, described by Giovanni Ricci, surely add up to something, even if the exact meaning of these exchanges or gestures is elusive.[112] In many ways, Pius's famous letter to Mehmed II fits well among these challenging pieces of evidence. Clearly, something was happening across the borders; Pius had to have been aware of at least some of these points of contact and began, himself, to consider his own foray.

In the same year that he wrote *Asia* (1461), Pius composed this letter, generally viewed as the most unusual and controversial work of his entire career. It opens with a disarmingly peaceful intention:

> As we set out to write a few things to you for your salvation and glory, and for the mutual comfort and peace of many nations, we encourage you to hear our words with kindness .... We do not seek you out with hatred .... We are hostile to your actions, not to you.[113]

After years of vilifying Mehmed, this is the first and only time he tried to separate the man from his reputed deeds and shine a more positive light on the Turks as a whole. The letter offers Mehmed papal support and legitimacy over his existing rule of "Greece and the East" in exchange for baptism, which he stunningly describes as both "a little thing" and "a little bit of water."[114] Had it been dispatched to the Ottoman Porte, it would constitute his only attempt to contact the sultan. There is no indication, however, that the letter was sent, much less received by Mehmed. A great many Christians, however, began to read it when it circulated around Europe in print in the 1470s.[115]

Unfortunately, little is known about the circumstances surrounding the Letter to Mehmed. Pius does not even mention its existence in the *Commentaries* or his other letters.[116] Only the text itself survives. As Housley aptly put it, the letter "remains enigmatic."[117] There are two main theories about Pius's intentions. One school of thought, to which I once ascribed, is that the letter was not conceived as a serious gesture to Mehmed, but as a refreshing exercise after the disappointments of Mantua, as Robert Schwoebel argues, or as a provocation to European Christians, as Franco Cardini contends. Some scholars in this camp have taken the letter as proof of Pius's cynical, self-promoting use of crusade.[118] The other view, put forward by R.W. Southern and, more recently, Benjamin Weber, takes the letter at face value, arguing that it was a sincere and fitting gesture for a pope to use his position for the purpose of proselytization.[119] Most scholars fall somewhere in the middle, but tend to believe that the letter shows a genuine, if brief, change of heart.

Perhaps we have all been thinking about Pius's letter to Mehmed in the wrong way. The first mistake is to assume that there is one voice and one agenda throughout: this, I now believe, is not the case. The letter contains irreconcilable tensions that have always made it difficult for scholars to prove it was either a sincere conversion attempt (aimed at Mehmed), or a calculated ruse (aimed at Christians). This problem stems from viewing the letter as a finished, coherent statement instead of reading it as a thought process that shifted as Pius wrote and polished it. If the latter is indeed the case, historians need not decide which message and intention was true: perhaps both were, at different times, and the traces of all these aspects remain.

With this in mind, I propose a modified reading that envisions Pius first approaching the letter with the sincere hope of not just converting Mehmed and the Turks but opening a line of communication. This hope, however brief, makes sense after the disappointments of Mantua and the disruption of the war in Naples; one can easily imagine Pius wishing to cut across all these obstacles with a direct appeal as the spiritual leader of Christendom. As Weber has shown, fifteenth-century popes, including Pius, not only focused on defending Europe from the Ottomans, but also made several overtures to non-Latin, and even non-Christian, powers.[120] Furthermore, one could argue that the least surprising aspect of the letter was Pius's semiformed notion that it lay in *his* power as pope to offer legitimacy to a great ruler, and even to elevate him to the rank of Eastern Roman Emperor, as Pope Leo III did for Charlemagne in the West in the year 800.[121] For a host of reasons, the prospect of negotiating one on one with Mehmed at this very moment in time—at least in theory—moved Pius enough to write or dictate this plea. It is entirely possible, then, that the letter began as a genuine attempt at outreach.

Nonetheless, I believe that these good intentions began to suffer almost as soon as the writing began. Somewhere along the line, the letter developed into a text Pius knew he could not send to Mehmed. Pius's off-putting treatment of Islam, his undiplomatic, condescending tone at several junctures, and his failure to consult with other contemporary experts on this topic are hard to explain if the final draft was intended for Mehmed's eyes. Critics might counter that Pius the pope was more dogmatic and patronizing than Aeneas the diplomat and, as pontiff, was prone to acting unilaterally rather than seeking input or assistance from other clergy. Why should this bullish letter surprise anyone? While Pius's inflated self-opinion cannot be denied, most scholars would agree that there is often a detectable difference between *his versions* of interactions, speeches, and letters and the actual texts that survive. Dramatic accounts of speeches in his *Commentaries*, in which he dresses down political adversaries or envoys should not be read as objective reports. In fact, Pius's tone in letters to rulers, like Louis XI, whose opposition infuriated him, was quite measured. In short, he never truly forgot his audience.[122]

Regarding his interpretation of Islam, one should also ask why Pius relied so heavily on Juan de Torquemada's harsh, polemical *Contra errores* when Nicholas of Cusa, who had written at length on the subject with greater subtlety, could readily be called upon as a cardinal in his curia. I would argue that if he began and ended the letter in good faith, he would have consulted more closely with Cusanus and possibly George of Trebizond who had gentler ideas. He might have also drawn on the work of the now deceased Juan de Segovia—a former friend from Basel who devoted his last years to a (sadly unfinished) Latin translation of the Qur'an in partnership with Muslim jurist Yça Gidelli.[123] Last but not least, Pius's contempt for Mehmed in all his other writings puts this letter so far out of character with the rest of his corpus that it is hard to read it as a wholly serious gesture. How on earth would he explain this to Christian princes if it became known? For all its verve, it is difficult to imagine Pius thought the finished version would be effective or prudent to send.[124] And yet, as we will see, the tract is not without moments of genuine appeal. Hence, while the letter to Mehmed is not the full-on "moment of vision" Southern describes, it offers a rare glimpse of Pope Pius II grappling with his doubts and considering a different strategy in future relations with the Turks.

How, then, did this moment of pause affect larger questions of cultural identity? It was no simple task for a man who had spent nearly a decade vilifying Mehmed, the Turks, and Islam to convince readers that it was possible to put all their differences aside and join in one religion and society. Even for Pius, who prided himself on the transformative powers of his rhetoric, this was a dilemma. But the possibility of peaceful negotiation and conversion enabled Pius to reexamine sources on the Turks in a positive light and unleashed his creativity. The greater challenge was finding a way to invite those he had vigorously excluded without undermining his previous arguments about the unique qualities of Europe and "the West"; if he ventured too far down the path of accommodation, he would look foolish and unstable. Pius needed to incorporate the Turks into Europe as worthy partners—something that baptism alone could not do, given all his previous objections about the Turks' character. The result is a work that revisits and even reinforces some views of self and other, while repositioning or abandoning others.

First, Pius had to find the words to address the leader of the Turks as a potential ally and friend. Any good stylist knew countless ways to flatter a powerful ruler (his address to Mehmed as "prince of the Turks" is a decent start), but Pius goes beyond stock rhetorical gestures. After praising some aspects of Islam, such as worship of one God and devotion to "the great prophet" Muhammad—a temporary reversal from his oration at Mantua—Pius laments,

> We grieve that you, an excellent man, illustrious scion of noble ancestors, famous for the glory of your deeds, endowed with a great empire, and excelling in many natural gifts do not walk in the paths of the Lord .... We do not believe you willingly go astray since we have faith that your nature is good.[125]

He excuses Mehmed by saying he was raised in ignorance of the truth but can now freely embrace it. Elsewhere, Pius praises Mehmed's intelligence (*sapientia*), and describes him as "not incapable of reasoning nor dull of intellect."[126] To be sure, Pius was not the first Catholic thinker to express faith in the ability of non-Christians to employ reason. But compared to his earlier characterizations of Mehmed as a cruel barbarian, whose only merits were discipline and ambition, it was quite a departure to describe the sultan's nature as "good."

When paired with his oration at Frankfurt, the letter speaks to his curiosity about Mehmed. As discussed in Chapter 2, positive views of the sultan probably came via accounts that circulated in Italy at the time. Greek refugees like Cardinal Bessarion, George of Trebizond, and especially Sagundino, who closely observed Mehmed during a diplomatic visit, were one conduit.[127] Such reports likely noted Mehmed's extensive education, his patronage of scholars, and his building projects.[128] Pius may have rejected such notions in 1454 at Frankfurt, but he seems more open to that side of Mehmed in the context of this letter. Perhaps when he invoked Aristotle, Zeno, or Hesiod, he was drawing on reports of the sultan's study of philosophy.

Yet his praise for the sultan has distinct limitations—a point that appears to have escaped the notice of most modern scholars. If Pius had indeed acquired information about Mehmed's education and patronage of learning, he refused to mention it. Unlike George of Trebizond's erudite letters to the sultan, Pius makes no effort to speak to Mehmed as an intellectual equal with a firm grasp of philosophy or history.[129] His overall tone is markedly condescending. Painting Mehmed as a noble, educable savage was hardly better than his previous efforts to cloak him in barbarism. Still, his letter to Mehmed, however patronizing it may be, shows some softening toward the sultan.

Pius's views of Islamic education, by contrast, had only hardened: "The study of the liberal arts greatly flourishes among us," he asserts toward the end of the letter, while Islam offers no divine truth and "has no understanding of the earthly, which it judges to be of no concern to heaven."[130] While some Western Europeans must have found this stereotype absurd, others likely took Pius's word on the subject and looked no further into the question. Pius, it seems, let himself be carried away by the notion that he could play the "civilized" learned counterpart to the barbarian convert—a Bishop Remigius to Gregory of Tours' caricature of Clovis. Much as the fantasy may have pleased Pius and European readers, it seems unlikely that he thought this approach would work with Mehmed; I see this particular assertion as a portion of the letter that reflects later editing and a change of heart and purpose. Unfortunately, as the letter stands (and was disseminated), it conveys a distorted view of Ottoman sultans and other leaders, who endowed madrasas in Asia and Europe as early as the reign of Orhan (c. 1342–62), with Mehmed taking steps to attach learned men to his government and promote them through the ranks.[131] His effort to create a class of scholars to serve the state was no different from the behavior of Christian Renaissance princes, but Pius makes no allowance for this. Hence, while less polemical than his other writings, the letter is still smug and uncompromising concerning the group identity of the Ottomans. They appear less worldly, intellectually curious, and learned than their Western counterparts—a misleading and damaging trope to say the least.

Perhaps the most radical assertion in the letter concerns the Scythians and concepts of ethnicity. Pius had invoked the theory at least eight times since 1453 that the Turks were barbaric descendants of the savage Scythians.[132] Yet in Book XIII of the letter to Mehmed, he creatively flips the script:

> We understand that your origin is Scythian and tradition holds that among the Scythians there were many renowned warriors who held Asia in tribute for many centuries and who pushed the Egyptians beyond the swamps. The Egyptians and Arabs cannot be compared with Scythians [*Scythico generi*] because there can be no comparison between a society of brave men and cowards .... An alliance with Christians will better suit you because the brave can easily be brought into alliance with the brave. Courage attracts courage. Friendships between equals are attractive and secure when their religion is the same and their cult of God the same.[133]

"Friendships between equals" is a surprising reversal from his tone in both the oration at Mantua and *Asia*. It has been argued that Pius could not view the Scythians in the same positive light as ancient writers due to his hatred for the Turks, and that he did not waver in this opinion after his election as pope.[134] In every other text, both these statements are true, except for the pronounced shift in the Letter to Mehmed.

I see two possible causes for this new stance on the Scythians. One, as noted earlier, is that Pius's research into classical sources for *Asia* left him uncertain about some of his assumptions. Recall that in *Asia*, Pius mocked the claim that the Scythians defeated the Persians and warred against the Egyptians, adding "Trogus speaks fine words, but I think that he was following certain Greeks who have the habit of exaggerating everything."[135] Yet in the letter to Mehmed, he *accepts* Trogus's account because it enables him to portray the Scythians as brave and daring. Even in *Asia* Pius may have started to temper some of his criticisms; he ended the section on the Scythians with this statement: "Nonetheless, I admit that they have produced many who have done great deeds; for those who live in a barren country readily migrate, and many are drawn by the prospect of better land."[136] In that particular case, he praised Scythian toughness to explain why the Huns and especially the Hungarians (who appear in the next passage) were successful, but he may have begun to reconsider his view of the Scythians more broadly.

The second reason for his shift on the Scythians relates to anxieties about bravery, masculinity, and ethnicity. With the letter to Mehmed, Pius's gendered language of the Turks comes full circle. In earlier works he tried to dismiss them as effeminate and unthreatening. Then he began to describe them in more ominous terms as savage barbarians. But the more he invoked the barbarian trope, the harder it became to reassure Christians that the Turks were weak and easily defeated. As a result, from 1455 onwards, Pius instead began to question the effectiveness and masculinity of nations *conquered by* the Turks: the Greeks and other Eastern Christians. In the letter to Mehmed, he lumps Arabs, Egyptians, and other Muslims in for good measure. This creates a dramatic contrast between "weak" Easterners and "strong" Westerners, with the Turks being granted an unexplained exemption.[137]

The letter to Mehmed, then, can be read as a fleeting attempt to decouple the Turks from the East. If Pius remained unwilling to cast the Ottomans as civilized or learned, he could at least grant them manliness—opening the door to other possibilities. A passage from his oration at Mantua in 1459, *Cum bellum hodie*, may hold the key to this changed point of view. Recall his claim that the manliness of the Romans, Germans, Spaniards, and Gauls enabled them to accept the "harder law" of Christianity.[138] While Pius made this bold assertion to encourage the Latin Christians in his audience to take up arms, in the letter to Mehmed it provides a newfound affinity between Western Europeans and Scythians. Was toughness the bridge by which the Ottomans could be brought into (European) Christian society?

This tactic is foreshadowed in book I of the letter to Mehmed with Pius's boasts about the resources and greatness of the "Christian people," specifically the Latins:

> I do not think you are so ignorant of our affairs as to be unaware of the strength of Spain, the warlike spirit of France, the vast populace of Germany, the bravery of Britain, the boldness of Poland, the tenacity of Hungary, and the wealth, energy, and experience in warfare of Italy.[139]

Hungary alone, he continues, was able to exhaust the Ottomans for eighty years. As he states few paragraphs later, "You will not fight against women if you invade Italy, Hungary, or another *western* province" (emphasis mine).[140] Pius had made similar statements to this effect about the merits of Europeans (without actually invoking Europe), but his language here is more focused and intentional with the addition of "western." On its own, this statement is a boast and a threat, but here it becomes an invitation to Mehmed to join strength with strength—after conversion, of course. For a brief moment, Pius argued that the Turks *already* shared enough with Western Europeans that they could easily "assimilate" after conversion. Pius's preoccupation with gender norms merits deeper examination, but here it seems to override questions about religious sincerity. He has, again, traded the humility of Christ and the apostles for masculinity. Perhaps he always knew his insistence on denying all good things about the Scythians was disingenuous in the face of several contradictory sources and decided, for once, to give those sources credence.

Did shared masculinity alone solve the problem of disparate geography? After years of arguing the differences between Europe and Asia, West and East, could Pius separate the Turks from the "East" just as he separated them from other Muslims? The answer would seem to be yes, but only if he brought North and South into the mix—which he implies rather than states. By breaking the (northern) Scythians and Turks away from their (southern) coreligionists, the Arabs and Egyptians, he plays into classical models that characterize northerners as hardy and strong and southerners as inherently weak, lazy, and effeminate.[141] By this facile logic, the northeastern Turks could be coopted by Europeans and repackaged as acceptable partners. Pius later builds on this conceit by claiming that if Mehmed converts, all other Muslims will follow, including "the Egyptian, leaning on his staff of reeds ... the unwarlike Arab and the naked African." While Pius praises Ethiopians as distinguished Christian co-religionists at another point in the letter and invokes the legend of Prester John, his generalizations about Egyptians, Arabs, and Africans are disturbingly off-handed and thoughtless.[142] A few sentences later he adds: "... but if you join us, in a short time all the East (*totus Oriens*) will return to Christ."[143] Hence, with Pius's help, Mehmed could convert and transform Western Asia, Africa, and beyond.

It seems that Pius let himself get carried away by his fantasy that kingdoms which were predominantly Islamic for centuries ("the whole East") would revert to Christianity in an instant. It suggests that the "natural state" of these areas was Christianity, and it only took the courage of one leader to nudge its inhabitants in the proper direction. This letter may be Pius's most serious effort to grapple with geography and character, but it also shows how muddled these distinctions could be. On the one hand, the North-South and East-West divides were not insurmountable if Christianity were the ultimate uniting force and "civilizer." And yet, there is a sense that geography truly mattered: that the highest level of Christian belief, civility, and manliness were all naturally found in Western Europe.[144] Since 1453, Pius had been slowly building an idea of Europeans having a collective personality, but this is perhaps the first time he articulates it so clearly. For Pius, then, Western Europeans set the standard, centuries before the modern colonial era.

After alluding to Europeans throughout the text, he finally mentions them by name near the end: "Above all it has been demonstrated that you cannot attain glory and power among Christians, which you seem to want, especially over Europeans and Western peoples [*Europeos et Occidentales populos*], if you remain in your religion."[145] Through this offer of legitimacy, Pius characterizes a sixth-generation ruler of large portions of southeast Europe as somehow external to the continent and "the West." Pius is clear, moreover, that a Muslim *cannot* rule Europeans and Westerners—at least not in any meaningful "hearts and minds" sense. Equally noteworthy is his word choice for the Turks in this passage: "Thus will you profit your soul and further the interests of the Turkish people [*Turcarum populo*]."[146] This phrasing, I believe, was not random: it is perhaps the only time Pius refers to the Turks as a "*populus*" – like the aforementioned Western peoples, or the Christian people, or a politically constituted entity like the Roman people. Only now, it seems, when they were on the hypothetical cusp of conversion and forming a bond with Europeans, did they rise in Pius's estimation from *gens* to *populus*. Should Mehmed accept Pius's offer, he continues, "your name [will] be celebrated for centuries. Thus, will all of Greece, Italy, and Europe marvel at you"[147]—as if they were not *already* marveling at the young conqueror.

In the end, the letter to Mehmed could only appeal to Western European readers of the period, offering them a fantasy of cultural and religious superiority as the Turks were threatening western borders. It is a testament to Pius's judgment that he, too, recognized the letter's inconsistencies and took no steps to explore a campaign of outreach much less to send this problematic text. But, even as he announced his plan to go on crusade and "wipe out" the Turks, he kept editing it, so much did the idea captivate him.[148] The letter remains a strange mix of praise and denigration, of invitation and menace. The two voices or mindsets of the epistle were never harmonized. Perhaps its popularity reflects a shared desire among Western readers for contact and connection with the Ottomans, if only on their own terms.

As far as its message on identity is concerned, the letter is truly an outlier among Pius's works. Meserve has rightly asserted that Pius sees the Turks as either barbaric, Scythian-descended rabble or the most fearsome, canniest, and best organized of all Muslims with no in between.[149] His letter to Mehmed, I would argue, is Pius's one attempt to reconcile the two tropes—to see them as stronger and better than other Muslims and more like Western Europeans *because* of that "barbaric" edge. The alliance could not be complete without conversion, but passages like this suggest that a radical cultural makeover was not necessary. They were already similar in certain perceived national or ethnic characteristics. But that brief window closed and Pius returned to his crusade.

The *Commentaries*: Pius's Autobiography Against the Backdrop of Europe

By 1462, two years had passed since the conclusion of the Congress of Mantua. Conflicts over Naples and struggles with France, Burgundy, Bohemia, and other powers continued unabated. Nonetheless, Pius remained convinced that his vision for the security and integrity of Europe was the only path forward. If he could persuade the relevant parties to share this vision, he could achieve his goal of crusade and strengthen the papacy, which was suffering from the reverberations of the Schism and conciliarism.[150] With so many obstacles and frustrations before him, Pius sought comfort in creative activities. One was a series of building projects in his hometown of Corsignano, which he renamed Pienza. There, with the help of the Florentine architect Bernardo Rossellino and likely input from famed humanists Leon Battista Alberti and Flavio Biondo, a new town square, a cathedral, and a palace for the Piccolomini family had just been completed. The buildings show a blend of Renaissance styles and Pius's own ideas, including inspiration from Gothic and Germanic architecture. To make Pienza more splendid, he ordered his cardinals to build their own palaces as well.[151]

Pius's ultimate creative outlet, of course, was writing, and in early 1462 he embarked upon his most ambitious work yet: an epic autobiography known as the *Commentaries*. The text borrowed its title, third-person narrative, and program of self-promotion from Caesar's first-century BCE *Commentaries on the Gallic Wars.* But instead of battles and military strategy, Pius recounts his winning debates and diplomatic coups. For all the similarities to Caesar's work, it is no carbon copy.[152] The *Commentaries* is a truly unique text if only for one reason: no reigning pope before or since has attempted to write his own life story.[153] The approach and tone of the work, however, were decidedly worldly. In his preface, Pius muses on the perfect happiness of the soul after death and asks, "Why then do we strive so hard to achieve the glory of a good name?"[154] Waving aside debates on the afterlife as the pastime of "argumentative types," he states, "the living take pleasure in earthly glory that is theirs today, and hope it will continue after death."[155] He declares his intention to refute detractors as a worthy task—untroubled, it would seem, by the pursuit of glory by a servant of the servants of Christ: "At his death he will be praised; he will be missed when he is no longer here ... the truth will out, and Pius will be numbered among the illustrious popes."[156]

But the *Commentaries* are more than a grandiloquent autobiography: they are an account of Pius's world writ large. Long digressions on the history of nations and cities and their rulers (primarily in Europe) fill almost as much space as his own agendas and actions. It is as if he merged his life with the continent itself—seeing its stories and his own as inextricable.[157] This point cannot be overstated. In the discussion that follows, his descriptions and evocations of places and peoples, that is, questions of identity, will be the main focus. I humbly submit that one could write an entire book on this subject and can imagine a host of topics that specialists will feel were wrongly ignored. The vast expanse of the *Commentaries* required some hard choices in this study, but hopefully the analysis that follows will help support my main thesis while stimulating further inquiry.

To date, the *Commentaries* have rarely been examined as a guide to Pius's *later* views on political and cultural identity. Scholars cannot be faulted for mining the *Commentaries* for colorful autobiographical sketches: if they wished to describe the young secretary in Scotland, what better source to use than his own words? But, as I noted in Chapter 1, this as a mistake, especially if one seeks to chart Pius's evolving concepts of group identity. As I hope to have demonstrated by now, the young traveler and secretary would never have framed his observations and activities in the elaborate way he did decades later. What he writes in the *Commentaries* is the product of years of reflection, the reading of new (to him) ancient texts, and the shock of events like 1453. For all these reasons, I have put off serious discussion of the places Pius visited and described in his *Commentaries* until now, in order to understand their proper context. They offer key insights into Pius's cherished view of Europe during his papacy.

Perhaps the clearest example of Pius's changed world view is the way he wrote about Scotland and England soon after his return in the 1430s versus his descriptions in later works. Recall that in a letter of 1436 he describes Scotland as "outside the world." By contrast, he allocated Scotland a place within Europe in the same titled work in 1458, describing King James, a legend regarding ducks, and the use of coal.[158] But in the 1460s in the

Commentaries, he cheerfully brought the distant country into the fold of Christian Europe even as he amplified its strangeness:

> [Scotland] is a cold country where few things grow and is for the most part barren of trees. Below ground there is a sulphurous rock which they dig for fuel. The cities have no walls. The houses are usually constructed without mortar, their roofs are covered with turf and in the country the doorways are closed with oxhides. The people, who are poor and rude, stuff themselves with meat and fish but eat bread as a luxury. The men are short and brave; the women fair, charming and lusty. In Scotland, a woman's kiss means less than a handshake does in Italy. They have no wine except what they import.[159]

Scottish ways, it would seem, could not be more foreign. If Pius is to be believed, moreover, the Northern English near the River Tweed found the young Italian as alien as he did them:

> All the men and women of the village came running as if to see a strange sight, and just as we marvel at Ethiopians or Indians, so they gazed in amazement at Aeneas, asking the priest where he came from, what his business was and whether he was a Christian.[160]

The people's wonder increased when Aeneas offered them loaves of bread and a jug of wine that he obtained from a monastery—things they had supposedly never seen before. If this is at all true, it is likely attributable to class differences between local peasants and clergy, but Pius does not explore this possibility, preferring a narrative of exoticism.

Had the young Aeneas really experienced, much less remarked on all these things in the 1430s, or were his memories and narratives supplemented with classical stereotypes—possibly acquired after 1457 via his readings in Rome? His description of the roughness of the Northern British peoples, their makeshift buildings, and their lack of access to bread and wine, for instance, smack of ancient assumptions about culture and society; the belief that bread and wine were among the highest markers of civilization as both required time, patient cultivation, and processing often led to harsh judgements of peoples who lacked such dietary staples.[161] While Pius seems to acknowledge that terrain and climate were responsible for these agricultural differences, he describes Scotland and parts of England as "utterly unlike the land we inhabit, being rude [*horrida*], uncultivated and untouched by the winter sun." [162] His use of "we" places the insular peoples and their "rude" land outside his main audience. He may also be echoing classical biases against northern people as uncultivated by nature and geography.

What was Pius getting at with these elaborate descriptions? Why did he portray these peoples as a cultural curiosity and not just fellow Christians? The most obvious answer is that the tale, which includes dramatic stories of escaping shipwreck, bandits, and the amorous embraces of several women, not to mention the strange habits of a host of "others," adds entertaining flair to his autobiography and establishes him as the intrepid, worldly traveler—much like his namesake in Virgil's epic. Perhaps in addition, Pius wanted to use this opportunity to show how far the Church's reach extended, even among modern day "barbarians." Sharing one faith with these strange inhabitants helped him get from place to place, to find common ground, and to make himself understandable—at least to educated clergy, with whom he could speak Latin. In many ways, Pius's majestic, detailed narratives of the countries and cities of Catholic Europe create a feeling of common enterprise and destiny; all these states, despite their tensions, were united under the Christian umbrella. All of them, for the most part, relied on the sacraments of the Roman Church and their relationship, however distant or strained, with the pope as its leader. And yet, Pius fully grasped their differences and ensured that his narrative did not flatten them.

Pius's colorful stories, moreover, enabled him to showcase his intimate knowledge of the remote corners of Europe and his skills as an ethnographer. His vivid description in the *Commentaries* of the Sarntal valley in the Italian Alps offers another rich example. The Sarntal appears in book I as a parish that Emperor Frederick III bestowed on Pius in 1443 when he was still just "Aeneas." As with most benefices, there was no expectation that Aeneas would attend to it in person, but it did provide him an income of sixty gold florins per year.[163] Importantly, he had little to say about the place in the 1440s when he received the Tyrolean parish, commenting in a few letters only on the basic logistics of the financial windfall.[164]

Yet, years later in the *Commentaries*, new details come to light for the first time about this intriguing hamlet. Without taking Pius completely at his word, one can appreciate the picture he paints:

> This valley lies in the alps separating Germany from Italy. It has only one entrance, which is very steep and rough, and for three quarters of the year it lies buried under snow and thick ice. The inhabitants remain in their houses all winter making boxes and other pieces of carpentry, in which art they are highly skilled, and which they sell in the summer in Bolzano and Trent. They while away a good deal of time playing chess and dice, games at which they are extraordinarily clever. They have no fear of war nor are they tormented by any ambitions nor consumed by greed for gold. Their wealth is in their flocks, which they feed on hay in the winter and which provide them with all the means of life. There are men among them who have never tasted wine: instead of drink, they have a milky food.[165]

Pius also describes their practice of burying the dead all at once in the spring, being unable to dig the frozen ground until the thaw. They would be the "happiest of mortals," he opines, if they lived more piously instead of indulging in fornication and feasting: no girl was supposedly married as a virgin in Sarntal.

Ady assumes that Pius must have visited the area, saying "his clever sketch of the remote Tyrolese parish is clearly based on personal knowledge."[166] Whether or not he spent time there is hard to say. He certainly had the opportunity to pass through or near it on his travels in the 1440s, but, like his writings on Scotland, his comments on both areas were extremely sparse at the time of such visits. It was only later, with the aid of ancient ethnographic models and the inspiration to think upon Europe as a unit, albeit one with countless curious and diverse pockets, that such full and engaging accounts were composed. Another unifying factor in many of his digressions on local culture or history are their direct connection to him, like this benefice or the sordid tale of the French Count of Armagnac's incestuous relationship with his sister and his attempts to obtain a dispensation to marry her, which more than one corrupt clergyman was willing to assist. Pius becomes a central figure in this extended discussion in book IV when he is approached by the duke himself, whom Pius roundly censures.[167]

Pius had a story to tell about nearly every corner of Europe, it seems. These and other examples suggest to me that Pius saw the *Commentaries* as a means to promote his intellectual authority, as well as his spiritual authority, over the continent—it was a powerful way of proving how well he knew his flock. His digressions showed his encyclopedic knowledge of his readers' homelands with a collection of first-hand observations from his many travels, including the amount of time it took to journey from one city to another, the route that was taken, and the friends he made from diverse parts of Europe, which smacks at times of name dropping. He is keen to comment on noteworthy churches and cathedrals as well as the ancient history and ruins of many places.[168] But, as noted, he did not gloss over the regional differences and tensions. Unlike papal monarchs of the medieval era, Pius seems to have understood the limits of Rome's authority and the changed world in which he lived.[169] Hence, the *Commentaries* seek to balance two disparate goals: presenting himself as the "head" that he previously lamented Christendom lacked and respecting each nation's unique past and future agenda.[170] Throughout, they contain fascinating insights into Pius's later views of Europe, Asia, individual nations, and their cultures.

As crucial as the *Commentaries* are to any study of Pius today, it is important to note that in his time they were not well known or highly circulated. The text, in fact, was only edited and printed in 1584; due to heavy redactions, many of Pius's more provocative statements were left out of that version. Hence, if one seeks to understand Pius's impact in the first century after his death, the *Commentaries* are not the best guide. There is no doubt, however, that they offer a valuable record of his views of Europe, its peoples, and its nations; they may be seen as a rich conduit of influence on later readers.

Imagined Communities: Pius and the Myths of Italy and Germany

The *Commentaries* contains many references to "Italy" and "Germany"—centuries before either would be unified into sovereign states. While these terms (along with "Italians" and "Germans") appeared in earlier texts by Pius, in the *Commentaries* they serve not only as national identities but as proxies for the North and South of Europe.[171] The most vivid use of "Italy" appears in Pius's account of private conversations with several cardinals during his own election: Italy looms large in his efforts to persuade or shame them into voting for him instead of the cunning and wealthy French (*Gallus*) cardinal of Rouen. After a poetic appeal to the cardinal of Pavia to consider St. Peter whose successor they were choosing, and affirming his own stoic acceptance of the outcome, he soon shifts to politics. Chiding the prelate for his planned support for Rouen, he states, "You've failed me. No, rather, you've failed yourself and your country [*patria*]—Italy!—unless you come to your senses."[172] Pius's campaign gathers steam through the maneuverings of the Venetian cardinal of San Marco: "spurred equally by patriotic fervor [*amor patriae*] and hatred of Rouen, he went round to all the Italian cardinals [*Italos cardinales*], urging and cajoling them not to abandon their country [*patriam*]."[173] In the end, if Pius is to be believed, most cardinals from the Italian peninsula were convinced that they were one "country" or "people" and therefore, should elect a fellow Italian lest the curia be uprooted to France again—even the Spanish cardinal Borgia is incited to hate the French and trust the "Italians." The terms *natio* and *patria* are repeatedly used in this section, but the description of Italy as *patria* or homeland/fatherland dominates.[174]

We cannot know Pius's exact words in this conclave given the secrecy of the proceedings and the lack of corroborating sources, but it is clear that by the time he began composing the *Commentaries* in 1462, the notion of Italy as a unified *patria* spoke to him, and he hoped that it would speak to his audience.[175] Most likely, his Italian birth and connections indeed helped his ascent to the papacy, even if some members like the cardinal of Rouen reportedly dismissed him as "only just come from Germany,"[176] insinuating that he was unknown or less "Italian" than others. Notably, Pius does not refer to himself in the *Commentaries* as "the German cardinal"—a badge he wore proudly around the time of his elevation in 1456, so fluid was his sense of personal identity. While the political forces that helped propel Pius to the throne of St. Peter were more complex than he admits, he seems to have gauged the shifting winds well enough to position himself effectively. But this jockeying came with a price. If his blatant appeal to "Italy" helped Pius win the papacy, it weakened his chances of convincing other European powers that he would be their pope as well.[177]

Despite his patriotic invocation of "Italy" in the Commentaries near the start of his papacy, Pius's use of the term is more ambiguous in the rest of the work. He describes a moment in 1456 "when all Italy was breathing more freely because of the recent peace [of Lodi],"[178] yet a few pages later, he characterizes Niccolò Piccinino's campaigns in Sienese territory as attacks on his *patria*—reverting to the narrower and more common sense of the word as one's regional homeland.[179] "Italy," however, appears more pointedly later in the text when the French (*Galli*) are boasting of a recent victory (1460) in the war against Ferrante of Naples. An exasperated Pius claims that he said to himself and his friends, "Look, people of Italy [*genus Italicum*]! How will you endure these men as masters, when as servants they are so bold? ... Woe to you, Italy, if you are forced beneath the [French] yoke!"[180] This is perhaps the only time where Pius refers to Italians as a *genus*, which implies "race" or common origin. Importantly, he describes this as an internal dialogue or a private conversation rather than a public speech or bull—just like his private conversations with the cardinals at his election. Did any of these discussions really take place in this way, or was this just a compositional device for Pius? Either way, the sense of Italians as a common descent group or possibly "race" only comes out in a moment of desperation.

Regardless of the intended audience, what these reported statements all share is that Pius most often used "Italy" when the peninsula was perceived to be in danger from some foreign adversary. It is largely a defensive gesture, much like his use of "Europe" when railing against the Turks. Was there a positive sense to Italy—as a homeland to all in times of safety? Perhaps, but in the *Commentaries*, it is an aspirational idea, like Petrarch gazing upon "Italy" (longingly, from a distance) in his famous "Ascent of Mt. Ventoux," or Machiavelli's call to his would-be prince to free Italy from the "barbarians." In the end, Pius knew as well as Machiavelli that "Italy" was hopelessly divided.

Standing in parallel to "Italy" is "Germany," Pius's former home. Here, too, Pius appears to have used this term much more than the average inhabitant of the region. While Pius developed a preference for the terms "Germany" and "Germans" (like other Italian and ancient Roman writers), imperial subjects seem to have been more sensitive to their regional differences.[181] There was a loose sense of unity among the vast number of federated states, the most important of which were represented by seven electors: the archbishops of Mainz, Trier, and Cologne, and the secular rulers of Bohemia, Brandenburg, Saxony, and the Palatine, but nomenclature could be tricky. In Pius's day, inhabitants of the land he called "Germany" were more likely to use a plural designation like "German lands" or "lands of the German tongues"; the phrase "German nation" does not seem to have taken root in the region itself until the late fifteenth century.[182] If Pius helped popularize such ideas, he by no means invented them. German writers had been crafting a notion of "German" political identity for well over a century before Pius set foot in the region. As Len Scales has argued, a number of later medieval thinkers like Alexander of Roes (d. c. 1288) articulated a concept of a German (or Teutonic) political identity—an imagined community that, in some ways, went beyond membership in the empire.[183] Such views likely influenced Pius's own evolving sense of "Germany" in the *Commentaries* and other writings. Importantly, "Germany" is not treated in quite the same way as France or Venice. Pius does not attempt to describe the whole of "Germany" in one brief section, as he does with several other countries in the *Commentaries* or even in *Europe*, and he rarely uses the term "German" to describe very specific political developments. As with Italy, "Germany" and "Germans" were more a future hope than a reality.

Sometimes Pius evokes the region as a self-promoting gesture, painting a rosy picture of "all the princes of Germany" celebrating his elevation to the cardinalate and papacy as they regarded him as "the champion and defender of the Germans."[184] This claim need not be taken seriously; many princes likely identified him as an advocate of the emperor, rather than "all of Germany." With many local rulers still supporting conciliarism, German princes and other rulers hardly held one view of the Church.[185] Pius was, perhaps, closer to the truth when writing of broadly shared "German" discontent with papal taxes and tithes.

The word choice that Pius attributes to German speakers, however, raises questions. He speaks of them expressing their concerns about crusade taxes and tithes at the Diet of Frankfurt (1454), adding a special flourish when they supposedly charged, "It was a fine trick, to swindle the Germans of their treasure by proclaiming a crusade against the Turks—as though the Germans were mere barbarians!"[186] While it is possible that Pius was paraphrasing words he heard spoken years earlier by Germans at Frankfurt, he was certainly not present on another occasion where he notes a similar speech pattern. This was at an imperial diet in 1461 in which Diether of Isenburg, archbishop elect of Mainz, complained about the papal fees and promises Pius extorted before he would confirm his position. Diether supposedly railed against both bankers and the pope saying, "The Italians are proving [lit. "obeying"] their own proverb, that one must use subtlety to squeeze gold from barbarians. And by 'barbarians,' they mean us!"[187]

It is hard to know if any of these statements were based on actual pronouncements by German speakers, but their resemblance to Pius's style places the likelihood in doubt. Regardless, it is fascinating that Pius invokes the word "barbarians" for Germans, even to push back on Italian stereotypes, when he uses the term so rarely in the *Commentaries* to describe the Ottoman Turks. It bears repeating that Pius, generally speaking, took few shots at Germans for being boorish or backward, as some Italian thinkers were inclined to do.[188] His general tone is one of complete respect. Even when he mentions the alarming custom of some bishops in Germany carrying arms and waging war in the *Commentaries*, he drily notes "Whether this is becoming or not we do not say. Great allowances must be made for custom ...."[189] Pius's invocation of German stereotypes in the *Commentaries* was perhaps part of his plan to offer local color and a note of exoticism, as seen in his descriptions of Scotland and Sarntal.

As with "Italy," "Germany" commonly appears in the *Commentaries* at moments of strife between local rulers. When Ludwig of Bavaria attacked Donauwörth in October 1458 and the emperor sent Albert of Brandenburg to confront him, both sides called up their allies to fight: "The pope [Pius] took this news badly, for he saw it meant the failure of the crusade and the ruin of the noble land of Germany."[190] A few pages later, he describes his legates chiding the princes for shedding the blood of Christians, unable to see "how [their] feuds weaken the whole of Christendom." The legates go on to state, or so Pius claims, that "the destruction of Germany is good news for the Turks ... the more you waste your energies, the stronger they become."[191] In these and other cases, Pius uses "Germany" as a foil for the Ottomans and their unnerving unity and progress. The connection comes up again after the Congress of Mantua when Bessarion is sent to work out terms of crusade in "Germany" but finds "war ablaze everywhere."[192] Taken all together, it is hard to escape the notion that Pius and others expected—or at least hoped— to find a single "country" at peace.

While four centuries would pass before Germany was unified into one nation, Pius repeatedly nudges its people in that direction. Recall that years before he simply used the term "empire" in most cases, for instance in *De Ortu* (1446), but here, transformed by the threat of 1453 and his experiences reading ancient ethnography as a cardinal in Rome, the terms "Germany" and "Germans" prevail. Pius's goal in this word choice is unclear, but to focus on "Germany" rather than "empire" could be seen as marginalizing the role of the emperor. The former offered a sense of cultural and ethnic coherence without a clear center or leader—a powerful, but potentially dangerous idea. Had Pius's views of the hallmarks of a nation-state shifted toward a pro-to-nationalist model since the 1440s? The *History of Bohemia* and the unfin-ished *History of Austria*, as Montecalvo has argued, provide some evidence for this view. But it is important to note the lack of definition in many of Pius's claims about what it means to be "German." One example concerns his description of the modern Belgian city of Liège, "which is half German, (but the people speak a corrupt form of French)."[193] The tantalizing concept of being "half-German" (*semi-Germanicus*) is left unexplained. Nonetheless, Pius's descriptions of common ethnic bonds in the *Commentaries* may have influenced or reinforced the beliefs of later readers, eager to see themselves or the "Germans" as a coherent nation-state.

In the fifteenth century there was little evidence of the nationalist use of ethnicity and bloodline as a myth to binding people across social class, but Pius and others before him, as Scales has shown, were promoting a notion of political unity and cultural bonds that transcended any given ruler, dynasty, or hard boundaries. While Pius's usages of "nation," "people," or "home-land" may not add up to a clear philosophy or system, his shift in terminol-ogy suggests an awareness of a changing political field. Leaders within the empire may have had little respect for their Habsburg emperor, but they seem to have possessed a growing awareness of their shared goals and an affinity with other "German" leaders.

A similar phenomenon can be found in his treatment of the Greeks, who were more clearly transitioning from "empire" to "nation" in his lifetime with the death of the last emperor in 1453. One poignant example is Pius's descrip-tion of the aged Isidore—the formerly Greek Orthodox metropolitan of Kiev, who became a unionist at the Council of Florence and was elevated to the rank of cardinal. Though convalescing at home from a stroke and unable to speak, he could not be prevented from walking to St. Peter's church to venerate the head of the apostle St. Andrew, an important relic that had recently arrived from Greece with the Despot Thomas. Pius, describing

Isidore as "a Greek by nation [*natione Grecum*], from the Peloponnese," says that he "was as delighted as if he had beheld the founder of his homeland [*patrie*]."[194] Whether this constitutes nationalist thought can be debated, but it certainly speaks to Pius's sense of one's country as a place of emotional attachment and patriotism. At moments like this in the *Commentaries*, the nation of one's birth is a permanent mark, no matter where else they might move or settle.

Bloodline, Ethnicity, and Race: Further Thoughts on Group Identity

An important question this study has not yet fully addressed is whether the category of race applies to Pius's views of the Turks and other peoples. Some thirty years ago the answer would have seemed simpler, given the prevailing definition of race as a modern construct that placed humans into fixed, bio-logically determined categories.[195] As we saw in previous chapters, there is little or no mention in Pius's works of physical traits, even among his most vilified group, the Turks, and his view of the lines between different "nations" was often fluid. By such definitions, it is hard to construe his views as particu-larly racial, and to my knowledge, no one has. Scholars, including me, have sometimes translated his use of *gens* as "race," but with the understanding that it had a different connotation in his time than it does today. In the past few decades, however, scholars like Geraldine Heng and Benjamin Isaac have argued that clear concepts of race existed in the ancient, medieval, and Renaissance periods that did not depend on biology or somatic traits, but nonetheless served as powerful markers of differentiation and discrimina-tion.[196] These broad new definitions of race and racism may place Pius's writ-ings in a new light, but questions remain. Was Pius's animosity toward the Ottomans discrimination or justified resentment against an aggressive power? One imagines a range of different responses from the scholarly community. Adding to the complexity, not all scholars agree that a clear concept of racial (as opposed to ethnic) identity existed in the minds of premodern thinkers.[197]

After much reading and reflection, I am still uncertain about where to place Pius's perceptions of human difference along the spectrum of ethnic and racial identity. My sense is that it is probably more accurate to categorize his views of the Ottomans and others as ethnic in nature—while being cogni-zant of the many other notions of identity that he examines, like civilization, barbarism, and religion. For centuries these categories have carried racial overtones, but not always and everywhere.[198] Yet I also wonder if Robert Bartlett has the right idea when he asserts that race and ethnicity overlapped in the minds of medieval folk, and that it is acceptable to speak of race and ethnicity as synonymous in this period "as long as it is made clear that race is not a biological category."[199] Is it splitting hairs to see Pius's use of *gens* as anything but race in modern parlance? Moreover, if I contend that his views are not racial, does this arise from a desire to defend him? Conversely, if I assert that his views are racial in nature, do I risk eliding and simplifying the subtle ways in which he saw and described difference? Sometimes race and ethnicity blended into one another in Renaissance imaginations, but many times they did not. William Jordan, concerned that presentism was clouding our view of the past, posed a question in 2001 that is still relevant today: "What payoff is there in regarding medieval attitudes toward people of different 'races' as 'racist'?"[200] Vanita Seth has likewise argued, "there are other ways of being in the world—ones that are not better or worse but different" from a twenty-first–century perspective.[201] Current scholarship on race in the Renaissance has greatly enriched our conversations about how people viewed themselves and others, but debates on how and where to apply these models are ongoing. In our quest to comprehend the periods we study, we must constantly ask if we are oversimplifying what we see to make it mirror our context or if we are refusing to see what is obviously quite similar.

Rather than erase that ambiguity in Pius's works and pick a side, as it were, I would like to offer a few observations and questions, first by saying a bit more about his view of the Ottomans, or specifically the Turks, as he calls them. One of the most interesting aspects about his generally polemical treatments of both the Turks and the Scythians is that he never attempts a somatic description of them—despite the fact that his favorite polemical source, Aethicus, describes the early Turks as having "a foul appearance as dark as soot with hair as black as a crow and very strong teeth."[202] Yet Pius ignores that passage, choosing to focus instead on their actions, diet, and other imagined *cultural* attributes. In truth, Renaissance texts as a group paid little attention to the Turks' physical appearance.[203] As Bronwen Wilson put it, the Turks were "too familiar to be made exotic."[204] Pius would have disagreed with some aspects of this statement, but it rings true, I believe, in regard to a perception of physical difference. Some might argue that Pius's obsession with the ethnic origins of the Turks shows a belief in a people's shared gene pool as indicative of their present character, but others might argue that his belief in the possibility of converting the Turks shows he could imagine them as part of the same extended family.[205] He certainly allowed for a cultural conversion of the Hungarians, whom he also saw as descendants of the Scythians. We are left unclear, then, as to whether Pius saw the bloodline of nations (as opposed to acquired traits) as a key component of identity. His view of Western Europeans and ethnic descent was also inconsistent; he seems to find the notion important when it comes to "the Germans" but has a much vaguer sense of how ancestry may have shaped "the Italians."

It is reasonable to ask if Pius associated climate and geography with a concept of race, given his obsession with East and West and his knowledge of ancient texts. Hippocrates and Aristotle claimed that the climate in which one lived played a significant role in their character and behavior, thereby establishing a doctrine that would be invoked for centuries to come.[206] Did Pius accept these theories? His mobility over the course of his life and his habit of calling himself "a German" at times renders this question even more problematic. If he believed his changing location or climate changed him, he never explicitly noted it. His letter to Mehmed contains a notion of the long-term impact of climate or geography on a people, with his dismissive comments about Egyptians and Africans, but it lacks the systematic categorization one sees in ancient tracts and modern racist treatises. The letter, I would argue, gestures at climate as formative without claiming it as definitive.[207] Not even Europe's enemies possessed a fixed, unchanging nature in Pius's view; he accepted a people's ability to change character—with conversion as a major conduit. As far as all the previous examples are concerned, the answer to whether or not Pius had a clear concept of race depends very much on one's own definition of what constitutes race in the Renaissance.

A few passages in the *Commentaries*, however, are less ambiguous and suggest a notion of identity in which somatic markers or heredity played some sort of role. At one point in 1462, when tensions peak between Emperor Frederick and his brother Albert, the duke of Austria, Frederick defends himself before the people of Vienna and pleads for their support by saying, "I who am your lord and of one blood with you, men of Vienna, am prevented from entering my own city."[208] This purported invocation of "one blood" among the Austrians would appear more racially motivated if Albert had been a foreigner rather than his own brother, but it is still interesting that Frederick (or Pius) claims a sense of shared ancestry between ruler and subjects—a notion later nationalist propagandists would exploit. For the most part, Pius only discusses bloodline in connection with dynasties as a way to set them apart from their people—noting, for instance, Alfonso of Aragon and Naples's *unique* claim to be directly descended from the Visigoths in Europe.[209]

As seen in Chapter 3, Pius seems more interested in linguistic groups and migration patterns and avoids viewing ethnic groups as discrete, unmixed entities. He rarely assumes that any ethnic group was defined by their physical features, but at one point in the *Commentaries* he describes a "handsome" delegation of young Polish nobles with "their blonde hair floating behind them in the wind" and the impression made by their clothing, arms, and steeds; he also notes the whiteness or fairness of Scottish women (*feminas albas*) and the short stature (and bravery) of the men.[210] But these are brief and, for him, most unusual statements. Pius rarely generalizes about skin, eye, or hair color, or the shape and size of the peoples he describes (unlike Tacitus who described the Germans as red-haired, blue-eyed, and large-framed people of unmixed stock).[211] Perhaps Pius's awareness of the physical variations among the Germanic and other peoples he had observed made it seem absurd to categorize them.

One moment of racialized language in the *Commentaries* stands out, however. There is a brief, but intriguing description of an unnamed black African soldier in the papal army whose heroism and resourcefulness won the battle of Isola in Lazio (1463). Pius describes him as an Ethiopian soldier (*miles ethyops*), which likely refers to his skin color rather than his national origin, judging by Pius's other uses of the word.[212] As Kate Lowe shows, black Africans were often described with a variety of imprecise terms in Renaissance Italy.[213] This soldier, Pius states, "had been for some years in [captain] Napoleone's service and had finally entered the army."²¹⁴ His critical role emerged when the city of Isola was taken, but the citadel held strong. Protected by a rushing river, the citadel seemed invulnerable until the African soldier presented a plan. Addressing his fellow soldiers as comrades (*commilitones*), he boldly offered to clear a path and urged them to follow his lead. He threw his lance across the river toward the citadel, disrobed, and "leapt naked into the river and swam swiftly to the other side. Then recovering his lance, he strove to climb the heap of ruins, a black and revolting [*tetro*] figure. Every bold man in the camp followed his example."²¹⁵ Two men drowned while trying to swim across, but this band of naked men overwhelmed and captured the citadel, much to the embarrassment of the defenders inside.

It is a fascinating portrait of daring and ingenuity, marred by voyeurism and denigration of the soldier's body, but Pius ends on a note of wonder and admiration: "An Ethiopian's courage stormed what was believed to be impregnable. Posterity will think it mythical ...."²¹⁶ The anonymous African soldier might be seen as a device—an underdog figure turning the tables in a moment of crisis. But this story is quite plausible, given the presence of West Africans in Renaissance Italy as domestic slaves, servants, and tradesmen like the gondoliers of Venice.²¹⁷ He was probably as real as Orietta Doria, the unnamed female fighter at Lesbos in Pius's *Asia* and *Commentaries*, turned out to be.

Was Pius thoughtlessly quoting another source or inserting his own view when he used the word *tetro*? Clearly, he did not witness the event. He seems more focused on the individual here than on his ethnicity or race, but that sentence is a jarring pause in his mostly color-blind account. It is difficult to say what Pius was getting at since he makes very few comments on skin color elsewhere in his works, but the remark does present a contrast to his equation of white skin and "fairness," particularly among women.²¹⁸ Throughout his works, there are only a handful of references to Africa or Africans. Interestingly, in the *Commentaries*, he compares the dramatic impression he made upon the Northern English to the response of (presumably) Italians to an Ethiopian or an Indian. Here, Ethiopians and Indians serve as consummate exotic others to convey a sense of wonderment, but he inserts them without physical descriptors or pejorative remarks.²¹⁹ Less ambiguous was Pius's aforementioned comment in his letter to Mehmed about the "naked African," who would meekly follow the sultan's example if he converted; it is hard to see that off-handed comment as anything but racist or ethnocentric.²²⁰ And yet Pius took the important step of condemning black slavery in 1462 as a great evil and ordered ecclesiastical sanctions against those who practiced it.²²¹ All things considered, Pius's relative neglect of Africa in his writings is puzzling considering his great interest in (Western) Asia; had a serious military threat had been coming from the South during his lifetime, his orientation would likely have been quite different. Either way, one wonders if Pius's indifference to Africa or his inability to include it as part of "the West" made an impact on his contemporaries just as Eurocentric concepts of world history were taking shape.

The question of race should also be raised in connection with European Jewish communities, who briefly appear in the *Commentaries* and other works. The brevity of Pius's comments on Jews may have led other scholars to ignore these moments, but I discern an intriguing pattern in his scattered references that may provide more texture to discussions of race, ethnicity, and especially belonging. Despite persecutions, banishments, and forced conversion attempts, many communities of Ashkenazi and Sephardic Jews were still living in parts of Western Europe in the mid fifteenth century.[222] In contrast to the Ottomans or Hussites, they posed no military threat, and unlike pagans on the peripheries of Europe, they had been living in Christian towns and villages for centuries. The question to ask here is whether Pius considered Jews a legitimate part of Europe.

In two letters from the 1440s, Pius noted the custom in which members of the Jewish community offered their law to the newly elected pope as he passed by in procession; the pope (in these cases Felix V in Basel and Nicholas V in Rome), following the predetermined script, praised their law while rejecting their interpretation of it.[223] Thus, the hierarchical relationship between the two parties was dramatized and Jews were publicly acknowledged as having the pope's protection. Pius also mentions Jews on a few occasions in the *Commentaries* in connection with the burdensome taxes levied upon them to support crusade.[224] Other references to Jews in Pius's works point to harsher realities. In one of his letters on Basel, he mentions stones with Hebrew inscriptions in the city walls—most likely gravestones of members of the Jewish community that was expelled in 1349. He soberly registers their absence, noting that there were once many Jews in Basel, just as one (still) sees in Italy.[225] Similarly, in his *Europe*, he mentions Ludwig IX of Bavaria's banishment of Jews from his dominions in 1450, without praise or censure.[226]

In the *Commentaries*, however, Pius criticizes one particular ruler who exploited the Jews in his kingdom:

> Giovanni Antonio [prince of Taranto] had been the worst of misers and so bent on gain that he kept the trade of his principality for himself alone. He bought from his subjects at his own price everything that was for sale and sold it to foreign merchants. He rarely paid his creditors. He kept in his dominion great numbers of Jews whom he could most easily plunder. He had commercial dealings with the Turks.[227]

Here, Pius groups Jewish and Christian subjects as common victims of economic exploitation. His use of the word "plunder" (*expilare*) for the prince's treatment of the Jews, moreover, suggests empathy and a recognition of injustice.

It is hard to determine Pius's overarching view of Jewish people from the few references he left in writing, but those snippets both reflect their presence in public life (albeit in a forced, humiliating ritual)[228] and highlight their vulnerability before powerful leaders. Arguably, what Pius does *not* say about Jews is equally important. At no point in *Europe* or the *Commentaries* does he question the Jews' right to live in Christian Europe, nor does he echo the falsehoods that other writers recklessly repeated: accusations of blood libel, child murder, or host desecration.[229] In fact, the only mention of these charges that Pius made, to my knowledge, appears in a letter from June 3, 1453, to Cardinal Carvajal: "In Bratislava all the Jews were reported to have been thrown in chains because they are said to have desecrated the Host. I suppose that it was invented to extort money for the new king [Ladislas Postumus]."[230] Pius's use of "invented" and his cynical comment on the corrupt purpose of such charges speaks volumes. At a time when some clergy supported such attacks or, like San Bernardino and other Franciscans, campaigned for the enforcement of the Fourth Lateran Council's requirement of badges for the Jews, Pius did not support such measures.[231]

At the risk of stretching the evidence at hand too far, I would venture to say that Pius accepted Jews as part of Europe and its nation states. He does not treat them as a separate race, nation, or some sort of threat. His mentions of them are all local and contingent on the conditions under which each community lived. As such, he describes Jews in some ways as citizens or subjects while calling attention to the limits of their rights. Pius was no champion of the Jews of Renaissance Europe, but he never attacks, belittles, or rejects them. In fact, one of his physicians during his papacy, Moses ben Joab da Rieti, was Jewish.[232] His reference to the Jews "one was accustomed to see in Italy" in his 1434 letter to Cesarini makes one wonder if he came into regular contact with their community as a student in Siena and on his travels in Northern Italian cities.[233]

Finally, I would like to offer a few thoughts on Pius's views of gender and ethnicity.[234] In exploring his works for examples of ethnic, cultural, national, and continental identity, I have been struck by the number of times he invokes masculine and feminine tropes in concert with various nations and groups—in some cases before 1453, but with much greater frequency afterward. His use of these stereotypes for different nations has already been noted. Germans, Italians, French, Spanish, Poles, and Hungarians—along with the ancient Romans—are all praised as especially manly. The Turks and their supposed Scythian ancestors wobble back and forth on Pius's spectrum of manliness and effeminacy, depending on the timing of his work and its goals. Greeks, Arabs, and Persians are progressively described as less manly or outright womanly—always in opposition to the hyper masculine Western Europeans. Reporting a conversation with a Burgundian delegate at Mantua in the *Commentaries*, he explains the Turks' easy victory over the Greeks because the latter were "unarmed and weak as women (*inermes atque effeminatos*)."[235] Some of these ideas no doubt came by way of ancient sources like Tacitus's *Germania*, which Nell Painter sees as sharing aspects of modern ethnogender stereotyping.[236] Apart from his diet oration at Wiener-Neustadt in 1455, Pius rarely imagined Western European soldiers as having any "feminine" attribute.[237]

A few examples, however, transcend the Europe-Asia and East-West binary. Pius seems to invoke the French-English debate about masculinity in his description of the battle of Agincourt (1415) where the toughened English bested the "effeminate nobility" of France; he later praises Henry V's rugged character.[238] His fascination with Joan of Arc may, at least in part, have some connection to his disdain for the French nobility and crown, but it also fits well among many other moments of admiration in his works for strong women who proved to be compelling leaders; Pius discusses Joan in *Europe* and at much greater length in the *Commentaries*, defending her against accusations of heresy and witchcraft and praising her bravery and resourcefulness.[239] Indeed, Pius's works show his pleasure in highlighting strong women and their stories; for example, Queen Margaret of Denmark, Sweden, and Norway, and the Duke of Carinthia's wife, who imprisoned her drunken, foolish husband twice.[240] Gendered behavior and sex were not synonymous for Pius.

In conclusion, my sense is that when Pius spoke of a *gens* or *natio*, he envisioned a coherent, but not closed, group identity; the membership of a given group was determined by such variables as geography and religion—categories that were neither static nor biologically preordained, although not easily changed. His interest and emphasis center more on the formation of states and the glue that held them together: common language, customs, and laws, for instance. And as we saw in Chapter 3, more than one *gens* could comprise a nation. When imagining Europe, Pius was probably informed by notions of the Roman Empire and Roman identity as a supra-ethnic designation; "Roman" was a name that the Hellenized Jew St. Paul and the Latin patrician Julius Caesar both claimed.[241] As he surveyed Europe's early history, Pius saw a place of great movement and resettlement over time—at least until the later Middle Ages, when it became more fixed by his definition, naturally excluding the Ottomans (and the Russians and Moors) from that pattern of change and absorption. If Pius saw the Turks as distinct outsiders, it is not clear that a notion of race rather than ethnic identity played a part in this.

At the same time, Pius began to place a greater emphasis on land, territory, and sovereignty than perhaps seen before this period, and he framed national narratives and identities in terms of their connection to that land.[242] As discussed in the previous chapter, he began to use the word "nation" for geographical settings as well as peoples. This represents a break from medieval notions of peoples or races, as "changing cultural communities, often in competition, often forming and reforming, overflowing and cutting across political boundaries," to cite Bartlett's definition.[243] By contrast, Pius saw the place of many nations as more static and defined by the land they inhabited and/or controlled. As such, Pius exemplifies and perhaps influenced a changing sense of what nation meant at this time. It was still movable and fluid, but shifting to a more permanent designation—with later ramifications for the notions of "blood and soil."[244] Pius, it is important to note, was not there yet. While scholars may wish to debate the exact nature of Pius's concepts of human difference and group identity, one thing that is clear is his imprint not just on the concept of Europe, but the notion of *Eurocentrism*. The attention and value he placed on Europe, at the expense of other continents and societies, was a lasting legacy.

The *Commentaries* and the Blurred Eastern Edges of Europe?

As described throughout this chapter, both the common practice of Christianity in (most of) Europe and Pius's copious knowledge of the continent give his narrative a sense of coherence: these were all, theoretically, "his" dominions. Even distant, exoticized Wallachia (roughly modern-day Romania) was an important part of Christian Europe: "The Wallachians speak Italian, but an imperfect, corrupted Italian. Some think that once Roman legions were sent there against the Dacians .... Their descendants, as has been said above, became more barbarous than the barbarians."[245] Despite Pius's concerns that its current leader, Vlad Dracul, had recently been imprisoned by Matthias Corvinus of Hungary and was attempting to collude with the sultan, the area in all its roughness was in Christian hands—for the time being. The anxiety this precarious region and Eastern borders as a whole provoked in him was obvious: it compelled him again and again to think of the integrity of Europe more than any other part of the continent.

Pius conveys greater distress when he describes how King Stephen of Bosnia's envoys begged him to send military aid against the Turks who were making inroads into his kingdom and winning over the peasants with their "kindly disposition." By promising "all who desert to them shall be free," he continues, "the inexperienced rustics do not understand their wiles and think their liberty will last forever."[246] If peasants continued to desert the nobles, Pius feared, their fortresses would soon fall. This indeed happened soon thereafter in 1463. It is as if Pius was trying to document which areas still belonged to Christian Europe, knowing full well they could splinter away any day. The price of losing any of these kingdoms, Pius implies, is to make the whole of Europe, Christendom, or "the West" vulnerable. After meeting with the legate of Bosnia, Pius informed his cardinals of the danger and purportedly stated, "We believe Stephen's embassy. The same reports are brought to us from many places. Mehmed, who has made his way through the eastern empire, now seeks that of the west."[247]

Pius particularly highlights the promise and vulnerability of Hungary, whose role as the wall or bulwark (*murum*) for the rest of Europe, hung in the balance.[248] Pius had looked to Hungary for this reason since the 1440s, but in the *Commentaries* it stands as Europe's last best hope; not only was the kingdom holding its own against the Ottomans, but it was one of the few Roman Catholic countries in the region. While Pius tried to be realistic, his hopes always rose when it came to Hungary: if enough aid were sent to the kingdom, Hungary could both protect its coreligionists to the west and become the site from which Mehmed would be "utterly driven from Europe" (*ab Europa prorsus eliminabitur*).[249] For all its strategic importance, when the Ottomans were not part of the discussion, Hungary held far less interest for Pius. Other aspects of Hungary's history, including recent dynastic struggles with the emperor, tend to come back to the Turkish threat:

All this was an annoyance to Pope Pius not only because feuds between kings are always to be condemned but because such dissension was increasingly an invitation to the Turks, who were stirred up against the empire of the west through their own inclination.[250]

A critical point in the *Commentaries* is that "West" and "Europe" always appear more frequently and urgently in his discussions of Eastern Europe and the frontier with the Ottomans than elsewhere in the work. Pius rarely invokes other Christian countries in this sprawling work as representatives of "Europe" or "the West." It is primarily at the flashpoint of danger and the threat of conquest by religious and cultural outsiders that this rhetoric is strongest. It is a tendency that had been brewing for years in his other writings, but here, in his largest and last major work, it comes into focus. When other issues such as deference to the pope or the stability of Italy provoke this usage, it is usually in tandem with the Turkish threat. For example, in a reported argument from 1463 between Pius and a Florentine ambassador about the need for Italians to aid Venice, now at war with the Turks, he raises the security of Europe several times.[251] It would be tedious to rehearse all the instances and ways in which the terms are used, but their constant repetition likely made an impact on his (European) readers.[252]

As expected, the Ottomans feature prominently in Pius's narrative. He no more successfully erases their imprint on the continent in the *Commentaries* than he did in *Europe*. In his accounts of countries in Eastern and Central Europe, the Turks are everywhere. It is surprising that so many scholars have read the *Commentaries* without remarking on the Ottoman presence throughout the text or the extent to which the threat of further expansion drives his thoughts about individual countries, "Europe," and "Western" culture. If one is alert to this issue, it is hard to miss this potent demonstration of self and other existing in dialectical tension. Yet, as in *Europe*, self and other only goes so far. The Ottomans may be cast as outsiders, but they just as often appear as essential and savvy players in continental politics.

Nonetheless, there are subtle, but significant differences in Pius's treatment of the Turks in the *Commentaries* as opposed to previous works. First, while Pius still claims that the Scythians were ancestors of the Turks at the start of book 2, there is no sign of his customary polemic or the dark fantasies he drew from Aethicus.[253] *Asia* would seem to be the last text in which Pius repeats Aethicus's spurious stories. Perhaps his reading of ancient authorities on the Scythians and his exercise of writing the letter to Mehmed finally shattered this tendentious belief. Similarly, Pius largely avoids the barbaric trope of the Ottomans in the *Commentaries*. By contrast, in fact, he calls European Christians barbaric on several occasions to indicate rough or cruel behavior while resisting that enticing label for the Turks.

Perhaps a more rational approach to the Turks better suited the tone of the *Commentaries*. As Pius clearly states at the beginning of book XIII, this work was not typical of histories of his day with its focus on recent events and stories that had begun, but not yet ended. Yet he urges his reader to "understand that we have kept to the law of history, not to depart from the truth."[254] A small demonstration of this intention may be found in his word choice for Turkish possessions as a "rule" or "dominion" (*Turcorum principatum*), which suggests either a growing acceptance of Ottoman rule or a resolution to provide a more honest description than the dismissive terms he had used in other works.[255] Indeed, for long stretches of the *Commentaries*, Pius seems less certain about his former opinions of the Turks and Mehmed. On several occasions, he uses such terms as *imperator*, *princeps*, and *dominus* to describe the sultan, whereas in previous texts, he tended to avoid such honorific titles.

Pius's references to Asia and the "East" are also more varied and less stark, but, at times, more reductive. For example, when he praises Francesco Sforza at the Congress of Mantua, he states that if all princes in attendance were like him, "they might actually take the offensive and recover without difficulty Greece and Asia, which had been lost by the negligence of their forefathers."[256] "Asia" here might only mean Asia Minor, but the idea of easily conquering even Anatolia was still a pipe dream and not to be taken seriously. The "East" is also employed in a sweeping fashion. At another point at the Congress of Mantua, Philip of Burgundy's envoys link his commitment to crusade to his ancestors' campaigns against "the peoples of the east" (*orientales*).[257] This is perhaps a convenient short cut to refer to both the Holy Land of earlier crusades and recent battles against the Ottomans, like Nicopolis (1396) where Philip's father was captured. Still, it creates a blocky sense of the enemy and suggests that such opposition would always be there so long as Muslims ruled in "the East." This vague but powerful notion occurs in a later passage when Pius describes the Knights of St. John at Rhodes: "Indeed, one may say that by their courage all our religion in the East was saved for Christ."[258] Such sweeping claims, it would seem, were common stock for Pius as he labored to raise support for his crusade.

The frequency of East, West, Asia, and Europe increase toward the end of the *Commentaries* as the pope prepares to depart for Ancona toward his would-be crusade. In the very last book he describes his decision to accompany the troops, sending ambassadors

> throughout Italy and to the Transalpine regions to ask aid of the faithful peoples and princes and to persuade them not to allow the Pope to go accompanied only by the Venetians, Hungarians, and Burgundians on a war so great that it seemed to demand all the strength of the West (*totas Occidentis vires*), since the Turks on their part were said to be ready to move the entire East (*universum Orientem*).[259]

In this framing, crusade has moved from a battle of the faiths to an epic battle of West versus East. This was Pius's state of mind when he composed his last crusade bull and tried to raise as much support as his persuasive rhetoric could achieve.

Borders Reaffirmed: Europe and "the West" vs. Asia and "the East" in Pius's Last Papal Bull

While Pius wrote or dictated his *Commentaries*, the *Asia*, and his unsent letter to Mehmed, the young sultan rapidly expanded his empire in Europe and the Mediterranean. Mehmed's conquest of Greece sent Emperor Constantine's brother, Despot Thomas Paleologus, and his family into flight. They arrived in the spring of 1461 in Rome, seeking refuge and aid to recover their state. As noted, the gift that Thomas gave in thanks for the pope's assistance was the precious relic of the head of St. Andrew the apostle. The reception of the apostle to the Greeks by the bishop of Rome became an elaborate pageant full of symbolism about the reunification of the churches and a spur to reconquer "Andrew's homeland." That same year, the Christian kingdom of Cyprus became an Ottoman tributary state when James of Lusignan pushed his sister Charlotte off the throne with the sultan's help. Pius describes the queen's arrival at the Vatican (Oct. 15, 1461), portraying her as a figure of feminine vulnerability despite her brave journey and determination to regain her throne.[260] Trebizond on the Black Sea also fell to the Ottomans in August of 1461, as did the island of Lesbos in September of 1462. According to some reports, Mehmed received the surrender of the island with the agreement that the inhabitants would keep their heads, but then proceeded to saw some four hundred Latins in half, thereby grimly preserving the letter of the pact.[261] Bosnia also fell to the Ottomans in May of 1463, and King Stephen was beheaded.

There was one encouraging development in the midst of such gloom: in May of 1462, a man named Giovanni di Castro, who knew Pius from his Basel days and had worked in the cloth dyeing industry in Constantinople, discovered alum in the hills of Tolfa north of Rome. This precious mineral, used as a mordant to make fabrics retain their dyes, was previously thought to exist only in Ottoman territory and procured at great cost. When di Castro presented his finding to Pius, he is said to have boasted, "Today, I bring you victory over the Turk." The profits from this new commodity, it was hoped, would fund the crusade.[262]

As all these developments took place, Pius grew increasingly impatient for action. Feeling that the crusade had been stalled for too long, he made his startling decision to be the first pope to accompany and help lead such an undertaking, "old and ill as we are." He first announced his decision to six of his most loyal cardinals in March of 1462, explaining that his goal was to force the duke of Burgundy to honor his promise to lead a crusade army if a prince of equal or greater stature also agreed to take part.[263] He made a lengthier speech to his cardinals again on September 23, 1463, reaffirming his intention to go on crusade. The speech is by turns humble and self-flattering, but the tone is largely religious. Rather than compare himself to a soldier— he had neither the intention nor the ability to fight—he portrayed himself as a potential martyr. As he recounts in the *Commentaries*, "We shall imitate our Lord and Master Jesus Christ, the holy and pure shepherd who hesitated not to lay down His life for His sheep."[264] And after lamenting the poor response from the princes he repeatedly tried to rouse, he states:

> It is not good to say 'Go'; perhaps they will listen better to 'Come.' We are resolved to try .... Perhaps when they see their master and father, the Pope of Rome, the Vicar of Jesus Christ, going into the war old and ill they will be ashamed to stay at home; they will take arms and embrace the defense of holy religion with brave hearts.[265]

Whatever momentary hesitation Pius may have felt regarding crusade when he began his Letter to Mehmed had vanished by early 1462.

Pius's crusade bull *Ezechielis prophetae* (Oct. 22, 1463) takes a more forceful tone than either his first bull or his oration to his cardinals, as he calls Christians to embark on crusade, with him as its leader. Owing, perhaps, to the unprecedented nature of a pope going off to war, the bull sparked great interest. It spread widely in manuscript and early print versions, including his *Opera omnia*, and it was translated into several languages.[266] Like in his first bull, religious elements appear with a host of Biblical references, the promise of indulgences, and an exhortation to protect the faith of Christ against the "abominable law of Muhammad."[267] Yet in many ways, in the bold and dramatic *Ezechielis*, Pius sounds more like his old humanist self. He had found a way at last to blend the office of the pope with the language of cultural and political identity.

Unsurprisingly, any gestures of legitimacy that Pius may have granted to Mehmed and the Turks in recent texts are absent from this bull. His goal was to incite men to anger and vengeance—there was no room for nuance. Mehmed II is described in the opening lines as a "monstrous dragon" poised to "devour the faithful."[268] Elsewhere the Turks are depicted as wolves and savage beasts who wish to tear the Lord's flock to pieces.[269] In addition to listing their atrocities in the sack of Constantinople and elsewhere—murder, rape, and desecration of churches—he adds specific details from reports of recent conquests. In Lesbos, he states, adult males were impaled with stakes, while in Bosnia, Mehmed "insatiable for human blood, by his own hand (it is said) cut the throat" of its last Christian king Stephen.[270] The legend of Mehmed's cruelty was already taking shape, and Pius was eager to help spread it; he spends no time here portraying Mehmed as a "prince," much less an "emperor."[271] As in most of Pius's works, the Ottomans as a group appear in the bull simply as "Turks" or *gens*, or worse, *foedam gentem* (foul race); and there is no use of nation, kingdom, or realm in reference to their state.[272]

By contrast, Pius employs more dignified terms for the group identity of his audience. They are the Christian people (*Christianus populus*) and the Christian republic (*respublica Christiana*). The theme of geography and the interconnectedness of European countries emerges in a long passage that bears quoting in full:

> Take pity on your brothers: bring help to those who are suffering. But if nothing in their situation moves you, at least consider your own safety.

Don't think that you are safe because you have obtained, perhaps, an abode that is distant from the Turks. No one is so remote that he cannot be found. If you dismiss your neighbor when he is in danger, the one who in front of you is closest to the fire, you too will be dismissed likewise by the neighbor who dwells behind you. We should behave towards others as we wish them to behave toward us. Don't expect the French to help you, Germans, unless you yourselves help the Hungarians, nor the Spaniards to help you, men of France, unless you help the Germans. For the same measure that you have meted out will be meted out again for you. And let no one flatter himself because he is powerful in principality or kingdom. The emperors of Constantinople and Trebizond, the king of Bosnia and the lords of Rascia, and many other rulers who were captured and cruelly put to death teach you what to expect. Nothing is so repugnant to Mehmed as the name of king: having won the empire of the East, he hastens toward the empire of the West.[273]

This passage begins with an eloquent plea for the interconnectedness of European countries, a sense of shared strength and vulnerability, and an almost gravitational pull toward mutual defense. Pius envisions a more complex geopolitical arrangement than a reciprocal, one-on-one alliance, however; instead, he proposes an unrealistic web of entanglements across Europe, offering no sense of how it might function long term. Pius's claim regarding Mehmed's hatred of the title "king" is poignant, but rather confusing. Was he suggesting that Mehmed was already far more powerful than a king, or that he could not tolerate (and coexist with) other rulers as powerful as himself, as kings in Europe had learned to do? It is left unclear as he does not refer to Mehmed as a king or emperor in this bull. Either way, Pius clearly seeks to keep the Turks *outside* of "the West." If his audience failed to do this, he continues, the Turks would seek to impose one empire and one law of Muhammad on "the West." [274] This suggests a fear of forced conversion—a strong allegation not seen in his previous statements about Ottoman rule over Christians.

To convince his audience of the seriousness of this threat and their advantages against the Turks, Pius, more firmly than ever, creates bipolar opposition between East and West. It begins with a familiar attempt to diminish the strength and manliness of the Turks:

But if you shudder at the yoke of a slave, if you cannot tolerate the insult to God and your neighbor, if you are ashamed that effeminate [*semiviros*] Asiatics (as they have never done before) have subdued the nation of the Greeks and have burst forth into such arrogance that they expect *the whole of Europe* to submit to them soon; if you have the heart of men, a noble heart, a mighty heart, a Christian heart, then follow the footsteps of your father [Pius], follow our camp [emphasis, mine]! Come to the aid of the faith! Come to the aid of your brothers![275]

He then proceeds to describe the Turks as less warlike and less well armed than has been presumed—a change from his recent, more realistic assessments of Ottoman strength.

The most powerful part of the bull in some ways is when Pius assigns a personality to "the West" that puts them in a position of authority over all Christians. The "Latins," he argues, in contrast to the Turks, have the best arms and armor and would assemble a formidable army. "If you western Christians [*Christiani occidentales*] stir yourselves and follow the shepherd of your souls, then many Greek and Asian Christians who do not doubt that the Roman pope is the true vicar of Christ will also be stirred."[276] This phrasing is key: it implies that "Latins" or "*western* Christians" were the natural leaders of this endeavor; Greeks and Asian Christians might join them, but only if they took the necessary first steps. In some ways, it is an early assertion of "Westerners" as saviors. Pius affirms this geographical distinction at the end of the bull when he calls upon the Lord to aid the crusade: "Give us victory over your enemies, so that when Greece is recovered, we may at last sing your worthy praises throughout all of Europe"—not Christendom, but Europe.[277] Greece, it should be noted, occupies an uncertain position: it is part of Europe, but not clearly part of "the West."

The language of this summons, like Pius's crusade orations, was a curious mixture of sacred and secular rhetoric. As Housley has shown, Pius "directs much of his bull's content to recruiting volunteers," not donations and spiritual support, and he even repeats the idea that criminous types would be welcomed on crusade.[278] Religious themes are prominent in the text, but unlike his first bull, *Vocavit nos Pius*, there is less emphasis on Christendom or the Holy Land and more on territorial boundaries. Europe is mentioned three times, and West and East in tandem also three times. On every occasion, East and West are invoked to contrast what Mehmed has brutally taken with the lands he aspires to conquer—but which still resist him for the time being.

Hence, on a smaller and more digestible scale than his great works, Pius's last major composition promotes the idea of a divided world—where differences between East and West, Asia and Europe were nigh insurmountable. For sure, the idea of protecting Christians beyond these borders was there, too, but not as much as the ones at home who constituted "us." His papal correspondence contains examples of these usages as well.[279] Becoming pope may have initially moved Pius away from this kind of language, but by the end of his reign and his life, it forcefully returned, making Christianity seem less universal than before. What might such stark rhetoric have meant to potential Muslim and Christian allies in East? One can only guess.

Conclusion

On June 18, 1464, Pius set out for Ancona. At age fifty-eight, he had been battling gout for three decades and was nearing the end of his physical endurance. The journey was a gamble for one so ill, but it was his last chance to launch a crusade. Despite his frailty, he was determined to inspire new recruits and meet up with his allies. As he announced in his bull, the crusade was supposed to include Duke Philip of Burgundy, Doge Cristoforo Moro of Venice, and King Matthias of Hungary. Asian leaders who opposed the Turks were also projected to take part.[280] This was not the large multistate enterprise that he had hoped to create in 1459, and, in fact, neither the Asian leaders nor Philip fully delivered on their promises, but what he did pull together was hardly a failure. Even with these defections, Pius assembled a smaller, but potentially effective combined force of ships and ground troops from three nation-states: Venice, Hungary, and small contingents from Burgundy and Milan. In addition, Pius was raising large numbers of volunteers from Saxony, Ghent, and other areas, eager to claim the spiritual benefits of fighting for the cross.[281] They streamed into the city despite the lack of preparations to receive them. But none of this activity could rally the ailing pope: Pius died on August 14, four weeks after his arrival.

Risky though the expedition was, it physically embodied Pius's efforts to bring Europeans together for a common purpose, and to lead them in whatever way he could. Pius's final journey to Ancona, as Baldi has rightly argued, should not be viewed as an idealistic attempt to return to medieval-style papal theocracy, but an effort to counterbalance the delicate political forces that comprised Christian Europe.[282] Had he survived the journey and been able to provide moral support to the mustering forces, an army would likely have sailed off to meet the Ottomans, with or without him. His primary goal, I believe, was to gather and bless these forces rather than to accompany them across the Adriatic.

But if Pius's determination to go to Ancona shows his commitment to protect the continent, the dissolution of the crusade upon his death reveals the fragility of that notion in the absence of a strong central leader. Just before dying he urged his cardinals, close friends, and relatives to keep his crusade alive with the words, "Woe unto you, woe unto you, if you desert God's work."[283] Yet, as I have argued throughout this study, what Pius could not achieve with his voice and his body during his lifetime, he arguably accomplished through his pen in the years that followed. While not the only writer of his time to speak of Europe and "the West" as an idea and a community, he did more than anyone at this time to promote this powerful and unique identity—alongside, but not always synonymous with, Christendom. His position as pope gave him the standing to normalize and amplify a concept that was just beginning to take shape.[284] Had a different man been elected pope, even another crusade advocate like his predecessor, this discourse would not have gathered strength and been disseminated in the same way.

I hope that I have also shown a lesser-known side of Pius's views of the Ottomans— moments when he wavered in his quest to reduce, essentialize, and "other" them. His letter to Mehmed and other works with subtler wording demonstrate moments of doubt or curiosity. His statements on Jewish communities also suggest a more nuanced view of Europe as a place where different religions might coexist. In addition, he demonstrated an ability to recognize the common humanity of almost all the people he described and avoided stark racialized dividers; for him, ethnicity seemed to have been as much about choice as it was about birth. For all their concerns about continental security, Pius's papal works portray diverse ethnicities as a source of strength and enrichment rather than division—at least within the confines of Europe.

Notes

1 *Commentaries*, ed. Margaret Meserve and Marcello Simonetta (Cambridge, MA: Harvard University Press, 2003), 1: 179. For more information on conclaves at this time, see Mary Hollingsworth, "Cardinals in Conclave," in *A Companion to the Early Modern Cardinal*, ed. Mary Hollingsworth, Miles Pattenden, and Arnold Witte (Leiden: Brill, 2020), 58–70.

2 *Commentaries*, ed. Meserve and Simonetta, 1: 179; 183.

3 Eugenio Garin, *Portraits of the Quattrocento*, tr. Victor A. and Elizabeth Velen (New York: Harper and Row, 1972), 30.

4 Charles L. Stinger, *The Renaissance in Rome* (Bloomington: Indiana University Press, 1985), 264–68.

5 *Commentaries*, Bk I, ch. 36. The national overtones that Pius uses in these arguments will be addressed later in this chapter.

6 For a discussion of the political and strategic factors that weighed on the cardinals in this period, see Marco Pellegrini, "Pio II, il Collegio cardinalizio e la Dieta di Mantova," in *Il Sogno di Pio II e il viaggio da Roma a Mantova*, ed. Arturo Calzona, Francesca Paolo Fiore, Alberto Tenenti, Cesare Vasoli (Florence: Leo S. Olschki, 2003), 15–76. See also Emily O'Brien, *Commentaries of Pope Pius II (1458–1464) and the Crisis of the Fifteenth-Century Papacy* (Toronto: University of Toronto Press, 2015), 97–98; 134; Barbara Baldi, *Pio II e la trasformazione dell'Europa cristiana, 1457–1464* (Milan: Unicopli, 2006), 107–112. On Capranica, see Thomas M. Izbicki, *Protector of the Faith: Cardinal Johannes de Turrecremata and the Defense of the Institutional Church* (Washington, DC: Catholic University of America Press, 1981), 22.

7 Some scholars depict Pius as a decent but tragic figure pursuing a hopeless cause. See Cecilia M. Ady, *Pius II: (Aeneas Silvius Piccolomini) The Humanist Pope* (London: Methuen and Co., 1913), 325; Ludwig Pastor, *The History of the Popes from the Close of the Middle Ages* (Kegan Paul, Trench, Trübner, & Co., 1900), 3: 374; Garin, *Portraits of the Quattrocento*, 50–51. Others view his crusade as a tool to exert greater papal control over Italy and Europe. See O'Brien, *Commentaries*, 98; Georg Voigt, *Enea Silvio de' Piccolomini als Papst Pius II und sein Zeitalter*, 3 vols (Berlin: De Gruyter, 1856–1863). By contrast, Pellegrini asserts Pius's importance in sustaining the Church and tying the papacy more firmly to Europe; "Unità europea, primate romano. Riflessi della teologia politica di Pio II Piccolomini," in *Enea Silvio Piccolomini: Arte, Storia e Cultura nell'Europa di Pio II*, edited by Roberta Di Paola, Arianna Antoniutti, and Marco Gallo (Rome: Libreria Editrice Vaticana, 2006), 431.

8 Baldi, *Pio II*, 260, 89; idem, "Il problema Turco dalla caduta di Costantinopoli (1453) alla morte di Pio II (1464)," in *La Conquista Turca di Otranto*, ed. Hubert Houben (Galatina, 2008), vol. 1: 75. See also Robert Schwoebel, *Renaissance Men and Ideas* (New York: St. Martin's Press, 1971), 68–79; Bisaha, "Pope Pius II and the Crusade," in *Crusading in the Fifteenth Century: Message and Impact*, ed. Norman Housley (New York: Palgrave Macmillan, 2004), 39–52. Kenneth Setton describes Pius's determination to go on crusade as "one of the nobler pictures of the Quattrocento, while also noting, "his efforts were doomed to failure." *The Papacy and the Levant (1205–1571)* (Philadelphia: American

Philosophical Society, 1978), 2: 261, 270. Norman Housley argues that, despite his flaws and missteps, he deserves the reputation that he, James Hankins, and others have given him as a great crusading pope; "Pope Pius II and Crusading" *Crusades* 11 (2012): 245; Margaret Meserve casts his shift from the imperial court to service to the pope as a sincere move in the interest of promoting crusade, while acknowledging its usefulness in furthering his other agendas; "Italian Humanists and the Problem of Crusade," in *Crusading in the Fifteenth Century*, ed. Housley, 24–25.

9   Baldi has also argued that his crusade plans and writing program are not unrelated; *Pio II*, 90.

10   Ady, *Pius II*, 154.

11   Benjamin Weber, "Toward a Global Crusade? The Papacy and the Non-Latin World in the Fifteenth Century," in *Reconfiguring the Fifteenth Century Crusade*, ed. Norman Housley (London: Palgrave Macmillan, 2017), 11–44.

12   "… fiet, mihi credite, fiet communi omnium Christianorum consensu passagium, si Romani pontificis hoc tempore surrexerit auctoritas ac bonorum predicatorum, inter quos esse vestram pietatem commune judicium habet, fideles ac diserte voces in fines orbis terre sonuerint." Rudolph Wolkan, ed., *Der Briefwechsel des Eneas Silvius Piccolomini*, in *Fontes Rerum Austriacarum*, ser. 2, vol. 68 (1918): 214–15; Eng. tr., with significant changes, *Reject Aeneas, Accept Pius: Selected Letters of Aeneas Sylvius Piccolomini (Pope Pius II)*, ed. and tr. Thomas M. Izbicki, Gerald Christianson, and Philip Krey (Washington, DC: Catholic University of America Press, 2006), 316–17.

13   The text of the bull is found in Lodrisio Crivelli's *De Expeditione Pii Papae II*, ed. Giulio C. Zimolo, in *Rerum Italicarum Scriptores*, New Series, vol. XXIII, pt. V (Bologna: Nicola Zanichelli, 1948–50), 91–96.

14   Ibid., 92.

15   "Ex altera parte, qua versus orientem Europa porrigitur, non potuit mare christianam religionem tueri." Ibid., 92.

16   Ibid., 92.

17   "Propter peccata nostra evenerunt nobis mala …. Quos diligit, corrigit atque castigat." Ibid., 93. Here he draws upon Hebrews, 12:6.

18   Housley, "Pope Pius II," 220–24.

19   Housley, "Pope Pius II," 228; Housley, *The Later Crusades: From Lyons to Alcazar 1274–1580* (Oxford: Oxford University Press, 1992), 105. The problems that ensued from this distinction are discussed later in this chapter.

20   See Colin Imber, *Crusade of Varna, 1443–1445* (Aldershot: Ashgate, 2006), 1.

21   Weber, "Toward a Global Crusade?" 23.

22   For details on Pius's plans to finance the crusade, see Weber, *Lutter contre les Turcs: Les formes nouvelles de la croisade pontificale au XVe siècle* (Rome: École Française de Rome, 2013), ch. 4. On the political problems he faced in Italy and Europe, see Baldi, *Pio II*, parts II and III.

23   He homes in on the danger to Hungary in *Vocavit nos Pius* twice; 94 and 95. See also his comments in June 1459 at the Congress of Mantua, as stated in *Commentaries*, ed. Meserve and Simonetta, 2:5; see also 2:59 and 2:89.

24   Norman Housley, "Aeneas Silvius Piccolomini, Nicholas of Cusa, and the Crusade: Conciliar, Imperial, and Papal Authority," *Church History* 86, no. 3 (Sept. 2017): 643.

25   Ady, *Pius II*, 159–64. For more on Mantua, see *Il Sogno di Pio II*, ed. Calzona et al.

26   Meserve, "Italian Humanists," 25; O'Brien, *Commentaries*, 161; 170–71. For an engaging account and analysis of the journey and Pius's perception of it, see Arthur White, *Plague and Pleasure: The Renaissance World of Pius II* (Washington, DC: Catholic University of America Press, 2014), ch. 6. For more on Pius and the Romans, see Anna Modigliani, "Pio II e Roma," in *Sogno di Pio*, ed. Calzona et al., 77–108.

27 Ady, *Pius II*, 164–65. For a translation of Ippolita Sforza's oration, see *Her Immaculate Hand: Selected Works by and About the Women Humanists of Quattrocento Italy*, ed. Margaret L. King and Albert Rabil, Jr. (Binghamton, NY: Center for Medieval and Early Renaissance Studies, 1981), 46–48.

28 Kate Simon, *A Renaissance Tapestry: The Gonzaga of Mantua* (New York: Harper and Row, 1981), 42–46.

29 "… locum palustrem atque insalubrem esse, cuncta aestu fervere, neque vina sapida neque res alias ad victum necessarias placere; aegrotare quam plurimos, febres admodum multos absumere; nihil audiri nisi ranas." *Commentaries*, vol. 2, ed. Meserve and Simonetta, 6; Eng. tr., 7. See his more generous comments about Mantua in ibid., 1: 368–69.

30 Setton. *Papacy*, 2:208.

31 Ady, *Pius II*, 171.

32 Ady, *Pius II*, 164–72.

33 Michael von Cotta-Schönberg, ed. and tr., "Cum bellum hodie" of Pope Pius II (26 September 1459, Mantua). Preliminary edition, 4th version. (Orations of Enea Silvio Piccolomini / Pope Pius II; 45). 2015. <hal-01184169v4>.

34 *Commentaries*, ed. Meserve and Simonetta, 2:147.

35 Johannes Helmrath, "Political-Assembly Speeches, German Diets, and Aeneas Sylvius Piccolomini" in *Beyond Reception: Renaissance Humanism and the Transformation of Classical Antiquity*, ed. Patrick Baker, Johannes Helmrath, and Craig Kallendorf (Berlin: De Gruyter, 2019), 83; on manuscripts and early print editions, see "Cum bellum hodie," ed. Cotta- Schönberg, 22–24.

36 Paul Chevedden argues that Urban II saw the Mediterranean region as a geographical and strategic whole. See "The View of the Crusades from Rome and Damascus: The Geo-Strategic and Historical Perspectives of Pope Urban II and ʿAlī ibn Tāhir al-Sulamī," *Oriens* 39 (2011): 257–329.

37 "Cum bellum hodie," ed. Cotta-Schönberg, 52–53.

38 Ibid., 52–53.

39 "Cum bellum hodie," ed. Cotta-Schönberg, 98–103. Some of these notions are repeated in Pius's letter to Mehmed (1461). On Torquemada and his influence on Pius's polemical view of Islam, see Izbicki, *Protector of the Faith*, passim, esp. 22–23.

40 Bisaha, "Pope Pius II and the Crusade"; Meserve, *Empires*, 197ff.

41 "Nam circa tempora Constantini magni natum ex Maria puerum Indi simul et Hispani colebant, nec Septentrio, nec Meridies Christum ignorabant. Vox Romani praesulis tamquam Jesu Christi vicarii maria penetrabat et terras gens sancta, gens electa, populus acquisitionis Christiani habebantur tributa ex gentibus accipientes, et in capite populorum positi. Haec fuit olim, o Christiani, majorum nostrorum gloria, hoc imperium, haec auctoritas." "Cum bellum hodie," ed. Cotta-Schönberg, 54; Eng. tr., 55.

42 Degeneraverat jam apud Graecos imperium, et Romana virtus sub aliud translate caelum elanguerat, quae res paulatim Christianas opes evertit. Manserunt tamen in Asia quamplures Christiani usque ad tempora Pipini, Francorum regis, qui anno ab hinc circiter sexcentesimo magno nomine et apud Germanos et apud Gallos regnavit." "Cum bellum hodie," ed. Cotta-Schönberg, 56; Eng. tr., 57.

43 Meserve, *Empires*, 198–99.

44 Juan Cole, *Muhammad, Prophet of Peace Amid the Clash of Empires* (New York: Nation Books, 2018).

45 "Graeci quoque, illustres quondam animae, haudquaquam vigorem antiquum retinent. Degeneraverunt ferme omnes, qui Turcis parent, neque in armis neque in litteris pristinum referunt spiritum. Ceciderunt omnia cum imperio. Non stant simul fortia pectora et servitus. Qui fortes viri in castris Turcorum militant ex Christianis sunt …." "Cum bellum hodie," ed. Cotta-Schönberg, 86; Eng. tr., 87.

46 Letter to Nicholas of Cusa (July 21, 1453), *Reject Aeneas*, tr. Izbicki et al., 310.

47 On the trope of Greek effeminacy in Renaissance writings on war, see Gerry Milligan, *Moral Combat: Women, Gender, and War in Italian Renaissance Literature* (Toronto: University of Toronto Press, 2018), 5, 128.

48 "Cum bellum hodie," ed. Cotta-Schönberg, 112–15.

49 "Confert et multum Romanorum auctoritas, qui, cum essent sapientissimi ac potentissimi et orbis domini collum evangelio minime submisissent, nisi aut rationibus victi aut miraculis tracti. Quis praeterea viros fortes eosdemque prudentes, Hispanos, Gallos, ac Germanos evangelium suscepisse crediderit, nisi magnis rationibus persuasos? Sane, cum lex gentium mollis esset, Christianorum durior, nemo hanc subire voluisset, nisi auctorem ejus Deum esse didicisset." "Cum bellum hodie," ed. Cotta-Schönberg, 116; Eng. tr., 117.

50 "Cum bellum hodie," ed. Cotta-Schönberg, 54–55.

51 Meserve, *Empires*, 201.

52 The supposed threat from Northern pagans comes from a letter from the king of Denmark to Calixtus, who used it as an excuse to get out of crusading against the Ottomans; "Cum bellum hodie," ed. Cotta-Schönberg, 61, n. 3.

53 "Cum bellum hodie," ed. Cotta-Schönberg, 60–61.

54 "Hi sunt termini vestri, o Christiani, sic circumdati estis, sic in angulum coartati, potentissimi quondam domini et orbis possessores. En quantum imperium amisistis, quot nobiles urbes, quot ditissimas provincias perdidistis, inter quas etiam Judaeam neglexistis, terram nobilem, terram sanctam, terram lacte et melle fluentem, terram, in qua primi fidei nostrae flores apparuere. Heu pudor!' Heu dolor!" "Cum bellum hodie," ed. Cotta-Schönberg, 62; Eng. tr., 63.

55 Substituting Cotta-Schönberg's vivid "be damned" with "pass away."

56 "Sed negligamus, si libet, antiquam ignominiam, vetusta damna, nec vos urgeat, quod non pupugit avos. Transeat omnis Asia, omnis Africa; Europam saltem inspiciamus, et nostri temporis rationem reddamus. An parum nostra aetate nostra culpa perditum est? Constantinopolim, Orientalis imperii caput, et totius Graeciae columen, non patres nostri, sed nos ipsi amisimus ...." "Cum bellum hodie," ed. Cotta-Schönberg, 68; Eng. tr., 69, with some modifications.

57 Baldi also argues that crusade and defense of Europe and its culture were part of Pius's policy goals and explain his effort at Mantua to create alliances; *Pio II*, 91ff. and 149.

58 On emissaries from Armenia and Georgia, who arrived in 1460, see Pius's *Asia*; *Descripción de Asia*, ed. and tr. Domingo F. Sanz (Madrid: Consejo Superior de Investigaciones Científicas, 2010), 160, 240. On papal outreach in the fifteenth century, see Weber, "Toward a Global Crusade," 21–28. Previous popes looked also toward North Africa and the Levant, but Pius zeroed in on Asia Minor and its environs. Ludovico da Bologna had traveled to Africa with Pope Nicholas's permission, bringing back eight Ethiopian friars. Calixtus was about to send him as far as Persia, when his death changed the direction of his next mission. Pius sent him to areas around Anatolia and the Black Sea in the hopes of building alliances and gathering intelligence; see ibid., 26–28.

59 Numquam ille arma deponet, nisi aut victus, aut omnium victor. Proxima illi quaeque victoria gradus erit alterius, donec subactis occidentalibus regibus, deleto Christi evangelio Maumetheam legem ubique gentium inserat. "Cum bellum hodie," ed. Cotta-Schönberg, 74; Eng. tr., 75.

60 "Soli fideles Hungari perseverant, non tamen diu stabunt, nisi adjuti. Et hi quidem muri loco vobis ad orientem remanserunt, quo diruto, neque Theutones, neque Bohemi, neque Poloni satis tuti erunt. Non asperi montes, non alta flumina iter impedient. Nihil erit, victa Hungaria, Turcis invium, nihil insuperabile orbis imperium quaerentibus." "Cum bellum hodie," ed. Cotta-Schönberg, 76; Eng. tr., 77.

61 "... ditem Italiam, nobilem Galliam, fortem Hispaniam, bellicosam et populosam Germaniam .... Illi enim, etsi omnes conatus adhibeant, supra tamen ducenta hominum milia non educent. Sed quos homines? Imbelles, sane, atque inermes, ex Asianis atque Graecis mixtos. Nostis quanti faciat Asianos Remus ille Virgilianus, cujus illa sunt verba: *O verae Phrygiae, nec enim Phryges* ...." "Cum bellum hodie," ed. Cotta-Schönberg, 82–843; Eng. tr., 83, 85.

62 Compare to Meserve's contention that he abandoned the effeminacy argument after Frankfurt. *Empires*, 98. This is true for the most part, but as this oration shows, he continued to allude to the idea in other ways.

63 Pius claims Caesar's famous "Veni, vidi, vici," was a pointed dismissal of his Pontic Asian adversaries and that Godfrey slaughtered more numerous Asian troops "like cattle." "Cum bellum hodie," ed. Cotta-Schönberg, 86; Eng. tr., 87.

64 Housley, *Later Crusades*, 106.

65 Housley, "Pope Pius II," 228–29; Housley, *Later Crusades*, 105.

66 See Jonathan Riley-Smith, *The First Crusade and the Idea of Crusading* (Philadelphia: University of Pennsylvania Press, 1986), 91–119.

67 Housley, "Aeneas Silvius Piccolomini," 666–67. Baldi, *Pio II*, 91. O'Brien argues that Pius wished to control the crusade to prevent any other Christian prince from gaining power or advantage over him; *Commentaries*, 99–111. But, as this study shows, Pius's desire for papal leadership of crusade extended back as far as Nicholas's reign, and he was willing to let practically any prince to lead it. There is no denying, however, that his efforts to seize the reins were often heavy handed.

68 Baldi, *Pio II*, 91–92.

69 Johannes Helmrath, "The German *Reichstage* and the Crusade," in *Crusading in the Fifteenth Century, Message and Impact*, ed. Norman Housley (New York: Palgrave Macmillan, 2004), 63. Helmrath cites the number of manuscripts here as over 120; see his more recent estimate of 110 above.

70 Contemporary Ludovico Foscarini praised the oration. See Joycelyne G. Russell, *Diplomats at Work: Three Renaissance Studies* (Wolfeboro Falls, NH: Alan Sutton Publishing Inc., 1992), 74–75. Favorable modern opinions include Helmrath, "German *Reichstage*," 63–64, and Ady, *Pius II*, 172. For more critical views of the oration see Housley, *Crusade and the Ottoman Threat*, 161, n. 207; Bisaha, "Pope Pius II and the Crusade," 44. My opinion of the literary quality this oration has improved, despite its inconsistencies.

71 Pius never secured French support for the crusade, but as Leona C. Gabel claims, he "emerged as victor, having gained the revocation of the obnoxious Sanction without yielding on the subject of Naples; he had shown himself a master of the new school of statecraft." *Memoirs of a Renaissance Pope: The Commentaries of Pius II, An Abridgement*, tr. Florence A. Gragg and ed. Leona C. Gabel (New York: Capricorn Books, 1962), 24. For more on Italian humanist attitudes toward France at this time, see Patrick Gilli, *Au miroir de l'humanisme: Les représentations de la France dans la culture savante italienne à la fin du moyen âge, c. 1360–c. 1490* (Bibliothèque des Écoles Françaises d'Athènes et de Rome. Rome: École Française de Rome, 1997).

72 For a full discussion of these events see Baldi, *Pio II*, 173–201. See also *Commentaries of Pius II*, tr. Florence Alden Gragg, ed. Leona C. Gabel (Northampton, Mass.: Smith College, 1937–1957): 640 ff and 674. Ady, *Pius II*, 206–14.

73 This charming vignette evokes the famous portrait of the duke and his young son by Pedro Berruguete, depicting Federigo dressed in armor and reading a large codex.

74 "Cumque de Asia quoque mentio fieret, quae Minor vocatur, nec de limitibus conveniret, pontifex postea nactus otii paululum apud Tibur, Asiam ipsam descripsit ex Ptolomaeo, Strabone, Plinio, Q. Curtio, Iulio Solino, Pomponio Mela et aliis veteribus auctoribus, quae sibi visa sunt ad rei cognitionem idonea, suscipiens." *Commentaries*, ed. Meserve, 3: 138; Eng. tr., 139.

75   Conti's account was included in Poggio Bracciolini's *De varietate fortunae*, which Bracciolini dedicated to Pius. See Thomas J. Mauro, "*Praeceptor Austriae*: Aeneas Sylvius Piccolomini (Pius II) and the Transalpine Diffusion of Italian Humanism Before Erasmus" (PhD diss., University of Chicago, 2003), 289. On the mappamundi of Fra Mauro, see Alessandro Scafi, "Pio II e la cartografia: un papa e un mappamondo tra Medioevo e Rinascimento," in *Enea Silvio Piccolomini: Pius Secundus Poeta Laureatus Pontifex Maximus*, ed. Manlio Sodi and Arianna Antoniutti (Rome: Libreria Editrice Vaticana, 2007), 239–64; see also the introduction to an Italian translation of Pius's *Asia (De Asia, 1461)*, ed. and tr. Remigio Presenti and Manlio Sodi, introduced by Serge Stolfe, appendix ed. by Francesco Dondoli (Rome: IF Press, 2016), 15.

76   *Commentaries*, ed. Margaret Meserve (Cambridge, MA: Harvard University Press, 2018), 3: 146–47.

77   For a discussion of Pius's approach to geography and history, including his sources, comparable works, and how he differed from them, see Konrad Benedikt Vollmann, "Piccolomini as a Historiographer: *Asia*," in *Pius II: 'El Più Expeditivo Pontifice: Selected Studies on Aeneas Silvius Piccolomini*, ed. Zweder Von Martels and Arjo Vanderjagt (Leiden: Brill, 2003), 41–54. The edition used here, with facing Spanish translation is *Descripción de Asia*, ed. and tr. Domingo F. Sanz.

78   Mauro, *Praeceptor*, 290.

79   It was printed in Italian in 1544; for more on *Asia*, see Nicola Casella, "Pio II tra geografia e storia: la *Cosmographia*." *Archivio della Società romana di storia patria*, vol. 95 (1972), 35–112.

80   Meserve, "From Samarkand to Scythia: Reinventions of Asia in Renaissance Geography and Political Thought," in *Pius II*, ed. Von Martels and Vanderjagt, 13–39; Nicola Casella, "Enea Silvio a difesa dell'Occidente Cristiano," in *Enea Silvio Piccolomini: Uomo lettere e mediatore di culture, Gelehrter und Vermittler der Kulturen*, ed. Maria Antonietta Terzoli (Basel: Schwab Verlag, 2006), 55–68; *Asia*, ed. and tr. Presenti et al., 15.

81   Casella, "Pio II tra geografia e storia," 46–48.

82   Meserve, "From Samarkand to Scythia," 23.

83   "… sed arbitramur Grecos eum aliquos secutum quibus mos est omnia in maius extollere. Scytharum natio barbara est, nec iusti nec recti tenax. Fedissima apud eos vita: religionum mille modi idola et serpentes colunt; in libidinem profusi; aurum non concupierunt donec fuit ignotum, ubi splendorem eius conspicati sunt, nihil non auri causa partravere; et propter regnum sepe parricidia commisere; neque inter se iusti neque cum aliis veraces; cui plus virium est, huic et iuris: magis potentie omnia cedunt." *Asia*, ed. Sanz, 176.

84   "Iordanis Europeos fuisse Gothos affirmat, quem sequi non pudet sue gentis intitia referentem." *Asia*, ed. Sanz, 180. On his preference for Aethicus, Meserve states, "It was Aeneas's hatred of the Turks, wedded to his dream of organizing a crusade to oust them from Eastern Europe and the Mediterranean, that caused him to doubt, and ultimately to reject, the admiration his classical authorities expressed for the Scythians—whom he believed were the Turks' forebears." See Meserve, "Samarkand," 25; see also Bisaha, *Creating East and West*, 76. Pius's favorable view of the Goths likely stemmed from his recent epitome of Jordanes's *History of the Goths*.

85   *Asia*, ed. Sanz, 178.

86   See *Asia*, ed. Sanz, 180; see also *Europe (c. 1400–1458)*, tr. Robert Brown, intro. and notes, Nancy Bisaha (Washington D.C.: Catholic University of America Press, 2013), 52.

87   "Multi hodie qui videri docti volunt Turcos appellant Teucros, quos Scytharum genus esse haud ambiguum est, quemadmodum postea dicemus cum de Turcis agemus." *Asia*, ed. Sanz, 316. See also ibid., 422 and 424.

88 Vollmann notes the theme of decline and loss under the Turks, especially regarding the Christian faith; "Piccolomini as Historian," 54.

89 On the Crusades, see for instance paragraphs 57 and 60 in *Asia*, ed Sanz, 272, 282; Meserve, "From Samarkand," 31.

90 Michel-Rolph Trouillot, *Silencing the Past: Power and the Production of History* (Boston: Beacon Press, 1995), 4–6, 95–97.

91 "Adeo Turcorum nomen auctum est ut que olim Asia vocabatur nunc Turciam vocitent." *Asia*, ed. Sanz, 424. On the theme of the damage to Christianity, see Vollman, "Aeneas as Historiographer," 53–54.

92 *Asia*, ed. Sanz, 266. Pius employed this phrase in his July 21, 1453, letter to Nicholas of Cusa, but it is a rare usage for him.

93 *Asia*, ed. Sanz, 260.

94 *Asia*, ed. Sanz, 424, 426.

95 Meserve sees the text as more "political polemic" than a work of scholarly criticism; "Samarkand," 19.

96 *Asia*, ed. Sanz, 420–28.

97 *Asia*, ed. Sanz, 240; 160

98 "Sed Hismael loci dominus non expectato impetu sese dedit quanvis legatum ad nos miserit multa pollicitus si sibi auxilia mitterentur. Sed longum est Christianos non modo armare, sed consulturos de sumendis armis congregare. Non miramur si apud obsessum principem plus instans metus quam spes longinqua et dubia potuit." *Asia*, ed. Sanz, 266. On Ismail and Uzun Hasan, see Setton, *Papacy*, 2: 237–38.

99 "Sed non omnes Turci Ottumanorum imperio subsunt, nam et Caramanus Cilicie dominus, qui magnam Cappadocie partem possidet, et Asambecus, qui prope Euphratem dominatar, et alii nonnulli reguli ab origine Turci cum Ottumani progenie diu de regni possessione certarunt." *Asia*, ed. Sanz, 424.

100 *Asia*, ed. Sanz, 424.

101 Ibid., 422; 424.

102 *Asia*, ed. Sanz, 424.

103 On Pius's interest in Uzun Hasan, see Meserve, *Empires*, 205 ff. On the problematic embassy of Ludovico da Bologna (1460–61), see Setton, *Papacy*, 2: 222, n. 80.

104 Meserve, *Empires*, 231.

105 *Asia*, ed. Sanz, 376.

106 "Sed affuit virgo virilibus armis induta que, mirabile dictu, salutem patrie peperit ... tedet non habere nomen: digna enim erat non minori memoria quam Sappho." *Asia*, ed. Sanz, 332, 334. Pius repeats this story, almost word for word in his *Commentaries*, Bk 10.

107 Doria is noted in a sixteenth-century compendium of famous women by Francesco Serdonati, *Libro di M. Giovanni Boccaccio delle donne illustri* (1596), 577–78; See Milligan, *Moral Combat*, 218.

108 Vollmann, "Piccolomini as a Historiographer," 44–45; 54.

109 As Meserve has argued about humanist historiography in regard to *Asia*, "Elements of classical antiquarianism and oriental romance, political agitation and racial polemic, all combined in the image of Asia and its peoples which the Renaissance humanists developed and which they bequeathed to the orientalist scholars of early modern Europe." See "From Samarkand," 39.

110 James H. Merrell, "Second Thoughts on Colonial Historians and American Indians," *William and Mary Quarterly* 3d ser., 69, no. 3 (July 2012): 451–512.

111 Claire Norton, "Blurring the Boundaries: Intellectual and Cultural Interactions between the Eastern and Western; Christian and Muslim Worlds," in *The Renaissance and the Ottoman World*, ed. Anna Contadini and Claire Norton (Burlington, VT: Ashgate, 2013), 20. See also Palmira Brummett's balanced examination in "The Lepanto Paradigm Revisited: Knowing the Ottomans in the Sixteenth Century," in ibid., 63–93.

112 See Anna Contadini, "Sharing a Taste? Material Culture and Intellectual Curiosity around the Mediterranean, from the Eleventh to the Sixteenth Century," in *Renaissance and the Ottoman World*, ed. Contadini and Norton, 23–61; see especially 60; Giovanni Ricci, *Appeal to the Turk: The Broken Boundaries of the Renaissance* (Rome: Viella, 2018).

113 "Scripturi ad te aliqua pro tua salute et gloria proque communi multarum gentium consolatione et pace, hortamur ut benigne audias verba nostra .... Non enim te odio persequimur .... Operibus tuis, non tibi sumus infensi ...." *Epistola ad Mahomatem II (Epistle to Mohammed II)*, ed. and tr. Albert R. Baca (New York: Peter Lang, 1990), 115; Eng. tr., 11. See also *Epistola ad Mahumetem*, ed. and tr. Reinhold Glei and Markus Köhler (Trier: Wissenschaftlicher Verlag, 2001).

114 "Parva res omnium qui hodie vivunt maximum et potentissimum et clarissimum te reddere potest ... id est aquae pauxillum, quo baptizeris et ad Christianorum sacra te conferas et credas Evangelio .... Nos te Graecorum et Orientis imperatorem appellabimus et quod modo vi occupas et cum iniuria tenes possidebis iure." *Epistola*, ed. Baca, 122; Eng. tr., 17–18.

115 It was first printed in or around 1470 in Cologne; in 1475 in Treviso; and in or around 1478 in Rome; *Epistola ad Mahumetem*, ed. and tr. Glei and Köhler, 102–03.

116 Pius's early biographers Platina and Campano briefly mention the letter; Baldi *Pio II*, 199. It seems safe to say that Pius neither hid nor called attention to the letter in his lifetime.

117 Housley, "Aeneas Silvius Piccolomini," 661.

118 See Robert Schwoebel, *The Shadow of the Crescent: The Renaissance Image of the Turk (1453–1517)* (New York: St. Martin's Press, 1967), 65–67; Franco Cardini, "La repubblica di Firenze, e la crociata di Pio II," *Rivista storica della chiesa in Italia* 33 (1979), 471–72; Bisaha, "Pius II's Letter to Sultan Mehmed II: A Reexamination." *Crusades* 1 (2002): 183–200. Schwoebel and I see it less as a self-serving gesture than a means to help his crusade goals in some way.

119 R.W. Southern, *Western Views of Islam in the Middle Ages* (Cambridge, Mass.: Harvard University Press, 1962); Benjamin Weber, "Conversion, croisade et oecuménisme à la fin du Moyen-âge: encore sur la lettre de Pie II à Mehmed II," *Crusades* 7 (2008): 181–99.

120 Weber, "Toward a Global Crusade," 11–44.

121 Rolando Montecalvo argues that Pius enacted his earlier theories of papal predominance in the letter to Mehmed, where he "reiterated the pope's right to designate the ultimate secular leaders of the East and the West." See "Between Empire and Papacy: Aeneas Silvius and German Regional Historiography (PhD diss., University of California, Berkeley, 2000), 123–29, especially 128–29. See also Southern, *Western Views*; Baldi, *Pio II*, 89–91.

122 See for example, his letters to Louis XI (Oct. 26, 1461) in *Opera omnia*, 861–62, and to Frederick III regarding Mantua: Pastor, *History of the Popes*, 3: 381. On Pius's tone with leaders and envoys, see also Ady, *Pius II*, 167–68, 211; Setton, *Papacy*, 2: 232.

123 For the views of Pius, Cusanus, Segovia, and Torquemada of the prophet in larger context, see John V. Tolan, *Faces of Muhammad: Western Perceptions of the Prophet of Islam from the Middle Ages to Today* (Princeton: Princeton University Press, 2019), 91; John Monfasani, *George of Trebizond: A Biography and a Study of His Rhetoric and Logic* (Leiden: E.J. Brill, 1976); Maarten Halff, "Did Cusanus Talk With Muslims? Revisiting Cusanus' Sources for the Cribratio Alkorani and Interfaith Dialogue," *Revista Española de Filosofía Medieval* 26 no. 1 (2019): 29–58. James E. Biechler, "A New Face toward Islam: Nicholas of Cusa and John of Segovia," in *Nicholas of Cusa in Search of God and Wisdom*, ed. Gerald Christianson and Thomas M. Izbicki (Leiden: E.J. Brill, 1991). On

Segovia, see Thomas E. Burman, *Reading the Qur'an in Latin Christendom, 1140–1560* (Philadelphia: University of Pennsylvania Press, 2007), 179. See also Southern, *Western Views of Islam*, 86–92; 98; Anne Marie Wolf, *Juan de Segovia and the Fight for Peace: Christians and Muslims in the Fifteenth Century* (Notre Dame, IN: University of Notre Dame Press, 2014).

124 Several of the preceding points were made at greater length in Bisaha, "Pius's Letter."

125 "Dolemus te virum excellentem, nobilitate maiorum illustrem, gestarum rerum gloria clarum, imperio magno praeditum et pluribus naturae dotibus eminentem, non incedere in viis Domini .... Nec te credimus libenter errare, cuius naturam bonam esse confidimus." *Epistola*, ed. Baca., 144; Eng. tr., 38. See ibid., book IV for his praises of Islam and Muhammad the prophet. Toward the end of the letter, however, Pius reverts to attributing Muhammad's "discoveries" to the devil.

126 "Tu ergo, princeps nobilis, qui non es rationis incapax neque ingenii obtusi ...." *Epistola*, ed. Baca, 211; Eng. tr., 101; for the previous passage, see ibid., 97, 207.

127 Contemporary Greek writers Doukas and Kritoboulos noted Mehmed's interest in scholarship, but their texts did not yet circulate in Italy.

128 See above, Chapter 2, on Sagundino and his oration to Alfonso where he notes Mehmed's learning.

129 Monfasani, *George of Trebizond*.

130 "Inter nos vero liberalium artium studia admodum florent"; "Tua lex neque de Deo sapit neque de caelestibus neque terrena satis intelligit, quae putat Superis curae non esse." *Epistola*, ed. Baca, 199; Eng. tr., 91.

131 See Abdurrahman Atçıl, *Scholars and Sultans in the Early Modern Ottoman Empire* (Cambridge, Cambridge University Press, 2017), 28–48 and 59–82.

132 Meserve, *Empires*, 99.

133 "Tua origo, sicut accepimus, Scythica est. Inter Scythas multos fuisse viros in armis claros memoriae traditur, qui vectigalem Asiam pluribus saeculis tenuerunt et Aegyptios ultra paludes eiecerunt. Non sunt comparandi aut Aegyptii aut Arabes Scythico generi; non est forti et ignavo aequa societas .... Conformior tibi cum Christianis societas erit. Fortibus viris facile amicantur fortes; virtus virtuti placet. Pulchra et stabilia sunt inter aequales consortia, si eadem religio est idemque Dei cultus." *Epistola*, ed. Baca, 180; Eng. tr., 74.

134 See Meserve, "Samarkand" 25; and idem., *Empires*, 113.

135 "Pulchre Trogus, sed arbitramur Grecos eum aliquos secutum quibus mos est omnia in maius extollere." *Asia*, ed. Sanz, 176.

136 "Fatemur tamen ab his exiisse quam plures qui res magnas gessere. Facile enim migrant quibus sterilis sedes est et melioris soli fama multos trahit." *Asia*, ed. Sanz, 178. See also Meserve, *Empires*, 80.

137 The one exception to this rule seems to be Saladin, whom Pius praises; *Epistola*, ed. Baca, 74; Latin, 180.

138 "Cum bellum hodie," ed. Cotta-Schönberg, 117.

139 "Nos non ita ignarum te credimus nostrarum rerum quin scias ... quam valida Hispania, quam bellicosa Gallia, quam populosa Germania, quam fortis Britannia, quam audax Polonia, quam strenua Hungaria, quam dives et animosa et bellicarum perita rerum Italia." *Epistola*, ed. Baca, 116; Eng. tr., 12.

140 "Non pugnabis contra feminas, aut Italiam, aut Hungariam, aut aliam in occidenti provinciam ingressus." *Epistola*, ed. Baca, 117; Eng. tr., 13, with a few modifications.

141 On Pius's view of the North, see Meserve, "From Samarkand," 20–22. On ancient precedents, see Christopher Krebs, "Borealism: Caesar, Seneca, Tacitus, and the Roman Discourse about the Germanic North," in *Cultural Identity in the Ancient Mediterranean*, ed. Erich S. Gruen, (Los Angeles: Getty Research Institute, 2011), 202–221.

142 "Quid faciet baculus Aegyptiorum arundineus, quando Christianum te viderit effectum? Quid inbellis Arabs? Quid nudus Afer? Omnibus his Aethiopes imminent, presbytero Johanni parentes, qui Christianus est ...." *Epistola*, ed. Baca, 125; Eng. tr., 20. Pius makes further comments on "Ethiopians" in his *Commentaries*, as will be discussed.

143 "Quodsi te nobis adiunxeris, brevi totus Oriens revertetur ad Christum ...." *Epistola*, ed Baca, 125; Eng. tr., 20.

144 Baldi, similarly argues that the letter strives to present a picture of Europe united in culture and religion despite its political divisions; if Mehmed were to convert, he, too, would have to adapt to "western" culture as well as the faith; see *Pio II e la trasformazione*, 199. For earlier attitudes on geography, see Suzanne Conklin Akbari, *Idols in the East: European representations of Islam and the Orient, 1100*–1450 (Ithaca: Cornell University Press, 2009).

145 "Ante omnia vero monstratum est non posse te assequi inter Christianos gloriam et potentiam, quam videris optare, maxime apud Europeos et Occidentales populos, dum tua in secta perseveraris ...." *Epistola*, ed. Baca. Latin, 211 (reading monstratum for Baca's monstratam and capitalizing Occidentales and Orientales, as Glei and Köhler have it; see *Epistola ad Mahumetem*, 24); Eng. tr., Baca, with some modifications, 101.

146 "Sic tuam animam lucrifacies, sic Turcarum populo bene consules ...." *Epistola*, ed. Baca, 211; Eng. tr., 101.

147 "Sic tuum nomen in saecula celebrabitur, sic te omnis Graecia, omnis Italia, omnis Europa demirabitur ...." *Epistola*, ed. Baca, 211–12; Eng. tr., 102.

148 Bisaha, "Pius II's Letter," 196.

149 Meserve, *Empires*, 199.

150 Baldi sees Pius as trying to form alliances at Mantua and in the period that ensued. She provides a blow-by-blow description of his words and actions following the congress; *Pio II*, 91 ff. Russell argues that his love of Italy overshadowed his other diplomatic efforts and that he spent most of his time trying to play one country off against another in an effort to maintain some control; *Diplomats at Work*, 76–82.

151 For a recent description of Pienza and Pius's vision, see White, *Plague and Pleasure*, 245–57.

152 See Emily O' Brien, "Arms and Letters: Julius Caesar, the *Commentaries* of Pope Pius II, and the Politicization of Papal Imagery," *Renaissance Quarterly* 62, no. 4 (Winter 2009): 1080–89; and idem, *Commentaries*.

153 With the possible exception of John XXIII's *Journal of a Soul*.

154 "Quid est igitur, quod tantopere boni nominis gloriam quaerimus?" *Commentaries*, ed. Meserve and Simonetta 1:2; Eng. tr., 3.

155 "At sentiant contentiosi de mortuis quicquid libuerit, dum viventes oblectari gloria quae adest, et quae post obitum futura speratur, minime negent!" *Commentaries*, ed. Meserve and Simonetta 1: 2; Eng. tr., 3.

156 "... extinctus laudabitur et desiderabitur cum haberi non poterit ... vera resurget fama Piumque inter claros pontifices collocabit." *Commentaries*, ed. Meserve and Simonetta 1: 2; Eng. tr., 3.

157 For a similar view of the *Commentaries*, see Rinaldo Rinaldi, "L'Italia 'Romana' del Piccolomini," in *Il Sogno di Pio*, ed. Calzona et al., 109–28.

158 Letter of April 9, 1436, to the Sienese government, Wolkan, *Briefwechsel*, 61: 41; Eng. tr., *Reject Aeneas*, tr. Izbicki et al., 83–84; *Europe*, tr. Brown and Bisaha, 211–12.

159 "... terram frigidam, paucarum frugum feracem, magna ex parte arboribus carentem; subterraneum ibi esse lapidem sulphureum, quem ignis causa defodiunt; civitates nullos habere muros, domos magna ex parte sine calce constructas, villarum tecta de caespitibus facta, ostia rusticana corio boum claudi; vulgus pauper et incultum carnes et pisces ad saturitatem, panem pro obsonio

commedere; viros statura parvos et audaces, feminas albas et venustas atque in venerem proclives; basiationes feminarum minoris illic esse, quam manus in Italia tractationes; vinum non haberi, nisi importatum." *Commentaries*, ed. Meserve and Simonetta, 1: 20; Eng. tr., 21.

160 "Et omnes tum feminae virque villae quasi ad rem novam accurrerant, atque ut nostri vel Aethiopes vel Indos mirari solent, sic Aeneam stupentes intuebantur quaerentes ex sacerdote, cuias esset, quidnam facturus venisset, Christianamne fidem saperet." *Commentaries*, ed. Meserve and Simonetta, 1: 24, Eng. tr., 25. More will be said on Pius's use of terms like "Ethiopian" in the *Commentaries*.

161 Brent Shaw, "'Eaters of Flesh, Drinkers of Milk': The Ancient Mediterranean Ideology of the Pastoral Nomad," *Ancient Society* 13/14 (1982/83): 5–31.

162 "… nam terra Scotia et Angliae pars vicina Scotis nihil simile nostrae habitationis habet—horrida, inculta atque hiemali sole inaccessa." *Commentaries*, ed. Meserve and Simonetta, 1: 26; Eng. tr., 27.

163 *Commentaries*, ed. Meserve and Simonetta, 1: 51.

164 See his letters to Kaspar Schlick (Dec. 28, 1443) and to Francesco Bossio (Dec. 30, 1443); Wolkan, *Briefwechsel*, 61: 260–61, 264.

165 "Sita in alpibus quae Germaniam ab Italia disterminant, ea vallis uno tantum aditu eoque alitissimo et perdifficili patens, nivibus et asperrima glacie tribus anni partibus obtecta rigescit. Loci accolae totas hiemes domi se continent, cistas et quae sunt opera carpentariorum solerter agentes, quae per aestatem Bulzani Tridentique vendunt. Scaccorum ac alearum ludo temporis plurimum terunt, illumque mirum in modum callent. Nullus hos belli metus occupat, neque honoris cupido cruciat, neque auri magna fames atterit. Horum opes pecora sunt, quae per hiemem faeno nutriunt, hisque vivunt; inter quos et homines invenire est, quos numquam bibisse constat, quibus pro potu est cibus lacteus." *Commentaries*, ed. Meserve and Simonetta, 1: 50, Eng. tr., 51, with a slight change.

166 Ady, *Pius II*, 106.

167 *Commentaries*, ed. Meserve and Simonetta, 2: 264–281.

168 During his papacy, Pius often traveled with papal secretary, humanist, and antiquarian, Flavio Biondo, who acted as a guide to ancient ruins. Ady, *Pius II*, 248.

169 O'Brien, *Commentaries*, 4–5, 9–10.

170 O'Brien, *Commentaries*, 18.

171 Leona C. Gabel notes "four major themes, largely political" in the *Commentaries*: Italy, the political schemes of France, the Holy Roman Empire, and the Ottoman Turks; see *Memoirs of a Renaissance Pope*, 23–25.

172 "Fefellisti me, immo vero te ipsum et patriam tuam, Italiam, nisi resipis!" *Commentaries*, eds. Meserve and Simonetta, 1: 190; Eng. tr., 191.

173 "… commotus amore patriae simul et odio quo Rhotomagensem prosequebatur, circuire Italos cardinales, hortari, monere, ne patriam relinquerent …." *Commentaries*, eds. Meserve and Simonetta, 1: 190; Eng. tr., 191.

174 For example, he asserts to the cardinal of Pavia, "A French pope will either go to France, leaving our beloved country [*dulcis patria nostra*] bereft of its splendor, or he'll stay among us, and Italy, the queen of nations [*regina gentium*], will serve a foreign master …. Are you too stupid to see that this will lay a yoke on your nation [*nationi tuae*] forever? … Where is your love for your country [*amor patriae*]?" *Commentaries*, ed. Meserve and Simonetta, 1: 188–91.

175 *Commentaries*, ed. Meserve and Simonetta, 1: 205. It did not speak to everyone: some Italian powers, like Florence and Venice, were displeased by his election, and several countries were unhappy due to their opposition to Frederick III or the empire, including Scotland, Denmark, Poland, France, Hungary, Cyprus, and Bohemia.

176 "Ex Germania recens venit, nescimus eum." *Commentaries*, ed. Meserve and Simonetta, 1: 180, Eng. tr., 181. This notion of Pius being perceived as more

German than Italian may be pure invention on his part. He seems to have enjoyed portraying himself in this way. See Chapter 3 for more on this subject.

177 See Russell, *Diplomats at Work*, 77–79.
178 "Per idem tempus, cum tota Italia recenti pace respirasset ...." *Commentaries*, ed. Meserve and Simonetta, 1: 150; Eng. tr., 151.
179 "Aeneas agreed [to broker a peace on behalf of Siena]. He did not want to fail his country in such a crisis ... (*Annuit Aeneas, ne patriae in tanto discrimine deesset ...*"). *Commentaries*, ed. Meserve and Simonetta, 1: 154, Eng. tr., 155.
180 "En genus Italicum, ferrene horum dominatum poteris quorum servitia adeo sunt insolentia? ... Vae tibi, Italia, si horum subire iugum cogaris!" *Commentaries*, ed. Meserve and Simonetta, 2: 300, Eng. tr., 301, with a slight modification.
181 On ancient Roman and Italian usages of *Germani* and *Teutonici*, see Peter H. Wilson, *The Heart of Europe: A History of the Holy Roman Empire* (Cambridge: Belknap Press, 2016), 256–58.
182 Thomas A. Brady, *German Histories in Age of Reformations, 1400–1650* (Cambridge: Cambridge University Press, 2009), 12, 19.
183 Len Scales, "Late medieval Germany: an under-Stated nation?" in *Power and the Nation in European History*, ed. Len Scales and Oliver Zimmer (Cambridge: Cambridge University Press, 2005), 166–91.
184 "Sed et Germani omnes principes Aeneae per epistolas congratulati sunt, tamquam in eo et Germania ipsa decorata fuisset. Nec decepti, nam Aeneas Germanorum semper et laudator et defensor extitit non modo in cardinalatu, verum etiam in pontificatu maximo, et Callistus eum prae ceteris cardinalibus in rebus Germanicis audivit." *Commentaries*, ed. Meserve and Simonetta, 1: 164, Eng. tr., 165.
185 Ady, *Pius II*, 221; see also O'Brien on the *Commentaries* painting a positive picture of German princes' relations with the papacy; *Commentaries*, 151–52; 158–59.
186 "... pulchrum id esse aucupium, expeditionem in Turchos decernere ut a Germanis aurum subtili ingenio, velut a barbaris, extrahatur ...." *Commentaries*, ed. Meserve and Simonetta, 1: 134; Eng. tr., 135.
187 "Parent suo proverbio Itali: aurum subtili ingenio extorquendum a barbaris dicunt, et nos appellant barbaros!" *Commentaries*, ed. Meserve, 3: 178; Eng. tr., 179.
188 On negative views by Petrarch and others, see Caspar Hirschi, *The Origins of Nationalism: An Alternative History from Ancient Rome to Modern Germany* (Cambridge: Cambridge University Press, 2012), 143 ff.
189 "An id deceat non asserimus: moribus multa tribuas necesse est..." *Commentarii rerum memorabilium que temporibus suis contigerunt*, ed. Adrian Van Heck (Vatican City: Biblioteca Apostolica Vaticana, 1984), 2: 691; Eng. tr., *Commentaries*, ed. Gragg and Gabel, 748.
190 "Quae res magno maerore pontificem affecit, cum et rem fidei hoc modo perituram, et nobilem Germaniam exustum iri animadverteret." *Commentaries*, ed. Meserve and Simonetta, 2: 14 and 16; Eng. tr., 15.
191 "Furore atque ira pleni non cernitis Christianae rei publicae vulnera, quae vestra inferunt odia .... [Pius] Intelligit sapiens praesul Germanorum calamitatem Turchorum esse felicitatem, tantumque vires illorum crescere quantum vestrae diminuantur ...." *Commentaries*, ed. Meserve and Simonetta, 2: 18; Eng. tr., 19.
192 "... bellis flagrare omnia repperit." *Commentaries*, ed. Meserve, 3:56; Eng. tr., *Commentaries*, Gabel and Gragg, 366.
193 "Per idem tempus in agro Leodiensi, qui semi-Germanicus est, quamvis sermone utatur Gallico eoque corrupto ...." *Commentaries*, ed. Meserve, 3: 212; Eng. tr., 213.
194 "Anno qui precesserat proximus percusserat apoplexis Isydorum, episcopum sabinensem, sancte romane ecclesie cardinalem, natione Grecum ex Peloponneso ... nam quasi patrie sue conditorem vidisset ita sibi ipsi complacuit ...." *Commentarii*, ed. Van Heck, 2: 483.

195 As Vanita Seth puts it, scholars saw the origins of racism as "tethered to the rise of centralized states, nationalism, anthropology, and biological science—in other words, the appendages of modernity"; "The Origins of Racism: A Critique of the History of Ideas," *History and Theory* 59, no. 3 (Sept. 2020): 344. See also see Lynn T. Ramey, *Black Legacies: Race and the European Middle Ages* (Gainesville: University of Florida Press, 2014), 25–38 and 131–32, n. 1.

196 Geraldine Heng, *The Invention of Race in the European Middle Ages* (Cambridge: Cambridge University Press, 2018), 3; Benjamin Isaac, *The Invention of Racism in Classical Antiquity* (Princeton, NJ: Princeton University Press, 2006). On the importance of discrimination as part of the definition, see Francisco Bethencourt, *Racisms: From the Crusades to the Twentieth Century* (Princeton, NJ: Princeton University Press, 2013), 6, 8.

197 See Seth, "Origins of Racism"; William C. Jordan, "Why "Race"?" *Journal of Medieval and Early Modern Studies*, 31, no. 1 (Winter 2001): 165–173; Nell Painter's work may also present an implicit challenge by showing how constructed and modern the idea of whiteness appears to be; see *History of White People* (New York: W.W. Norton & Co., 2010).

198 As Paul Freedman has noted, there were a great many "others" in the Middle Ages; see Freedman, "The Medieval Other" in Timothy S. Jones and David Sprunger, eds. *Marvels, Monsters, and Miracles* (Kalamazoo, MI: Medieval Institute Publications, 2002), 4.

199 Robert Bartlett, "Medieval and Modern Concepts of Race," *Journal of Medieval and Early Modern Studies* vol. 31, no. 1, (Winter 2001): 43, 44.

200 Jordan, "Why "Race"?" 165.

201 Seth, "Origins," 368.

202 "Habent enim statura fuligine teterrima, crines corvini similitudinis, dentes stertissimos …." Otto Prinz, ed. *Die Kosmographie des Aethicus* (Munich: Monumenta Germaniae Historica, 1993), 121–22; Eng. tr., Meserve, *Empires*, 103. The Latin here is unclear, and the translation especially of "stertissimos" which may relate to teeth or snoring, is an educated guess. Thanks to Rob Brown and Curtis Dozier for their help on this question.

203 This is my sense from the texts I have read over the years; Paul Kaplan, who has studied the question more carefully, confirms it. See Kaplan, "'Black Turks': Venetian Perceptions of Ottoman Ethnicity," in *The Turk and Islam in the Western Eye 1450–1750*, ed. James G. Harper (Burlington, VT: Ashgate, 2011), 44–45.

204 Brownen Wilson, *The World in Venice: Print, the City, and Early Modern Identity* (Toronto: University of Toronto Press, 2005), 147.

205 Compare this, in a less violent way, to Robert Chazan's arguments about attempts to forcibly convert the Rhineland Jews and bring them fully into Christian society in 1096; see *European Jewry and the First Crusade*, (Berkeley, CA: University of California Press, 1987).

206 Bartlett, "Concepts of Race," 46; see also Benjamin Isaac, "Racism: a rationalization of prejudice in Greece and Rome," in *The Origins of Racism in the West*, ed. Miriam Eliav-Feldon, Benjamin Isaac, and Joseph Ziegler (Cambridge: Cambridge University Press, 2009), 42.

207 As Anthony Pagden argues for Spanish colonists in the Americas, there was a notion of climate as determining only disposition; see "The peopling of the New World: ethnos, race and empire in the early-modern world," in *Origins of Racism in the West*, ed. Eliav-Feldon et al., 297.

208 "Vester sanguis et dominus, viri viennenses, propriam civitatem ingredi prohibeor." *Commentarii*, ed. Van Heck, 2: 568; Eng. tr. *Commentaries*, ed. Gabel and Gragg, 629.

209 *Europe*, tr. Bisaha and Brown, 307; on Gothic identity in medieval Europe, see Patrick J. Geary, *The Myth of Nations: The Medieval Origins of Europe* (Princeton, NJ: Princeton University Press, 2002), 133–34.

210 On the Poles, ("... ac flavis crinibus post tergum vento dimissis...") see
     Commentaries, ed. Meserve, vol. 3: 328; Eng. tr., 329 with some modification. On
     the Scots, see *Commentaries*, ed. Meserve and Simonetta: 20–21 and 24–25.

211 Tacitus, *Germania*, 1, 4.

212 In *Europe*, he mentions a rumor that the ruler of Piombino was cuckolded by his
     mistress with a Moorish (*maurus*) fluteplayer in his household, which was dis-
     covered when she gave birth to an "Ethiopian" (*Ethiopem*) baby; *Europe*, tr.
     Bisaha and Brown, 255; *De Europa*, ed. Van Heck, 227. On early connotations
     of "Moor," see Bethencourt, *Racisms*, 17–18.

213 Kate Lowe, "Visible Lives: Black Gondoliers and Other Black Africans in
     Renaissance Venice," *Renaissance Quarterly* 66, no. 2 (Summer 2013): 412–452.

214 "Tum miles ethyops qui pluribus annis inter servitia Neapoleonis fuerat tandem-
     que militie sese dederat ...." *Commentarii*, ed. Van Heck, 2: 719; Eng. tr.,
     Commentaries, ed. Gabel and Gragg, 773.

215 "... proiectis vestibus, nudus in aquam prosiliit celerique natatu traiecto flumine,
     comprehensa lancea, tetro niger aspectu superare molem nititur. Sequuntur
     exemplum quicunque sunt in castris audaces ...." *Commentarii*, ed. Van Heck: 2:
     720; Eng. tr., *Commentaries*, ed. Gabel and Gragg, 773–74.

216 Virtus Ethyopis quod inexpugnabile credebatur munimentum expugnationi
     subiecit. Posteritas fabulosum putabit ...." *Commentarii*, ed. Van Heck, 2, 720;
     Eng. tr., *Commentaries*, ed. Gabel and Gragg, 774.

217 See *Black Africans in Renaissance Europe*, ed. T.F. Earle and Kate Lowe
     (Cambridge: Cambridge University Press, 2005); Lowe, "Visible Lives." Lowe
     notes the challenge of identifying Africans or people of African descent in the
     documentary record by name only. She also mentions Africans as having the
     reputation of being skilled boatmen and swimmers in Venice.

218 See also Pius's description of the heroine Lucretia as white-skinned and beauti-
     ful in *Tale of Two Lovers* (1444).

219 *Commentaries*, ed. Meserve and Simonetta, I: 25.

220 *Epistola ad Mohomatem*, ed. Baca, 20; 125.

221 Nelson Minnich, "The Catholic Church and the pastoral care of black Africans
     in Renaissance Italy," in *Black Africans in Renaissance Europe*, ed. Earle and
     Lowe, 281.

222 Jews were expelled in England (1290) and twice in France (1322 and 1394), and
     were beginning to be expelled from different parts of the Holy Roman Empire in
     the fifteenth century.

223 The first mention comes from a letter to Juan de Segovia (August 13, 1440); see
     Reject Aeneas, tr. Izbicki et al., 130; the second is found in a letter to Emperor
     Frederick III (1447); ibid., 270.

224 On the twentieth, see *Commentarii*, ed. Van Heck, 222 and 758.

225 In Pius's letter to Cesarini describing Basel (July 1434), discussed in Chapter 1;
     Wolkan, *Briefwechsel*, 61: 35.

226 *Europe*, tr. Bisaha and Brown, 193.

227 "Avarissimus enim fuerat Iohannes Antonius adeoque lucris intentus, ut sibi soli
     mercaturas sui principatus reservaverit. A subditis emit, quanti voluit pretii,
     quecunque venalia fuerunt eaque vendidit negotiatoribus externis. Creditoribus
     raro satisfecit. Iudeos, quos posset expilare facilius, complures in ditione sua
     sustinuit. Cum Turcis commertia habuit." *Commentarii*, ed. Van Heck, 2: 789;
     Eng. tr., *Commentaries*, ed. Gabel and Gragg, 841.

228 Interestingly, Pius makes no mention in the *Commentaries* of such an occurrence
     during his own papal coronation ceremonies.

229 See Magda Teter's perceptive argument about the impact of written works that
     repeated these lies on the growing insecurity of Jews in Christian Europe: "Blood
     Libel and its Legacies," in *Whose Middle Ages: Teachable Moments for an*

Ill-Used Past, ed. Andrew Albin et al. (New York: Fordham University Press, 2019), 44–57.

230 In Vratislavia omnes Judei in vincula conjecti referuntur, quia in sacramentum domini debaccati dicuntur. Puto id inventum esse ad extorquendas novello regi pecunias." Wolkan, *Briefwechsel*, 68: 171–72.

231 For a discussion of the friars' role in propaganda, see Robert Bonfil, *Jewish Life in Renaissance Italy*, tr. Anthony Oldcorn (Berkeley, CA: University of California Press, 1994), 21–29. On Capistrano and Bernardino, see Cecil Roth, *History of the Jews of Italy* (Philadelphia: Jewish Publication Society of America, 1946), 162–63; Roth notes that Pius forbade the baptism of Jews under age twelve but was uncompromising on their tax levy; ibid., 177–78.

232 Moses was also a writer. See Bonfil, *Jewish Life*, 155; Roth, *History of the Jews of Italy*, 202.

233 Roth, *History of the Jews of Italy*, 133. Such statements may speak to the differences in attitudes toward Jews that characterized Northern versus Southern Europe, according to Gavin Langmuir; see *Toward a Definition of Antisemitism* (Los Angeles: Center for Medieval and Renaissance Studies, 1990), 308.

234 This is a potentially rich subject that unfortunately goes beyond the scope of the present work.

235 *Commentaries*, ed. Meserve and Simonetta, 2: 54–55. See Milligan, *Moral Combat*, 128 on allegations of Greek effeminacy in other works of the time.

236 Painter, *History of White People*, 28.

237 Recall that he urged listeners at Wiener-Neustadt to repent, abandon pride, and to take as their companion "the modest and beautiful maiden whom we call humility." "In hoc florentissimo," ed. Cotta-Schönberg, Eng., tr., 69.

238 *Commentaries*, ed. Gabel and Gragg, 430, 435.

239 See *Commentaries*, ed. Meserve, 3: 239 ff. on Joan of Arc and ibid., 495, n. 43 on Gabel's surprise at Pius's free rein with some of the details. Joan's reputation had been rehabilitated by the papacy by this time. See also *Europe*, tr. Bisaha and Brown, 202.

240 In *Europe*, tr. Bisaha and Brown, 123, 167–68.

241 Geary, *Myth of Nations*, 63–64.

242 Rolando Montecalvo, "The New Landesgeschichte: Aeneas Silvius Piccolomini on Austria and Bohemia," in *Pius II*, ed. Von Martels and Vanderjagt, 55–86.

243 Bartlett, "Concepts of Race," 54.

244 There are certainly earlier examples of attaching a people to a territory, like Gerald of Wales's famous prediction about the Welsh occupying the land until the end of time; see "Description of Wales," in *The Journey Through Wales and the Description of Wales*, tr. Lewis Thorpe (New York: Penguin, 2004), 274.

245 "Valachi lingua utuntur italica, verum imperfecta et admodum corrupta. Sunt qui legiones romanas eo missas olim censeant adversus Dacos ... quorum posteri, ut ante relatum est, barbariores barbaris evasere." *Commentarii*, ed. Van Heck, 681; Eng. tr., *Commentaries*, ed. Gabel and Gragg, 737. For his earlier reference to the Wallachians, see Gabel and Gragg, 580–81.

246 "... in agrestes mitem animum ostendunt. Dicunt futuros liberos quicunque ad se deficiunt blandeque complectuntur. Rusticorum rude ingenium non intelligit artes et libertatem perpetuo duraturam existimat." *Commentarii*, ed. Van Heck, 684; Eng. tr., *Commentaries*, ed. Gabel and Gragg, 741.

247 "Habemus fidem legationi Stephani: eadem multis ex locis nuntiantur. Occidentis imperium querit Maumethes qui orientale pervasit." *Commentarii*, ed. Van Heck, 685; Eng. tr., *Commentaries*, ed. Gabel and Gragg, 741, with some modifications.

248 See, for example, Book XI: 25, *Commentarii*, ed. Van Heck, 713; *Commentaries*, ed. Gabel and Gragg, 768.

249 *Commentarii*, ed. Van Heck, 763; Eng. tr., *Commentaries*, ed. Gabel and Gragg, 816.

250 "Molesta ea res Pio pontifici fuit cum propter odia regum nullo tempore non detestanda, tum quod ea dissensio Turcos ad imperium Occidentis suopte inge- nio erectos magis ac magis invitabat." *Commentarii*, ed. Van Heck, 748; Eng. tr., *Commentaries*, ed. Gabel and Gragg, 801, with some changes. For a description of Frederick III's claims to the throne, see *Commentarii*, ed. Van Heck, 2: 794-ff. For his assertion that the Turks (like invaders of the past) wanted to use Hungary as a launch point to attack "the empire of the west," see ibid., 1: 190–91. For other pairings of Hungary and Europe, see ibid., 2: 741 and 760.

251 *Commentarii*, ed. Van Heck, 2:758 ff.; *Commentaries*, ed. Gabel and Gragg, 813–17. On the idea of Europe uniting under papal leadership against the Ottomans in the *Commentaries*, see Rinaldo Rinaldi, "L'Italia 'romana' del Piccolomini," 110–11, in *Sogno di Pio*, ed. Calzona et al.; Casella "Pio II," 35.

252 There are a few cases where Pius uses "Europe" in other ways. For instance, regarding the death of Guarino da Verona, he states that pupils "flocked to him from all of Europe"; (*Commentaries*, ed., Meserve: 3:55). Regarding Genoa, he states that no city in all of Europe has changed princes so many times (ibid., 3: 69).

253 *Commentaries*, ed. Meserve and Simonetta, 1:208, 209.

254 "Tu qui lecturus es, quamvis non leges historiam qua res novas exponimus, his- torie tamen legem servatam scito, cuius est a veritate non aberrare." *Commentarii*, ed. Van Heck, 2: 794; Eng. tr., *Commentaries*, ed. Gabel and Gragg, vol. 5: 845.

255 *Commentarii*, ed. Van Heck, 2:762.

256 "… sed ultro eos invadentes et Graeciam et Asiam maiorum negligentia per- ditam facile recuperarent." *Commentaries*, ed. Meserve and Simonetta, 2:83, Eng. tr., 84.

257 "… maiores, quotiens in orientales duxere, ex Gallia, Germania et Anglia copias quaesivisse." *Commentaries*, ed. Meserve and Simonetta, 2:52, Eng. tr., 53.

258 "Quorum virtute quicquid in Oriente nostre religionis est, Christo servatum fateri licet." *Commentarii*, ed. Van Heck, 493; Eng. tr., *Commentaries*, ed. Gabel and Gragg, 545.

259 "Publicato apud urbem Romam Pii pontificis decreto belli contra Turcos gerendi legati per omnem Italiam et ad regiones transalpinas missi sunt, qui ex fidelibus populis ac regibus auxilia impetrarent suaderentque ne solum pontificem cum Venetis, Hungaris, atque Burgundis ad tantum bellum proficisci permitterent, quod totas Occidentis vires videretur exquirere, siquidem Turci ex altera parte universum Orientem commoturi ferebantur." *Commentarii*, ed. Van Heck, 2:794; Eng. tr., *Commentaries*, ed. Gabel and Gragg, 845–46.

260 See *Commentaries*, book VII.

261 Setton, *Papacy*, 2:238.

262 Ady, *Pius II*, 309–18; *Commentaries*, ed. Meserve, 3:436–37. As the mines became productive, Pius forbade the importation of alum from the East and resolved to use all the profits from the alum trade for crusade; Setton, *Papacy*, 2: 240. See also Romualdo Luzi, "Giovanni di Castro: la sua "patria: e la sua for- tuna," in *Enea Silvio Piccolomini: Arte, Storia e Cultura nell'Europa di Pio II*, ed. Roberta Di Paola, Arianna Antoniutti, and Marco Gallo (Rome: Libreria Editrice Vaticana, 2006), 165–205.

263 *Commentarii*, ed. Van Heck, 460–63; *Commentaries*, ed. Gabel and Gragg, 515–18.

264 "Nos autem magistrum et dominum nostrum Iesum Christum, pium et sanctum pastorem, imitabimur qui pro suis ovibus animam ponere non dubitavit." *Commentarii*, ed. Van Heck, 769; Eng. tr., *Commentaries*, ed. Gabel and Gragg, 822.

265 "Non belle dicitur: ite! Fortasse melius audient: venite! Hoc temptare libet… Fortasse cum viderint magistrum et patrem suum, romanum pontificem, Iesu Christi vicarium, senem et egrotum, in bella vadentem, pudebit eos manere

domi; arma capient defensionemque sacre religionis fortibus animis amplecten-
tur." *Commentarii*, ed. Van Heck, 2:772; Eng. tr., *Commentaries*, ed. Gabel and
Gragg, 824. The text of this oration to his cardinals was also preserved and circulated on its own. See, Michael Cotta-Schönberg. Oration "Sextus agitur
annus" of Pope Pius II (23 September 1463, Rome). 5th version. (Orations of
Enea Silvio Piccolomini / Pope Pius II; 75). 2019. ffhal-01240577f.

266 Helmrath, "Political-Assembly Speeches," 84.

267 "abominabilem Mahometis ... legem"; *Bulla de profectione in Turcos, Ezechielis
prophetae*, in *Opera omnia*, 918. See especially 918–19 for biblical references and
921 for indulgences.

268 "... nec sinerent immanem draconem Mahometem fideles devorare animas."
Ezechielis, 914. Recall that Pius described Mehmed as a dragon in 'Vocavit nos
Pius' as well.

269 "Turci tanquam lupi et immanes bestiae ovile Dominicum, id est Christianam
plebem lacerare conantur et lacerant." *Ezechielis*, 916.

270 "In Lesbon multitudo puberum palo transfixa. In Bosna Regem qui salutem
pactus sese dederat cum patruo suo, Mahometes ipse humano sanguine insatia-
bilis, sua manu (ut fertur) iugulavit." *Ezechielis*, 915.

271 Whether or not some or all of these stories were at least partly true is a question
that goes beyond the limits of this study, but the sources that popularize stories
of Mehmed's inordinate cruelty are often Latin Christian. See Franz Babinger,
Mehmed the Conqueror and this Time. (1953; tr. Princeton, 1978), 427–32.

272 See *Ezechielis*, 918; on 916 Pius calls both Turks and Saracens the foulest of
peoples (*foedissimae gentes*).

273 "Misere fratrum tuorum: Affer opem iam dura ferentibus. Quod si nihil horum
te trahit, at saltem de tua salute cogita. Nec te tutum idcirco existimes, quia
mansionem fortasse procul à Turcis sortitus es. Nemo tam remotus est quin rep-
eriri queat. Si vicinum dimiseris in periculo, qui ante te proximus est igni, dimit-
teris et ipse similiter à vicino qui retro te habitat. Tales oportet nos esse in alios,
quales ergo nos illos cupimus invenire. Nolite auxilia Gallorum sperare
Theutones, nisi et vos Ungaris, nec vos Galli Hispanorum, nisi Theutonicis
opem fertis. Qua enim mensura mensi fueritis eadem remetietur et vobis. Nec
propterea sibi quispiam blandiantur [*sic*], quoniam principatu polleat aut regno.
Constantinopolitanus Imperator et Trapezuntius, et Rex Bosnae et Rasciae
Domini, et alii quamplures principes capti et crudeliter occisi, quid sit expectan-
dum edocent. Nihil tam contrarium Mahometi quam nomen regium: Orientis
adeptus imperium, ad Occidentale festinat." *Ezechielis*, 919.

274 *Ezechielis*, 920.

275 "At si servile iugum horretis, si contumeliam Dei et proximi tolerare nequit, si
pudet semiviros Asiaticos Graecorum gentem (quod nunquam antea fecerunt)
subegisse eoque superbiae prorupisse, ut Europam sibi totam brevi tempore
paritura sperent. Si cor virile vobis est, cor nobile, cor altum, cor Christianum,
sequimini vestigia patris vestri, sequimini castra nostra: Venite in auxilium fidei:
Venite in auxilium fratrum vestrorum." *Ezechielis*, 920.

276 "Si movebimini vos Christiani occidentales, et animarum vestrarum pastorem
secuti fueritis, movebuntur et multi ex Graecia atque Asia Christiani, qui verum
esse Christi vicarium Romanum Pontificem non dubitant." *Ezechielis*, 920.

277 "Da nobis victoriam de tuis hostibus, ut tandem recuperata Graecia per totam
Europam dignas tibi cantemus laudes ...." *Ezechielis*, 923.

278 Housley, "Pope Pius II," 233–34.

279 Some examples from his correspondence include the use of Europe twice in a
letter to Florence (1460); *Documenti sulle relazioni delle città toscane coll'Oriente
cristiano e coi Turchi.*, ed. Giuseppe Müller (1879. Reprint, Rome: Società
Multigrafica Editrice, 1996), 185; Pius's successor, Paul II uses Europe, too;
ibid., 202. See also Pius's letter to Leonardo Tocco of Arta (1459), in *Ungedruckte*

Akten zur Geschichte der Päpste, ed. Ludwig Pastor (Freiburg im Breisgau: Herdersche Verlagshandlung, 1904), 119. Letters and orations to Pius also using "Europe" in ways that echo Pius's rhetoric include Nicola Loschi's 1463 poem to Pius, "Constantinus Supplex," which mentions the danger to the coasts and cities of Europe; Agostino Pertusi, ed. *Testi inediti e poco noti sulla caduta di Costantinopoli* (Bologna: Pàtron Editore, 1983), 276; and Venice's instructions to their ambassador in Rome (1459), *Ungedruckten Akten*, ed. Pastor, 118.

280   *Ezechielis*, 917.

281   See Housley, *Later Crusades*, 106–09, 410; "Pope Pius II," 232–45; Stefan Stantchev, shows the republic's lack of interest in crusade before this time, which arguably points to Pius's role in bringing them on board; "Venice and the Ottoman Threat, 1381–1453," in *Reconfiguring the Fifteenth-Century Crusade*, ed. Housley, 161–205. Had Pius survived and Ancona been prepared to receive the numerous recruits who arrived there, the campaign would have likely been larger.

282   Baldi, *Pio II*, 260.

283   Ady, *Pius II*, 336. The quote comes from a letter of Iacopo Ammanati Piccolomini to Cardinal Francesco Piccolomini (late August/ early September 1464); see *Lettere (1444–1479)*, ed. Paolo Cherubini (Rome: Ufficio Centrale per i beni archivistici, 1997), 2: 521.

284   Other authors besides Pius were using "Europe" in a provocative way, like Flavio Biondo in his oration to Alfonso of Naples (1453) and his dedication of his *Roma Triumphans* in 1459 to Pius, but his audience was smaller. Catherine Castner shows the importance and influence of Biondo's works, but also acknowledges that his work circulated in pieces and was not directly cited for centuries; "The Fortuna of Biondo Flavio's Italia Illustrata," in *A New Sense of the Past: The Scholarship of Biondo Flavio (1392–1463)*, ed. Angelo Mazzocco and Marc Laureys (Leuven: Leuven University Press, 2016), 188–90.

Conclusion

Niall Ferguson claims that

> it is not 'Eurocentrism' or (anti-)'Orientalism' to say that the rise of Western civilization is the single most important historical phenomenon of the second half of the second millennium after Christ. It is a statement of the obvious. The challenge is to explain how it happened.[1]

Too often, "the West" is described as a tangible reality whose history can be mapped out, when, in fact, it is only a construct. Unlike Ferguson, I find it not only Eurocentric but problematic to speak of "Western civilization" as a universally accepted fact, much less one of singular importance. Our challenge should be to explain what gave rise to this notion and why some continue to defend its most hegemonic manifestations so vigorously. This study has explored the life and works of Pope Pius II in an effort to understand one of the earliest articulations of a European and Western identity. While others contend that the ancient Greeks or Enlightenment thinkers defined the concept of Europe, I have argued that it was a Renaissance pope who helped inaugurate a major turning point when many inhabitants of Europe began thinking of themselves not only as Christians, but as "Europeans."

When Pius was born, the peoples of Europe already formed a recognizable collective, tied together by a history of alliances, exchanges, and wars; a dominant religion; and shared traditions in governance, learning, customs, and the common, though elite, language of Latin. One could travel across large areas of the continent and be able to recognize familiar buildings and concepts, even if they did not know the language or precise local practices. In many ways, Europe was "made" or "born" in the Middle Ages, as Robert Bartlett and Jacques LeGoff, have convincingly argued.[2] And yet, what was missing at this time was a clear *awareness* of a common European culture. Scholars concur that one does not see a widespread use of "Europe" and "European," in fact, until the sixteenth century. Pius, however, was employing this rhetoric in the mid-fifteenth century. His written works, as I have shown, offer a critical connection between medieval developments and an early modern discourse. He was not the only writer of his time to use these terms and present a notion of European identity, but he had a uniquely

DOI: 10.4324/9781003315865-6

defined vision of this identity and its potential importance. LeGoff highlights his role when he states, "Only Pope Pius II... possessed a clear idea of Europe."[3]

Pius came to this view over the course of many years, and several factors played into it. It is often assumed that this crusading pope always supported holy war against the Turks, but all signs point to personal skepticism in his early years of those who took the cross. While serving as secretary at Emperor Frederick III's court, he showed little enthusiasm for the Crusade of Varna (1444), describing it as a tool for Pope Eugenius IV and the king of Poland and Hungary's political ambitions. He slowly began to warm up to idea a few years later, but it was the Ottoman conquest of Constantinople in 1453 that really changed his mind. After 1453, Pius became strongly pro-crusade, which fueled his desire to speak of a united Europe and a defense of shared borders and culture. While scholars agree that the Ottoman advance changed crusading from an offensive to a defensive concept, I contend that Pius's emphasis on Europe as sacred homeland helped to define what exactly Christians of disparate nations were fighting for.

Yet the Ottoman advance alone was not enough to offer Pius a distinct idea of Europe. As this study has shown, the conquest of Constantinople was one of three major elements that combined to shape his interests and insights regarding European identity—the other two were his extensive travels and his humanist education, as discussed in chapter 1. They provided the material and the tools to craft this vision. Still, 1453 was a critical moment for Pius, as chapter 2 shows. His genuine shock and despair at disturbing reports of the sack of this illustrious and ancient Christian city and the enslavement of men, women, and children echo in several of his writings. This outrage, coupled with an intense desire to correct this injustice or at least halt the Ottomans' progress, changed his life and his view of the continent he inhabited and had traveled so extensively. It made him see its countries as having a shared destiny. We can see that transformation taking place through a close reading of his letters from 1453–1455. These missives demonstrate his emotional turmoil and desperation for a large-scale military response. At times he became sick with worry, showing that he personally identified with the defense of Europe, his homeland.

Before 1453, Pius tended to treat the Ottomans as just another political power within the continent, with occasional expressions of pro-crusade language. After the conquest, he became convinced that the Ottomans had nothing in common with Europeans. Even though Europeans visited their share of violence on other Christian cities, Pius and other contemporaries reserved special horror for the Ottomans, who could be conveniently painted in this case as an uncivilized "other." One wonders if Mehmed had been able to restrain his troops and curb the enslavement of locals if Pius and others would have viewed them any differently—as heirs to the New Rome rather than barbarians. From this point on, Pius rarely described the Ottomans as anything other than a foreign presence to be expelled.[4] Importantly, then, 1453 compelled Pius to consider what was at stake, not just in Greece, but in all of Europe, and to think anew about all the regions he had visited. It turned his gaze inward as well as outward. My comparison of Pius's reaction to that of other humanists in chapter 2 also helps to demonstrate how unique and well-developed his geographical focus was at this early stage.

This study has also examined Pius's fertile intellectual period in Rome shortly before he became pope (1455–58). His direct access to texts by Tacitus, Strabo, and Pliny exposed him to the riches of ancient ethnography, bringing subtlety and structure to his writings on group identity, but also varying levels of accuracy. When writing of Europeans, his works took on a dialogic quality, as described by Shirin Khanmohamadi, whereby one could sense them not just as objects of Pius's works, but looking back at him, as it were.[5] This was almost never the case with the Ottomans; his curiosity about them grew by leaps and bounds, and he wrote prodigiously about them, but he remained content to repeat the same untrustworthy sources, like the early medieval Aethicus's fantastical description of the Scythians, whom Pius and others viewed as the ignoble ancestors of the Turks.

In this period, Pius also showed increasing interest in early nationalist thought, describing the histories, traditions, and aspirations of several nation-states in his *Germania*, the *History of Bohemia*, and *Europe*. He moved back and forth between nation and continent in his efforts to describe the peoples of Europe, showing both the tensions and positive connections between the two broader collectives. As I argued in chapter 3, he was keener to pinpoint the boundaries of Europe than he was to define the borders or rightful rulers of Christian nations. He was less troubled, it seems, by movement or upheaval within Europe so long as it was Europeans doing it to one another. His emphasis on European security kept internal boundaries loose and flexible. Catholic Christians (even Hussites or Eastern Orthodox, in some cases), automatically belonged. Even Jews seem to have a place in Europe within the Christian political hierarchy, but not Muslims. At their best, these "European" nations formed a team: interestingly, Ukraine or "Ruthenia" was part of Europe for Pius, but Russia was not.

In writing these works Pius drew on his own recollections, and probably notes, as well as contemporary oral and written sources, although he rarely cited them. Few men covered as many miles and even fewer were in a position to take stock of the similarities and differences they witnessed along the way. Pius was unusually perceptive in his ability to grasp many of the same threads that Bartlett and LeGoff cite as proof of the formation of Europe—a feat they accomplished with the benefit of archival research and centuries of hindsight. Whether he was describing European nations or the entire continent, Pius began to conflate lands and their peoples in ways that are still invoked today, while maintaining a view of ethnicity that was more flexible than that of later nationalist and racial theorists.

Once he became pope in 1458, Pius spoke more passionately of Christendom and its future, but he continued to advocate for Europe and its unique identity, haranguing audiences to defend it in his orations, bulls, and other writings. At times he clearly prioritized the safety and security of Europe over other Christian regions; his elevation to the See of St. Peter did not convert him to a dramatically inclusive vision of the Christian world. His writings on identity in this period and the fame that his earlier writings now acquired helped promote a vision of Europe and Christianity as tied together. In Pius's writings, Europe was more than a group of Christian countries, it was depicted as the natural leader of the Christian world. Ironically, however, during his papacy Pius began to show a slightly more nuanced view of the Ottomans. As seen in chapter 4, he praised the Turks' strength and briefly considered the possibility of converting and bringing them into the fold of European society before abandoning the idea with his famous, unsent letter to Mehmed II. The word choice in some of his texts also suggest a subtle recognition of their legitimacy as rulers in Europe and not just squatters, as it were. Perhaps Pius's access to more accurate, or at least more nuanced, reports of Ottoman activities and movements complicated his efforts to cast them as illegitimate outsiders. In the end, however, Pius returned to his mantra of expelling the Turks from Europe in his last, well-circulated papal bull.

What emerges from Pius's writings over time is a sense of Europe or Europeans as having a personality that was strong, pronouncedly masculine at times, highly educated, civilized, and, with very few exceptions, Christian. The gendering of Europe is especially fascinating as it leads to a reflexive feminizing of most other cultures; the Turks drift back and forth across that line of demarcation in Pius's framing. Ultimately, his goal was to show Europeans as distinctly different, and of course, better than their neighbors. It was also, in many ways, to put Europe first in his reader's imaginations. Even in his treatise on Asia (1461), the standard by which he judges the continent and its history is wholly Eurocentric.

In the decades following Pius's death, the prospect of "European" identity became increasingly attractive to many inhabitants of the continent. The Protestant Reformation fractured the shaky solidity of Christendom, pushing contemporaries to seek alternate designations for the larger collective of neighboring nations. Exploration and imperialism also intensified the need to distinguish between larger landmasses and their inhabitants. This is all in addition to the Ottoman threat as an ongoing source of anxiety about borders and inter-continental relations.[6] Amid the voices and concerns that contributed to the rising use and emotional content of the term "Europe," Pius's words and ideas continued to circulate. Other concepts of Europe competed with Pius's vision but because of his position as pope and the many printings of his texts into the later sixteenth century, his views received more attention than many others. While a number of scholars have perceived the importance of Pius's vision, this monograph is the first in-depth examination of the long and intricate process by which he achieved it.

Pius's precise impact, however, is an elusive question. It is difficult to know if contemporary or later authors who echo his rhetoric were quoting or paraphrasing him, channeling his ideas indirectly, or if they were influenced by an entirely different source or set of stimuli. Ultimately, Pius's legacy is something I gesture toward in this study rather than seek to prove. Perhaps experts on readership and transmission, with the help of increasing digitization, will take on this question on in the future. I hope that if they do it will not contradict my sense that his message on European and Western identity found many interlocutors, who picked it up and continued to develop it in their own ways.[7] In the meantime, it seems reasonable to believe that many people were reading Pius a century or more after his death, or there would have been no market for the many manuscript and printed copies of his works. Isabella Walser-Bürgler argues for Pius's impact in several ways, including the prominence and growing usage of the terms "Europe" and "European" that his works inspired, and the ethnographic stereotyping that he and his later followers frequently employed.[8] We know that Christopher Columbus, Erasmus of Rotterdam, François de la Noue, René de Lucinge, and Nicolas Nicolay, for instance, read him. Erasmus, who frequently criticized fellow European Christians and even defended the Turks, may well have bristled at Pius's chauvinism, but Columbus and Nicolay seem to have been sympathetic to the pope's mantra of positional superiority.[9] My goal is not to assign full credit for this shift in identity to Pius, but to use his works to help unpack its earliest manifestations.

It also bears repeating that the myth of Europe as a culturally distinct and advanced society—a shared idea co-authored, as it were, by Pius—was but one school of thought on the continent at this time. Differing Renaissance views of Europe and its neighbors complicated the discourse he helped to create. As studies on Machiavelli, Montaigne, and other writers show, not everyone felt smugly superior to or separate from the Ottoman world.[10] Noel Malcolm and John Tolan discuss other writers who praised the Ottoman Empire and Islam, and used Muslim writings to provoke their readers rather than lull them into complacency about their supposed superiority.[11] As we saw at several points in this study, even Pius had occasional doubts about his message and considered the other side with curiosity. However much he tried to convince his readers of the foreignness and separation of the Ottomans, he undercut that message with his descriptions of their intense engagement in Europe, not just as conquerors, but as rulers, allies, and neighbors. Careful readers could detect the overlapping interests, networks, and "shared world" of Islamic and Christian regions in Europe and the Mediterranean, especially in Pius's historical works.[12] They might even come away wondering if the Ottomans' greatest threat was not their alleged barbarism, but their sophistication and adaptability. If Pius's ultimate goal was to eject the Ottomans from Europe, he at least gave them a bright spotlight along the way.

Despite these moments of nuance or curiosity, the dominant message in Pius's works about the Ottomans was grim, and it is hard to imagine many of his premodern readers focusing on the few positive or neutral characterizations and tuning out the steady drumbeat of negativity. This is because Pius himself focused on negative reports and chose to change or erase parts of recent Ottoman history at will. Fortunately, other writers helped balance out Pius's blind spots and harshness—he did not speak for all Europeans by any means. Nonetheless, his words may have fed a false sense of security for some that "Europeans" were inherently better than Asians.[13] This was a coping mechanism to be sure, but what began in shock and fear for Pius eventually transformed into one upmanship and false bravado.

Whether or not Pius directly influenced later generations' perceptions of Europe, we do see important later trends that square with his world view. First, the political. While in reality, European countries were far from united, and colonial projects in other continents would only serve to intensify those rivalries,[14] Pius's words offered a comforting myth of common values and modes of life. Above all, he articulated a notion of self-defense as *mutual defense*.[15] His vision of what might be called "Europe first" ("let all of Asia and Africa fall away") when he preached crusade as pope, shifted the location and goal of crusade to the home front or "our soil."[16] This notion clearly failed to prevent a host of wars within Europe, but this exclusive ideal of what Europe ought to be resonates to this day among many thinkers.

In the long-term, Pius's writings may also have impacted modern "western" conceptions of time and geographical space. In terms of time, popular definitions of the Renaissance and modernity—two charged and contested terms—share similarities with Pius's elitist definitions of culture and civilization that reflected his own narrow context. And in terms of space, whenever Pius spoke of the high culture of his day, he *only* thought of Europe, even as other humanists, poets, artists, and scientists were exhibiting a growing appreciation of Asian and African learning and culture. Nineteenth-century Swiss scholar Jakob Burckhardt, who coined the term "Renaissance," and his followers would reenact this myopic narrative, thereby excluding the contributions of non-Europeans and silencing their role in histories of the Renaissance.[17]

Pius may have played a hand in this process by defining high culture as the contemporary study of rhetoric and classical texts. Like other peninsular humanists, he saw their studies as a movement that began in Italy, then migrated to the North and other areas. For Pius, it was a cultural phenomenon specific to Europe. In recent decades, scholars have emphasized the crucial role of non-Europeans as co-creators in the Renaissance, showing their inspiration of a host of developments that were long claimed as indigenous to Christian Europe.[18] Yet there is still a tendency today among some thinkers to see outside influences as temporal rather than geographical—emanating from the ancient Greek and Roman past, but not from another continent or non-Christian faith. Some of this resistance, to be sure, derives from other 19th century biases that influenced Burckhardt when he wrote his seminal work, but Pius's frequent appearances in his *Civilization of the Renaissance in Italy* suggest that the pope's praises of Europe and his insistence on the inferiority and foreignness of the Ottomans also played a role in the modern foundations of this academic discipline. Pius was distinctly uninterested in Islamic learning and paid little attention to Africa. His view of the character of European culture and his use of the word "West" bear more than a passing resemblance to later notions of "Western Civilization" as well as "the Renaissance." Whether or not we can measure Pius's direct influence among other voices in the early modern period, his corpus helps us understand the moment when this shift began.

Despite these resonances, we must be clear just how distant Pius's world is from our own. The circumstances that sparked his defensive evocation of Europe could not be more different from the agendas of some thinkers who seek to defend "European" and "Western" society today. From 1453 on, Pius lived in dread of invasion from a large and imperial power. Without excusing his cultural biases, one might at least understand his anxiety and defensiveness from the standpoint of security and self-rule. He was, after all, trying to prevent the very real prospect of a harsh take-over. Italy, Hungary, Greece, and its neighbors were under direct threat: before Mehmed II died in 1481, he nearly completed the conquest of the Balkans, sent raids into Friuli in Northern Italy, and his troops took Otranto in Southern Italy by force and held it for a year. Half of Hungary fell under the control of his great grandson, Suleyman, and Vienna was attacked in 1529 and 1683. For these reasons, when one hears echoes of Pius's rhetoric in the speeches of modern-day xenophobes in America and Europe it is both fascinating and disturbing.

Modern "western" pundits and politicians who tout their cultural superiority and call for separation and the closing of borders to immigrants and refugees are unconsciously invoking a centuries-old discourse born from fear of an organized, massive armed incursion. The irony is, indeed, heavy. An awareness of that historical context could help us examine new situations from a place of reason and critical thought instead of raw emotion and defensive rhetoric. There are many inclusive, progressive definitions of Europe that can displace the reactionary ones—and some of them are found in Pius's writings. Walser-Bürgler describes his *Europe* (1458) as offering "an astounding panorama of beauty and diversity shaping the continent," setting the trend for "all later pluralistic descriptions of [Europe]."[19]

Perhaps the most important thread that links Pius's rhetoric with modern associations are his repeated efforts to fuse Christianity with the "European" and "Western" identity, with some room, it would seem, for Jewish communities. Despite the claim of most modern western countries to have secular, enlightened governments that protect religious freedom, Jews, Muslims, Hindus, Buddhists, and others often feel pressured to argue for their rights and dignity in these countries in ways that members of Christian sects, even the most radical, do not. It is just assumed that Christians "belong" in western countries. Other developments surely contributed to this Christian bias, but Pius's forceful and early articulation of religion as an inseparable part of "Western" identity merits further consideration.[20] In many ways, he promoted a positive view of Europe with calls for peace between neighboring nations, shared responsibility for defense, and a rich history and cultural traditions, but it is still not a community in which all feel welcome.

Somewhere between the formation of a "European society" and a widespread use of that phrasing lies Pius's life, his works, and his dogged efforts to convince his neighbors that Europe was theirs, that it was better than other continents, and that it was worth protecting. Modern thinkers would do well to deconstruct the harmful implications of his message, while considering the more generous aspects of his vision and the better instincts that lay beneath it. Hopefully this study has shown the power of the seemingly innocent words we use to describe our and others' identities, and the value of questioning them again and again.

Notes

1 Niall Ferguson, *Civilization: The West and the Rest* (New York: Penguin Press, 2011), 8.
2 Robert Bartlett, *The Making of Europe: Conquest, Colonization and Cultural Change 950–1350* (Princeton: Princeton University Press, 1993); Jacques Le Goff, *The Birth of Europe*, tr. Janet Lloyd. (Malden, MA: Blackwell: 2005).
3 LeGoff, *Birth of Europe*, 1. For a list of other scholars who credit Pius with playing a central role in forging the idea of Europe, see the present study's introduction.
4 As discussed in chapter 1 and 2, Pius may well have been influenced by Hungarian rhetoric about expelling the Turks from Europe.
5 Shirin A. Khanmohamadi, *In Light of Another's Word: European Ethnography in the Middle Ages* (Philadelphia: University of Pennsylvania Press, 2014).
6 Denys Hay, *Europe: The Emergence of an Idea* (Edinburgh: Edinburgh University Press, 1957), 97–100; Norman Housley, *The Later Crusades: From Lyons to Alcazar 1274–1580* (Oxford: Oxford University Press, 1992).
7 Isabella Walser-Bürgler in her research on Neo-Latin texts similarly notes the enormous scale of such a quantitative and qualitative study (or series of studies) on the concept of Europe in this period. Until that is done, we cannot answer these big questions about who was reading whom and in what way; *Europe and Europeanness in Early Modern Latin Literature: Fuitne Europa tunc unita?* (Leiden: Brill, 2021), 116–17.
8 Walser-Bürgler, *Europe*, 32, 34.
9 See Bisaha, *Creating East and West*, epilogue for more on these writers.
10 John M. Najemy, "Machiavelli Between East and West," in *From Florence to the Mediterranean and Beyond: Essays in Honor of Anthony Molho*, ed. Diogo Ramada Curto, Eric Dursteler, Julius Kirschner, and Francesca Trivellato (Florence: Leo S. Olschki, 2009), 127–46; Marcus Keller, "France, Europe, and the Orient in the *Essays*, Montaigne's Dialectics," in *The Dialectics of Orientalism in Early Modern Europe*, ed. Marcus Keller and Javier Irigoyen-Garcia (London: Palgrave Macmillan, 2018), 121–36. See also Margaret Meserve, *Empires of Islam in Renaissance Historical Thought* (Cambridge, MA: Harvard University Press, 2008).
11 Noel Malcolm, *Useful Enemies: Islam and the Ottoman Empire in Western Political Thought, 1450–1750* (Oxford: Oxford University Press, 2019), 417; John V. Tolan, *Faces of Muhammad: Western Perceptions of the Prophet of Islam from the Middle Ages to Today* (Princeton, NJ: Princeton University Press, 2019).
12 Gilles Veinstein, "The Great Turk and Europe," in *Europe and the Islamic World: A History*, ed. John Tolan, Gilles Veinstein, and Henry Laurens (Princeton: Princeton University Press, 2013), 111–253; Molly Greene, *A Shared World: Christians and Muslims in the Early Modern Mediterranean* (Princeton, NJ: Princeton University Press, 2000); Eric Dursteler, *Renegade Women: Gender, Identity and Boundaries in the Early Modern Mediterranean* (Baltimore: Johns Hopkins University Press, 2011).
13 Pius makes this exact comment in his *Germania*; see chapter 3 above.

14 Vanita Seth, *Europe's Indians: Producing Racial Difference, 1500–1900* (Durham, NC: Duke University Press, 2010), 36 and 58.
15 Malcolm, *Useful Enemies*, 11, 29.
16 See chapter 4 on his oration at Mantua, *Cum bellum hodie* (1459).
17 Michel-Rolph Trouillot, *Silencing the Past: Power and the Production of History* (Boston, MA: Beacon Press, 1995).
18 See Anna Contadini and Claire Norton, eds. *The Renaissance and the Ottoman World* (Burlington, VT: Ashgate, 2013); Walter G. Andrews, and Mehmet Kalpakli, *The Age of Beloveds: Love and the Beloved in Early-Modern Ottoman and European Culture and Society* (Durham: Duke University Press, 2005); Deborah Howard, *Venice and the East: The Impact of the Islamic World on Venetian Architecture 1100–1500* (New Haven: Yale University Press, 2000); Rivka Feldhay and F. Jamil Ragep, eds. *Before Copernicus: The Cultures and Contexts of Scientific Learning in the Fifteenth Century* (Montreal: McGill University Press, 2017).
19 Walser-Bürgler, *Europe and Europeanness*, 80.
20 See Talal Asad, *Formations of the Secular: Christianity, Islam, Modernity* (Stanford, CA: Stanford University Press, 2003).

Bibliography

Works Authored by Pius II

Asia (De Asia, 1461). Edited and translated by Remigio Presenti and Manlio Sodi, introduced by Serge Stolfe, appendix edited by Francesco Dondoli. Rome: IF Press, 2016.

"Audivi" (16 November 1436, Basel). Edited and translated by Michael V. Cotta-Schönberg. Final edition, 2nd version. (Orations of Enea Silvio Piccolomini/Pope Pius II; 1). 2019. ⟨hprints-00683151⟩

Commentaries, vols. 1 and 2. Edited by Margaret Meserve and Marcello Simonetta. Cambridge, MA: Harvard University Press, 2003; 2007.

Commentaries, vol. 3. Edited by Margaret Meserve. Cambridge, MA: Harvard University Press, 2018.

Commentaries of Pius II. Translated by Florence Alden Gragg and edited by Leona C. Gabel. Northampton, MA: Smith College, 1937–1957.

Commentarii rerum memorabilium que temporibus suis contigerunt, vols. 1–2. Edited by Adrian Van Heck. Vatican City: Biblioteca Apostolica Vaticana, 1984.

"Constantinopolitana Clades" of Enea Silvio Piccolomini (15 October 1454, Frankfurt). Edited and translated by Michael von Cotta-Schönberg. 3rd ed.: (Orations of Enea Silvio Piccolomini/Pius II; 19). Ed. and transl. by Michael von Cotta-Schönberg. 2nd ed. 2015. <hal-01097147v3>

Cugnoni, Giuseppe, ed. *Aeneae Silvii Piccolomini Senensis qui postea fuit Pius II Pont. Max., Opera inedita*. Rome: Salviucci, 1883.

"Cum bellum hodie" (26 September 1459, Mantua), Edited and translated by Michael von Cotta-Schönberg. 2nd ed.: (Orations of Enea Silvio Piccolomini/Pope Pius II; 38). 2015. <hal-01184169v2>

De Europa. Edited by Adrian Van Heck. Vatican City: Biblioteca Apostolica Vaticana, 2001.

De gestis concilii Basiliensis commentariorum libri II. Edited by Denys Hay and W.K. Smith. Oxford: Clarendon Press, 1967.

De viris illustribus. Edited by Adrian Van Heck. Vatican City: Biblioteca Apostolica Vaticana, 1991.

Descripción de Asia. Edited and translated by Domingo F. Sanz. Madrid: Consejo Superior de Investigaciones Científicas, 2010.

Epistola ad Mahomatem II (Epistle to Mohammed II). Ed. and tr. Albert R. Baca. New York: Peter Lang, 1990.

Epistola ad Mahumetem. Edited and translated by Reinhold Glei and Markus Köhler. Trier: Wissenschaftlicher Verlag, 2001.

Europe (c. 1400–1458). Translated by Robert Brown. Introduced and annotated by Nancy Bisaha. Washington, DC: Catholic University of America Press, 2013.

"Ezechielis prophetae." In *Opera quae extant omnia*, 914–23. Basel: 1571.

Germania. Edited by Maria Giovanna Fadiga. Florence: SISMEL, 2009.

Historia Bohemica, vols. 1–3. Edited by Joseph Hejnic and Hans Rothe. Cologne: Bohlau Verlag, 2005.

"In hoc florentissimo" of Enea Silvio Piccolomini (25 February 1455, Wiener Neustadt). Orations of Enea Silvio Piccolomini before the pontificate; 18. Edited and translated by Michael von Cotta-Schönberg. 2015. <halshs-01141255v2>

Lettere scritte durante il cardinalato. Edited by Ettore Malnati e Ilaria Romanzin. Brescia: M. Serra Tarantola, 2007; a facsimile of *Enee Siluii Piccolominei qui et Pius Secu[n]dus fuit Epistole in cardinalatu* (Rome, 1475).

Memoirs of a Renaissance Pope: The Commenatries of Pius II, An Abridgement. Translated by Florence A. Gragg and edited by Leona C. Gabel. New York: Capricorn Books, 1962.

"Moyses vir Dei" of Enea Silvio Piccolomini (24 April 1452, Rome). Edited and translated by Michael von Cotta-Schönberg: Orations of Enea Silvio Piccolomini; 14. 2014. <halshs-01064759>

"On the Origin and Authority of the Roman Empire." In *Three Tracts on Empire: Engelbert of Admont, Aeneas Silvius Piccolomini, and Juan de Torquemada*. Translated and edited by Thomas M. Izbicki and Cary J. Nederman, 95–112. Bristol, UK: Thoemmes Press, 2000.

Opera quae extant omnia. Basel: 1571.

Pentalogus. Edited by Christoph Schingnitz. Hannover: Harrassowitz, 2009.

"Quamvis omnibus" (16 May 1454, Regensburg). Edited and translated by Michael von Cotta-Schönberg (Orations of Enea Silvio Piccolomini/Pope Pius II; 16). 2014. <hal-01086738>

Reject Aeneas, Accept Pius: Selected Letters of Aeneas Sylvius Piccolomini (Pope Pius II). Introduced & translated by Thomas M. Izbicki, Gerald Christianson, and Philip Krey. Washington, D.C.: Catholic University of America Press, 2006.

"Res Bohemicas" (1455, Rome). Edited and translated by Michael von Cotta-Schönberg. Preliminary edition, 2nd version. (Orations of Enea Silvio Piccolomini/Pope Pius II; 28). 2015. <hal-01180832>

"Solent plerique" (13 August 1455, Rome). Edited and translated by Michael von Cotta-Schönberg. (Orations of Enea Silvio Piccolomini/Pope Pius II; 21). 2015. <hal-01176055>

"Vocavit nos Pius." In Lodrisio Crivelli, *De Expeditione Pii Papae II*. Edited by Giulio C. Zimolo, in *Rerum Italicarum Scriptores*, New Series, vol. XXIII, pt. V, 91–96. Bologna: Nicola Zanichelli, 1948-50.

Wolkan, Rudolf, ed. *Der Briefwechsel des Eneas Silvius Piccolomini*. In *Fontes Rerum Austriacarum*, ser. 2, vols. 61, 62, 67, 68 (Vienna, 1909-18).

Other Primary Sources

Barbaro, Niccolò. *Diary of the Siege of Constantinople*. Edited and translated by J.R. Jones. New York: Exposition Press, 1969.

Bessarion. *Kardinal Bessarion als Theologe, Humanist und Staatsmann, Fund und Forschungen*. Edited by Ludwig Mohler, vols. 1–3. Paderborn: Ferdinand Schöningh, 1967.

Biondo, Flavio. "Scritti inediti e rari." Edited by Bartolomeo Nogara. In *Studi e testi*, vol. 48. Rome: Tipografia Poliglotta Vaticana, 1927.

Campano, Giovanni Antonio. "Vita Pii Pontificis Maximi." In *Le Vite di Pio II*. Edited by Giulio Zimolo. Bologna: Zanichelli, 1964. (*Rerum Italicarum Scriptores*, vol. 3: part 3, General ed. L.A. Muratori).

Crivelli, Lodrisio. "De Expeditione Pii Papae II." Edited by Giulio C. Zimolo. In *Rerum Italicarum Scriptores*, New Series, vol. XXIII, pt. V. Bologna: Nicola Zanichelli, 1948–50.

Drace-Francis, Alex, ed. *European Identity: A Historical Reader*. Hampshire: Palgrave Macmillan, 2013.

Doukas. *Decline and Fall of Byzantium*. Edited and translated by Harry Magoulias. Detroit: Wayne State University Press, 1975.

Filelfo, Francesco. *Collected Letters, Epistolarum Libri XLVIII*. Edited by Jeroen De Keyser, vols. 1–4. Alessandria: Edizioni dell'Orso, 2015–2017.

Froissart, Jean. *Chronicles*. Translated and edited by Geoffrey Brererton. London: Penguin Press, 1978.

Grund, Gary, ed. and tr. *Humanist Comedies*. Cambridge, MA: Harvard University Press, 2005.

Herodotus. *The Histories*. Translated by Aubrey de Selincourt, revised by John Marincola. New York: Penguin Books, 1972.

Imber, Colin, ed. and tr. *The Crusade of Varna, 1443–1445*. Aldershot: Ashgate, 2006.

Jones, J.R. Melville, ed. and tr. *The Siege of Constantinople 1453: Seven Contemporary Accounts*. Amsterdam: Adolf M. Hakkert, 1972.

Kritovoulos. *The History of Mehmed the Conqueror*. Edited and translated by Charles T. Riggs. Princeton, NJ: Princeton University Press, 1954.

Monfasani, John, ed. *Collectanea Trapezuntiana: Texts, Documents, and Bibliographies of George of Trebizond*. Binghamton, NY: Medieval and Renaissance Texts and Studies, 1984.

Müller, Giuseppe, ed. *Documenti sulle relazioni delle città toscane coll'Oriente cristiano e coi Turchi*. 1879. Reprint, Rome: Società Multigrafica Editrice, 1996.

Pastor, Ludwig, ed. *Ungedruckte Akten zur Geschichte der Päpste*. Freiburg im Breisgau: Herdersche Verlagshandlung, 1904.

Pertusi, Agostino, ed. *La caduta di Costantinopoli*, vols. 1–2. Milan: Arnoldo Mondadori Editore, 1976.

———, ed. *Testi inediti e poco noti sulla caduta di Costantinopoli*. Bologna: Pàtron Editore, 1983.

Peters, Edward, ed. *The First Crusade: The Chronical of Fulcher of Chartres and Other Source Materials*. 2nd ed. Philadelphia: University of Pennsylvania Press, 1998.

Philippides, Marios, ed. and tr. *Mehmed II the Conqueror and the Fall of the Franco-Byzantine Levant to the Ottoman Turks*. Tempe: ACMRS, 2007.

Piccolomini, Iacopo Ammanati. *Lettere (1444–1479)*. Edited by Paolo Cherubini. Rome: Ufficio Centrale per i beni archivistici, 1997.

Platina, Bartolomeo. "Vita Pii Pontificis Maximi." Edited by Giulio Zimolo. In *Le Vite di Pio II*. Bologna: Zanichelli, 1964. (Rerum Italicarum Scriptores, vol. 3: part 3, General ed. L.A. Muratori).

Portable Renaissance Reader. Edited and with an introduction by James Bruce Ross and Mary Martin McLaughlin. New York: Penguin Books, 1981. (1st ed. Viking Press, 1953).

Purchas, Samuel. *Hakluytus posthumus, or Purchas his Pilgrimes: contayning a history of the world in sea voyages and lande travells by Englishmen and others*. Glasgow: J. MacLehose and Sons, 1905–1907.

Quirini, Lauro. *Lauro Quirini umanista*. Edited by Konrad Krautter, Paul Oskar Kristeller, Agostino Pertusi, Giorgio Ravegnani. Helmut Roob, Carlo Seno. Florence: Leo S. Olschki Editore, 1977.

Sphrantzes, George. *The Fall of the Byzantine Empire: A Chronicle by George Sphrantzes 1401–1477*. Translated by Marios Philippides. Amherst: University of Massachusetts Press, 1980.

Strauss, Gerald, ed. and tr. *Manifestations of Discontent in Germany on the Eve of the Reformation*. Bloomington, IN: Indiana University Press, 1985.

Tierney, Brian, ed. *The Crisis of Church and State 1050–1300*. Toronto: University of Toronto Press, 1988.

Tursun, Beg. *History of Mehmed the Conqueror*. Edited and translated by Halil Inalcik. Minneapolis: Bibliotheca Islamica, 1978.

Valla, Lorenzo. *Correspondence*. Translated and edited by Brendan Cook. Cambridge, MA: Harvard University Press, 2013.

Secondary Sources

Ady, Cecilia M. *Pius II: (Aeneas Silvius Piccolomini) The Humanist Pope*. London: Methuen and Co., 1913.

Akbari, Suzanne Conklin. "From Due East to True North." In *Postcolonial Middle Ages*, edited by Jeffery Jerome Cohen. New York: St. Martins Press, 2000.

———. *Idols in the East: European Representations of Islam and the Orient, 1100–1450*. Ithaca: Cornell University Press, 2009.

Albin, Andrew, Mary C. Erler, Thomas O'Donnell, Nicholas L. Paul, Nina Rowe, eds. *Whose Middle Ages: Teachable Moments for an Ill-Used Past*. New York: Fordham University Press, 2019.

Anderson, Benedict. *Imagined Communities: Reflections on the Origin and Spread of Nationalism*. London: Verso, 1983.

Andrews, Walter G. and Mehmet Kalpaklı, *The Age of Beloveds: Love and the Beloved in Early-Modern Ottoman and European Culture and Society*. Durham: Duke University Press, 2005.

Ansary, Tamim. *Destiny Disrupted: A History of the World Through Islamic Eyes*. New York: Public Affairs, 2009.

Antognini, Roberta. *Il progetto autobiografico delle Familiares di Petrarca*. Milan: Edizioni Universitarie di Lettere Economia Diritto, 2008.

Appiah, Kwame Anthony. "There is no such thing as western civilization." *The Guardian*, Nov. 9, 2016. https://www.theguardian.com/world/2016/nov/09/western-civilisation-appiah-reith-lecture

———. "Muslims and European Identity." In *The Idea of Europe From Antiquity to the European Union*, edited by Anthony Pagden, 209–27. Cambridge: Cambridge University Press, 2002.

Asad, Talal. *Formations of the Secular: Christianity, Islam, Modernity*. Stanford, CA: Stanford University Press, 2003.

Atçıl, Abdurrahman. *Scholars and Sultans in the Early Modern Ottoman Empire*. Cambridge: Cambridge University Press, 2017.

Babinger, Franz. *Mehmed the Conqueror and This Time*. Translated by Ralph Manheim. 1953; tr. Rev. ed., Princeton, NJ: Princeton University Press, 1978.

Baldi, Barbara. "Enea Silvio Piccolomini e il *De Europa*: umanesimo, religione e politica." *Archivio Storico Italiano* 598 (2003): 619–83.

———. *Pio II e la trasformazione dell'Europa cristiana, 1457–1464*. Milan: Unicopli, 2006.

———. "Il problema Turco dalla caduta di Costantinopoli (1453) alla morte di Pio II (1464)." In *La Conquista Turca di Otranto*, edited by Hubert Houben. Galatina, 2008, vol. 1, 55–76.

———. "Un umanista alla corte di Federico III. Il Pentalogus di Enea Silvio Piccolomini." *Cahiers d'études italiennes* 13 (2011): 161–71. http://cei.revues.org/85?lang=en

———. *Il "cardinale tedesco": Enea Silvio Piccolomini fra impero, papato, Europa (1442–1455)*. Milan: Edizioni Unicopli, 2012.

Baker, Patrick. *Italian Renaissance Humanism in the Mirror*. Cambridge: Cambridge University Press, 2015.

Baron, Hans. *The Crisis of the Early Italian Renaissance Civic Humanism and Republican Liberty in an Age of Classicism and Tyranny*. Princeton, NJ: Princeton University Press, 1966.

Bartlett, Robert. *The Making of Europe: Conquest, Colonization and Cultural Change 950–1350*. Princeton, NJ: Princeton University Press, 1993.

———. "Medieval and Modern Concepts of Race." *Journal of Medieval and Early Modern Studies* 31, no. 1 (Winter 2001): 39–56.

Basten, Harry. "'Nationis Teutonicae': The German Nation and the Holy Roman Empire through the eyes of an Italian humanist." Master's thesis, Leiden University, 2016.

Bernstein, Eckhard. *German Humanism*. Boston: Tayne, Publishers, 1983.

Biechler, James E. "A New Face Toward Islam: Nicholas of Cusa and John of Segovia." In *Nicholas of Cusa in Search of God and Wisdom*, edited by Gerald Christianson and Thomas M. Izbicki. Leiden: E.J. Brill, 1991.

Biow, Douglas. *Doctors, Ambassadors, and Secretaries: Humanism and Professions in Renaissance Italy*. Chicago: University of Chicago Press, 2002.

Bisaha, Nancy. "Petrarch's Vision of the Muslim and Byzantine East." *Speculum* 76, no. 2 (2001): 284–314.

———. "Pius II's Letter to Sultan Mehmed II: A Reexamination." *Crusades* 1 (2002): 183–200.

———. *Creating East and West: Renaissance Humanists and the Ottoman Turks*. Philadelphia: University of Pennsylvania Press, 2004a.

———. "Pope Pius II and the Crusade." In *Crusading in the Fifteenth Century: Message and Impact*, edited by Norman Housley, 39–52. New York: Palgrave Macmillan, 2004b.

———. "'Discourses of Power and Desire': The Letters of Aeneas Silvius Piccolomini (1453)." In *Florence and Beyond: Culture, Society, and Politics in Renaissance Italy*, edited by David Peterson and Daniel Bornstein, 121–34. Toronto: Centre for Reformation and Renaissance Studies, 2008.

———. "European Cross-Cultural Contexts Before Copernicus." In *Before Copernicus: The Cultures and Contexts of Scientific Learning in the Fifteenth Century*, edited by Rivka Feldhay and F. Jamil Ragep, 29–41. Montreal: McGill University Press, 2017a.

———. "Reactions to the Fall of Constantinople." In *The Routledge Handbook of Christian-Muslim Relations*, edited by David Thomas, 219–26. New York: Routledge, 2017b.

————. "Reactions to the Fall of Constantinople and the Concept of Human Rights." In *Reconfiguring the Fifteenth-Century Crusade*, edited by Norman Housley, 285–324. London: Palgrave Macmillan, 2017c.

Black, Antony . *The West and Islam*. Oxford: Oxford University Press, 2008.

Black, Robert. *Benedetto Accolti and the Florentine Renaissance*. Cambridge: Cambridge University Press, 1985.

Black, Robert, ed. *Renaissance Thought: A Reader*. London: Routledge, 2001.

Black, Jeremy. *Maps and History: Constructing Images of the Past*. New Haven, CT: Yale University Press, 1997.

Bonfil, Robert. *Jewish Life in Renaissance Italy*. Translated by Anthony Oldcorn. Berkeley: University of California Press, 1994.

Bottici, Chiara and Benoit Challand. *Imagining Europe: Myth, Memory and Identity*. Cambridge: Cambridge University Press, 2013.

Boulting, William. *Aeneas Silvius (Enea Silvio de' Piccolomini—Pius II)*. London: Archibald Constable and Co., Ltd. 1908.

Boyar, Ebru and Kate Fleet. *A Social History of Ottoman Istanbul*. Cambridge: Cambridge University Press, 2010.

Brady Jr., Thomas A. *German Histories in Age of Reformations, 1400–1650*. Cambridge: Cambridge University Press, 2009.

Brann, Noel. "Humanism in Germany." In *Renaissance Humanism: Foundations, Forms and Legacy*, edited by Albert Rabil, vol. 2, 123–55. Philadelphia: University of Pennsylvania Press, 1988.

Brummett, Palmira. "The Lepanto Paradigm Revisited: Knowing the Ottomans in the Sixteenth Century." In *The Renaissance and the Ottoman World*, edited by Anna Contadini and Claire Norton, 63–93. Burlington, VT: Ashgate, 2013.

————. *Mapping the Ottomans: Sovereignty, Territory, and Identity in the Early Modern Mediterranean*. Cambridge: Cambridge University Press, 2015.

Burke, Peter. "Did Europe Exist Before 1700?" *History of European Ideas* 1, no. 1 (1980): 21–29.

Burman, Thomas E. *Reading the Qur'an in Latin Christendom, 1140–1560*. Philadelphia: University of Pennsylvania Press, 2007.

Cahen, Claude. *Pre-Ottoman Turkey: A General Survey of the Material and Spiritual Culture and History, c. 1071–1330*. Translated from the French by J. Jones-Williams. New York: Taplinger Publishing Co., 1968.

Calzona, Arturo, Francesca Paolo Fiore, Alberto Tenenti, Cesare Vasoli, eds. *Il Sogno di Pio II e il viaggio da Roma a Mantova*. Florence: Leo S. Olschki, 2003.

Campopiano, Michele, and Henry Bainton, eds. *Universal Chronicles in the High Middle Ages*. Writing History in the Middle Ages. York: York Medieval Press, 2017.

Cardini, Franco. "La repubblica di Firenze, e la crociata di Pio II." *Rivista storica della chiesa in Italia* 33 (1979): 455–82.

————. *L'Invenzione dell' Occidente*. Chieti: Marino Solfanelli Editore, 1995.

Casella, Nicola. "Pio II tra geografia e storia: la *Cosmographia*." *Archivio della Società romana di storia patria* 95 (1972): 35–112.

————. "Enea Silvio a difesa dell'Occidente Cristiano." In *Enea Silvio Piccolomini: Unomo lettere e mediatore di culture, Gelehrter und Vermittler der Kulturen*, edited by Maria Antonietta Terzoli, 55–68. Basel: Schwab Verlag, 2006.

Castner, Catherine J. "The *Fortuna* of Biondo Flavio's *Italia Illustrata*." In *A New Sense of the Past: The Scholarship of Biondo Flavio (1392–1463)*, edited by Angelo Mazzocco and Marc Laureys, 177–95. Leuven: Leuven University Press, 2016.

Celenza, Christopher. *The Lost Italian Renaissance: Humanists, Historians, and Latin's Legacy*. Baltimore, Md: Johns Hopkins University Press, 2004.

Celenza, Christopher. *Renaissance Humanism and the Papal Curia: Lapo da Castiglionchio the Younger's "De curiae commodis"*. Ann Arbor, MI: University of Michigan Press, 1999.

————. "What Did It Mean to Live in the Long Fifteenth Century?" In *Before Copernicus: The Cultures and Contexts of Scientific Learning in the Fifteenth Century*, edited by Rivka Feldhay and F. Jamil Ragep, 17–28. Montreal: McGill University Press, 2017.

Chabod, Federico. *Storia dell'idea d'Europa*. 1961. Rev. ed. by Ernest Sestan and Armando Saitta, 4th edition. Rome: Edizioni Laterza, 2001.

Chambers, D.S. *Popes, Cardinals and War*. London: I.B. Tauris & Co., 2006.

Chazan, Robert. *European Jewry and the First Crusade*. Berkeley, CA: University of California Press, 1987.

Chevedden, Paul. "The View of the Crusades from Rome and Damascus: The Geo-Strategic and Historical Perspectives of Pope Urban II and ʿAlī ibn Ṭāhir al-Su-lamī." *Oriens* 39 (2011): 257–329.

Clough, Cecil. "The Chancery Letter-files of Aeneas Silvius Piccolomini." In *Enea Silvio Piccolomini Papa Pio II*, edited by Domenico Maffei, 117–131. Siena: Varese, 1968.

Cochrane, Eric. *Historians and Historiography in the Italian Renaissance*. Chicago: University of Chicago Press, 1981.

Cole, Juan. *Muhammad, Prophet of Peace Amid the Clash of Empires*. New York: Nation Books, 2018.

Contadini, Anna and Claire Norton, eds. *The Renaissance and the Ottoman World*. Burlington, VT: Ashgate, 2013.

Contadini, Anna. "Sharing a Taste? Material Culture and Intellectual Curiosity Around the Mediterranean, From the Eleventh to the Sixteenth Century." In *The Renaissance and the Ottoman World*, edited by Anna Contadini and Claire Norton, 23–62. Burlington, VT: Ashgate, 2013.

Crouzet, Denis, Elisabeth Crouzet-Pavan, Philippe Desan, and Clémence Revest, eds. *L'humanisme à l'épreuve de 'Europe (xvᵉ- xviᵉ siècle)*. Ceyzérieu: Champs Vallon, 2019.

Dakhlia, Jocelyne, and Bernard Vincent, eds. *Les Musulmans dans l'histoire de l'Europe I. Une integration invisible*. Paris: Albin Michel, 2011.

Dalché, Patrick Gautier. "Strabo's Reception in the West (Fifteenth-Sixteenth Centuries)." In *The Routledge Companion to Strabo*, edited by Daniela Dueck, 367–83. London: Routledge, 2017.

Darling, Linda. "The Renaissance and the Middle East." In *A Companion to the Worlds of the Renaissance*, edited by Guido Ruggiero, 55–69. Oxford: Blackwell Publishing, 2002.

Dávid, Géza and Pál Fodor. *Ransom Slavery Along the Ottoman Borders*. Leiden: Brill, 2007.

Delanty, Gerard. *Inventing Europe: Idea, Identity, Reality*. London: Palgrave Macmillan, 1995.

Detering, Nicolas, Clementina Marsico, Isabella Walser-Bürgler, eds. *Contesting Europe: Comparative Perspectives on Early Modern Discourses on Europe, 1400–1800*. Leiden: Brill, 2020.

DeVries, Kelly. *Guns and Men in Medieval Europe 1200–1500*. Aldershot: Ashgate, 2002.

Di Paola, Roberta, Arianna Antoniutti, and Marco Gallo, eds. *Enea Silvio Piccolomini: Arte, Storia e Cultura nell'Europa di Pio II*. Rome: Libreria Editrice Vaticana, 2006.

Drozdiak, William. *Fractured Continent: Europe's Crises and the Fate of the West*. New York: W.W. Norton, 2017.

Dursteler, Eric. "Language and Gender in the Early Modern Mediterranean." *Renaissance Quarterly* 75, no. 1 (Spring, 2022): 1–45.

———. *Venetians in Constantinople: Nation, Identity, and Coexistence in the early Modern Mediterranean*. Baltimore, MD: Johns Hopkins University Press, 2006.

———. *Renegade Women: Gender, Identity and Boundaries in the Early Modern Mediterranean*. Baltimore: Johns Hopkins University Press, 2011.

Earle, T.F. and Kate Lowe, eds. *Black Africans in Renaissance Europe*. Cambridge: Cambridge University Press, 2005.

Elden, Stuart. *The Birth of Territory*. Chicago: University of Chicago Press, 2013.

Eliav-Feldon, Miriam, Benjamin Isaac, and Joseph Ziegler, eds. *The Origins of Racism in the West*. Cambridge: Cambridge University Press, 2009.

Elukin, Jonathan M. *Living Together, Living Apart: Rethinking Jewish-Christian Relations in the Middle Ages*. Princeton, NJ: Princeton University Press, 2007.

Enenkel, Karl. "Landeskunde als Politische Argumentation: Enea Silvio Piccolominis *De Europa*." In *Monumenta Illustrata Raumwissen und antiquarische Gelehrsamkeit*, edited by Dietrich Boschung and Alfred Schäfer, 13–43. Leiden: Wilhelm Fink, 2019.

Fadiga, Maria. "*L'Hist Bohemica*: la genesi di un'idea?" In *Il Ritorna dei classici nell'umanesimo: Studi in memoria di Gianvito Resta*, edited by Gabriella Albanese, Claudio Ciociola, Mariarosa Cortesi, and Claudia Villa, 245–55. Florence: Sismel, 2015.

Feldhay, Rivka and F. Jamil Ragep, eds. *Before Copernicus: The Cultures and Contexts of Scientific Learning in the Fifteenth Century*. Montreal: McGill University Press, 2017.

Ferguson, Niall. *Civilization: The West and the Rest*. New York: Penguin University Press, 2011.

Fine, John V.A. *Late Medieval Balkans*. Ann Arbor: University of Michigan Press, 1987.

François, Etienne and Thomas Serrier, eds. *The European Way Since Homer: History, Memory, and Identity*. London: Bloomsbury Academic, 2021.

Freedman, Paul. "The Medieval Other." In *Marvels, Monsters, and Miracles*, edited by Timothy S. Jones and David Sprunger, 1–24. Kalamazoo, MI: Medieval Institute Publications, 2002.

Freely, John. *The Grand Turk: Sultan Mehmet II—Conqueror of Constantinople and Master of an Empire*. New York: Overlook Press, 2009.

Friedman, John Block, *The Monstrous Races in Medieval Art and Thought*, 2nd ed. Syracuse, NY: Syracuse University Press, 2000.

Fubini, Riccardo, "The Italian League and the Policy of the Balance of Power at the Accession of Lorenzo de' Medici." *Journal of Modern History* 67, no. supplement (December 1995): S166–99.

———. *Humanism and Secularization*. Durham, NC: Duke University Press, 2003.

———. "Enea Silvio Piccolomini nei suoi rapporti con la cultura umanistica del tempo." In *Pio II Piccolomini: il Papa del Rinascimento a Siena*, edited by Fabrizio Nevola, 131–50. Siena: Protagon Editore, 2009.

Fudge, Thomas A. "Seduced by the Theologians: Aeneas Sylvius and the Hussite Heretics." In *Heresy in Transition: Transforming Ideas of Heresy in Medieval and Early Modern Europe*, edited by Ian Hunter, John C. Laursen, Cary J. Nederman, 89–101. Aldershot, UK: Ashgate, 2005.

———. "'O Cursed Judas': Formal Heresy Accusations Against Jan Hus." In *Religion, Power, and Resistance From the Eleventh to the Sixteenth Centuries: Playing the Heresy Card*, edited by Karen Bollermann, Thomas M. Izbicki, and Cary J. Nederman, 55–80. New York: Palgrave Macmillan, 2014.

Gaeta, Franco. "Sulla 'Lettera a Maometto' di Pio II." *Bulletino dell'Istituo storico italiano per medioevo e archivio muratoriano* 77 (1965): 127–227.

Garin, Eugenio. *Portraits of the Quattrocento*. Translated by A. Victor and Elizabeth Velen. New York: Harper and Row, 1972.

Geary, Patrick J. "What Happened to Latin?" *Speculum* 84: 4 (Oct. 2009): 859–873.

Geary, Patrick J. *The Myth of Nations: The Medieval Origins of Europe*. Princeton, NJ: Princeton University Press, 2002.

Giustiniani, Vito. "Gli umanisti Italiani e la Germania." In *Pio II e la cultura del suo tempo*, edited by Luisa Rotondi Secchi Tarugi, 229–41. Milan: Guerini e Associati, 1991.

Glendinning, Robert. "Love, Death, and the Art of Compromise: Aeneas Sylvius Piccolomini's *Tale of Two Lovers*." *Fifteenth Century Studies* 23 (1996): 101–20.

Goffman, Daniel. *The Ottoman Empire and Early Modern Europe*. Cambridge, UK: Cambridge University Press, 2002.

Gould, Evlyn and George Sheridan, eds. *Engaging Europe: Rethinking a Changing Continent*, Lanham, MD: Rowman and Littlefield, 2005.

Gouwens, Kenneth. "Perceiving the Past: Renaissance Humanism After the 'Cognitive Turn.'" *American Historical Review* 103, no. 1 (1998): 55–82.

Grafton, Anthony, April Shelford, and Nancy Siraisi. *New Worlds, Ancient Texts: The Power of Tradition and the Shock of Discovery*. Cambrdige, MA: Belknap Press, 1992.

Grafton, Anthony. "The Winged Eye at Work: Leon Battista Alberti Surveys Old Saint Peter's." *Renaissance Quarterly* 73, no. 4 (2020 [2021]): 1137–78.

Gray, Hanna. "Renaissance Humanism: The Pursuit of Eloquence." *Journal of the History of Ideas* 24 (1963): 497–514.

Greenblatt, Stephen. *Marvelous Possessions: The Wonder of the New World*. Chicago: Chicago University Press, 1991.

———. *The Swerve: How the World Became Modern*. New York: W.W. Norton and Co., 2011.

Greene, Molly. *A Shared World: Christians and Muslims in the Early Modern Mediterranean*. Princeton, NJ: Princeton University Press, 2000.

Grendler, Paul F. *Universities of the Italian Renaissance*. Baltimore: Johns Hopkins University Press, 2002.

Groebner, Valentin. "The carnal knowledge of a coloured body: sleeping with Arabs and Blacks in the European Imagination, 1300–1550." In *The Origins of Racism in the West*, edited by Miriam Eliav-Feldon, Benjamin Isaac, and Joseph Ziegler, 217–31. Cambridge: Cambridge University Press, 2009.

Gruen, Erich S., ed. *Cultural Identity in Ancient Mediterranean*. Los Angeles: Getty Research Institute, 2011.

Gusejnova, Dina and Charles West. "European History And 'Eurocentrism'—A Conversation Between Dina Gusejnova (LSE) and Charles West (Sheffield)." *History Matters: History brought alive by the University of Sheffield*. May 12, 2021. http://www.historymatters.group.shef.ac.uk/eurocentrism-conversation/

Halff, Maarten. "Did Cusanus Talk With Muslims? Revisiting Cusanus' Sources for the Cribratio Alkorani and Interfaith Dialogue." *Revista Española de Filosofia Medieval* 26, no. 1 (2019): 29–58.

Hale, John R. *Civilization of Europe in the Renaissance*. New York: Atheneum, 1994.

Hankins, James. "Renaissance Crusaders: Humanist Crusade Literature in the Age of Mehmed II." *Dumbarton Oaks Papers* 49 (1995): 111–207.

Harris, Jonathan. *Constantinople: Capital of Byzantium*. London: Hambledon Continuum, 2007.

Hastings, Adrian. *The Construction of Nationhood: Ethnicity, Religion, and Nationalism*. Cambridge: Cambridge University Press, 1997.

Hay, Denys. *Europe: The Emergence of an Idea*. Edinburgh: Edinburgh University Press, 1957.

Held, Joseph. *Hunyadi: Legend and Reality*. Boulder: East European Monographs, 1985.

Helmrath, Johannes. *Das Basler Konzil, 1431–1449*. Cologne: Böhlau Verlag, 1987.

———. "Pius II. und die Türken." In *Europa und die Türken in der Renaissance*, edited by Bodo Guthmüller and Wilhelm Kühlmann, 79–138. Tübingen: Max Niemeyer, Verlag, 2000.

———. "The German *Reichstage* and the Crusade." In *Crusading in the Fifteenth Century, Message and Impact*, edited by Norman Housley, 53–69. New York: Palgrave Macmillan, 2004.

———. "Enea Silvio Piccolomini (Pius II.) - Ein Humanist als Vater des Europagedankens?" In *Themenportal Europäische Geschichte*, 361–69, 2007. www.europa.clio-online.de/essay/id/fdae-1327

———. "Political-Assembly Speeches, German Diets, and Aeneas Sylvius Piccolomini." In *Beyond Reception: Renaissance Humanism and the Transformation of Classical Antiquity*, edited by Patrick Baker, Johannes Helmrath, and Craig Kallendorf, 71–94. Berlin: De Gruyter, 2019.

Heng, Geraldine. *The Invention of Race in the European Middle Ages*. Cambridge: Cambridge University Press, 2018.

Hirschi, Caspar. *The Origins of Nationalism: An Alternative History From Ancient Rome to Modern Germany*. Cambridge: Cambridge University Press, 2012.

Holt, Andrew. "Crusading Against Barbarians: Muslims as Barbarians in Crusade Era Sources." In *East Meets West in the Middle Ages and Early Modern Times*, edited by Albrecht Classen, 443–56. Berlin: Walter De Gruyter, 2013.

Horden, Peregrine and Sharon Kinoshita, eds. *A Companion to Mediterranean History*, ed. Malden, MA: Wiley Blackwell, 2014.

Horsfall, Nicholas. *Virgil, Aeneid 3: A Commentary*. Leiden: Brill, 2006.

Housley, Norman. *The Later Crusades: From Lyons to Alcazar 1274–1580*. Oxford: Oxford University Press, 1992.

———. *Religious Warfare in Europe, 1400–1536*. Oxford: Oxford University Press, 2002.

———. *Crusading in the Fifteenth Century, Message and Impact*. New York: Palgrave Macmillan, 2004.

———. *Crusading and the Ottoman Threat, 1453–1505*. Oxford: Oxford University Press, 2012a.

———. "Pope Pius II and Crusading." *Crusades* 11 (2012b): 209–47.

———. "Aeneas Silvius Piccolomini, Nicholas of Cusa, and the Crusade: Conciliar, Imperial, and Papal Authority." *Church History* 86, no. 3 (Sept., 2017): 643–67.

Howard, Deborah. *Venice and the East: The Impact of the Islamic World on Venetian Architecture 1100–1500*. New Haven: Yale University Press, 2000.

Hunt, Lynn. *History: Why it Matters*. Cambridge: Polity Press, 2018.

Imber, Colin. *Ottoman Empire, 1300–1650: The Structure of Power*. Hampshire: Palgrave Macmillan, 2002.

Isaac, Benjamin. "Racism: A Rationalization of Prejudice in Greece and Rome." In *The Origins of Racism in the West*, edited by Miriam Eliav-Feldon, Benjamin Isaac, and Joseph Ziegler, 32–56. Cambridge: Cambridge University Press, 2009.

Isom-Verhaaren, Christine. *Allies With the Infidel: The Ottoman and French Alliance in the Sixteenth Century*. London: IB Tauris, 2011.

Itkowitz, Norman. *The Ottoman Empire and Islamic Tradition*. Chicago: University of Chicago Press, 1972.

Izbicki, Thomas M. *Protector of the Faith: Cardinal Johannes de Turrecremata and the Defense of the Institutional Church*. Washington, DC: Catholic University of America Press, 1981.

———. "'Reject Aeneas!' Pius II on the Errors of His Youth." In *Pius II: 'El Più Expeditivo Pontifice: Selected Studies on Aeneas Silvius Piccolomini*, edited by Zweder Von Martels and Arjo Vanderjagt, 187–204. Leiden: Brill, 2003.

———. "The Missing Anti-pope: The Rejection of Felix V and the Council of Basel in the Writings of Aeneas Sylvius Piccolomini and the Piccolomini Library." *Viator* 41, no. 1 (2009): 301–14.

———. "Badgering for Books: Aeneas Sylvius Piccolomini and Leonardo Bruni's Translation of Aristotle's *Politics*." In *Essays in Renaissance Thought and Letters in Honor of John Monfasani*, edited by Alison Frazier and Patrick Nold, 12–22. Leiden: Brill, 2015.

Jensen, Janus Møller. *Denmark and the Crusades 1400–1650*. Leiden: Brill, 2007.

Joachimsen, Paul. "Humanism and the Development of the German Mind." In *Pre-Reformation Germany*, edited by Gerald Strauss, 162–224. New York: Palgrave Macmillan, 1972.

Jordan, William Chester. "Why "Race"?" *Journal of Medieval and Early Modern Studies*, 31, no. 1 (Winter 2001): 165–73.

———. "Europe' in the Middle Ages." In *The Idea of Europe from Antiquity to the European Union*, edited by Anthony Pagden, 72–90. Cambridge: Cambridge University Press, 2002.

Kafadar, Cemal. "The Ottomans and Europe." In *Handbook of European History 1400–1600*, vol. 1, edited by Thomas A. Brady, Jr., Heiko A. Oberman, James D. Tracy, 589–636. Leiden: Brill, 1994.

———. *Between Two Worlds: The Construction of the Ottoman State*. Berkeley: University of California Press, 1995.

———. "A Death in Venice (1575): Anatolian Muslim Merchants Trading in the Serenissima." In *Merchant Networks in the Early Modern World*, edited by Sanjay Subrahmanyam, 97–124. Aldershot: Variorum, 1996.

Kaminsky, Howard. "Pius Aeneas Among the Taborites." *Church History* 28, no. 3 (1959): 281–309.

Kaplan, Paul. "'Black Turks': Venetian Perceptions of Ottoman Ethnicity." In *The Turk and Islam in the Western Eye 1450–1750*, edited by James G. Harper, 44–55. Burlington, VT: Ashgate, 2011.

Kedar, Benjamin Z. *Crusade and Mission: European Approaches Toward the Muslims*. Princeton, NJ: Princeton University Press, 1984.

Kedar, Benjamin. "The Jerusalem Massacre of 1099 in Western Historiography of the Crusades," *Crusades* 3 (2004): 15–75.

Keller, Marcus. "France, Europe, and the Orient in the *Essays*: Montaigne's Dialectics." In *The Dialectics of Orientalism in Early Modern Europe*, edited by Marcus Keller and Javier Irigoyen-Garcia, 121–36. London: Palgrave Macmillan, 2018.

Khanmohamadi, Shirin A. *In Light of Another's Word: European Ethnography in the Middle Ages*. Philadelphia: University of Pennsylvania Press, 2014.

Kia, Mehrdad. *Daily Life in the Ottoman Empire*. Santa Barbara: Greenwood Press, 2011.

Kikuchi, Catherine. "Des humanists italiens au-delà des Alpes des imprimés voyageurs entre le xve et le début du xvie siècle." In *L'humanisme à l'épreuve de 'Europe (xve- xvie siècle)*, edited by Denis Crouzet, Elisabeth Crouzet-Pavan, Philippe Desan, Clémence Revest, 41–58. Ceyzérieu: Champs Vallon, 2019.

Kisch, Guido. "Enea Silvio Piccolomini e la giurisprudenza." In *Enea Silvio Piccolomini Papa Pio II*, edited by Domenico Maffei, 195–97. Siena: Varese, 1968.

Kraye, Jill, ed., *Renaissance Humanism*. Cambridge: Cambridge University Press, 1996.

Krebs, Christopher B. "Borealism: Caesar, Seneca, Tacitus, and the Roman Discourse About the Germanic North." In *Cultural Identity in the Ancient Mediterranean*, edited by Erich S. Gruen, 202–21. Los Angeles: Getty Research Institute, 2011a.

———. *A Most Dangerous Book: Tacitus's Germania, From the Roman Empire to the Third Reich*. New York: W.W. Norton & Co., 2011b.

Kristeller, Paul Oskar and L.D. Reynolds. *Renaissance Thought: The Classic, Scholastic, and Humanistic Strains*. 1955. Reprint. New York: Harper and Row, 1961.

Kristeller, Paul Oskar. "Tacitus." In *Texts and Transmission: A Survey of Latin Classics*, edited by L.D. Reynolds, et al. Oxford: Clarendon Press, 1983.

Langmuir, Gavin. *Toward a Definition of Antisemitism*. Los Angeles: Center for Medieval and Renaissance Studies, 1990.

Lausberg, Heinrich. *Handbook of Literary Rhetoric: A Foundation for Literary Study*, edited by David E. Orton and R. Dean Anderson; Translated by Matthew T. Bliss, Annemiek Jansen, David E. Orton. Leiden: Brill, 1998.

Le Goff, Jacques. *The Birth of Europe*. Translated by Janet Lloyd. Malden, MA: Blackwell, 2005.

Lines, David. "Humanism and the Italian Universities." In *Humanism and Creativity in the Renaissance*, edited by Christopher Celenza and Kenneth Gouwens, 327–46. Leiden: Brill, 2006.

Lowe, Kate. "Visible Lives: Black Gondoliers and Other Black Africans in Renaissance Venice." *Renaissance Quarterly* 66, no. 2 (Summer 2013): 412–52.

Lowry, Heath W. "The 'Soup Muslims' of the Ottoman Balkans: Was There a 'Western' and 'Eastern' Ottoman Empire?" In *Beyond Dominant Paradigms in Ottoman and Middle Eastern/North African Studies: A Tribute to Rifa'at Abou-El-Haj*, edited by Donald Quataert and Baki Tezcan, 97–133. Istanbul: ISAM, 2010.

Maffei, Domenico, ed. *Enea Silvio Piccolomini Papa Pio II*. Siena: Varese, 1968.

Malcolm, Noel. *Useful Enemies: Islam and the Ottoman Empire in Western Political Thought, 1450–1750*. Oxford: Oxford University Press, 2019.

Mallet, Michael E. *The Borgias: The Rise and Fall of a Renaissance Dynasty*. New York: Barnes & Noble: 1969.

Martines, Lauro. *The Social World of the Florentine Humanists 1390–1460*. Princeton: Princeton University Press, 1963.

Matar, Nabil. *Europe Through Arab Eyes, 1578–1727*. New York: Columbia University Press, 2009.

Matar, Nabil, ed. and tr. *Lands of the Christians: Arabic Travel Writing in the Seventeenth Century*. New York: Routledge, 2003.

Mattingly, Garrett. *Renaissance Diplomacy*. 1955. Reprint. New York: Dover Publications, 1988.

Mauro, Thomas J. *"Praeceptor Austriae*: Aeneas Sylvius Piccolomini (Pius II) and the Transalpine Diffusion of Italian Humanism Before Erasmus." PhD diss., University of Chicago, 2003.

Mazzocco, Angelo and Marc Laureys, eds. *A New Sense of the Past: The Scholarship of Biondo Flavio (1392–1463)*. Leuven: Leuven University Press, 2016.

Mazzocco, Angelo. "Rome and the Humanists: The Case of Biondo Flavio." In *Rome in the Renaissance: The City and the Myth*, edited by P.A. Ramsey, 185–95. Binghamton, NY: Center for Medieval and Early Renaissance Studies, 1982.

McCahill, Elizabeth. *Reviving the Eternal City: Rome and the Papal Court, 1420–1447*. Cambridge, MA: Harvard University Press, 2013.

Merrell, James H. "Second Thoughts on Colonial Historians and American Indians." *William and Mary Quarterly* 69, no. 3 (July 2012): 451–512.

Meserve, Margaret. "From Samarkand to Scythia: Reinventions of Asia in Renaissance Geography and Political Thought." In *Pius II: 'El Più Expeditivo Pontifice: Selected Studies on Aeneas Silvius Piccolomini*, edited by Zweder Von Martels and Arjo Vanderjagt, 13–40. Leiden: Brill, 2003.

———. "Italian Humanists and the Problem of Crusade." In *Crusading in the Fifteenth Century, Message and Impact*, edited by Norman Housley, 13–38. New York: Palgrave Macmillan, 2004.

———.*Empires of Islam in Renaissance Historical Thought*. Cambridge, MA: Harvard University Press, 2008.

———. "Nestor Denied: Francesco Filelfo's Advice to Princes on the Crusade Against the Turks." *Osiris* 25, no. 1: 47–65.

Milligan, Gerry. *Moral Combat: Women, Gender, and War in Italian Renaissance Literature*. Toronto: University of Toronto Press, 2018.

Minnich, Nelson. "The Catholic Church and the pastoral care of black Africans in Renaissance Italy." In *Black Africans in Renaissance Europe*, edited by T.F. Earle and Kate Lowe, 280–300. Cambridge: Cambridge University Press, 2005.

de Miramon, Charles. "Noble dogs, noble blood: the invention of the concept of race in the late Middle Ages." In *The Origins of Racism in the West*, edited by Miriam Eliav-Feldon, Benjamin Isaac, and Joseph Ziegler, 200–16. Cambridge: Cambridge University Press, 2009.

Mitchell, R.J. *The Laurels and the Tiara: Pope Pius II 1458–64*. New York: Doubleday and Co., 1962.

Molho, Anthony, Diogo Ramada Curto, and Niki Koniordos, ed. *Finding Europe: Discourses on the Margins, Communities, Images, ca. 13th–18th Centuries*. New York: Bergahn Books, 2007.

Monfasani, John. *George of Trebizond: A Biography and a Study of His Rhetoric and Logic*. Leiden: E.J. Brill, 1976.

Montecalvo, Rolando. "Between Empire and Papacy: Aeneas Silvius and German Regional Historiography." PhD diss., University of California, Berkeley, 2000.

———. "The New *Landesgeschichte*: Aeneas Silvius Piccolomini on Austria and Bohemia." In *Pius II: 'El Più Expeditivo Pontifice: Selected Studies on Aeneas Silvius Piccolomini*, edited by Zweder Von Martels and Arjo Vanderjagt, 55–86. Leiden: Brill, 2003.

Musumeci, Antonio. "L'epistolario di Enea Silvio Piccolomini: il discorso sulla letteratura." In *Pio II e la cultura del suo tempo*, edited by Luisa Rotondi Secchi Tarugi, 373–93. Milan: Guerini e Associati, 1991.

Najemy, John. *Between Friends: Discourses of Power and Desire in the Machiavelli-Vettori Letters of 1513–1515*. Princeton, NJ: Princeton University Press, 1993.

————. "Arms and Letters: The Crisis of Courtly Culture in the Wars of Italy." In *Italy and the European Powers: The Impact of War, 1500–1530*, edited by Christine Shaw, 207–38. Leiden: Brill, 2006.

————. "Machiavelli Between East and West." In *From Florence to the Mediterranean and Beyond: Essays in Honor of Anthony Molho*, edited by Diogo Ramada Curto, Eric Dursteler, Julius Kirschner, and Francesca Trivellato, 127–46. Florence: Leo S. Olschki, 2009.

Nardi, Paolo. "Enea Silvio Piccolomini e lo *Studium* di Siena nel terzo decennio Quattrocento." In *Pio II Piccolomini: il Papa del Rinascimento a Siena*, edited by Fabrizio Nevola, 151–66. Siena: Protagon Editore, 2009.

Nederman, Cary. "Humanism and Empire: Aeneas Sylvius Piccolomini, Cicero, and the Imperial Ideal." *The Historical Journal* 36 no. 3 (Sept. 1993): 499–515.

Nevola, Fabrizio, *Siena: Constructing the Renaissance City*. New Haven, CT: Yale University Press, 2007.

————. ed. *Pio II Piccolomini: il Papa del Rinascimento a Siena*. Siena: Protagon Editore, 2009.

Nicol, Donald. *The Immortal Emperor: The Life and Legend of Constantine Palaiologos, Last Emperor of the Romans*. Cambridge: Cambridge University Press, 1992.

————. *The Byzantine Lady: Ten Portraits 1250–1500*. Cambridge: Cambridge University Press, 1994.

Nirenberg, David. *Communities of Violence: Persecution of Minorities in the Middle Ages*. Princeton, NJ: Princeton University Press, 1996.

————. "Was there race before modernity? The example of 'Jewish' blood in late medieval Spain." In *The Origins of Racism in the West*, edited by Miriam Eliav-Feldon, Benjamin Isaac, and Joseph Ziegler, 232–64. Cambridge: Cambridge University Press, 2009.

Norton, Claire. "Blurring the Boundaries: Intellectual and Cultural Interactions Between the Eastern and Western; Christian and Muslim Worlds." In *The Renaissance and the Ottoman World*, edited by Anna Contadini and Claire Norton, 3–22. Burlington, VT: Ashgate, 2013.

Norwich, John J. *Byzantium: The Decline and Fall*. New York: Alfred A. Knopf, 1996.

O'Brien, Emily. "Aeneas Sylvius Piccolomini and the Histories of the Council of Basel." In *The Church, the Councils, and Reform: The Legacy of the Fifteenth Century*, edited by Gerald Christianson, Thomas Izbicki, and Christopher Belitto, 60–81. Washington, DC: Catholic University of America Press, 2008.

————. "Arms and Letters: Julius Caesar, the *Commentaries* of Pope Pius II, and the Politicization of Papal Imagery." *Renaissance Quarterly* 62, no. 4 (Winter 2009): 1080–89.

————. *Commentaries of Pope Pius II (1458–1464) and the Crisis of the Fifteenth-Century Papacy*. Toronto: University of Toronto Press, 2015.

O'Doherty, Marianne and Felicitas Schmieder, eds. *Travels and Mobilities in the Middle Ages: From the Atlantic to the Black Sea*. Turnhout: Belgium, 2015.

Ohler, Norbert. *The Medieval Traveller*. Translated by Caroline Hillier. Woodbridge, UK: Boydell Press, 1989.

Onar, Nora Fisher. "Turkey in the Post-Ottoman Mediterranean: Transcending the 'West'/'Islam' Binary." In *Mediterranean Frontiers: Borders, Conflict and Memory in a Transnational World*, edited by Dimitar Bechev and Kalypso Nicolaidis, 57–68. London: I.B. Tauris, 2010.

Oschema, Klaus. *Bilder von Europe im Mittelalter*. Ostfildern: Jan Thorbecke Verlag, 2013.

Pagden, Anthony, ed. *The Idea of Europe From Antiquity to the European Union.* Cambridge: Cambridge University Press, 2002.

———. "The Peopling of the New World: Ethnos, Race and Empire in the Early-Modern World." In *The Origins of Racism in the West*, edited by Miriam Eliav-Feldon, Benjamin Isaac, and Joseph Ziegler, 292–312. Cambridge: Cambridge University Press, 2009.

Painter, Nell. *The History of White People.* New York: W.W. Norton & Co., 2010.

Paparelli, Gioacchino. *Enea Silvio Piccolomini: l'umanesimo sul soglio di Pietro.* Ravenna: Longo Editore, 1978.

Partner, Peter. *The Pope's Men: The Papal Civil Service in the Renaissance.* Oxford: Clarendon Press, 1990.

Passerini, Luisa. "From the Ironies of Identity to the Identities of Irony." In *The Idea of Europe from Antiquity to the European Union*, edited by Anthony Pagden, 191–208. Cambridge: Cambridge University Press, 2002.

Pastor, Ludwig. *History of the Popes From the Close of the Middle Ages*, vols. 1–2. London: Kegan Paul, Trench, Trübner, and Co., 1899.

———. *The History of the Popes From the Close of the Middle Ages*, vol. 3. London: Kegan Paul, Trench, Trübner, & Co., 1900.

Paviot, Jacques. "Burgundy and the Crusade." In *Crusading in the Fifteenth Century: Message and Impact*, edited by Norman Housley, 70–80. New York: Palgrave Macmillan, 2004.

Pellegrini, Marco. "Pio II, il Collegio cardinalizio e la Dieta di Mantova." In *Il Sogno di Pio II e il viaggio da Roma a Mantova*, edited by Arturo Calzona, Francesca Paolo Fiore, Alberto Tenenti, Cesare Vasoli, 15–76. Florence: Leo S. Olschki, 2003.

———. "Unità europea, primato romano. Riflessi della teologia politica di Pio II Piccolomini." In *Enea Silvio Piccolomini: Arte, Storia e Cultura nell'Europa di Pio II*, edited by Roberta Di Paola, Arianna Antoniutti, and Marco Gallo, 423–32. Rome: Libreria Editrice Vaticana, 2006.

———. "Un gentiluomo "piesco" tra la patria senese e la corte papale: Goro Lolli Piccolomini." In *Pio II Piccolomini: il Papa del Rinascimento a Siena*, edited by Fabrizio Nevola, 79–108. Siena: Protagon Editore, 2009.

Pernot, Laurent. *Rhetoric in Antiquity.* Translated by W.E. Higgins. Washington, DC: Catholic University of America Press, 2005.

Peterson, David S. "Out of the Margins: Religion and the Church in Renaissance Italy." *Renaissance Quarterly* 53, no. 3 (Autumn 2000): 835–79.

Pettegree, Andrew. *The Book in the Renaissance.* New Haven: Yale University Press, 2010.

Philippides, Marios. "Urbs Capta: Early 'Sources' on the Fall of Constantinople (1453)." In *Peace and War in Byzantium Essays in Honor of George T Dennis, SJ*, edited by Timothy S. Miller, and John Nesbitt, 209–24. Washington, DC: Catholic University of America Press, 1995.

———. "The Fall of Constantinople 1453: Bishop Leonardo Giustiniani and his Italian Followers." *Viator* 29 (1998): 189–225.

———. *Constantine XI Dragaš Palaeologus: The Last Emperor of Byzantium.* London: Routledge, 2019.

Philippides, Marios and Walter K. Hanak. *The Siege and the Fall of Constantinople in 1453.* Burlington, VT: Ashgate, 2011.

———. *Cardinal Isidore, c. 1390–1462.* New York: Routledge, 2018.

Pick, Lucy K. *Conflict and Coexistence: Archbishop Rodrigo and the Muslims and Jews of Medieval Spain.* Ann Arbor: University of Michigan Press, 2004.

Pippidi, Andrei. *Visions of the Ottoman World in Renaissance Europe*. London: Hurst and Co., 2012.

Pirenne, Henri. *A History of Europe*. Translated by Bernard Miall, vol. 1. Garden City, NY: Doubleday Anchor Books, 1956.

Pocock, J.G.A. "Some Europes in Their History." In *The Idea of Europe From Antiquity to the European Union*, edited by Anthony Pagden, 55–71. Cambridge: Cambridge University Press, 2002.

Rabil, Albert R., ed. *Renaissance Humanism: Foundations, Forms, and Legacy*, vols. 1–3. Philadelphia: University of Pennsylvania Press, 1988.

Ramey, Lynn T. *Black Legacies: Race and the European Middle Ages*. Gainesville: University of Florida Press, 2014.

Ricci, Giovanni. *Appeal the to the Turk: The Broken Boundaries of the Renaissance*. Rome: Viella, 2018.

Rietbergen, Peter. *Europe: A Cultural History*. London: Routledge, 1998.

Riley-Smith, Jonathan. *First Crusade and the Idea of Crusading*. Philadelphia: University of Pennsylvania Press, 1986.

Rinaldi, Rinaldo. "L'Italia 'romana' del Piccolomini." In *Il Sogno di Pio II e il viaggio da Roma a Mantova*, edited by Arturo Calzona et al., 109–28. Florence: Leo S. Olschki, 2003.

Ristuccia, Nathan J. *Christianization and Commonwealth in Early Medieval Europe*. Oxford: Oxford University Press, 2018.

Roberts, Sean. *Printing a Mediterranean World: Florence, Constantinople, and the Renaissance of Geography*. Cambridge, MA: Harvard University Press, 2013.

Rodinson, Maxime. *Europe and the Mystique of Islam*. Translated by Roger Veinus. Seattle: University of Washington Press, 1987.

Rothman, E. Nathalie, *Brokering Empire: Trans-imperial Subjects Between Venice and Istanbul*. Ithaca, NY: Cornell University Press, 2012.

Ruggiero, Guido, ed. *A Companion to the Worlds of the Renaissance*. Oxford: Blackwell Publishing, 2002.

Runciman, Steven. *The Fall of Constantinople: 1453*. Cambridge: Cambridge University Press, 1965.

Russell, Joycelyne G. *Diplomats at Work: Three Renaissance Studies*. Wolfeboro Falls, NH: Alan Sutton Publishing Inc., 1992.

Ryder, Alan. *Alfonso the Magnanimous, King of Aragon, Naples and Sicily, 1396–1458*. Oxford: Clarendon Press, 1990.

Said, Edward. *Culture and Imperialism*. New York: Vintage Books, 1994.

Scafi, Alessandro. "Pio II e la cartografia: un papa e un mappamondo tra Medioevo e Rinascimento." In *Enea Silvio Piccolomini: Pius Secundus Poeta Laureatus Pontifex Maximus*, edited by Manlio Sodi and Arianna Antoniutti, 239–64. Rome: Libreria Editrice Vaticana, 2007.

Scales, Len. "Late medieval Germany: an under-Stated nation?" In *Power and the Nation in European History*, edited by Len Scales and Oliver Zimmer, 166–91. Cambridge: Cambridge University Press, 2005.

Schwoebel, Robert. *The Shadow of the Crescent: The Renaissance Image of the Turk (1453–1517)*. New York: St. Martin's Press, 1967.

———. *Renaissance Men and Ideas*. New York: St. Martin's Press, 1971.

Seigel, Jerrold. *Rhetoric and Philosophy in Renaissance Humanism*. Princeton, NJ: Princeton University Press, 1968.

Sensi, Mario. "Niccolò Tignosi dal Foligno, l'opera e il pensiero." *Annali della facoltà di lettere e filosofia della Università degli Studi di Perugia* 9 (1971–72): 361–495.

Seth, Vanita. *Europe's Indians: Producing Racial Difference, 1500–1900*. Durham, NC: Duke University Press, 2010.

———. "The Origins of Racism: A Critique of the History of Ideas." *History and Theory* 59, no. 3 (Sept. 2020): 343–68.

Setton, Kenneth. *The Papacy and Levant (1205–1571)*, vol. 2. Philadelphia: American Philosophical Society, 1978.

Shaw, Brent. "Eaters of Flesh, Drinkers of Milk': The Ancient Mediterranean Ideology of the Pastoral Nomad." *Ancient Society* 13/14 (1982/83): 5–31.

Sidwell, Keith. "Il *De curialium miseriis* di Enea Silvio Piccolomini e il *De mercede conductis* di Luciano." In *Pio II e la cultura del suo tempo*, edited by Luisa Rotondi Secchi Tarugi, 329–42. Milan: Guerini e Associati, 1991.

———."Aeneas Silvius Piccolomini's *De curialium miseriis* and Peter of Blois." In *Pius II: 'El Più Expeditivo Pontifice: Selected Studies on Aeneas Silvius Piccolomini*, edited by Zweder Von Martels and Arjo Vanderjagt, 87–106. Leiden: Brill, 2003.

Sieber-Lehmann, Claudius. "An Obscure but Powerful Pattern: Crusading, Nationalism and the Swiss Confederation in the Late Middle Ages." In *Crusading in the Fifteenth Century: Message and Impact*, edited by Norman Housley, 81–93. New York: Palgrave Macmillan, 2004.

Sodi, Manlio and Arianna Antoniutti, eds. *Enea Silvio Piccolomini: Pius Secundus Laureatus Pontifex Maximus*. Rome: Libreria Editrice Vaticana, 2007.

Southern, R.W. *Western Views of Islam in the Middle Ages*. Cambridge, MA: Harvard University Press, 1962.

Soykut, Mustafa. *The Image of the "Turk" in Italy: A History of the "Other" in Early Modern Europe: 1453–1683*. Berlin: Klaus Schwarz Verlag, 2001.

Spiller, Elizabeth. *Reading and the History of Race in the Renaissance*. Cambridge: Cambridge University Press, 2011.

Stantchev, Stefan. "Venice and the Ottoman Threat, 1381–1453." In *Reconfiguring the Fifteenth-Century Crusade*, edited by Norman Housley, 161–206. London: Palgrave Macmillan, 2017.

Starn, Randolph, "The European Renaissance." In *Companion to the Worlds of the Renaissance*, edited by Guido Ruggiero, 39–54. Oxford: Blackwell Publishing, 2002.

Statwald, Kurt. *Roman Popes and German Patriots*. Geneva: Librairie Droz, 1996.

Stieber, Joachim. *Pope Eugenius IV, The Council of Basel and the Secular and Ecclesiastical Authorities in the Empire*. Leiden: E.J. Brill, 1978.

Stinger, Charles L. *The Renaissance in Rome*. Bloomington: Indiana University Press, 1985.

Stolf, Serge. *Les lettres et la tiare: E.S. Piccolomini, un humaniste au XVe siècle*. Paris: Classiques Garnier 2012.

Tarugi, Luisa Rotondi Secchi, ed. *Pio II e la cultura del suo tempo*. Milan: Guerini e Associati, 1991.

Tarugi, Luisa Secchi, ed. *Pio II nell'epistolografia del Rinascimento*. Florence: Franco Cesati Editore, 2015.

Tavakoli-Targhi, Mohamad. "Orientalism's Genesis Amnesia." *Comparative Studies of South Asia, Africa, and the Middle East* (formerly *South Asia Bulletin*) xvi, no. 1 (1996): 1–13.

Teter, Magda. "Blood Libel, a Lie and Its Legacies." In *Whose Middle Ages: Teachable Moments for an Ill-Used Past*, edited by Andrew Albin et al., 44–57. New York: Fordham University Press, 2019.

Toewes, John. "The View of Empire in Aeneas Sylvius Piccolomini (Pope Pius II)." *Traditio* 24 (1968): 471–87.

Tolan, John V. "Constructing Christendom." In *The Making of Europe: Essays in Honour of Robert Bartlett*, edited by John Hudson and Sally Crumplin, 277–98. Leiden: Brill, 2016.

———. *Faces of Muhammad: Western Perceptions of the Prophet of Islam From the Middle Ages to Today*. Princeton, NJ: Princeton University Press, 2019.

Tolan, John, Gilles Veinstein, and Henry Laurens. *Europe and the Islamic World: A History*. Translated by Jane Marie Todd with a Foreword by John L. Esposito. Princeton, NJ: Princeton University Press, 2013.

Trexler, Richard C. *Public Life in Renaissance Florence*. Ithaca, NY: Cornell University Press, 1980.

Trouillot, Michel-Rolph. *Silencing the Past: Power and the Production of History*. Boston: Beacon Press, 1995.

Van Heck, Adrian. "Amator vetusti ritus et observator diligens. Stile e modelli stilisitic di Pio II." In *Pio II e la cultura del suo tempo*, edited by Luisa Rotondi Secchi Tarugi, 119–49. Milan: Guerini e Associati, 1991.

Veinstein, Gilles. "The Great Turk and Europe." In *Europe and the Islamic World: A History*, edited by John Tolan, Gilles Veinstein, and Henry Laurens, 111–253. Princeton, NJ: Princeton University Press, 2013.

Voigt, Georg. *Enea Silvio de' Piccolomini als Papst Pius II und sein Zeitalter*, vols. 1–3. Berlin: De Gruyter, 1856–1863.

Vollmann, Benedikt Konrad. "Aeneas Silvius Piccolomini as a Historiographer: Asia." In *Pius II 'El Più Expeditivo Pontifice: Selected Studies on Aeneas Silvius Piccolomini*, edited by Zweder Von Martels and Arjo Vanderjagt, 41–54. Leiden: Brill, 2003.

Von Martels, Zweder. "The Fruit of Love. Aeneas Silvius Piccolomini About His Illegitimate Child." In *Pius II 'El Più Expeditivo Pontifice: Selected Studies on Aeneas Silvius Piccolomini*, edited by Zweder Von Martels and Arjo Vanderjagt, 229–48. Leiden: Brill, 2003.

Von Martels, Zweder and Arjo Vanderjagt, eds. *Pius II 'El Più Expeditivo Pontifice: Selected Studies on Aeneas Silvius Piccolomini*. Leiden: Brill, 2003.

Wagendorfer, Martin. *Die Schrift des Eneas Silvius Piccolomini*. Vatican City: Biblioteca Apostolica Vaticana, 2008.

Walser-Bürgler, Isabella. *Europe and Europeanness in Early Modern Latin Literature: Fuitne Europa tunc unita?* Leiden: Brilll, 2021.

Watt, William Montgomery. *The Influence of Islam on Medieval Europe*. Edinburgh: Edinburgh University Press, 1994.

Weber, Benjamin. "Conversion, croisade et oecuménisme à la fin du Moyen-âge: encore sur la lettre de Pie II à Mehmed II." *Crusades* 7 (2008): 181–99.

———. *Lutter contre les Turcs: Les formes nouvelles de la croisade pontificale au XVe siècle*. Rome: École Française de Rome, 2013.

———. "Toward a Global Crusade? The Papacy and the Non-Latin World in the Fifteenth Century." In *Reconfiguring the Fifteenth Century Crusade*, edited by Norman Housley, 11–44. London: Palgrave Macmillan, 2017.

Weinig, Paul. *Aeneam suscipite, Pium recipite: Aeneas Silvius Piccolomini: Studien zur Rezeption eines humanistischen Schriftstellers im Deutschland des 15. Jahrhunderts*. Wiesbaden: Harrassowitz, 1998.

Wells, Peter S. *The Barbarians Speak: How the Conquered Peoples Shaped Roman Europe*. Princeton, NJ: Princeton University Press: 1999.

Wheatcroft, Andrew. *The Enemy at the Gate: Habsburgs, Ottomans and the Battle for Europe*. New York: Basic Books, 2008.

Whitaker, Cord J. *Black Metaphors: How Modern Racism Emerged From Medieval Race-thinking.* Philadelphia: University of Pennsylvania Press, 2019.

White, Arthur. *Plague and Pleasure: The Renaissance World of Pius II.* Washington, DC: Catholic University of America Press, 2014.

Whitley, Antonia. "Mind over matter. Living with ill health: the case of Pius II." In *Pio II Piccolomini: Il Papa del Rinascimento a Siena*, edited by Fabrizio Nevola, 269–79. Siena: Protagon Editore, 2009.

Widmer, Berthe. *Enea Silvio Piccolomini Papst Pius II.* Basel: Benno Schwabe & Co. Verlag, 1960.

Wilson, Brownen. *The World in Venice: Print, the City, and Early Modern Identity.* Toronto: University of Toronto Press, 2005.

Wilson, Peter H. *The Heart of Europe: A History of the Holy Roman Empire.* Cambridge: Belknap Press, 2016.

Witt, Ronald G. *In the Footsteps of the Ancients: The Origins of Humanism From Lovato to Bruni.* Leiden: Brill Academic Publishers, 2003.

Wolf, Anne Marie. *Juan de Segovia and the Fight for Peace: Christians and Muslims in the Fifteenth Century.* Notre Dame, IN: University of Notre Dame Press, 2014.

Yurdusev, A.N. "Ottoman Concepts of War and Peace in the Classical World." In *Just Wars, Holy Wars, and Jihads: Christian, Jewish, and Muslim Encounters and Exchanges*, edited by Sohail H. Hashmi, 190–218. Oxford: Oxford University Press, 2012.

Zippel, Giovanni "E.S. Piccolomini e il mondo Germanico." *Cultura* 19 (1981): 267–350.

Index

Printed in Great Britain
by Amazon

24028127R00170